Information Discovery on Electronic Health Records

Chapman & Hall/CRC
Data Mining and Knowledge Discovery Series

SERIES EDITOR
Vipin Kumar
University of Minnesota
Department of Computer Science and Engineering
Minneapolis, Minnesota, U.S.A

AIMS AND SCOPE

This series aims to capture new developments and applications in data mining and knowledge discovery, while summarizing the computational tools and techniques useful in data analysis. This series encourages the integration of mathematical, statistical, and computational methods and techniques through the publication of a broad range of textbooks, reference works, and handbooks. The inclusion of concrete examples and applications is highly encouraged. The scope of the series includes, but is not limited to, titles in the areas of data mining and knowledge discovery methods and applications, modeling, algorithms, theory and foundations, data and knowledge visualization, data mining systems and tools, and privacy and security issues.

PUBLISHED TITLES

UNDERSTANDING COMPLEX DATASETS: Data Mining with Matrix Decompositions
David Skillicorn

COMPUTATIONAL METHODS OF FEATURE SELECTION
Huan Liu and Hiroshi Motoda

CONSTRAINED CLUSTERING: Advances in Algorithms, Theory, and Applications
Sugato Basu, Ian Davidson, and Kiri L. Wagstaff

KNOWLEDGE DISCOVERY FOR COUNTERTERRORISM AND LAW ENFORCEMENT
David Skillicorn

MULTIMEDIA DATA MINING: A Systematic Introduction to Concepts and Theory
Zhongfei Zhang and Ruofei Zhang

NEXT GENERATION OF DATA MINING
Hillol Kargupta, Jiawei Han, Philip S. Yu, Rajeev Motwani, and Vipin Kumar

DATA MINING FOR DESIGN AND MARKETING
Yukio Ohsawa and Katsutoshi Yada

THE TOP TEN ALGORITHMS IN DATA MINING
Xindong Wu and Vipin Kumar

GEOGRAPHIC DATA MINING AND KNOWLEDGE DISCOVERY, Second Edition
Harvey J. Miller and Jiawei Han

TEXT MINING: CLASSIFICATION, CLUSTERING, AND APPLICATIONS
Ashok N. Srivastava and Mehran Sahami

BIOLOGICAL DATA MINING
Jake Y. Chen and Stefano Lonardi

INFORMATION DISCOVERY ON ELECTRONIC HEALTH RECORDS
Vagelis Hristidis

Chapman & Hall/CRC
Data Mining and Knowledge Discovery Series

Information Discovery on Electronic Health Records

Edited by
Vagelis Hristidis

 CRC Press
Taylor & Francis Group
Boca Raton   London   New York

CRC Press is an imprint of the
Taylor & Francis Group, an **informa** business

A CHAPMAN & HALL BOOK

Chapman & Hall/CRC
Taylor & Francis Group
6000 Broken Sound Parkway NW, Suite 300
Boca Raton, FL 33487-2742

© 2010 by Taylor and Francis Group, LLC
Chapman & Hall/CRC is an imprint of Taylor & Francis Group, an Informa business

Library of Congress Cataloging-in-Publication Data

Information discovery on electronic health records / editor, Vagelis Hristidis.
    p. cm. -- (Chapman & Hall/CRC data mining and knowledge discovery series)
   Includes bibliographical references and index.
   ISBN 978-1-4200-9038-3 (alk. paper)
   1. Medical records--Data processing. 2. Data mining. I. Hristidis, Vagelis.

R864.I53 2010
610.285--dc22   2009025359

Visit the Taylor & Francis Web site at
http://www.taylorandfrancis.com

and the CRC Press Web site at
http://www.crcpress.com

To my wife Jelena and my family.

Contents

Preface

Electronic health records (EHRs) are a key component of the information technology revolution occurring in healthcare. EHRs can help improve the quality of healthcare and reduce healthcare costs. Most of the research efforts so far have studied the important and critical problem of standardization of EHRs and interoperability of healthcare information management systems. However, little work has been conducted on the problem of leveraging the rich information found in EHRs, which can improve the quality of medical practice at the point-of-care, or facilitate research. The information stored in EHRs is valuable for practitioners and researchers from the areas of medicine, public health, nursing, law, and health insurance.

In this book, we study the problem of information discovery on EHRs, which involves (a) *searching* the EHR collection given a user query and returning relevant fragments from the EHRs and (b) *mining* the EHR collection to extract interesting patterns, group entities to various classes, or to decide whether an EHR satisfies a given property. An example of searching would be "find the patients related to 'asthma.'" This seemingly simple query turns out to be challenging for many reasons. Should we rank higher a patient with "asthma" in the diagnosis of a past hospitalization, or a patient for whom "asthma" is mentioned in her medical history, or a patient whose EHR refers to "respiratory distress," which is a term related to "asthma"? An example of mining would be "identify patients with high probability of developing asthma." Answering this question involves learning correlations in the EHR collection and using classification algorithms. Most of the book focuses on textual or numeric data of EHRs, where more searching and mining progress has occurred. We also include a chapter on the processing of medical images.

Information discovery on EHRs has some unique challenges compared to information discovery on other domains such as the Web or a bibliographic database. Some of these challenges are medical privacy concerns, lack of standardization for the representation of EHRs, missing or incorrect values, availability of multiple rich health ontologies, and the often small statistical samples. Addressing these challenges requires interdisciplinary collaboration, which is often difficult to achieve, and this has led to relatively little and narrow public information on this important topic.

In this book, we have assembled an extraordinary interdisciplinary team including scientists from the areas of computer science, medicine, law, math, decision sciences, and biomedical engineering. The book, therefore, covers multiple aspects of information discovery on EHRs, such as ethics/privacy, EHR creation, and EHR processing.

To ensure consistent style and flow across the book, I have, in addition to being the editor, coauthored four chapters, and closely reviewed the rest of the chapters. One of the key goals was to minimize the use of technical jargon in most of the book, so that readers from different disciplines and disparate backgrounds can appreciate the content. In each chapter, we have tried to push the technical material to the second half of the chapter, to allow both experts and nonexperts of the specific chapter's material to satisfy their learning needs. Chapters present state-of-the-art research topics from the perspective of the chapter authors, but also present a survey of the achievements in that area.

The book is organized as follows. Chapter 1 presents an overview of the Extensible Markup Language (XML), which is the data model adopted by most of the recent EHR formatting standards. Chapter 2 presents an overview of EHRs, including what information they include, how they are formatted, and what software systems manage them. Chapter 3 defines the term "information discovery," clarifies related terminology, and presents an overview of the challenges and solutions in different aspects of information discovery on EHRs. Chapter 4 discusses data quality and integration issues in EHRs, including how EHRs are created, which help the reader better understand the processing and discovery challenges of EHRs. Chapter 5 discusses the ethical, legal, and social issues around EHRs, which must be known to everyone who processes or manages EHRs. Chapters 6 to 10 present in detail various aspects of information discovery on EHRs. Chapters 6 and 7 discuss the problems for searching and mining EHRs, respectively. Chapter 8 focuses on how data mining techniques, such as those discussed in Chapter 7, can be adapted in a way that the privacy of the data is preserved; that is, specific data for a specific patient are not revealed. Chapter 9 investigates a different setting, where EHR data are collected or processed by mobile devices. The real-time data analysis needs are also discussed. Finally, Chapter 10 tackles the problem of searching and processing medical images, and in particular the problem of medical image segmentation.

Target Audience

A key goal set before the writing of this book was to make it appropriate for multiple disciplines and a wide audience. This is why we tried to minimize the technical jargon and explain the used terminology where possible. Some chapters are more technical than others. In particular, we believe that Chapters 1 to 5 are appropriate for any audience with basic scientific backgrounds. In Chapters 6 to 10, which are more technical, we tried to contain the more technical material to the second half of the chapter, in order to allow nontechnical readers to absorb the key ideas of the chapters.

The following are some examples of the target audience of this book.

- Medical informaticians, who are interested on how the EHR data can be searched and mined
- Computer science students and researchers, who want to make the jump to healthcare research
- Medical students who want to learn about EHRs and the way they are leveraged to extract useful knowledge
- Medical, statistical, or other types of researchers who study medical trends or patterns
- Medical, computer science, or information technology students taking a course on "mining medical data"

Vagelis Hristidis

Acknowledgments

I would like to thank all the contributors of this book for their effort and dedication and for believing in the success of this book. Obviously, this book would not be possible without their support. I would also like to thank Randi Cohen and Professor Vipin Kumar, who are the executive and series editors for this book series, for their support.

About the Editor

 **Vagelis Hristidis** (also Evangelos Christidis) received his bachelor's degree in electrical and computer engineering at the National Technical University of Athens in 1999. He later moved to San Diego, California, where he finished his master's and doctoral degrees in computer science in 2000 and 2004, respectively, at the University of California, San Diego. Since 2004, he has been an assistant professor at the School of Computing and Information Sciences at Florida International University in Miami, Florida.

Dr. Hristidis is an expert in database systems and information retrieval (IR). His main research contribution is his work on bridging the gap between databases and IR, by facilitating keyword searching on structured databases. He has successfully applied these techniques to bibliographic, biomedical, and clinical databases, in collaboration with domain experts from the areas of medicine and biology. Dr. Hristidis has also worked in the areas of ranked queries, query results exploration, Web search, storage and parsing of XML data, and spatial databases. Dr. Hristidis's work has resulted in more than 40 publications, which have received more than 1000 bibliographic citations according to Google Scholar. His work has been funded by the National Science Foundation.

Dr. Hristidis has served on numerous program committees of conferences including the Institute of Electrical and Electronics Engineers (IEEE) International Conference on Data Engineering, the International Conference on Extending Database Technology, the IEEE International Conference on Data Mining, the Association for Computing Machinery Special Interest Group on Spatial Information, the International Conference on Advances in Geographic Information Systems, and on the review board of the Proceedings of Very Large Databases Endowment. He has also served as cochair of the International Workshop on Ranking in Databases, and as proceedings, finance, and publicity chair of major database conferences.

Contributors

Filipa Canario Almeida
Department of Biostatistics and
   Medical Informatics
Universidade do Porto
Porto, Portugal

Daniele Apiletti
Dipartimento di Automatica e
   Informatica
Politecnico di Torino
Torino, Italy

Elena Baralis
Dipartimento di Automatica e
   Informatica
Politecnico di Torino
Torino, Italy

Donald J. Berndt
Department of Information
   Systems
University of South Florida
Tampa, Florida

Giulia Bruno
Dipartimento di Automatica e
   Informatica
Politecnico di Torino
Torino, Italy

Redmond Burke
Miami Children's Hospital
Miami, Florida

Tania Cerquitelli
Dipartimento di Automatica e
   Informatica
Politecnico di Torino
Torino, Italy

Rong Chen
Department of Biomedical
   Engineering
Linköping University
Linköping, Sweden

Altamiro Costa-Pereira
Department of Biostatistics and
   Medical Informatics
Universidade do Porto
Porto, Portugal

Ricardo João Cruz-Correia
Department of Biostatistics and
   Medical Informatics
Universidade do Porto
Porto, Portugal

Reid Cushman
Department of Medicine
University of Miami School of
   Medicine
Miami, Florida

Fernando Farfán
School of Computing and
   Information Science
Florida International University
Miami, Florida

Alessandro Fiori
Dipartimento di Automatica e
   Informatica
Politecnico di Torino
Torino, Italy

Alberto Freitas
Department of Biostatistics and
   Medical Informatics
Universidade do Porto
Porto, Portugal

James Gardner
Department of Mathematics and
    Computer Science
Emory University
Atlanta, Georgia

Vagelis Hristidis
School of Computing and
    Information Sciences
Florida International University
Miami, Florida

Xiaolei Huang
Department of Computer Science
    and Engineering
Lehigh University
Bethlehem, Pennsylvania

Pawel Jurczyk
Department of Mathematics and
    Computer Science
Emory University
Atlanta, Georgia

James J. Lu
Department of Mathematics and
    Computer Science
Emory University
Atlanta, Georgia

Stephen L. Luther
Department of Veterans Affairs
Tampa, Florida

Pedro Pereira Rodrigues
Department of Biostatistics and
    Medical Informatics
Universidade do Porto
Porto, Portugal

Monica Chiarini Tremblay
Department of Decision Sciences
    and Information Systems
Florida International University
Miami, Florida

Gavriil Tsechpenakis
Department of Computer Science
University of Miami
Miami, Florida

Ramakrishna Varadarajan
Department of Computer Sciences
University of Wisconsin–Madison
Madison, Wisconsin

Li Xiong
Department of Mathematics and
    Computer Science
Emory University
Atlanta, Georgia

1

Overview of XML

Fernando Farfán and Vagelis Hristidis

CONTENTS

1.1 Introduction

XML, which stands for Extensible Markup Language, is a general purpose language that allows the creation of other new languages to be used in several domains. It is flexible, simple, and designed to meet the challenges of large-scale electronic publishing, facilitating the exchange of data among heterogeneous computer systems (particularly over the Internet), while maintaining the capability of being human-readable.

XML uses a combination of notes and special symbols (called "markup") to express information about the data itself. These markups are basically strings of characters called tags, which are put together to delimit the main portions of data, called elements.

XML is extensible because it lets users to define their own tags, element types, and overall document structure. This extensibility has allowed the development of many application languages for a large number of application domains, ranging from Mathematics (MathML [1]), Graphs and Graphics (GraphML [2]; GML [3]; SVG [4]), Finance (FIXML [5]; FinXML [6]; SwiftML [7]), Internet-related languages (RSS [8]; XHTML [9]), to medicine (CDA [10]).

Figure 1.1 shows an example of an XML document. An XML document consists of the following:

XML elements. XML elements are the basic building blocks of XML markup. Lines 5 to 8, for example, correspond to a *name* XML element. The elements may be seen as containers. Each element may have attributes, and may contain other elements, character data, or other types of information. This containment specifies the structure

```
1.    <? xml version="1.0" ?>
2.    <ClinicalDocument>
3.      <id extension="49912" root="2.16.840.1.113883.3.933"/>
4.      <patient>
5.        <name>
6.          <given>Peter</given>
7.          <family>Patient</family>
8.        </name>
9.        <genderCode code="M" codeSystem="2.16.840.1.5.1"/>
10.       <birthTime value="20020924"/>
11.     </patient>
12.     <component>
13.       <StructuredBody>
14.         <component>
15.           <section>
16.             <code code="10160-0" codeSystem="2.16.840.1.113883.6.1"
                    codeSystemName="LOINC" />
17.             <title>Medications</title>
18.             <entry>
19.               <Observation>
20.                 <code code="84100007" codeSystem="2.16.840.1.113883.6.96"
                       codeSystemName="SNOMED CT" displayName=" medication history"/>
21.                 <value xsi:type="CD" code="195967001" codeSystem="2.16.840.1.113883.6.96"
                       codeSystemName="SNOMED CT" displayName="Asthma">
22.                   <originalText>
23.                     <reference value="m1"/>
24.                   </originalText>
25.                 </value>
26.               </Observation>
27.             </entry>
28.             <entry>
29.               <Observation>
30.                 <code code="84100007" codeSystem="2.16.840.1.113883.6.96"
                       codeSystemName="SNOMED CT" displayName="medication history"/>
31.                 <value xsi:type="CD" code="32398004" codeSystem="2.16.840.1.113883.6.96"
                       codeSystemName="SNOMED CT" displayName="Bronchitis">
32.                   <value xsi:type="CD" code="91143003" codeSystem="2.16.840.1.113883.6.96"
                         codeSystemName="SNOMED CT" displayName="Albuterol" />
33.                 </value>
34.               </Observation>
35.             </entry>
36.             <entry>
37.               <SubstanceAdministration>
38.                 <text>
39.                   <content ID="m1">Theophylline</content>20 mg every other day, alternating
                         with 18 mg every other day. Stop if temperature is above 1103F.
40.                 </text>
41.                 <consumable>
42.                   <manufacturedProduct>
43.                     <manufacturedLabeledDrug>
44.                       <code code="66493003" codeSystem="2.16.840.1.113883.6.96"
                            codeSystemName="SNOMED CT" displayName="Theophylline"/>
45.                     </manufacturedLabeledDrug>
46.                   </manufacturedProduct>
47.                 </consumable>
48.               </SubstanceAdministration>
49.             </entry>
50.           </section>
51.         </component>
52.       </StructuredBody>
53.     </component>
54.   </ClinicalDocument>
```

FIGURE 1.1
Sample XML document.

and hierarchy to the document. The *ClinicalDocument* element that starts in line 2, for example, contains all the other XML elements in the document; the elements in lines 6 and 7 contain text data. The element in line 9 includes two attributes, *code* and *codeSystem*, but does not contain any further information; it is called an empty element.

Tags. Each element is delimited with a *start-tag* and an *end-tag*. Line 5 corresponds to the start-tag of the element name, whereas line 8 corresponds to the end-tag of the same element. We can see how the start-tag "opens" the container that is later closed by the end-tag. In the case of empty elements, a pair of *start-tag/end-tag* can be used, or it could be represented by an *empty-element tag* abbreviation, as it is the case in line 9. The attributes are always included in the start-tag, as seen in the element in line 3.

Attributes. Element attributes describe the properties of an element. Each attribute is comprised of a name-value pair. For example, the start-tag in line 9 has two attributes: code="M" and codeSystem="2.16.840.1.5.1". *code* is an attribute name and "M" is its attribute value. Attribute values must be character strings. Note that it is often a design decision whether a piece of information is represented as an attribute or as a subelement.

It is important to understand that XML is not a programming language; hence XML does not do anything by itself. XML is a data representation format.

The syntax (format) of XML is standardized and formally defined by the World Wide Web Consortium (W3C) [11], which is supported by large software vendors as well as the academic community. This is a key reason for the success of XML.

According to the W3C [12], the key characteristics of XML are

- XML is a markup language much like Hypertext Markup Language (HTML).
- XML was designed to carry data, not to display data.
- XML tags are not predefined. You must define your own tags.
- XML is designed to be self-descriptive.
- XML is a W3C Recommendation.

1.1.1 Does XML Have Semantics?

XML has a strict and formally defined syntax, which specifies when a document qualifies to be an XML document. Furthermore, an XML element has a tag that generally specifies the type of the element and some value. For instance, in Figure 1.1, we can tell that "Peter" is the "name" of a "patient." However, all of these factors do not mean that XML has semantics. This is a common misunderstanding. Intuitively, the reason is that a computer does not know what a "patient" is. Furthermore, two persons may use different tag names to denote the same real-life entity, for example, "patient" versus "client" for a hospital database. To add semantics to XML data, we need to define the semantic meaning of the XML tags. One popular means of doing this is by using ontologies (which will be discussed in Chapter 2).

1.1.2 Related Work and Further Readings

The W3C [11] is an international organization devoted to the definition of Web standards. This consortium, which was formed by industry giants, academia, and the general public, creates standards for the World Wide Web. Within these standards and recommendations, W3C has defined markup languages such as Standard Generalized Markup Language (SGML) [13] and XML [14], as well as technologies and query languages around XML, such as the Document Object Model [15] for document parsing, XML Path Language [16] and XML Query Language [17]. Also, application and domain languages based on XML have been defined by the W3C, such as Extensible Hypertext Markup Language [9], Scalable Vector Graphics [4], and the Resource Descriptor Framework (RDF; [18]).

The storage of XML documents has received attention from academia and industry, with several directions being followed. Many independent works have studied new native storage solutions for XML [19], or created native XML databases and storage systems, such as Lore [20], TIMBER [21], Natix [22, 23], and eXist [24]. Another direction exploits the maturity of relational systems to store XML [25]. Some of these works include STORED [26] and those carried out by Florescu and Kossmann [27] and Tatarinov et al. [28]. Moreover, major commercial Relational Database Management Systems (RDBMSs), such as Microsoft SQL Server [29], Oracle [30], and IBM DB2 [31], provide support to store and query XML data.

In addition, XML schema has been considered as an adequate means to close the gap between relational databases and XML. Some works exploit XML schema to create mappings from XML to RDBMSs [32], or to represent relational data as XML [33, 34].

Several query languages for XML have been developed by W3C, such as XPath [16] and XQuery [17]. A large amount of scholarly work has been devoted to optimizing the processing of XPath and XQuery queries. Works on optimizing XPath query processing include BLAS [35], the Natix project [23, 36], and the work done by Barton et al. [37]. Similarly, XQuery process optimization has been addressed by May et al. [38] (Natix), Zhang et al. [39] (Rainbow), and Liu et al. [40].

Another popular topic in XML research is the study and optimization of XML parsing, which especially considers tree-based representations of XML documents. Nicola and John [41] have identified the XML parsing process as a bottleneck to enterprise applications. Their study compares XML parsing in several application domains to similar applications that use relational databases as their backend. Operations such as shredding XML documents into relational entities, XPath expression evaluation, and XSL Transformations [42, 43] processing are often determined by the performance of the underlying XML parser [41], limiting the massive embracement of native XML databases into large-scale enterprise applications.

Noga et al. [44] presented the idea of *lazy parsing*. The virtual document tree can potentially be stored on disk to avoid the preparsing stage; however, the virtual document tree has to still be read from disk. Schott and Noga [45] applied these ideas to XSL Transformations. Kenji and Hiroyuki [46] have also proposed a lazy XML parsing technique applied to XSL Transformation stylesheets, constructing a pruned XML tree by statically identifying the nodes that will be referred to during the transformation process. We extended these ideas and developed a double-lazy parser [47, 48], which treats both phases of the DOM processing (*preprocessing* and *progressive parsing*) in a lazy fashion.

Lu et al. [49] presented a parallel approach to XML parsing, which initially preparses the document to extract the structure of the XML tree, and then perform a parallel full parse. This parallel parsing is achieved by assigning the parsing of each segment of the document to a different thread that can exploit the multicore capabilities of contemporary CPUs. Their preparsing phase is more relaxed than the one proposed by Noga et al. [44] and that we use throughout our work; this relaxed preparsing only extracts the tree shape without additional information, and is used to decide where to partition the tree to assign the parsing subtasks to the threads. This partitioning scheme differs from ours since it is performed after the preparsing phase is executed, whereas ours is performed a priori, with the objective of optimizing such preparsing stage.

There have been efforts in developing XML pull parsers [50] for both Simple API for XML (SAX) and DOM interfaces. Also, a new API [51] has been presented that is built just one level on top of the XML tokenizer, hence claiming to be the simplest, quickest, and most efficient engine for processing XML.

Another important direction related to XML is the definition of languages that represent semantics such as the RDF [18]. RDF provides a technique for describing resources on the Web. Hence, this development has spanned topics such as generation of metadata [52], storage and querying of RDF schemas [53], and use of RDF for network infrastructure [54].

1.2 XML versus HTML

Although both XML and HTML may look alike, there exist important differences between them. Both XML and HTML are derived from SGML. SGML is an older and more complex markup language, codified as an international standard by the International Organization for Standardization (ISO) as ISO 8879. HTML is, indeed, an application of SGML, and a new version of HTML

4, called XHTML, is an application of XML. Although SGML, HTML, XML, and XHTML are all markup languages, only SGML and XML can be considered metalanguages—they can be used to create new languages (HTML is a single and predefined markup language).

Figure 1.2 presents a sample HTML document showing information similar to that in Figure 1.1. Although the document looks similar to that in Figure 1.1, we observe that the set of tags used here is different: the *head* element in line 2 contains general information (metainformation) about the document, and the *body* element in line 6 contains all the contents in the document. The rest of the elements in the HTML document are presentation-oriented, and hence we have the elements *h1*, *h2*, and *h3* (lines 7, 8, and 28, respectively) that

```
1.  <html xmlns="http://www.w3.org/1999/xhtml">
2.  <head>
3.    <meta http-equiv="Content-Type" content="text/html; charset=utf-8" />
4.    <title>Clinical Document</title>
5.  </head>
6.  <body>
7.    <h1>Clinical Document</h1>
8.    <h2>Patient</h2>
9.    <table border="1" cellspacing="0" cellpadding="0">
10.     <tr>
11.       <td width="120">Given Name</td>
12.       <td width="120"><strong>Peter</strong></td>
13.     </tr>
14.     <tr>
15.       <td>Family Name</td>
16.       <td><strong>Patient</strong></td>
17.     </tr>
18.     <tr>
19.       <td>Gender</td>
20.       <td><strong>MALE</strong></td>
21.     </tr>
22.     <tr>
23.       <td>Birth Time</td>
24.       <td><strong>09-24-2002</strong></td>
25.     </tr>
26.   </table>
27.   <h2>Clinical Encounter</h2>
28.   <h3>Medications</h3>
29.   <table width="640" border="1" cellspacing="0" cellpadding="0">
30.     <tr>
31.       <th>Illness</th>
32.       <th>Medication</th>
33.     </tr>
34.     <tr>
35.       <td>Asthma</td>
36.       <td>Theophylline</td>
37.     </tr>
38.     <tr>
39.       <td>Bronchitis</td>
40.       <td>Albuterol</td>
41.     </tr>
42. </table>
43. </body>
44. </html>
```

FIGURE 1.2
Sample HTML document.

correspond to different levels of header formatting in the document. HTML tags are predefined and have specific presentation meaning, whereas XML tags are defined by the user and have no specific presentation meaning.

We can observe how even when the captured information is similar, the HTML document does not describe any logical structure or semantics about what the document is about, whereas the XML document richly describes the data it contains. The tags in the XML document directly correspond to concepts in the domain of electronic health records.

It is important to say that XML is not a replacement for HTML. Both were designed with different goals: HTML's goal is to display data and it focuses on how data looks; XML's goal is to transport and store data, focusing on the data content and not on its presentation.

1.3 XML versus Relational Data Model

In database management, the *relational model* is, nowadays, the dominant model for commercial data processing applications. Originally proposed by E. F. Codd in 1970 [55], this model specifies that the data are stored in the database as a collection of Tables (formally, mathematical relations). Each Table (relation) can be seen as a set of records (tuples) [56]. The relational model uses a schema to model the data in terms of table name, name of each field, and type of each field.

For example, we can create a relation to store the information about patients in a hospital as follows:

Patients(*patient_id*: integer, *first_name*: string, *last_name*: string,

date_of_birth: date, *gender*: string)

This schema specifies that each tuple in the Patients relation has five fields, whose names and types are explicitly indicated. An example instance (content at a specific time) of this relation is depicted in table 1.1.

One of the advantages of XML over other data models is its ability to exchange data between heterogeneous platforms. In contrast to proprietary systems and

TABLE 1.1

Sample Instance of a *Patients* Relation

Patient_Id	First_Name	Last_Name	Date_of_Birth	Gender
60135	Jacqueline	Jones	2002-02-12	Female
76638	Andrew	Smith	2003-05-25	Male
76639	Jason	Smith	2003-06-18	Male
76640	Melinda	Galvin	2004-01-12	Female

formats, whose data are incompatible among others, XML data are stored in plain text in a standardized format, which provides software and hardware independence in storing and sharing data. Moreover, as discussed previously, XML combines the data schema and the instance of the data in the same file. This self-containment also makes XML more appropriate for data exchange than other data models such as the relational model. The structure of XML files also makes it a convenient means to represent complex hierarchical data.

1.4 XML Syntax

We now present the basic syntactic elements of XML. For a complete and detailed overview, see World Wide Web Consortium [14], Birbeck et al. [57], and W3Schools [12]. In addition, an annotated version of the first edition of the XML Recommendation is given by Bray [58].

As shown in Figures 1.1 and 1.2, XML elements and their content look very similar to those of HTML. But looking further, it becomes obvious that XML documents provide more information within the document, since the element types (tags) give additional information about the data.

All XML documents that follow certain basic rules specified in the XML 1.0 Recommendation [14] are known as *well formed* [57]. To be well formed, an XML document must follow more than 100 rules; however, most of them are trivial. To summarize, an XML document is well formed if it satisfies the following conditions:

- Every start-tag has a matching end-tag. Moreover, all elements must be properly nested (no overlapping in element definitions), and there are no instances of multiple attributes with the same name for one element.

- It conforms to all rules of XML specification, meaning that start-tags and end-tags are always matched, there is no overlapping in elements, attributes have unique names, and markup reserved characters are properly escaped.

- It has a unique root element, with all the elements forming a hierarchical tree under the root element.

Tree representation of XML. A special exception to the hierarchical tree property cited in the last bulleted item may be achieved when internal links are introduced to the file. XML has mechanisms to introduce internal and external pointers. For example, an ID/IDREF attribute combination can be used to establish a link from one element to another. For example, the document in Figure 1.1 includes an ID/IDREF link: the *content* element in line 39 has an ID attribute that is referenced by the IDREF attribute in line 23. In this case, the document cannot be represented as a hierarchical tree, but becomes a graph.

As discussed, the XML document can be represented as a hierarchical tree. In this model, every XML element is represented as a node, and the parent–child relationships between elements are captured as edges. We call these *containment edges*. The use of ID/IDREF attributes creates an additional edge between elements that are not directly connected by a parent–child relationship. We call these edges *ID/IRDEF edges*. This introduces a new edge into the representation and transforms the tree into a graph, since a cycle is created within the graph. ID-IDREF edges dramatically complicate the processing of XML data given that many algorithmic problems, such as shortest path and proximity search, become very expensive if we move from trees to graphs. Figure 1.3 shows the tree representation for the document in Figure 1.1. Note how we have an ID/IDREF edge between the *content* element (line 39) and the *reference* element (line 23).

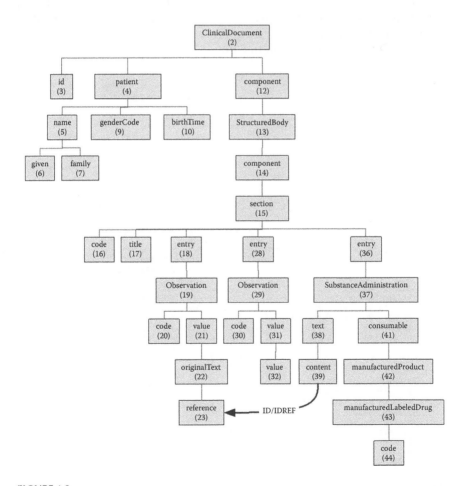

FIGURE 1.3
Tree representation of the XML document in Figure 1.1.

1.5 XML Schema

In general, we can think of data schema as the detailed description of rules and constraints that data instances have to comply in order to be valid. In addition to being well formed, an XML document can, in occasions, meet certain further validity rules. In this case, the document is said to be *valid*. A valid XML document is a well-formed document that also complies with a Document Type Definition (DTD; [59]) file or XML Schema file [60]. Note that the validity of an XML document can only be checked against an XML schema.

DTD was the first method used to specify the schema of XML documents. A DTD file specifies a set of rules that define how the data in the XML document should be structured, by defining a list of valid elements and attributes, what attributes can describe each element, and the nesting of the elements.

Figure 1.4 shows a fragment of the DTD document that specifies the validity of the XML document shown in Figure 1.1.

```
<!ELEMENT ClinicalDocument          (id, patient, component) >
<!ELEMENT id                        (#PCDATA) >
<!ATTLIST id                        extension   CDATA #REQUIRED
                                    root  CDATA #REQUIRED >
<!ELEMENT patient                   (name, genderCode, birthTime) >
<!ELEMENT component                 (StructuredBody, section) >
<!ELEMENT name                      (given, family) >
<!ELEMENT genderCode                EMPTY >
<!ATTLIST genderCode                code  CDATA #REQUIRED
                                    codeSystem  CDATA #REQUIRED >
<!ELEMENT birthTime                 EMPTY >
<!ATTLIST birthTime                 value CDATA #REQUIRED >
<!ELEMENT StructuredBody            (component) >
<!ELEMENT section                   (code, title, entry) >
<!ELEMENT given                     (#PCDATA) >
<!ELEMENT family                    (#PCDATA) >
<!ELEMENT code                      EMPTY >
<!ATTLIST code                      code  CDATA #REQUIRED
                                    codeSystem  CDATA #REQUIRED
                                    codeSystemName    CDATA #REQUIRED >
<!ELEMENT title                     (#PCDATA) >
<!ELEMENT entry                     (Observation, SubstanceAdministration) >
<!ELEMENT Observation               (code, value) >
<!ELEMENT SubstanceAdministration   (text, consumable) >
<!ELEMENT value                     (value, originalText, #PCDATA) >
<!ATTLIST value                     type  CDATA #REQUIRED
                                    code  CDATA #REQUIRED
                                    codeSystem  CDATA #REQUIRED
                                    codeSystemName    CDATA #REQUIRED
                                    displayName CDATA #REQUIRED >
<!ELEMENT text                      (content, #PCDATA) >
<!ELEMENT consumable                (manufacturedProduct) >
<!ELEMENT originalText              (reference) >
<!ELEMENT content                   (#PCDATA) >
<!ATTLIST content                   ID    ID #REQUIRED
<!ELEMENT manufacturedProduct       (manufacturedLabeledDrug) >
<!ELEMENT reference                 (EMPTY) >
<!ATTLIST reference                 IDREF value #REQUIRED
<!ELEMENT manufacturedLabeledDrug   (code) >
```

FIGURE 1.4
DTD specification for the XML document in Figure 1.1.

A more recent approach to specifying the structure of XML documents is XML Schema. This is a W3C Recommendation aimed to provide a more powerful and flexible language by which to define the XML document structure. XML Schema is more expressive than DTD, allowing new features such as richer specification of data types (e.g., nonNegativeInteger vs. PCDATA), namespaces and number, and order of child elements. XML Schemas are themselves XML documents, which is another advantage since there is no need to learn a new language to specify the structure of the document. XML Schema provides an object-oriented approach to defining the data schema.

For a detailed description of DTDs and XML Schema, see Birbeck et al. [57].

1.6 XML Parsing

In computer science and linguistics, the process of analyzing a sequence of tokens to determine the grammatical structure with respect to a given formal grammar is called *syntactic analysis* or *parsing*. In the case of XML, this means that the XML file is analyzed and the sequence of tokens is checked to validate that all the constraints noted in the previous section about XML syntax are satisfied. As the document is parsed, the data contained in the document is made available to the application that is parsing it [61].

The XML 1.0 Recommendation [14] defines two levels of parsing:

1. *Nonvalidating* makes sure that the document is well formed, but does not require an external schema to be present.
2. *Validating* Ensures that the document is both well formed and valid, according to a DTD or XML Schema.

Another distinction between parsers is the implementation that they use to process the data:

- *Tree-based parsers.* This class of parsers creates an in-memory representation of the XML tree. This allows user-friendly navigation of the tree, but may require large amounts of memory to represent the tree.
- *Event-driven parsers.* The data are processed sequentially, and the data component is handled one at a time. The memory requirements are minimal, but the interface may not be as user-friendly.

Two popular representatives of these two parsing implementations are the Document Object Model [15, 62] and the SAX [63], respectively. As with many other solutions to real-world problems, the vast number of possibilities and requirements make these two approaches necessary and compatible. Every different scenario can benefit from these implementations or a combination of both. In general, DOM is easier to program with, whereas SAX is more efficient and scalable.

1.7 XML Querying

Another mechanism of accessing XML data is to use query languages. Several query languages have been proposed, again covering a vast range of requirements. Two of the most popular XML query languages are XPath [16] and XQuery [17].

XPath is a language for selecting nodes from an XML document, and is based on the tree representation of the XML document, providing the ability to navigate the XML tree. XPath also provides a series of functions for manipulating strings, numbers, Booleans, and node sets.

XQuery, on the other hand, is a query language designed to access an XML document or a collection of XML documents in a manner similar to what a relational database does with relations. XQuery tries to exploit the flexibility and hierarchical structure of XML documents. By defining its own data model and algebra, XQuery uses path expressions (based on XPath), conditional expressions, and complex constructs, recursion, and other mechanisms to deliver a powerful, yet easy-to-learn query language. XQuery is generally more complex than SQL, which is used for querying relational databases, and hence it has so far not been widely accepted in practice.

1.8 XML Advantages and Disadvantages

Now that we have presented XML, we can summarize the advantages and disadvantages of this data model.

One of the advantages for XML that has majorly contributed to its popularity is its orientation to data exchange. XML has been designed to be platform independent by storing its contents as data files. This reduces the complexity of exchanging data, by allowing XML documents to be shared among incompatible platforms, making it resistant to software or hardware updates.

XML is also defined to be self-contained: both metadata and data are included in the XML document. Hence, there is no need to store any additional resources to interpret the data.

XML is standardized. It was created as a W3C Recommendation, backed up by the industry giants and academic researchers, and accepted by the community in general. This has also contributed to its quick popularization.

XML can represent complex, nested data in scenarios where representing the same on relational databases would be extremely cumbersome.

On the other hand, the expensive processing and querying of XML documents is also its major drawback. The need for large amounts of memory and processing power to parse and query XML data makes it unfeasible for some configurations.

Also, to date there is still no popular and efficient XML-native database systems. Instead, all the major RDBMS vendors, such as Oracle, IBM DB2, and Microsoft SQL Server, incorporate XML storage modules.

Moreover, in many cases, the complexity and overhead of XML makes it simply suboptimal for simple and small environments.

1.9 Chapter Summary

In this chapter, we have introduced the XML, which has revolutionized the manner in which data are stored, exchanged, and processed in distributed systems. We have reviewed the XML syntax, data model, and semantic aspects of its definition.

We reviewed some related work, both in industry and academia, which are based in XML or extend XML in new and more powerful directions. We also compared XML and HTML, outlining the differences in approach and syntax of these two languages.

We talked about XML storage, parsing, and querying, and based on this we identified the advantages and disadvantages of this metalanguage, which has become the *lingua franca* of the World Wide Web.

References

1. World Wide Web Consortium. W3C Math Home. 2008. http://www.w3.org/Math/(Accessed Aug. 2, 2008).
2. GraphML Working Group. 2007. GraphML. http://graphml.graphdrawing.org/(Accessed Aug. 2, 2008).
3. Open Geospatial Consortium. 2008. Geography Markup Language. http://www.opengeospatial.org/standards/gml, (Accessed Sept. 1, 2009).
4. World Wide Web Consortium. Scalable Vector Graphics. 2008. http://www.w3.org/Graphics/SVG/(Accessed Aug. 2, 2008).
5. FIX Protocol. 2008. FIXML Resources for FIX 4.4 Specification. http://www.fix-protocol.org/specifications/fix4.4fixml, (Accessed Sept. 1, 2009).
6. OASIS XML Cover Pages. 1999. FinXML—The Digital Language for Capital Markets. http://xml.coverpages.org/finXML.html, (Accessed Sept. 1, 2009).

7. OASIS XML Cover Pages. 2001. SwiftML for Business Messages. http://xml. coverpages.org/swiftML.html, (Accessed Sept. 1, 2009).
8. Wikipedia. RSS Web feed format. 2008. http://en.wikipedia.org/wiki/RSS_ (file_format), (Accessed Sept. 1, 2009).
9. World Wide Web Consortium. 2002. XHTML 1.0 The Extensible HyperText Markup Language (Second Edition). http://www.w3.org/TR/xhtml1/ (accessed Aug. 2, 2008).
10. Dolin, R. H., Alschuler, L., Boyer, S., Beebe, C., Behlen, F. M., Biron, P. V., and Shabo, A. 2006. HL7 Clinical document architecture, Release 2. *International Journal of the American Medical Informatics Association* 13(1):30–39.
11. World Wide Web Consortium. W3C Homepage. 2008. http://www.w3.org/ (Accessed Aug. 4, 2008).
12. W3 Schools. 2008. Extensible Markup Language. http://www.w3schools.com/ XML (Accessed Aug. 2, 2008).
13. World Wide Web Consortium. 2004. Overview of SGML Resources. http:// www.w3.org/MarkUp/SGML/(Accessed Aug. 2, 2008).
14. World Wide Web Consortium. 2006. Extensible Markup Language (XML) 1.0 (Fourth Edition). http://www.w3.org/TR/REC-xml/(Accessed Aug. 2, 2008).
15. World Wide Web Consortium. Document Object Model (DOM). http://www. w3.org/DOM/(Accessed Aug. 4, 2008).
16. World Wide Web Consortium. 1999. XML Path Language (XPath). http://www. w3.org/TR/xpath (Accessed Aug. 4, 2008).
17. World Wide Web Consortium. XQuery 1.0: An XML Query Language. 2007. http://www.w3.org/TR/xquery/(Accessed Aug. 4, 2008).
18. World Wide Web Consortium. 2004. Resource Descriptor Framework (RDF). http://www.w3.org/RDF/(Accessed Aug. 5, 2008).
19. Bhadkamkar, M., Farfán, F., Hristidis, V., and Rangaswami, R. 2009. Storing semi-structured data on disk drives. *ACM Transactions on Storage* 5(2):1–35.
20. McHugh, J., Abiteboul, S., Goldman, R., Quass, D., and Widom, J. 1997. Lore: A database management system for semistructured data. *ACM SIGMOD Record* 26(3):54–66.
21. Jagadish, H. V., Al-Khalifa, S., Chapman, A., et al. 2002. TIMBER: a native XML database. *VLDB Journal* 11(4):274–291.
22. Fiebig, T., Helmer, S., Kanne, C.-C., et al. 2002. Natix: a technology overview, revised papers from the NODe 2002 Web and Database-Related Workshops on Web, Web-Services, and Database Systems, pp. 12–33.
23. Data ex machina. 2008. The NATIX XML Repository. http://www.data-ex-machina.de/natix.html, (Accessed Sept. 1, 2009).
24. Meier, W. 2002. eXist: An open source native XML database. In *Web, Web-Services, and Database Systems*, E. R. Chaudri, M. Jeckle, and R. Unland, Eds., Springer LNCS Series.
25. Shanmugasundaram, J., Tufte, K., He, G., Zhang, C., Dewitt, D., and Naughton, J. 1999. Relational databases for querying XML documents: limitations and opportunities. In *Proceedings of the 25th VLDB Conference*.
26. Deutsch, A., Fernandez, M. F., and Suciu, D. 1999. Storing semistructured data with STORED. In *Proceedings of the ACM International Conference on Management of Data (SIGMOD)*.

27. Florescu, D., and Kossmann, D. 1999. Storing and querying XML data using an RDMBS. *IEEE Data Engineering Bulletin* 22:27–34.
28. Tatarinov, I., Beyer, K., and Shanmugasundaram, J. 2002. Storing and querying ordered XML using a relational database system. In *Proceedings of the ACM SIGMOD*.
29. Microsoft Developer Network. 2005. XML Support in Microsoft SQL Server 2005. http://msdn.microsoft.com/en-us/library/ms345117.aspx, (Accessed Sept. 1, 2009).
30. Oracle Corporation. XML Technology Center. http://www.oracle.com/technology/tech/xml/index.html, (Accessed Sept. 1, 2009).
31. IBM Corporation. 2008. pureXML. http://www-306.ibm.com/software/data/db2/xml/, (Accessed Sept. 1, 2009).
32. Bohannon, P., Freire, J., Roy, P., and Simeon, J. 2002. From XML schema to relations: a cost-based approach to XML storage. In *Proceedings of International Conference on Data Engineering*.
33. Carey, M. J., Florescu, D., Ives, Z. G. et al. 2000. XPERANTO: publishing object-relational data as XML. In International Workshop on the Web and Databases.
34. Lee, D., Mani, M., Chiu, F., and Chu, W. W. 2001. Nesting-based relational-to-XML schema translation. In *International Workshop on the Web and Databases WebDB*.
35. Chen, Y., Davidson, S. B., and Zheng. Y. 2004. BLAS: an efficient XPath processing system. In *Proceedings of ACM SIGMOD*.
36. Brantner, M., Helmer, S., Kanne, C.-C., and Moerkotte, G. 2005. Full-fledged algebraic XPath processing in Natix. In *Proceedings of the 21st International Conference on Data Engineering ICDE*.
37. Barton, C., Charles, P., Goyal, D., Raghavachari, M., and Fontoura, M. 2003. Streaming XPath processing with forward and backward axes. In *Proceedings of the International Conference on Data Engineering ICDE*.
38. May, N., Helmer, S., Kanne, C.-C., and Moerkotte, G. 2004. XQuery processing in Natix with an emphasis on join ordering. In *Proceedings of International Workshop on XQuery Implementation, Experience and Perspectives XIME-P*.
39. Zhang, X., Mulchandani, M., Christ, S., Murphy, B., and Rundensteiner, E. A. 2002. Rainbow: mapping-driven XQuery processing system. In *Proceedings of the ACM SIGMOD*.
40. Liu, Z. H., Krishnaprasad, M., and Arora, V. 2005. Native XQuery processing in oracle XMLDB. In *Proceedings of ACM SIGMOD*.
41. Nicola, M., and John, J. 2003. XML parsing: a threat to database performance. In *Proceedings of the 12th Conference on Information and Knowledge Management*.
42. World Wide Web Consortium. Extensible Stylesheet Language (XSL) 2007. http://www.w3.org/TR/xsl/(Accessed Aug. 5, 2008).
43. World Wide Web Consortium. XSL Transformations. 2007. http://www.w3.org/TR/xslt (Accessed Aug. 5, 2008).
44. Noga, M., Schott, S., and Löwe, W.. Lazy XML processing. In *ACM DocEng*, 2002.
45. Schott, S., and Noga, M. 2003. Lazy XSL transformations. In *ACM DocEng*.
46. Kenji, M., and Hiroyuki, S. 2005. Static optimization of XSLT Stylesheets: template instantiation optimization and lazy XML parsing. In *ACM DocEng*.

47. Farfán, F., Hristidis, V., and Rangaswami, R. 2007. Beyond lazy XML parsing. In *Proceedings of DEXA*.

48. Farfán, F., Hristidis, V., and Rangaswami, R. 2009. 2LP: A double-lazy XML parser. *Information Systems* 34:145–163.

49. Lu, W., Chiu, K., and Pan, Y. 2006. A parallel approach to XML parsing. In *IEEE/ ACM International Conference on Grid Computing Grid*.

50. XML Pull Parsing. 2006. http://www.xmlpull.org/index.shtml (Accessed Aug. 5, 2008).

51. XML Pull Parser (XPP). 2004. http://www.extreme.indiana.edu/xgws/xsoap/ xpp/(Accessed Aug. 5, 2008).

52. Jenkins, C., Jackson, M., Burden, P., and Wallis, J. 1999. Automatic RDF meta-data generation for resource discovery. *International Journal of Computer and Telecommunications Networking* 31(11–16):1305–1320.

53. Broekstra, J., Kampman, A., and van Harmelen, F. 2002. Sesame: a generic architecture for storing and querying RDF and RDF Schema. In *Proceedings of the Semantic Web Conference ISWC*.

54. Nejdl, W., Wolf, B., Qu, C., et al. 2002. EDUTELLA: a P2P networking infrastructure based on RDF. In *Proceedings of the International WWW Conference*.

55. Codd, E. F. 1970. A relational model of data for large shared data banks. *Communications of the ACM* 13(6):377–387.

56. Ramakrishnan, R., and Gehrke, J. 2000. *Database Management Systems*, 3rd ed. New York, NY: McGraw-Hill Higher Education.

57. Birbeck, M., Duckett, J., and Gudmundsson, O. G. et al. 2001. *Professional XML*, 2nd edn. Birmingham, England: Wrox Press Inc.

58. Bray, T. 1998. Introduction to the Annotated XML Specification: Extensible Markup Language (XML) 1.0. http://www.xml.com/axml/testaxml.htm, (Accessed Sept. 1, 2009).

59. W3Schools. Introduction to DTD. 2003. http://www.w3schools.com/DTD/ dtd_intro.asp (Accessed Aug. 4, 2008).

61. McLaughlin, B., and Loukides, M. 2001. *Java and XML. (O'Reilly Java Tools)*. O'Reilly & Associates.

60. World Wide Web Consortium. 2006. XML Schema. http://www.w3.org/XML/ Schema (Accessed Aug. 4, 2008).

62. W3 Schools. 2008. XML DOM Tutorial. 2008. http://www.w3schools.com/ dom/default.asp (Accessed Aug. 4, 2008).

63. Official SAX Website. 2004. http://www.saxproject.org/about.html, (Accessed Sept. 1, 2009).

2

Electronic Health Records

Fernando Farfán, Ramakrishna Varadarajan, and Vagelis Hristidis

CONTENTS

2.1 Introduction

An electronic health record (EHR) is an individual patient's medical record stored in digital format. It can be viewed as a longitudinal report that can be generated in one or more encounters in any care delivery setting. The EHR can contain several types of patient data, such as the patient's demographic information, clinical data such as vital signs, medical history, immunizations, laboratory and radiology data, problems and progress notes, accounting and billing records, and even legal documents such as living wills and health powers of attorney.

The purpose of EHRs is to automate and streamline the healthcare workflow by putting together a complete record of a clinical patient encounter, increasing

TABLE 2.1

Sample Instance of a *Patients* Relation

Patient_Id	First_Name	Last_Name	Date_of_Birth	Gender
60315	Jacqueline	Jones	2002-02-12	Female
76638	Andrew	Smith	2003-05-25	Male
76639	Jason	Smith	2003-06-18	Male
76640	Melinda	Galvin	2004-01-12	Female

the physician's efficiency, and reducing costs. Moreover, the adoption of EHRs seeks standardization in the representation of clinical information.

EHRs have several advantages of over conventional paper records. The costs of physically storing paper (and other media) records and centralizing them in a convenient location are highly minimized when an EHR solution is implemented. The poor legibility and medical errors induced by hand-written medical records is also minimized by the extensive use of terminologies, dictionaries, and abbreviations in EHRs. Other benefits of EHRs are the improved interaction between physicians and patients, flagging of potentially harmful drug interactions, and the ability to exploit these electronic records in decision support systems and information discovery systems.

In recent years, many EHR standard representation languages have been proposed based on Extensible Markup Language (XML) (presented in Chapter 1). Two of the most popular XML-based data representations are the Clinical Document Architecture (CDA) [1] proposed by the Health Level 7 (HL7) group and the American Society for Testing and Materials (ASTM) International's Continuity of Care Record (CCR) [2]. CDA is an XML-based document markup standard that specifies the structure and semantics of clinical documents, such as discharge summaries and progress notes, for the purpose of storing and exchanging data. It is an American National Standard Institute–approved HL7 standard, intended to become the *de facto* EHR representation standard.

Even though recent EHR standards increasingly use XML representation, many existing EHR systems use the relational data model, where data is organized in tables (relations) with rows (also called records or tuples) and columns (also called attributes or fields). As an example, we can observe a relation of medical records in Table 2.1. An instance of a relation is the actual content of the relation at a specific time. It is also possible that an EHR system uses both XML and relation representation of the EHR data, given that XML is more suitable for the exchange of data, whereas the relational model is more efficient for storage in a Relational Database Management System (RDBMS).

2.1.1 Terminology Discussion

There has been some debate regarding the terminology and acronyms used in the health informatics field. Both terms, EHR and electronic medical records (EMRs), have become popular synonyms in many circles. For many users, there is a clear and important distinction between these terms. According to the Healthcare Information and Management Systems Society [3, 4], the term EHR should be assigned to a global concept and EMR to a discrete localized record [5]. In particular, an EMR can be seen as a legal record created in a healthcare facility that will be the source of data for an EHR [3]. In other words, an EMR is considered to be one of several components of an EHR. In the rest of this book, we refer to EHR as a global and complete record of an individual, comprising several types of information and often fed by different EMRs.

A new related term is personal health record (PHR), a health record intended to be maintained by an individual [6]. Many public and private records, such as Microsoft HealthVault [7], Google Health [8], and Records for Living HealthFrame [9], provide systems and portals that allow individuals to manage PHRs, by gathering and managing data from a series of healthcare providers.

2.1.2 History of EHRs

Since the 1990s, there has been an increased interest in implementing and popularizing medical informatics systems to help reduce preventable medical errors. In a 1999 report [10], the Institute of Medicine challenged the healthcare industry to reduce preventable medical errors by 50% by 2004. One proposed method to achieve this goal was to use technology to reduce these rates. Since that report, several standards and systems have been defined and although there is still much room for improvement, the reduction in medical errors has been partially achieved in many cases.

Recently, new initiatives from information technology industry giants have appeared: Google Health [8] and Microsoft HealthVault [7], conceived to bring EHRs to the general public in the form of PHRs, were intended as a solution to organize, centralize, and manage the health information of every person, as well as to make patient-physician communication more fluid. These two portals represent a new trend of end user products that allow the creation and management of PHRs, by managing information regarding basic demographics, medical history and conditions, medications, allergies, etc. Microsoft HealthVault, in particular, allows interaction with mobile health devices such as heart rate monitors and fitness devices. Google Health also provides an engine to detect possible harmful interactions between the recorded medications.

2.1.3 Adoption of EHRs

According to the report "Health Information Technology in the United States: The Information Base for Progress" [11], in 2006 almost 25% of physicians used EHRs to improve the quality of care they delivered. This report stated that EHR is still not widely adopted because of financial, technical, and legal obstacles. This study, which was led by researchers from Massachusetts General Hospital and George Washington University, estimated that 25% of physicians use EHRs, but only 10% would define their solutions as "fully functional." The report also identified that only 5–10% of hospitals have implemented computerized physician order entry systems, which can reduce medical errors and facilitate care delivery. An interesting discovery of this report is that large clinical practices (grouping nine physicians or more) have significantly higher rates of having an EHR system in place; small practices (n = 1–9 physicians), however, account for 80% of physicians in the nation.

2.2 Related Work and Further Reading

This section presents important pointers for topics related to EHRs.

2.2.1 EHR Standards

In addition to the EHR standards discussed in this chapter, there are other standardization efforts in progress. The following is a nonexhaustive list of these efforts:

- ISO/TC 215 [12] is the International Organization for Standardization's Technical Committee on health informatics. It has worked on the standardization of Health Information and Communications Technology, defining the technical specification ISO 18308, which describes the requirements for EHR architectures.
- OpenEHR [13] is a next-generation public specifications and implementations for EHR systems and communication, based on a complete separation of software and clinical models.
- American National Standard Institute X12 (EDI) [14] is a set of transaction protocols used for transmitting virtually any aspect of patient data. Several of the transactions became required by the Health Insurance Portability and Accountability Act (HIPAA; [15]) for transmitting data to Medicare.
- CONTSYS [16] is a system of concepts that supports continuity of care. It has been adopted by the European Union and is filed as the standard EN 13940.
- EHRcom, also referred to as the European standard EN 13606, is the standard for the communication of information from EHR systems.

- HISA refers to the "Standard Architecture for Healthcare Information Systems" (EN 12967), a services standard for intersystem communication in a clinical information environment.

Benefits of using EHR systems. Use of EHR systems improves the legibility and accessibility of medical data [17]. It also improves the availability, timeliness, accuracy, and completeness of medical documentation [18]. Although the current perception is that the use of the EHR system increases the time spent by clinicians on related activities, this resistance, which is based on lack of familiarity, will diminish as physicians become more proficient with computers [19]. One critical use of EHR systems is in preventive care recommendations [18]. EHR systems can integrate evidence-based recommendations for preventive services in patient data to identify patients needing specific services. The main benefits of using EHR systems is to reduce drug costs (such as identifying the least expensive drug within a class) and prevent adverse drug events [19].

Barriers to the use of EHR systems. A major obstacle is the initial cost of EHR systems, and identifying who will shoulder this investment is difficult [18, 19]. This barrier has been studied by many groups. For example, data entry may take additional time [19]. The learning curve for system usage may be steep [19]. Concern about security and confidentiality of electronic information is another issue and much work remains in the development of access security strategies [19].

Experience in deploying EHRs. Many positive experiences have been documented worldwide. Burke and White [20] described a specialized EHR system for cardiac departments that uses the World Wide Web to collect, store, and exchange patient information. Boulus and Bjorn [21] identified and characterized the factors that allowed the adaptation of EHR systems in Norway and Canada. Ludwick and Doucette [22] performed an exhaustive survey on experiences in implementing health information systems, and discovered the concerns complicating the deployment of health information systems.

Medical ontologies and terminologies. Further reading resources analyzing the impact of medical ontologies are sampled as follows: Open Clinical [23] presents a detailed survey on medical ontologies. Gangemi et al. [24] report on ONIONS, a methodology for ontology analysis and integration applied to large ontologies such as the Unified Medical Language System project. MEDCIN [25], developed by Medicomp Systems, is a system of standardized medical terminology including more than 250,000 clinical data elements such as symptoms, history, physical examination, tests, diagnoses, and therapy. The National Drug Code [26] is a universal product identifier used in the United States and maintained by the U.S. Food and Drug Administration with a current list of all drugs intended for human use. For more information, see Hristidis et al. [26a].

2.3 Content and Format of EHRs

A *medical record* or *health record* [27] is a systematic documentation of a patient's medical history and care. The purpose of maintaining the health records of a patient is to allow healthcare providers access to the medical history of the patient and to serve as a basis for planning patient care, documenting communication between the healthcare provider and any other health professional contributing to the patient's care.

2.3.1 Content of an EHR

The specific content of a medical record [28] may vary depending on the specialty and location of the healthcare provider. It usually contains the patient's identification information and other demographics, the patient's health history (what the patient tells the healthcare providers about his or her past and present health status), and the patient's medical examination findings (what the healthcare providers observe when the patient is examined). In addition, a medical record may include laboratory test results, prescribed medications, list of allergies (including immunization status), referrals ordered to healthcare providers, patient's insurance and billing details, plans for future care, etc. In addition to text and numeric data, an EHR may also contain multimedia data such as medical images or videos. Generally, separate standards are used to represent multimedia data of EHRs.

2.3.2 EHR Formats and Standards

Traditionally, medical records have been written on paper and kept in folders. These folders are typically divided into useful sections, with new information added to each section chronologically as the patient experiences new medical issues. The advent of EHRs has not only changed the format of health records, but has increased accessibility of files. There are many standards relating to specific aspects of EHRs and EMRs. Note that the format of EHRs has a major impact on its exchange and interoperability among various healthcare providers.

There are many organizations that work on developing the standards for representing, storing, and exchanging EHRs among heterogeneous systems. The HL7 organization develops Conceptual Standards [i.e., HL7 Reference Information Model (RIM) [29]], Document Standards (i.e., HL7 CDA; [1]), Application Standards [i.e., HL7 Clinical Context Object Workgroup (CCOW); [30], and Messaging Standards (i.e., HL7 v2.x and v3.0). HL7 messages [27, 31] are used for interchange between hospital and physician record systems and between EHR systems and practice management systems. HL7 specifies a message model for exchange of text-based medical data, and is currently widely used for intrainstitution data exchange. The goal of HL7 version 2 standard is to support hospital workflows. HL7 v2.x (collectively all HL7 2 versions are known as version 2.x) mostly uses a proprietary (non-XML) encoding syntax based on delimiters.

The HL7 RIM is the grammatical specification of HL7 messages, constituting the building blocks of the language entities and the relationship among them. RIM can be represented as a network of classes, expressed using a notation similar to Unified Modeling Language [32]. Figure 2.1 shows the RIM core class diagram, consisting of six "core" classes and a set of relationships between them. In addition to the core classes depicted in the figure, the HL7 RIM also provides a set of classes to define a communication infrastructure. Table 2.2 summarizes the function of each core class and provides examples for each case.

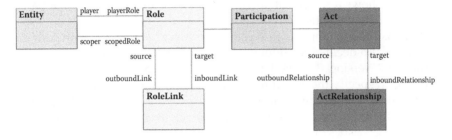

FIGURE 2.1
HL7 RIM core class diagram.

TABLE 2.2

Examples and Description of RIM Core Classes

Core Class	Description	Examples
• *Act*	• Actions and happenings to be documented. Analogous to a verb.	• Clinical observation • Assessment of health condition
• *Entity*	• Physical thing or being. Analogous to a noun.	• Person • Chemical substances
• *Role*	• Ties an *Entity* to the *Acts* that it plays or provides. Each *Role* is played by one *Entity*.	• Patient • Employee
• *RoleLink*	• Specifies the connections and dependencies that exist between two different *Role* objects.	• Manager has authority over analyst (using *RoleLink* "direct authority")
• *Participation*	• Specifies a relationship between a particular *Role* instance and a particular *Act* instance.	• Surgeon • Author
• *ActRelationship*	• Associates a pair of *Act* objects representing a connection from one *Act* to another.	• Theophylline mitigates asthma (using *ActRelationship* of type "mitigates")

Next, we present several formats and standards of modern EHR systems as a whole, organized according to the type of information that they store or represent.

2.3.2.1 Standards for Textual Information

Some of the most prominent EHR standards cover the basic structure and textual information contained in the record. Two of the most prominent standards in this category are the ASTM International CCR and HL7 CDA, which are described below.

ASTM International CCR [2] is a patient health summary standard based on XML. The CCR can be created, read, and interpreted by various EHR systems, allowing easy interoperability between otherwise disparate entities. Figure 2.2 shows a sample of an ASTM CCR document, depicting a partial EHR for a fictional patient.

CCR has become popular in recent years after Microsoft HealthVault and Google Health decided to adopt it and use it in their PHR portals.

The HL7 version 3 CDA [1] is another XML-based markup standard intended to specify the encoding, structure, and semantics of clinical documents, such as discharge summaries and progress notes, for the purpose of electronic exchange. According to the developers of CDA version 2.0, the main characteristics of the CDA standard are

- *Persistence.* The clinical documents exist in an unaltered state for a period defined by local and regulatory requirements.
- *Stewardship.* A clinical document is maintained by an organization entrusted with its care.
- *Authentication.* The clinical records are intended to be legally authenticated.
- *Context.* The clinical document specifies its own default context.
- *Wholeness.* Authentication of a clinical document applies to the whole instance and the full context. Also, it is a complete and persistent set of information including text, images, sound, and other multimedia content.
- *Human readability.* A clinical document is human-readable.

Figure 2.3 presents a sample CDA document, showing the partial health record to a fictional patient.

We can observe that even though both CCR and CDA documents are XML-based and store the same information, the set of XML tags is different, and so is the organization of each format. For example, references to external sources (dictionaries and ontologies) are treated differently by the two formats. In the case of CCR, a whole subtree is devoted to an external code, as exemplified by lines 35–39 in Figure 2.2. This XML subtree references

```
1.    <?xml version="1.0" encoding="UTF-8" ?>
2.    <ContinuityOfCareRecord xmlns="urn:astm-org:CCR">
3.        <Language><Text>English</Text></Language>
4.        <Version>V1.0</Version>
5.        <DateTime>
6.            <ExactDateTime>2009-04-14T13:05:31-05:00</ExactDateTime>
7.        </DateTime>
8.        <Patient>
9.            <ActorID>ID-8dd1b1b8-007c-4778-92e4-9f605bb8ae24</ActorID>
10.       </Patient>
11.       <Actors>
12.           <Actor>
13.               <Person>
14.                   <Name>
15.                       <CurrentName>
16.                           <Given>John</Given>
17.                           <Family>Doe</Family>
18.                       </CurrentName>
19.                       <DisplayName>John Doe</DisplayName>
20.                   </Name>
21.                   <DateOfBirth><ExactDateTime>1986-02-26</ExactDateTime></DateOfBirth>
22.                   <Gender>
23.                   <Text>Male</Text>
24.                   <Code>
25.                       <Value>C0024554</Value>
26.                       <CodingSystem>UMLS</CodingSystem>
27.                       <Version>2005AC</Version>
28.       </Code></Gender></Person></Actor></Actors>
29.       <Body>
30.           <Alerts>
31.               <Alert>
32.                   <Type><Text>Allergy</Text></Type>
33.                   <Description>
34.                       <Text>Penicillin</Text>
35.                       <Code>
36.                           <Value>6369005</Value>
37.                           <CodingSystem>SNOMEDCT</CodingSystem>
38.                           <Version>2005</Version>
39.                   </Code></Description>
40.                   <Status><Text>Active</Text></Status>
41.                   <Agent>
42.                       <Products>
43.                           <Product>
44.                               <ProductName>
45.                                   <Text>Penicillin</Text>
46.                                   <Code>
47.                                       <Value>6369005</Value>
48.                                       <CodingSystem>SNOMEDCT</CodingSystem>
49.                                       <Version>2005</Version>
50.                                   </Code>
51.       </ProductName></Product></Products></Agent></Alert></Alerts>
52.       </Body>
53.   </ContinuityOfCareRecord>
```

FIGURE 2.2
Sample continuity of care record document.

the International Systematized Nomenclature of Human and Veterinary Medicine (SNOMED) CT ontology (described later this chapter) concept "Penicillin," showing the coding system, code, and version of this entry. On the other hand, a reference to an external source in CDA documents is depicted in line 21 of Figure 2.3, again, showing a reference to a SNOMED Clinical Terms (SNOMED CT) concept. Here, a single XML element contains all the information about the coding system, code, and textual description, although version information is not present. Note that these minor

```
1.   <? xml version="1.0" ?>
2.   <ClinicalDocument>
3.      <id extension="49912" root="2.16.840.1.113883.3.933"/>
4.      <patient>
5.        <name>
6.          <given>Peter</given>
7.          <family>Patient</family>
8.        </name>
9.        <genderCode code="M" codeSystem="2.16.840.1.5.1"/>
10.       <birthTime value="20020924"/>
11.     </patient>
12.     <component>
13.       <StructuredBody>
14.         <component>
15.           <section>
16.             <code code="10160-0" codeSystem="2.16.840.1.113883.6.1"
                  codeSystemName="LOINC" />
17.             <title>Medications</title>
18.             <entry>
19.               <Observation>
20.                 <code code="84100007" codeSystem="2.16.840.1.113883.6.96"
                      codeSystemName="SNOMED CT" displayName=" medication history"/>
21.                 <value xsi:type="CD" code="195967001" codeSystem="2.16.840.1.113883.6.96"
                      codeSystemName="SNOMED CT" displayName="Asthma">
22.                   <originalText>
23.                     <reference value="m1"/>
24.                   </originalText>
25.                 </value>
26.               </Observation>
27.             </entry>
28.             <entry>
29.               <Observation>
30.                 <code code="84100007" codeSystem="2.16.840.1.113883.6.96"
                      codeSystemName="SNOMED CT" displayName="medication history"/>
31.                 <value xsi:type="CD" code="32398004" codeSystem="2.16.840.1.113883.6.96"
                      codeSystemName="SNOMED CT" displayName="Bronchitis">
32.                   <value xsi:type="CD" code="91143003" codeSystem="2.16.840.1.113883.6.96"
                      codeSystemName="SNOMED CT" displayName="Albuterol" />
33.                 </value>
34.               </Observation>
35.             </entry>
36.             <entry>
37.               <SubstanceAdministration>
38.                 <text>
39.                   <content ID="m1">Theophylline</content>20 mg every other day, alternating
                      with 18 mg every other day. Stop if temperature is above 1103F.
40.                 </text>
41.                 <consumable>
42.                   <manufacturedProduct>
43.                     <manufacturedLabeledDrug>
44.                       <code code="66493003" codeSystem="2.16.840.1.113883.6.96"
                          codeSystemName="SNOMED CT" displayName="Theophylline"/>
45.                     </manufacturedLabeledDrug>
46.                   </manufacturedProduct>
47.                 </consumable>
48.               </SubstanceAdministration>
49.             </entry>
50.           </section>
51.         </component>
52.       </StructuredBody>
53.     </component>
54.   </ClinicalDocument>
```

FIGURE 2.3
HL7 clinical document architecture sample.

representation differences between the two formats cannot be viewed as an advantage of one standard over the other.

2.3.2.2 Standards for Medical Images

The Digital Imaging and Communications in Medicine (DICOM) [27, 33] is a standard for representing radiology images and reporting. It is a comprehensive specification of information content, structure, encoding,

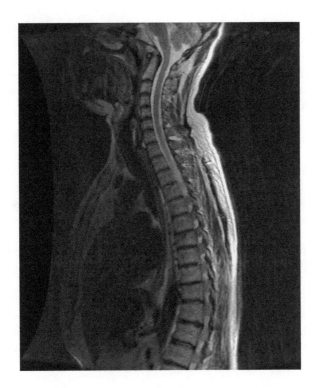

FIGURE 2.4
DICOM-formatted medical image from an EHR. (Image taken from DICOM Files [65].)

and communications protocols for electronic interchange of diagnostic and therapeutic images and image-related information. DICOM differs from other data formats in that it groups information into data sets. This means that a file of a chest x-ray image, for example, actually contains the patient ID within the file, so that the image can never be separated from this information by mistake. Figure 2.4 shows a medical image that can be represented using DICOM.

The DICOM specification provides several services, such as storage, query and retrieval, printing, offline handling, and network transmission. JPEG Interactive Protocol [34] allows users to transmit specific tiles of image with specific resolution and quality. JPEG Interactive Protocol is used by DICOM.

2.3.2.3 Messaging Standards

Messaging standards are particularly important because they define how information is packaged and communicated from one party to another. The CEN/TC 251/PT3-033 (European Standardization Committee: Technical Committee for Healthcare, Project Team 22) Request and Report Messages for Diagnostic Service Departments document specifies a semantic data model and model-based compositional rules for messages, but only provides partial guidelines for electronic document interchange. HL7 defines its own messaging standards. Unfortunately, the HL7 and CEN/TC 251 specifications leave major communications issues unresolved. Implementers depend on bilateral negotiation between information system vendors to determine parameters for the unspecified details.

2.3.2.3.1 Context Management and Integration Standards

A technique called "context management" CCOW [30] allows information in separate healthcare applications to be unified so that each application is referring to the same patient, encounter, or user. CCOW does not handle data exchange between remote users but only synchronizes data access for a single user. Finally, IHE (Integrating the Healthcare Enterprise) [35] is an initiative that promotes and supports the integration of systems in the healthcare enterprise. Recently, the research community has been working on other EHR integration solutions. For example, Hristidis et al. [36] proposed a flexible mechanism for EMR exchange, which allows generating a customized EHR using a generic approach independent of existing healthcare applications. They proposed a declarative communication engine called Communication Virtual Machine, which negotiates the capabilities of the involved parties and underlying networks to guarantee quality of service and presentation compatibility.

2.4 Issues and Challenges in EHR Adoption and Use

As will be discussed in Chapter 5, health records are personal documents and there are many ethical, social, political, and legal issues surrounding them. Even though several EHR standards have been proposed, adoption of EHRs and other health information technologies has been minimal in the United States. A vast majority of healthcare transactions in the United States still take place on paper, a system that has remained unchanged since the 1950s. The main issues accounting for this slow adoption of EHRs can be briefly attributed to the following [37]:

- *Privacy*—Patients are reluctant to give full access to their historical medical data. A major concern is the adequate confidentiality of the individual records being electronically managed. Multiple access points over an open network like the Internet increases possible patient data interception. HIPAA [15] requires any EHR exchange between health providers to follow a privacy policy. HIPAA establishes national standards for EHR system transactions and national identifiers for providers, health insurance plans, and employers. It also protects health insurance coverage for workers and their families when they change or lose their jobs. Patients also do not want to give providers access to their whole medical record but only to the most recent part, since they believe that it would be unnecessary and intrusive [38]. Privacy issues are discussed in detail in Chapter 5.

- *Interoperability*—Healthcare provider institutions are reluctant to open their systems to mediators or any type of external access, due to security, privacy (HIPAA; [15]) and competitive advantage–related reasons. Also, a unique patient id is not possible due to privacy-related and political reasons [38, 39].

- *Making existing health records electronic*—Older paper health records ideally should be incorporated into the patient's record. Paper records involve extensive handwritten content; some of the content is illegible following conversion. The material may exist in any number of formats, sizes, media types, and qualities, which further complicates accurate conversion. The digital scanning process involved in the conversion of these physical records to EHR is an expensive, time-consuming process, which must be carried out to exacting standards to ensure exact capture of the content.

- *Budget limitations*—Historically, implementation and maintenance of an EHR system was difficult to afford in small, budget-conscious, multiple-location healthcare organizations. In recent times, new marketing plans are focusing on bringing EHR technology to the mainstream, motivated in particular by the initiative of President Barack Obama's administration in trying to jump-start the adoption of EHRs with economic incentives [40].

- *Preservation*—The physical medical records are the property of the medical provider (or facility) that prepares them. HIPAA provides federal right to patients with respect to information in their health records, including copying and access. In addition, those responsible for the management of EHRs are responsible for ensuring that the hardware, software, and media used to manage the information remain usable and are not degraded. This requires backup of the data and protection of copies.

2.5 Healthcare Information Systems

EHR systems, which are part of broader healthcare information systems, provide many benefits to different institutions in the healthcare industry. For simplicity, we use the terms healthcare information systems and EHR systems interchangeably in this chapter. The American Health Information Management Association (AHIMA) [41] defines the three essential capabilities of an EHR system:

- To capture data at the point of care
- To integrate data from multiple internal and external sources
- To support caregiver decision making

Bates et al. [19] focused on the requirements of EHR systems in the U.S. primary care. This work, which was developed by the National Alliance for Primary Care Informatics, provides guidelines for implementing EHR systems in primary care. Hillestad et al. [18] examined the potential benefits of EHR systems, placing emphasis on the financial benefits that can be obtained by using EHR systems. McDonald [42] focused on the available standards in healthcare and the need for standardizing the information messaging in order to benefit the EHR systems. He also focused on coordination among different healthcare institutions. Miller and Sim [17] elaborated on physicians' use of electronic records, and the problems and related solutions based on a quantitative study of the practices of physicians who have implemented an EHR system.

There are many modern EHR systems available in the market. The following is a list of some of the vendors providing EHR solutions: Synamed [43], Teges [44], Medical Communication Systems (Medcomsoft) [45], StreamlineMD [46], eClinicalWorks [47], Practical Partner [48], MediNotes [49], Misys PLC HealthCare [50], NextGen [51], Allscripts [52], OmniMD [53], GE Healthcare [54], InteGreat [55], and Cerner [56]. These EHR system solutions offer different features and choosing the appropriate vendor is a challenging job. The AC Group [57] has been ranking EHR systems since 2002. The ranking is carried out after conducting extensive surveys on participating vendors as well as physicians using those EHR systems. The ranking is based on the following criteria: (1) product functionality, (2) end user satisfaction, (3) company financial viability, (4) client base, (5) technology, and (6) price. The choice of product is also dependent on the number of physicians in the practice. The AC Group [57] ranks the EHR system in the following category: 1–5 physicians, 6–19 physicians, 20–99 physicians, and more than 100 physicians. In the category of 1–5 physicians practice, Medical Communications System [45] is the highly ranked vendor. In all other categories, NextGen [51] is highly ranked. It did not rank highly in the category of 1–5 physicians because of its high price.

Features of healthcare information systems. We briefly describe the main features found in health information systems. Synamed [43] is a U.S. healthcare information technology company, established in 1999, that provides Web-based EHRs and practice management system to medical practitioners in the United States. Some of the products and services provided by Synamed [43] are

- EHRs
- Practice management system
- Scheduling DICOM—digital imaging system
- Patient portal
- Document management system
- Inventory management
- Electronic prescribing
- Electronic laboratory interface
- Patient and financial reporting

Teges Corporation's [44] area of expertise lies in providing Web-based resources for clinicians to manage and monitor critically ill patients in real time. Some of the features provided are: Comprehensive Patient Database for the Intensive Care Unit, Real-time Outcomes and Performance Measurement Tool, Remote Patient Monitoring, Physician Documentation Solution, Integrated Clinical Information System, and Optimized for Clinical Research. Figures 2.5 and 2.6 show two screenshots of the *Teges iRounds* EHR system.

MedcomSoft Inc. [45] is another leading developer of interoperable software tools for the ambulatory care environment. In 2002, the company released an EMR product for the U.S. market called MedcomSoft Record. MedcomSoft Record is a fully interoperable, fully integrated clinical automation suite, which includes the following features: Electronic Medical Record System; Practice Management System; Provider Order Entry; Document Management System; Referral and Authorization Management; Disease Management and Health Maintenance Systems; and Tools for interoffice workflow, clinical decision support, coding, and compliance checking. All of the functionality is supported by a single, stable database.

NextGen Healthcare [51] provides integrated EMR (NextGen EMR) and practice management (NextGen EPM) systems. They provide solutions, including revenue cycle management, for medical practices of all sizes and specialties. They help physicians build complete EHRs and integrate with their practice management system. NextGen EMR streamlines workflow, increases productivity, and enhances quality of care. Listed below are the many features of NextGen EMR: Advanced security, Appointment scheduling, CCR/PHR capabilities, Clinical Decision Support, Disease Management, Document Generation, Image Management, Health maintenance, Lab Order entry, remote patient care, patient registry, and patient education module.

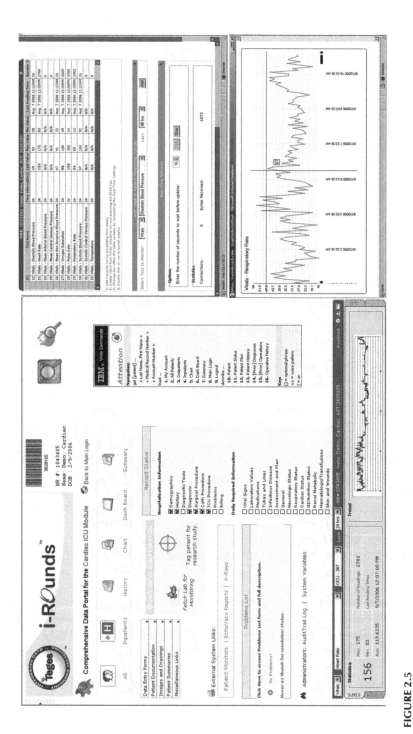

FIGURE 2.5

Screenshot of Teges i-Rounds EHR system for the cardiac intensive care unit of a hospital. (Courtesy of Teges Corporation.)

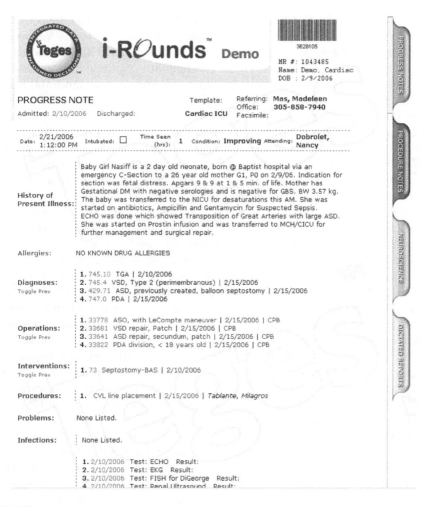

FIGURE 2.6
Screenshot of Teges i-Rounds showing a patient's HER. (Courtesy of Teges Corporation.)

2.6 Health Ontologies

In this section, some key health and biomedical ontologies used to standardize the terminology and provide semantics in EHRs are presented. Using ontologies in EHR systems can offer many benefits by disambiguating terms and standardizing concepts. As will be discussed in Chapters 3 and 6, ontologies play a key role in improving the quality of information discovery in EHRs. Ontologies can also help in integrating EHR systems by matching identical terms and entities across systems.

SNOMED CT. The SNOMED CT was created in 2001 [57a] as the conjunction of SNOMED RT and the United Kingdom's Clinical Terms Version 3, and has grown into a comprehensive set of more than 150,000 records in 12 different chapters or axes. These concepts are organized into anatomy (topology), morphology (pathologic structure), normal and abnormal functions, symptoms and signs of disease, chemicals, drugs, enzymes and other body proteins, living organisms, physical agents, spatial relationships, occupations, social contexts, diseases/diagnoses, and procedures [58]. Within the disease/diagnosis axis, many disease concepts have cross-references to other concepts in the terminology that are essential characteristics of the disease. These form a useful basis for the further formalization and development of a reference terminology [59].

SNOMED has created and is committed to spreading the adoption and implementation of SNOMED CT, a universal healthcare terminology and infrastructure whose objective is making healthcare knowledge usable wherever and whenever it is needed. It provides a common language that enables a consistent way of capturing, sharing, and aggregating health data across specialties and sites of care. The SNOMED CT structure is concept-based; each concept represents a unit of meaning, having one or more human language terms that can be used to describe the concept. Every concept has interrelationships with other concepts that provide logical computer-readable definitions, including hierarchical relationships and clinical attributes. Figure 2.7 shows a fragment (subgraph) of the SNOMED CT ontology graph. Each node in the graph corresponds to a clinical concept (e.g., "Asthma," "Respiratory Finding"), and the edges in the graph correspond to the different types of relationships among clinical concepts (e.g., "Is a," "Finding Site of").

At the moment, SNOMED CT contains more than 325,000 concepts, with 800,000 terms in English, 350,000 in Spanish, and 150,000 in German. Also, there are 1,200,000 relationships connecting these terms and concepts. The SNOMED CT ontology is used to standardize concepts in EHRs. As an example, SNOMED CT terms are routinely referenced in CDA documents and CCR documents by their numeric codes, that is, the SNOMED CT vocabulary is referenced as an external domain according to HL7 V3 processes.

Logical Observation Identifiers Names and Codes (LOINC). LOINC is a voluntary effort housed in the Regenstrief Institute, associated with Indiana University. It was initiated in 1994 by the Regenstrief Institute and developed by Regenstrief and the LOINC committee as a response to the demand for electronic movement of clinical data. LOINC facilitates the exchange and pooling of results, such as blood hemoglobin, serum potassium, or vital signs, for clinical care, outcomes management, and research. Currently, most laboratories and other diagnostic services use HL7 to send their results electronically from their reporting systems to their care systems. However, most laboratories and other diagnostic care services identify tests in these messages via their internal and idiosyncratic code values. Thus, the care system cannot fully "understand" and properly file the results they receive unless

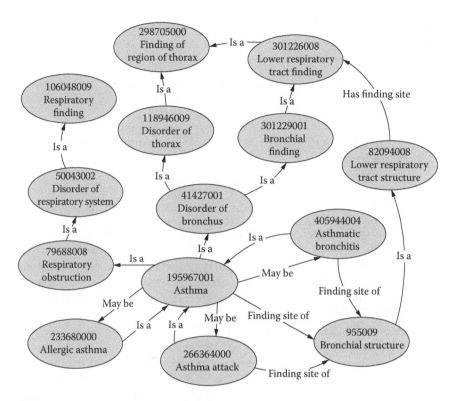

FIGURE 2.7
SNOMED CT Ontology fragment around the concept "Asthma."

they either adopt the producer's laboratory codes (which is impossible if they receive results from multiple sources), or invest in the work to map each result producer's code system to their internal code system. LOINC codes are universal identifiers for laboratory and other clinical observations that solve this problem.

The LOINC laboratory terms set provides a standard set of universal names and codes for identifying individual laboratory and clinical results. LOINC codes allow users to merge clinical results from many sources into one database for patient care, clinical research, or management. The LOINC database currently contains about 41,000 terms, which include 31,000 observational terms related to laboratory testing.

Each record in the LOINC database identifies a clinical observation and contains a formal six-part name, including: the name of the component, the property observed, the timing of the measurement, the type of sample, the scale of measurement, and where relevant, the method of measurement. In addition, each record has a unique name for tests, identifying code with check digits, synonyms, and other useful information. Table 2.3 presents a few examples of complete LOINC codes, showing the six examples previously

TABLE 2.3

LOINC Code Examples

Code	Name of Component	Property Observed	Timing	Type of Sample	Scale	Method
4764-5	GLUCOSE^3H POST 100 G GLUCOSE PO	SCNC	PT	SER/PLAS	QN	
5955-0	COAGULATION THROMBIN INDUCED	TIME	PT	PPP^CONTROL	QN	TILT TUBE
13969-1	CREATINE KINASE.MB	MCNC	PT	SER/PLAS		

Note: SCNC, substance concentration; MCNC, mass concentration; SER/PLAS, serum/ plasma; PPP^CONTROL, platelet poor plasma; PT, point in time; QN, quantitative.

described. It can be seen that the property observed can be time, substance concentration, or mass concentration, among others; the type of sample can be serum/plasma, platelet poor plasma, etc. For further explanation, please see the *LOINC User's Guide* [60].

Currently, LOINC codes are being used in the United States by laboratories and federal agencies, and are part of the HIPAA Attachment Proposal [61, 62]. Elsewhere, LOINC has been adopted in Switzerland, Hong Kong, Australia, Canada, and Germany. Similar to SNOMED CT, LOINC is used by CDA documents, CCR documents, and other EHR standards as a vocabulary domain, encoding EHR components and terminologies into a standard database of terms.

RxNorm. RxNorm [63] is a standardized nomenclature for clinical drugs produced by the National Library of Medicine. A clinical drug is a pharmaceutical product administered to a patient with a therapeutic or diagnostic intent. The definition of a clinical drug combines its ingredients, strengths, and form. The form refers to the physical form in which the drug is administered in a prescription or order. For example, two possible definitions of clinical drugs are

- Acetaminophen 500 mg oral tablet, for a generic drug name
- Acetaminophen 500 mg oral tablet (Tylenol) for a branded drug name

The purpose of RxNorm is to standardize the information exchange both between systems within the same organization and between different organizations, allowing various systems using different drug nomenclature to share data efficiently. It is intended to cover all prescription medications approved for use in the United States. RxNorm is constituted by concepts, collections of names identical in meaning at a specified level of abstraction. Each concept can be mapped to different string values in different systems,

TABLE 2.4

MeSH Code Examples

Code	Description
D009175	Mycoplasma infections
D009956	Ornithosis
D011001	Pleuropneumonia
D011024	Pneumonia, viral

all naming things that are the same. It also provides a linkage to terms from other vocabularies—for example, the concept *Ortho-Novum 7/7/7 21 Tablets* is a term from the SNOMED vocabulary; it is not within RxNorm at all, except as being related to RxNorm within the RXNREL table [63].

Medical Subject Headings (MeSH). MeSH [64] is the National Library of Medicine's controlled vocabulary (or metadata system) used to index journal articles and books in life sciences. It consists of a hierarchical structure of terms that allows searching at various levels of specificity.

As of 2008, MeSH has more than 24,700 main descriptors with their corresponding short definition. Each term also includes links to related descriptors and list of synonyms. In addition, there are more than 172,000 headings called Supplementary Concept Records (formerly Supplementary Chemical Records) within a separate thesaurus. These do not belong to the controlled vocabulary and hence are not used for indexing MEDLINE articles. There are also more than 97,000 entry terms that assist in finding the most appropriate MeSH Heading, for example, "Vitamin C" is an entry term to "Ascorbic Acid." Table 2.4 presents a few examples of MeSH codes with their respective description.

Note that MeSH is the ontology used to describe MEDLINE/PubMed entries, whereas SNOMED, LOINC, and RxNorm are more commonly used in EHRs to standardize terminology.

2.7 Chapter Summary

We have introduced the technologies, standards, and challenges involved in creating and processing EHRs. We have reviewed the concepts, history, and purpose of EHRs, as well as the challenges and experiences in implanting such systems in hospitals and clinical practices.

We discussed the content and format of EHRs as well as the most common and widespread standard formats that have been developed in recent years. We also presented state-of-the-art EHR systems and the issues that arise when developing such systems. Finally, we introduced key biomedical ontologies that have been used to introduce semantics to the EHRs.

References

1. HL7 Clinical Document Architecture, Release 2.0 (2004). http://lists.hl7.org/read/attachment/61225/1/CDA-doc%20version.pdf (Accessed Sept. 25, 2008).
2. Chheda, N. C. 2005. Electronic Medical Records and Continuity of Care Records—the Utility Theory. http://www.emrworld.net/emr-research/articles/emr-ccr.pdf, (Accessed Sept. 1, 2009).
3. Garets, D., and Davis, M. 2006. Electronic medical records vs. electronic health records: yes, there is a difference. HIMSS Analytics White Paper.
4. Healthcare Information and Management Systems Society. http://www.himss.org/, (Accessed Sept. 1, 2009).
5. Wikipedia. 2008. Electronic Health Record. http://en.wikipedia.org/wiki/Electronic_health_record, (Accessed Sept. 1, 2009).
6. Personal Health Records. http://en.wikipedia.org/wiki/Personal_health_record, (Accessed Sept. 1, 2009).
7. Microsoft HealthVault. 2008. http://www.healthvault.com/, (Accessed Sept. 1, 2009).
8. Google Health. 2008. http://www.google.com/health/, (Accessed Sept. 1, 2009).
9. Records for Living. HealthFrame. http://www.recordsforliving.com/HealthFrame/, (Accessed Sept. 1, 2009).
10. Kohn, L. T., Corrigan, J. M., and Donaldson, M. 1999. *To Err is Human: Building a Safer Health System.* Washington, DC: Institute of Medicine.
11. Blumenthal, D., DesRoches, C., Donelan, K. et al. 2006. Health Information Technology in the United States: The Information Base for Progress. Report for the Robert Wood Johnson Foundation. http://www.rwjf.org/files/publications/other/EHRReport0609.pdf, (Accessed Sept. 1, 2009).
12. Wikipedia. ISO/TC 215 Standard. http://en.wikipedia.org/wiki/ISO_TC_215, (Accessed Sept. 1, 2009).
13. Wikipedia. OpenEHR. 2008. http://en.wikipedia.org/wiki/Openehr, (Accessed Sept. 1, 2009).
14. Wikipedia. ASC X12. 2008c. http://en.wikipedia.org/wiki/ANSI_X12, (Accessed Sept. 1, 2009).
15. United States Department of Health and Human Services: Office of Civil Rights—HIPAA. 2006. http://www.hhs.gov/ocr/hipaa/, (Accessed Sept. 1, 2009).
16. European eHealth Continuity Site. 2009. CONTsys. http://www.contsys.eu/.
17. Miller, R. H., and Sim, I. 2004. Physicians use of electronic medical records. Barriers and solutions. *Health Affairs* 23:116–126.
18. Hillestad, R., Bigelow, J., Bower, A., Girosi, F., Meili, R., Scoville, R., and Taylor, R. 2005. Can electronic medical record systems transform health care? Potential health benefits, savings and costs. *Health Affairs* 24:1103–1117.
19. Bates, D. W., Ebell, M., Gotlieb, E., and Zapp, J. 2003. A proposal for electronic medical records in U.S. primary care. *Journal of the American Medical Informatics Association* 10:616.
20. Burke, R. P., and White, J. A. 2004. Internet rounds: A congenital heart surgeon's web log. *Seminars in Thoracic and Cardiovascular Surgery* 16(3):283–292.
21. Boulus, N., and Bjorn. P. 2008. A cross-case analysis of technology-in-use practices: EPR-adaptation in Canada and Norway. *International Journal of Medical Informatics*, in press. (Available online July 31, 2008.)

22. Ludwick, D. A., and Doucette, J. 2008. Adopting electronic medical records in primary care: lessons learned from health information systems implementation experience in seven countries. *International Journal of Medical Informatics* 78(1):22–31.

23. Open Clinical. 2007. Ontologies. http://www.openclinical.org/ontologies. html, (Accessed Sept. 1, 2009).

24. Gangemi, A., Pisanelli, D. M., and Steve, G. 1998. Ontology integration: experiences with medical terminologies. In *Formal Ontology in Information Systems*, N. Guarino, ed. Amsterdam: IOS Press, pp. 163–178.

25. Medicomp Systems. MEDCIN. http://en.wikipedia.org/wiki/MEDCIN, (Accessed Sept. 1, 2009).

26. U.S. Food and Drug Administration. The National Drug Code Directory. http://www.fda.gov/cder/ndc/, (Accessed Sept. 1, 2009).

26a. Hristidis, V., Farfán, F., Burke, R., Rossi, A., and White, J. 2007. Information discovery on electronic medical records. In National Science Foundation Symposium on Next Generation of Data Mining and Cyber-Enabled Discovery for Innovation, NGDM.

27. Eichelberg, M., Aden, T., Riesmeier, J., Dogac, A., and Laleci, G.B. 2005. A survey and analysis of Electronic Healthcare Record standards. *ACM Computing Surveys* 37(4):277–315.

28. Wikipedia. Medical Record. 2008. In http://en.wikipedia.org/wiki/Medical_ record, (Accessed Sept. 1, 2009).

29. HL7 Reference Information Model. 2008. http://www.hl7.org/library/ datamodel/RIM/C30204/rim.htm (Accessed Sept. 25, 2009).

30. HL7 CCOW Technical Committee. 2007. Clinical Context Object Workgroup (CCOW). http://www.hl7.org/special/Committees/ccow_sigvi.htm (Accessed Sept. 25, 2009).

31. Health Level Seven Inc. 2006. Health Level Seven (HL7). http://www.hl7.org/ (Accessed Sept. 1, 2008).

32. Unified Modeling Language. 2008. http://www.uml.org/, (Accessed Sept. 1, 2009).

33. DICOM Standards Committee. 2006. Digital Imaging and Communications in Medicine (DICOM). http://medical.nema.org/(Accessed Sept. 1, 2009).

34. JPEG Interactive Protocol (JPIP). 2006. http://www.jpeg.org/jpeg2000/ j2kpart9.html, (Accessed Sept. 1, 2009).

35. Integrating the Healthcare Enterprise. 2006. http://www.ihe.net/ (Accessed Sept. 25, 2009).

36. Hristidis, V., Clarke, P. J., Prabakar, N., Deng, Y., White, J. A., and Burke, R. P. 2006. A flexible approach for electronic medical records exchange. In *Proceedings of the Workshop on Health and Information Knowledge Management (HIKM) 2006*, in conjunction with CIKM 2006.

37. Wikipedia. Electronic Medical Record. 2008e. http://en.wikipedia.org/wiki/ Electronic_Medical_Record, (Accessed Sept. 1, 2009).

38. Waegemann, C. P. 2003. EHR vs. CCR: what is the difference between the electronic health record and the continuity of care record? Medical Records Institute, http://www.medrecinst.com/pages/libArticle.asp?id=42 (Accessed Oct. 2, 2008).

39. Conn, J. 2006. Identity crisis? Renewed debate over national patient ID. *Modern Healthcare Magazine*, http://www.modernhealthcare.com/article. cms?articleId=39954, (Accessed Sept. 1, 2009).

40. U.S. House of Representatives. 2009. "The American Recovery and Reinvestment Act of 2009." Committee on Rules.

41. American Health Information Management Association (AHIMA) 2008. http://www.ahima.org/, (Accessed Sept. 1, 2009).
42. McDonald, C. J. 1997. The barriers to electronic medical record systems and how to overcome them. *Journal of the American Medical Informatics Association* 4:213–221.
43. Synamed. 2008. http://www.synamed.com/, (Accessed Sept. 1, 2009).
44. Teges Corporation. 2008. http://www.teges.com/, (Accessed Sept. 1, 2009).
45. MedcomSoft. 2008. http://www.medcomsoft.com/, (Accessed Sept. 1, 2009).
46. StreamlineMD. 2008. http://www.streamline-md.com/, (Accessed Sept. 1, 2009).
47 Practice Partner. 2008. http://www.practicepartner.com/(Accessed Aug. 2, 2008).
48. Practice Partner. 2008. http://www.practicepartner.com/(Accessed Aug. 2, 2008).
48. eClinicalWorks. 2008. http://www.eclinicalworks.com/, (Accessed Sept. 1, 2009).
49. MediNotes. 2008. http://www.medinotes.com/, (Accessed Sept. 1, 2009).
50. Misys PLC Health Care. 2008. http://www.misyshealthcare.com/, (Accessed Sept. 1, 2009).
51. NextGen. 2008. http://www.nextgen.com/, (Accessed Sept. 1, 2009).
52. Allscripts. 2008. http://www.allscripts.com/, (Accessed Sept. 1, 2009).
53. OmniMD. 2008. http://www.omnimd.com/, (Accessed Sept. 1, 2009).
54. GE HealthCare. 2008. http://www.gehealthcare.com/, (Accessed Sept. 1, 2009).
55. InteGreat. 2008. http://www.igreat.com/, (Accessed Sept. 1, 2009).
56. Cerner. 2008. http://www.cerner.com/, (Accessed Sept. 1, 2009).
57. AC Group website. 2008. http://www.acgroup.org (Accessed Aug. 2, 2008).
57a. Wang, A. Y., Barret, J. W., Bentley, T., Markwell, D., Price, C., Spackman, K. A. et al. 2001. Mapping between SNOMED RT and clinical terms, version 3: A key component of the SNOMED CT development process. In *Proceedings/AMIA Annual Symposium.*
58. SNOMED Clinical Terms (SNOMED CT). 2008. http://www.snomed.org/snomedct/index.html, (Accessed Sept. 1, 2009).
59. Spackman, K. A., Campbell, K. E., and Cote, R. A. 1997. SNOMED-RT: a reference terminology for health care. In *Proceedings of the 1997 AMIA Annual Fall Symposium*, pp. 640–644.
60. McDonald, C. J., Huff, S., Mercer, K., Hernandez, J. A., and Vreeman, D., ed. 2009. *Logical Observation Identifiers Names and Codes (LOINC) User's Guide.* Indianapolis, IN: Regenstrief Institute.
61. Health Insurance Portability and Accountability Act. 2008. http://www.hipaa.org/, (Accessed Sept. 1, 2009).
62. McDonald, C. J., Huff, S. M., Suico, J. G. et al. 2003. LOINC, a universal standard for identifying laboratory observations: a 5-year update. *Clinical Chemistry* 49(4):624–633.
63. RxNorm. 2008. United States National Library of Medicine. http://www.nlm.nih.gov/research/umls/rxnorm/index.html (Accessed Sept. 1, 2008).
64. United States National Library of Medicine. Medical Subject Headings (MeSH) Fact List. http://www.nlm.nih.gov/pubs/factsheets/mesh.html (Accessed Sept. 1, 2008).
65. DICOM Files. DICOM Sample Image Sets. http://pubimage.hcuge.ch:8080/, (Accessed Sept. 1, 2008).

3

Overview of Information Discovery Techniques on EHRs

Vagelis Hristidis

CONTENTS

3.1 Introduction

In this chapter, we give an overview of information discovery on electronic health records (EHRs). Chapters 6 to 10 present this topic in detail. We do not discuss privacy concerns in this chapter. By *information discovery*, we generally mean:

Searching the EHR collection given a user question (query) and return relevant fragments from the EHRs, or

Mining the EHRs collection to extract interesting patterns, group entities
to various classes, or decide whether an EHR satisfies some given
property.

3.1.1 Searching

The following is an example of a user query to search the EHR collection:
Find information related to "Asthma" in the collection. This type of query is
very similar to the queries users are used to in Web search engines, and are
typically expressed as a list of keywords—hence called *keyword queries*.

Expressing search queries. In addition to keyword queries, other methods
for the user to express a search query have been proposed. Ideally, the
user should be able to write a natural language question and receive a
precise answer. For instance, a natural language query is "Find patient
records with frequent low blood pressure and family history of Ventricular
Septal Defect." Unfortunately, there are no effective systems to accurately
answer natural language queries, given the complexity of natural languages. Between the two extremes of plain keyword queries and natural
language queries, a large number of query languages have been proposed.
For instance, some languages specify attribute name, value pairs, such
as *blood pressure* = "low" *AND history CONTAINS* "Ventricular Septal
Defect."

Answering search queries. In this book, we do not address the problem of
answering natural language search queries. We assume a simpler query
model: the keyword query model or simple extensions to it where conditions on the attributes are allowed, for example, *find information related to*
"asthma" *in EHRs with last name* = "Smith." Boolean conditions such as
name = "Smith" are easy to handle efficiently using well-studied indexes
such as the inverted index or database indexes (B+ tree or hash indexes).
On the other hand, the handling of imprecise (fuzzy) conditions such as
"related to 'asthma'" is much more challenging because an EHR may be
related to "asthma" in many different ways—for example, "asthma" may
be part of the patient history field, or part of a patient's diagnosis field,
or may not even be present in an EHR but a related concept ("respiratory
obstruction") is. Furthermore, assuming that there are EHRs for all of the
above types of relationships to the query keyword, which one should be
displayed first?

Ranking of the results is a critical component of the search process.
Ranking has become the most challenging task in searching in the past
decades due to the information overload problem, which is more dramatically present in the Web. The manner in which search engines rank
the results has become more challenging than crawling or indexing the
fast-expanding Web. Similarly, ranking is a key challenge when searching possibly very large collections of EHRs. Is an EHR containing the

query keyword "asthma" in the history section more relevant than the one containing the same term in the medications section? This becomes even more critical given that fragments within an EHR may be returned instead of the whole EHR document. Also, fragments of an EHR may be combined to form a result. Hence, an EHR search engine must rank all possible fragment combinations within each EHR. This makes the ranking task challenging not only in terms of quality, but also in terms of performance (execution time).

As discussed below, the search problem has been traditionally studied by the information retrieval (IR) community.

3.1.2 Mining

The types of user requests that we refer to as mining requests can range from searching for interesting/unusual patterns to mining associations between elements of the database to clustering (grouping) the EHRs, and so on. A typical clustering request would be "group EHRs into groups based on their properties." A pattern discovery request would be "find any interesting pattern in medication time series." An association mining request would be "find medications that frequently co-occur in EHRs." A classification mining request would be "decide if there is a need for an MRI exam for this patient given her EHR."

The key challenge of applying such problems to the EHR domain is to appropriately exploit the domain semantics. For instance, finding a correlation between a patient's blood pressure and her name does not seem like an interesting result. Also, clustering patients by their weight may not be meaningful for an EHR collection of a cardiac clinic.

Another interesting mining problem is the *analysis of real-time EHR data* to monitor vital signs and generate alerts. This class of problems has additional challenges such as the critical nature of fast data processing as well as the limited processing power of the mobile devices that read and process vital sign data. Furthermore, learning techniques are necessary to predict alarming conditions by comparing a patient's progress to that of other patients.

3.1.3 Other Types of Data

Text data, which may be numeric or free text, is the main focus of this book. However, other types of data are becoming increasingly important as more and more multimedia files are stored in electronic format in EHR systems. In Chapter 10, we present some of the challenges and solutions in searching medical images. Medical video is another multimedia data type of interest, which has received little attention to date and is not studied in this book.

3.2 Related Work and Further Readings

Detailed related work on searching and mining of EHRs is provided in the next chapters.

3.2.1 Information Discovery

One of the first definitions for the concept of *information discovery* was presented by Proper and Bruza (1999). According to them, IR traditionally focused on searching relevant documents in a fixed document collection, usually textual documents. In contrast, information discovery is performed in an open network environment, where the collection of documents is not fixed and the documents may be of a heterogeneous or aggregate nature.

3.2.2 Searching

The problem of searching in digital collections has been studied for decades. In addition to the traditional IR methods (Salton, 1989; Singhal, 2001), where a query is typically a set of keywords (as in Web search engines), other query models have been proposed. One of the most well-studied and promising version is the question answering approach, which is the task of automatically answering a question posed in natural language. Clearly, this is a very hard task given the complexity of natural language. This problem has been studied in several ways.

First, there are some rules-based systems that are trained for a fixed set of question types (e.g., "what," "where") and try to match document sentences to the questions based on their rules. The AskMSR system from Microsoft is one such example (Banko et al., 2002).

Second, this problem has been studied by the natural language processing community (Manning and Schütze, 1999), within which a syntactic and semantic analysis of natural language text has been attempted.

Third, the problem of question answering has been studied by the semantic web community (Berners-Lee et al., 2001), where knowledge is represented as Resource Description Framework (RDF) triplets (Lassila and Swick, 1999). For instance, the sentence "NIH is the creator of the resource http://www. ncbi.nlm.nih.gov/pubmed/." is represented as the RDF triplet:

Subject (Resource): http://www.ncbi.nlm.nih.gov/pubmed/

Predicate (Property): Creator

Object (literal): "NIH"

Representing knowledge as RDF triplets allows combining knowledge to answer queries. One of the drawbacks is the cost of converting existing knowledge into RDF format.

Coiera et al. (2008) have recently conducted a study showing that metasearch filters improve the effectiveness of searching the medical literature. A metasearch filter can be thought of as encodings of search strategies that capture expert knowledge on how to search for an answer. For instance, a filter may specify which data sources to use for a query.

Pfeiffer et al. (2003) present an excellent survey of the requirements of a search engine for EHRs.

3.2.3 Mining

Cios and Moore (2002) present a comprehensive study on why medical data have unique characteristics in terms of data mining. Some of these unique characteristics include volume and complexity, physician's interpretation, poor mathematical characterization of medical data, ethical and privacy issues.

Inokuchi et al. (2007) present an online analytical processing system for clinical data. In particular, they store EHRs in tables (in a relational database system) and allow navigation and aggregation of the data for decision purposes.

3.3 Searching EHRs

Figure 3.1 shows a sample Extensible Markup Language (XML)-based EHR document. A sample search query is "find information related to 'lung.'" The word "lung" is mentioned in the text paragraph on History of Present Illness. How much relevance should we assign to this EHR document for containing the query word? Furthermore, there is an "Asthma" observation element, and given that "Asthma" is related to "lung," the relevance of this document to the query should be increased. This example shows some of the challenges encountered when searching and ranking EHR data. The following sections present an overview of how traditional searching (IR) techniques can be applied to EHR collections, and how searching EHRs can be improved by incorporating structural (tags hierarchy in XML) and ontological knowledge. More details are provided in Chapter 6.

3.3.1 Searching Using Traditional IR Techniques

Searching of documents is the focus in IR. IR is a relatively old discipline dating back to 1960. A key focus of IR is how to rank the documents of a collection according to their "goodness" with respect to a query. The "goodness" of a result, which is inherently subjective, depends on such factors as relatedness to the query, specificity, and importance. The query is usually expressed as a list of keywords, similar to the case of Web search. Other types of queries

```
<?xml version="1.0" encoding="UTF-8" standalone="no"?>
- <ClinicalDocument NS2:schemaLocation="urnchl7-orgv3 CDA.ReleaseTwo.Committee.2004.xsd"
    templateId="2.16.840.1.113883.3.27.1776" xmlns="urnchl7-orgv3" xmlns:NS2="http://www.w3.org/2001/XMLSchema-instance">
    <id extension="c266" root="2.16.840.1.113883.3.933"/>
  + <recordTarget>
  - <component>
    - <StructuredBody>
      - <section>
          <code code="10160-0" codeSystem="2.16.840.1.113883.6.1" codeSystemName="LOINC"/>
          <title>Medications</title>
        - <Observation>
            <code code="84100007" codeSystem="2.16.840.1.113883.6.96" codeSystemName="SNOMED CT"
              displayName="Medications"/>
          - <value NS2:type="CD" code="195967001" codeSystem="2.16.840.1.113883.6.96" codeSystemName="SNOMED CT"
              displayName="Asthma">
            - <originalText>
                <reference value="m1"/>
            </originalText>
          </value>
        </Observation>
      + <Observation>
      - <SubstanceAdministration>
        - <text>
            <content ID="m1">Theophylline</content>
            20 mg every other day, alternating with 18 mg every other day, for 2 weeks. Stop if temperature is above
            103F.
          </text>
        - <consumable>
          - <manufacturedProduct>
            - <manufacturedLabeledDrug>
                <code code="66493003" codeSystem="2.16.840.1.113883.6.96" codeSystemName="SNOMED CT"
                  displayName="Theophylline"/>
              </manufacturedLabeledDrug>
            </manufacturedProduct>
          </consumable>
        </SubstanceAdministration>
      </section>
    - <component>
      - <section>
          <code code="10164-2" codeSystem="2.16.840.1.113883.6.1" codeSystemName="LOINC"/>
          <title>History of Present Illness</title>
          <text>3 month old baby who has been transferred to MCH CICU for VSD repair. He was born FT, but had resp.
          distress requiring mehcanical ventilation for 3 days for ? pulmonary edema. He was diagnosed then to have a
          large VSD. He was admitted in the hospital for about a month for his resp. issues. He was sent home but after
          3 weeks developed bronchiolitis and had been in the hospital since then. During this admission he was also
          diagnosed to have GE Reflux and Aspiration. He was also found to have Chronic lung disease --possibly due
          to aspiration. he also had complex partial seizures--?? due to resp. distress which were being treated with
          Phenobarb. For the last 4 days his feeds were switched to NJ-- He was now transferred to Miami for surgery
          on 11/15/06 to have the VSD closed.</text>
      </section>
    </component>
  </StructuredBody>
  </component>
</ClinicalDocument>
```

FIGURE 3.1
Sample excerpt of an XML-based EHR document.

are possible; however, we assume keyword queries throughout this chapter unless we specify otherwise. The ranking factors in IR are generally combined using a ranking function in order to assign a score to each document. The documents are then output in decreasing order of their IR score.

Boolean model. The simplest query model of traditional IR is the Boolean model, where the query consists of a Boolean expression of keywords combined with AND and OR operators. For instance, "lung and Miami" returns all documents that contain both keywords. However, the Boolean model has no ranking, which makes it ineffective for the information overload problem.

Vector space model. The biggest advancement in traditional IR is probably the vector space model, which was proposed in 1968. A document is represented as a vector. Each dimension corresponds to a separate term. If a term occurs in the document, its value in the vector is nonzero. The definition of term depends on the application. Typically, terms are single words, keywords, or longer phrases. If the words are chosen to be the terms, the dimensionality of the vector is the number of words in the vocabulary (the number of distinct words occurring in the corpus). For instance, if the vocabulary is {"cardio," "exam," "patient"}, and there are two documents, D1 ("cardio exam") and D2 ("patient exam"), then the respective vectors for the two documents are $D1 = (1,1,0)$ and $D2 = (0,1,1)$.

In the above example, a Boolean 0 and 1 scheme was used to create the vector. Several different ways of computing these values, also known as (term) weights, have been developed. One of the best known schemes is *tf-idf* weighting. *tf*, which stands for term frequency, is the number of times a query keyword appears in the document. The higher the tf, the higher the score of a document. *idf*, which stands for inverse document frequency, is the inverse of the number of documents in the collection that contain a query term. The higher the idf, the higher the score—that is, high idf translates to a small number of documents containing the keyword, which means that this keyword is infrequent in the collection, and should hence be assigned a higher weight than a frequent keyword (e.g., the word "hospital" in an EHR collection). For instance, the tf of "lung" for the document in Figure 3.1 is 1, whereas the idf of "lung" equals the number of documents containing "lung."

The score of a document with vector D given a query with vector Q is proportional to the angle between these two vectors. Smaller angle corresponds to higher similarity. This is why the cosine (D,Q) is often used, because cosine is inversely proportional to the angle, for example, cosine (0) = 1 and cosine (90°) = 0. More details and examples are provided in Chapter 6.

Clearly, the vector space model can be refined in many ways. For instance, considering the proximity between the query keywords in the document or their order is important. Such improvements are already used by popular Web search engines.

3.3.2 Exploit the Structure of the EHR Documents in Searching

Traditional IR views a document as a bag of words. This abstraction was acceptable for plain text documents but it is inadequate for XML-based EHRs, where there is a hierarchical element structure, and each element has a tag, attributes, and a value. The proximity between two words in an XML-based EHR document can be measured using the number of other words between them, the distance in terms of containment (parent-child) edges between the elements that contain them, or using a combination of the two methods. For instance, the distance between "History" and "lung" in the document in Figure 3.1 is about 96 words, whereas the distance in terms of edges is 2: title-section and section-text containment edges. Hence, this document should receive a relatively high score for the query "History lung."

The intuition for counting the distance in terms of containment edges comes from the fact that each such edge typically corresponds to a tight semantic distance between the two elements. Variations of these measures can be considered. For instance, if an element has many children, then its semantic distance to its children should be smaller than for an element that only has a few children.

Minimal information unit. In addition to using the structure to come up with alternative semantic distance measures, the structure is important when defining a query result. It is challenging to define the granularity of a piece of information in a way that it is self-contained and meaningful, but at the same time specific. For example, given query "History lung" and the document in Figure 3.1, we could output as a result just the parent *section* element instead of the whole EHR document. Alternatively, if we know that the users like to see the name of the patient, we could output the *section* element along with the patient name (in Figure 3.1, the name is in the *recordTarget* element, which is not expanded). This problem is commonly referred to as the minimal information unit problem.

Furthermore, for some queries it is required to include into the result some elements that do not contribute in connecting the query keywords or are part of the minimal information unit of such a connecting node.

3.3.3 Exploit Ontologies and Thesauri in Searching EHRs

EHR (e.g., HL7 Clinical Document Architecture EHRs) documents routinely contain references to external dictionary and ontology sources through numeric codes. As an example, the document in Figure 3.1 includes references to Logical Observation Identifiers Names and Codes and Systematized Nomenclature of Human and Veterinary Medicine Clinical Terms (SNOMED CT). Consider the line

```
<code code="84100007" codeSystem="2.16.840.1.113883.6.96"
codeSystemName="SNOMED CT" displayName="Medications" />
```

2.16.840.1.113883.6.96 is the code for the SNOMED CT ontology. 84100007 is the code for the "Medications" concept in the SNOMED CT ontology.

The purpose of including such ontological references is to allow more intelligent operations and queries on the EHRs, given that it is much easier for computers to understand and process codes than natural language terms.

To date, the existence of such ontological references has not been exploited much. At the minimum, such codes allow using a single reference for a real-life concept. For instance, "cardiac arrest," "cardiorespiratory arrest," and "cardiopulmonary arrest" should have the same code and hence a smart search engine would be able to search for all of them when the user query only specifies one of them.

Note that, to date, there has been little use of these ideas, for reasons ranging from inadequate EHR representations, to data integration issues, to the complexity of accessing and querying medical ontologies.

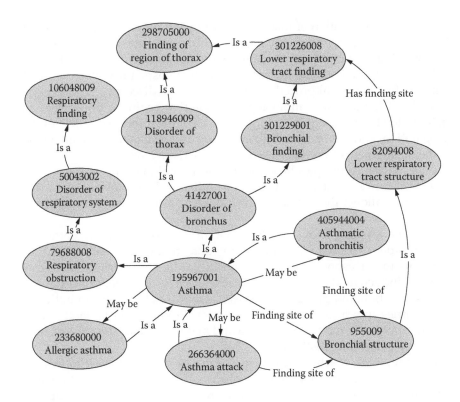

FIGURE 3.2
Subset of SNOMED CT ontology.

Consider the query "Respirator Obstruction" and the document in Figure 3.1. When using traditional IR techniques, this document will not be returned. However, as we see in the subset of SNOMED CT graph in Figure 3.2, "Asthma" *is a* "Respirator Obstruction," and hence the document in Figure 3.1, which contains "Asthma," should be returned for this query. Naturally, it should be ranked lower than a document that contains the phrase "Respirator Obstruction." Hence, we should not answer a query considering the EHR document in isolation. The query keywords may refer to text in the EHR document or an ontology that is connected to the Clinical Document Architecture document through a code reference.

3.4 Data Mining on EHRs

Data mining can be described as the inductive approach to uncovering patterns in data. In the particular case of data mining on EHRs, the process requires the application of machine learning techniques, or more precisely, knowledge discovery in databases. As will be presented in Chapter 7, the use of data mining techniques could allow the classification of patients by risk category, or could help predict the length of hospitalization for a specific patient after a surgical procedure. The knowledge discovery process is presented in Chapter 7 as a multistep life cycle that begins with problem and data understanding, explicitly highlights the large effort necessary for data preparation, and then proceeds to modeling and evaluation. The final phase is the deployment of predictive models into existing systems.

Data mining techniques lie at the intersection of machine learning, artificial intelligence, database systems, and statistics. The combination of these disciplines allows the extraction of hidden patterns from the underlying data.

Machine learning uses an inductive approach to uncovering patterns in data in order to search for mapping functions that relate a set of input data elements to corresponding output variables. Machine learning algorithms provide inductive, data-driven approaches to a wide variety of tasks, such as classification and prediction. Classification tasks try to group individual data entries into a known set of categories. Predictive tasks look into the future, applying a model to new data and making a qualitative classification or even a quantitative estimation.

In addition to machine learning, databases and data warehouses also play a key role in the data mining process. The original roles of database systems—data collection and database creation—shifted toward improved data management, incrementing their functionality with sophisticated transaction processing techniques and technologies that allow the knowledge discovery process. In the healthcare industry, data warehousing tools have been successfully applied for planning and decision support in both the private and public sectors.

Modern data mining incorporates many statistical techniques that aid in the tasks of feature selection and extraction. Statistical techniques—such as correlation analysis, histograms, and principal component analysis—and tests are incorporated for the processes of data visualization, attribute selection, and outlier investigation, and also to correct models so that they do not "over fit" the data; and finally, statistical techniques are used to evaluate data mining models and to express their significance.

Chapter 7 presents some of the most widely used supervised and unsupervised data mining techniques. These techniques include decision tree induction, neural networks, support vector machines, association rule mining, data clustering, and text mining. All these techniques are presented along with examples to better anchor the discussion firmly in the medical informatics area. Data clustering and classification are especially relevant to data mining on EHRs. The objective of these techniques is to find natural groupings within sets of records, uncovering "hidden" attributes or features that appropriately divide the cases. These divisions or groupings can often provide insights, such as finding patient subpopulations. Clustering can also be thought of as a data reduction technique that takes a vector of dimensions describing a set of data points and results in a single cluster label.

Chapter 7 also presents methods to evaluate the accuracy of data mining techniques, both for classification and predictor models. These strategies assess and ensure that the discovered models do not result from good or bad luck. For example, in a classification model, *accuracy* is the percentage of cases correctly classified by a model. Metrics to describe this accuracy, such as *sensitivity, specificity,* and *precision,* are described.

For more details on data mining on EHRs, see Chapter 7. Chapter 8 discusses about privacy preserving searching and data mining, where the goal is to achieve the information discovery goals while respecting the privacy concerns of EHR data.

3.5 Analysis of Real-Time EHR Data: Mobile Devices' Special Characteristics—Monitoring Vital Signs

Patient's vital signs need to be continuously acquired and analyzed in real time to facilitate out-of-hospital monitoring. Medical sensors allow an individual to closely monitor changes in her or his vital signs for extended periods and to provide information on patient health behavior and people activities. The combination of information technologies and telecommunications enables the design and exploitation of smart mobile devices, which are able to ubiquitously collect real-time streams of physiological signals. These devices, integrated in *ad hoc* health system architectures, can continuously evaluate patient health conditions by enhancing people's comfort, efficiency of healthcare, and illness prevention.

Chapter 9 outlines the different architectures of mobile healthcare systems to analyze physiological signals and for ubiquitous patient monitoring. Relevant literature on healthcare applications has also been reviewed, along with advantages and disadvantages of proposed works. Relevant knowledge discovery applications and patient data modeling techniques are introduced. Requirements and pitfalls of mobile clinical data analysis are also discussed.

A major challenge is how to provide better healthcare services to an increasing number of people using limited financial and human resources. To this challenge, healthcare services have become more mobile, ubiquitous, and user-friendly through the wireless technologies. Medical staff and patients could benefit from the monitoring process by applying automatic real-time analysis. There is still only limited success in exploiting the knowledge hidden within data for improving medical processes and quality of care, even though the data collection processes are well established in medicine and the amount of collected medical data is considerable. Many research activities have been focused on the architecture and the connectivity among devices, whereas less attention has been devoted to the design and development of analysis techniques to automatically detect unsafe situations in real time.

Each patient wears a set of sensors that monitor physiological signals and activities. These sensors, which are integrated into non-invasive objects, are connected to a user's device (also called personal server, e.g., a smart phone or a personal digital assistant) through a short-range communication link in charge of transmitting recorded signals. The communication between the user's mobile device and the remote centers is made possible via a wired or wireless network infrastructure. Finally, through the mobile phone network, an alert message may be sent to the closest medical center to request for prompt medical intervention when a risk situation is detected. An alert message can also be sent by the patient himself/herself, if he/she needs the physician intervention.

Intelligent systems in medicine exploit two main technologies, both based on data processing and search: optimization and machine learning. They are used for different types of medical problems such as clinical data mining, diagnosing, medical imaging, and signal processing. Signals for patient activity recognition can be obtained from different types of detectors. These include electromyography, audio sensors, image sensors, and accelerometers. In the intensive care context, there is the need for algorithms that automatically detect risk situations, because clinicians have to process large amounts of clinical data.

An important issue with mobile activity recognition systems is customization or personalization. An individual training phase may be needed for high accuracy recognition of some activities. Patient data modeling techniques are especially useful to suit the characteristics of patients presenting particular conditions. Given historical physiological data related to a single patient, the framework automatically learns both common and uncommon behaviours, and builds a behavioral model tailored to the specific patient. When a dangerous situation is detected, an immediate intervention is requested by triggering an alarm (e.g., a phone call, a short message).

Due to potentially life-threatening situations, the reliability of message delivery to healthcare professionals is one of the most crucial requirements of patient monitoring. Furthermore, the network should deliver the messages carrying vital signs within a certain time depending on the level of emergency. It is necessary to contain the delays that could rise under frequent monitoring or for a large number of monitored patients. Although this satisfies the reliability requirement of patient monitoring, it is important to conserve device power. This implies that sensors have to be extremely power efficient. Other issues related to requirements are the scalability in terms of the number of patients, the managing of both routine and emergency vital signs, and the manageable cognitive load for healthcare professionals. Another critical requirement is that, as information is being transmitted over wireless networks, efforts should be made to keep it confidential and private.

For more details, see Chapter 9.

3.6 Information Discovery on Medical Images

Performing information discovery on medical images is generally more difficult than on text data. The reason is that specialized tools are needed to extract the relevant information from a medical image.

As discussed in the excellent survey of Duncan and Ayache (2000), initially, the efforts in the area of medical image processing were seen as applying pattern analysis and computer vision techniques to another interesting dataset. However, over the past two to three decades, the unique nature of the problems presented within this area of study has led to the development of a new discipline in its own right. Examples of these include the following: the types of image information that are acquired, the fully three-dimensional image data, the nonrigid nature of object motion and deformation, and the statistical variation of both the underlying normal and abnormal ground truth. The past 20 years of research on medical image processing can be divided into four time frames:

1. Up to 1984: 2D Image analysis.
2. 1985–1991: Knowledge-based strategies came to the forefront and the advent of magnetic resonance imaging.
3. 1992–1998: Analysis of fully 3D images became the key goal and more mathematical model–driven approaches became computationally feasible.
4. 1999 and beyond: Advanced imaging and computing technology is facilitating work in image-guided procedures and more realistic visualizations.

In Chapter 10, we discuss a key problem in analyzing and information discovery on medical images. We present solutions for the problem of *automated image segmentation*, which is aimed at automated extraction of region boundary features and plays a fundamental role in understanding image content for searching and mining in medical image archives. A challenging problem is to segment regions with boundary insufficiencies, that is, missing edges and/or lack of texture contrast between regions of interest and background. To address this problem, several segmentation approaches have been proposed in the literature, with many of them providing rather promising results.

3.7 Chapter Summary

In this chapter, we defined what information discovery on EHRs entails. We explained the differences between searching and mining and their subproblems. Furthermore, we provided an overview of the next chapters of the book to offer a holistic view to the reader.

We also discussed about real-time EHR data and the role of mobile devices for monitoring such data. Most of this book handles textual data, such as medication or procedure names, physician notes, numeric vital sign values, and so on. However, note that information discovery on nontextual EHR data is also challenging and critical. In Chapter 10, we discuss some of the challenges and solution of analyzing medical images, which can be part of an EHR.

References

Banko, M., Brill, E., Dumais, S., and Lin, J. 2002. AskMSR: guestion answering using the Worldwide Web. In *Proceedings of 2002 AAAI Spring Symposium on Mining Answers from Texts and Knowledge Bases.*

Berners-Lee, T., Hendler, J., and Lassila, O. 2001. The semantic Web. *Scientific American* 284(5):34–43.

Cios, K. J., and Moore, W. G. 2002. Uniqueness of medical data mining. *Elsevier Artificial Intelligence in Medicine* 26(1):1–24.

Coiera, E., Westbrook, J. I., and Rogers, K. 2008. Clinical decision velocity is increased when meta-search filters enhance an evidence retrieval system. *Journal of the American Medical Informatics Association* 15(5):638–646.

Duncan, J. C., and Ayache, N. 2000. Medical image analysis: progress over two decades and the challenges ahead. *IEEE Transactions on Pattern Analysis Machine Intelligence* 22(1):85–106. DOI:http://dx.doi.org/10.1109/34.824822.

Inokuchi, A., Takeda, K., Inaoka, N., and Wakao, F. 2007. MedTAKMI-CDI: interactive knowledge discovery for clinical decision intelligence. *IBM Systems Journal* 46(1):115–134.

Lassila, O., and Swick, R. R. 1999. Resource Description Framework (RDF) Model and Syntax Specification. W3C. http://www.w3.org/TR/1999/REC-rdf-syntax-19990222/.

Manning, C., and Schütze, H. 1999. *Foundations of statistical natural language processing.* Cambridge, MA: MIT Press.

Pfeiffer, K. P., Goebel, G., and Leitner, K. 2003. Demand for intelligent search tools in medicine and health care. *Lecture Notes in Computer Science* 2818:5–18.

Proper, H. A., and Bruza, P. 1999. What is information discovery about? *Journal of the American Society for Information Science and Technology* 50(9):737–750.

Salton, G. 1989. *Automatic text processing: the transformation, analysis, and retrieval of information by computer.* Boston, MA: AddisonWesley Longman.

Singhal, A. 2001. Modern information retrieval: a brief overview. *Bulletin of the IEEE Computer Society Technical Committee on Data Engineering* 24(4):35–42.

4

Data Quality and Integration Issues in Electronic Health Records

Ricardo João Cruz-Correia, Pedro Pereira Rodrigues, Alberto Freitas, Filipa Canario Almeida, Rong Chen, and Altamiro Costa-Pereira

CONTENTS

4.1 Introduction

Thirty years ago, Komaroff [1] warned that medical data collected on paper records were defined and collected with a marked degree of variability and inaccuracy. He claimed that the taking of a medical history, the performance of the physical examination, the interpretation of laboratory tests, even the definition of diseases, was surprisingly inexact [1]. A decade ago, Hogan and Wagner [2] argued that electronic health records (EHRs) were not properly evaluated regarding data accuracy. Some studies have been published meanwhile showing that many of the problems found by Komaroff can still be found today.

EHRs are usually used for purposes other than healthcare delivery, namely, research or management. This fact has an important impact on the manner in which data are introduced by healthcare professionals, on how data are recorded on databases, and also on the heterogeneity found when trying to integrate data from different Information Systems (IS). This chapter focuses on DQ and data integration issues when using EHRs on research. The sections of this chapter describe the potential problems of existing EHRs, how to detect them, and some suggestions to overcome them. Some original studies are included in this chapter and are identified as case studies.

4.2 Fundamental Concepts

To better understand the issues covered in this chapter, it is important to understand how patient information flows in healthcare, what are IS (such as the EHR), what is the nature of health-related information, and who are the different actors involved in the process.

4.2.1 The Information Flow

Healthcare is information- and knowledge-driven. Good healthcare depends on taking decisions at the right time and place, according to the right patient data and applicable knowledge [3]. Communication is of utmost relevance in today's healthcare settings, as health-related activities, such as delivery of care, research, and management, depend on information sharing and teamwork [4].

Providing high-quality healthcare services is an information-dependent process. Indeed, the practice of medicine has been described as being dominated by how well information is processed or reprocessed, retrieved, and communicated [5]. An estimated 35% to 39% of total hospital operating costs has been associated with patient and professional communication activities [6]. Physicians spend over a quarter [7, 8] and nurses half [9] of their time writing up patient charts.

A patient record is a set of documents containing clinical and administrative information regarding one particular patient, supporting communication and decision-making in daily practice and having different users and purposes [10]. It exists to memorize and communicate the data existing on a particular individual, in order to help in the delivery of care for this person.

Records are not only an IS but also a communication system that enables communication between different health professionals and between the past and the present [11, 12]. Patient records, the patient, and published evidence are the three sources needed for the practice of evidence-based medicine [3]. They are used for immediate clinical decisions (either by the author or by others), future clinical decisions, quality improvement, education, clinical research, management, and reimbursement, and to act as evidence in a court case.

In practice, quite frequently patients are incorrectly registered or data items can be inaccurately recorded or not recorded at all. The quality of patient data in computer-based patient records has been found to be rather low in several health IS [2, 13, 14]. Most sources of poor DQ can be traced back to human error [13, 15] or bad system design [14]. Moreover, the assessment of the correctness of collected patient data is a difficult process even when we are familiar with the system under which it was collected [16].

Figure 4.1 represents the information flow diagram from patient observation to the use of data by the researcher (based on Hogan and Wagner [17] and Savage [18]). In each step of the information flow (represented by the arrows in the figure), it is possible to encounter problems resulting in data loss or data misinterpretation. It becomes obvious that there is a long way to go from the actual patient data to the data used by the researcher. It should be emphasized that, currently, we just do not have people who are entering information into a computer, we also have computers entering data into each other [19].

4.2.2 What Are Models and IS?

To better understand the relation between human artifacts (e.g., IS) and the real world (e.g., healthcare delivery) a description of the steps needed to create a human artifact is presented. These steps stress the fact that the quality of the artifacts is highly dependable on the quality of several models:

1. Create a model of the real world with whom the artifact will interact (e.g., information flow in the obstetrics department).
2. Create a model of the artifact (e.g., Unified Modeling Language diagrams describing the behavior of the obstetrics department IS to be implemented).
3. Implement the artifact based on the model (e.g., implement an Obstetrics Patient Record to be part of the information flow in the obstetrics department).
4. Use the implemented artifact on the real world (e.g., use the implemented Obstetrics Patient Record on a daily basis on a particular obstetrics department).

Mathematical and computational models exist to describe behaviors, that is, to explain how a real-world system or event works. They simplify or ignore

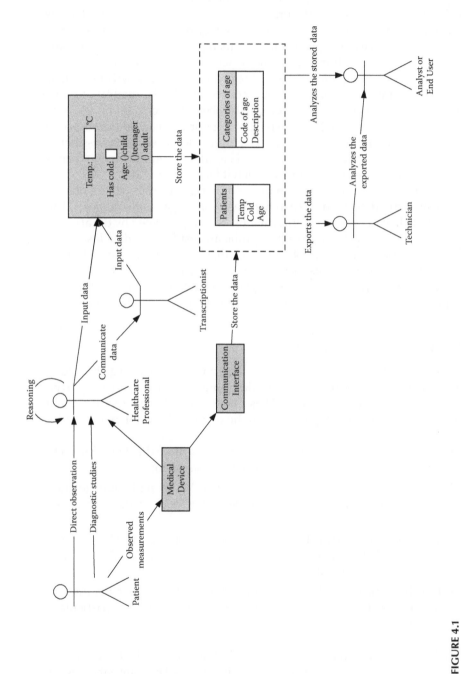

FIGURE 4.1
Information flow diagram from patient observation to the use of data by the researcher.

some details in order to make them more understandable. Generally, they allow complex systems to be understood and make their behaviors predictable. Models can be presented as equations, diagrams, or schemes. They can give false descriptions and predictions when used in situations they were not planned for.

IS are models and being so, they are wrong, that is, they ignore some details not needed for the purpose of the IS. The problem arises when the data collected by the IS are used for different purposes than the ones it was designed for, and for new purposes that ignored details have relevance.

A data model is a plan for building a database. Data modeling produces a formal description of the data that represent concepts of interest to a specific domain (people, places, etc.), and indicates how entities are conceptually related to one another. Data modeling in healthcare is a difficult and time-consuming task due to the vastness of the domain, the complexity of the knowledge, and the wide variety of participants, all with slightly differing views about the process [20]. In this context of healthcare systems, databases must address two important requirements: rapid retrieval of data for individual patients and adaptability to the changing information needs of an institution [21]. There are four basic steps to generic data modeling for a clinical IS: to develop a detailed schema of the medical data, to filter out concepts and relations that do not vary across patient records, to transform the detailed schema into a generic schema, and to implement the generic schema using a database management system [20].

An introduction to healthcare IS can be found in Chapter 2. It focuses on Extensible Markup Language (XML)–based representation of EHR, which is the most promising future representation. However, most existing EHR systems still use the relational model, which stores data in tables, with rows and columns (columns are also called attributes). Even though some parts of our discussion assume a relational model for EHR, the same principles also apply for XML-based EHR representation.

Another important lesson is that it is difficult to propose which data must be structured and which terms must be offered for data entry, before knowing the purpose for which data will be used. In prospective studies, the study is designed before the data are collected, whereas retrospective studies rely on data already collected for a different purpose. Table 4.1 presents some of the differences between retrospective and prospective studies: (1) the time when the meaning of each data fields is known to the researcher, (2) the existence of a research protocol for data collection, (3) the control on the types of users, and (4) the purpose for data collection. Clinical research will often require data that have a high granularity and are recorded uniformly, which will not always correspond to the format in which data are recorded for patient care. Completeness, accuracy, and required uniformity of data, therefore, remain functions of the use of the data. Nevertheless, we must conclude that structuring narrative data does not per se guarantee a thoroughness

TABLE 4.1

Retrospective versus Prospective Studies

Retrospective	Prospective
1. Researcher has to find meaning of each data field	Researcher sets the meaning of each data field
2. Data are collected without protocol	Protocol is predefined
3. Users are heterogeneous	Users are controlled
4. Data are collected for different purposes	Data are collected for research

and retrievability of routinely recorded clinical data for subsequent use in clinical research [22].

4.2.3 The Nature of Health Information

Information is described as the interpretation of data and knowledge that intelligent systems (human and artificial) perform to support their decisions. Data are central to all medical care because they are crucial to the process of decision-making. Data provide the basis for categorizing the problems a patient may have or identifying a subgroup within a population of patients. All medical care activities involve gathering, analyzing, or using of data. They also help the physician to decide what additional information is needed and what actions should be taken to gain a greater understanding of a patient's problem or to treat more effectively the disease that has been diagnosed [23]. Health informatics can help doctors with their decisions and actions, and improves patient outcomes by making better use of information, making more efficient the manner in which patient data and medical knowledge is captured, processed, communicated, and applied.

Health-related data are not homogeneous in nature. They range from narrative, textual data to numerical measurements, recorded biological signs, and images.

Narrative data accounts for a large component of the information that is gathered in the care of patients. They include the patient's symptoms, his/her description of the present illness, medical history, social and family history, the general review of systems, and physical examination findings. Data collected from physical examination are loosely coded with shorthand conventions and abbreviations known to health professionals and reflect the stereotypical examination process. The other narrative data are extremely difficult to standardize and significant problems can be associated with nonstandard abbreviations once they can have different meanings depending on the context in which they are used. Some attempts have been made to use conventional text notation as a form of summarization and complete phrases are used as loose standards. The enforcement to summarize heterogeneous conditions characterizing a simple concept about a patient is often unsuccessful [23].

Many data used in medicine are numerical. These include vital signs such as temperature or blood pressure, laboratory tests results, and some measurements taken during physical examination. This type of data is easier to formalize and some can be acquired and stored automatically. However, when numerical data are interpreted, the problem of precision and validity becomes important. In some fields of medicine, especially intensive care medicine, data are acquired in the form of continuous signals such as electrocardiogram or pulse oximetry wave. When these data are stored in medical records, a graphical tracing is frequently included. How this type of data is best managed in computer storage and clinical decision systems is an important challenge.

Visual images, acquired from machines or drawn by the health professionals to locate abnormalities or describe procedures, are an important type of data. Radiology images can be stored in electronic patient records using formalized compressing protocols. The possibility of acquiring and storing sketched images is an important challenge in the development of an electronic patient record due to its heterogeneity and lack of standardization.

Medical practice is medical decision-making [24]. Information exists to support decisions and actions such as procedures; if it fails to do this, it becomes irrelevant noise. The process of diagnosis is a probabilistic clinical reasoning based on three types of information: patient data, medical knowledge, and "directory" information (e.g., available surgical rooms at the hospital) [25]. This is why the diagnosis and the consequent clinical decision are an uncertain dynamic and an evolutive process. Although this type of information can be coded and structured, its storage in a patient record can be difficult to formalize due to this uncertainty, the existence of more than one diagnosis hypotheses, and the time-related evolution of the final diagnosis. Clinical procedures are easier to formalize and are usually represented with codes.

In general, health information can be divided into different groups. To each group, it is possible to associate a usual method to obtain such data and also the difficulty of formalization. Table 4.2 summarizes some of the characteristics of these groups.

4.2.4 Understanding What Is Recorded

Poor presentation of clinical data can also lead to poorly informed clinical practice, inappropriate repeated investigation, or unnecessary referrals, and wastes clinical time and other resources [3]. What humans understand is profoundly shaped by the manner in which data are presented, and by the way we react to different data presentations [4]. Thus, it is probably as important to structure the data in a way so that it can be best understood, as it is to ensure that the data are correct in the first place. The manner in which data are presented should take into consideration the current clinical context and anticipate the users' needs, thus creating an intelligent ambient [26].

TABLE 4.2

Groups of Health-Related Data

Type of Health Data	Method to Obtain Data	Formalization Difficulty	Type of Computer Data	Example of Standards
Narrative data	Ask the patient	Difficult to formalize	Free text	Some loose standards of conventional text notation
Physical examinations	Observation and measurements	The measurements are easier to formalize than the observations that are narrative data	Text and numeric data	LOINC, HL7, openEHR
Diagnosis	Reasoning	Some parts are difficult to formalize (e.g., uncertainty)	Numeric coded data	Several international codification standards such as SNOMED and ICD. Attempt to structure diagnosis using different classification branches
Procedures	Result of actions	Easy to formalize	Numeric coded data	Several international codification and classification standards on medical and surgical procedures as well as pharmacological therapy
Laboratory reports	Tests mainly done automatically	Easy to formalize	Numeric	LOINC
Images and biological signals	Measures made by machines	Easy to formalize	Numeric	DICOM

Note: DICOM, Digital Imaging and Communications in Medicine; HL7, Health Level Seven; ICD, International Classification of Diseases; LOINC, Logical Observation Identifiers Names and Codes; SNOMED, Systematized Nomenclature of Human and Veterinary Medicine.

In order to properly interpret EHR data, it is very important for the researcher to understand how the EHR IS works, that is, the software, hardware, people, and the processes. Thus, researchers using EHR data should have access to documentation describing database models, user forms, devices used in data collection, a description of the users, and the protocols used in data collection.

Moreover, to safely interpret health data from heterogeneous systems for research use, it is important to be able to share and communicate the meaning of data. Due to a potentially very large amount of data and necessary reasoning of the data, it is crucial that the semantics of the data are computer-interpretable. Such semantic concerns can generally be divided into data values, data structures, and terminology-related semantics.

To improve data accuracy, EHR should allow the association of a reliability measure to some data (e.g., "Suspect influenza"). Some authors have even proposed that associated to each value in a database, there should be a second value describing the reliability of the value [27]. The proposed categories are good, medium, poor, unknown, and not applicable.

4.3 Data Quality

With the development of informatics technology, medical databases tend to be more reliable. However, issues regarding DQ have become more relevant than ever as the utilization of these databases is increasing both in magnitude and importance. DQ is relative to each objective and can be defined as "fitness for use," that is, data can be considered of appropriate quality for one purpose but they may not hold sufficient quality for another situation [28]. This is especially true in medical databases; a medical database can be of quality for economic analyses but may be insufficient quality for a clinical study.

For data to have quality, Wyatt and Liu [29] stated that they should be accurate, complete, relevant, timely, sufficiently detailed, appropriately represented (e.g., consistently coded using a clinical coding system), and should retain sufficient contextual information to support decision-making. Other authors consider four dimensions of DQ [28]: accuracy, as the degree of correctness and precision with which real-world data are represented; completeness, as the degree to which all relevant data are recorded; consistency, as the degree to which data satisfy specified constraints and business rules; and timeliness, as the degree to which the recorded data are up-to-date [30, 31].

In another perspective, it is possible to analyze DQ concerning three roles about data: production, custodian, and consumer. Data producers are those that generate data (e.g., medical, nursing, or administrative staff); data custodians are those that provide and manage computing resources for storing and processing data (e.g., database administrators and computer scientists); and data consumers are those who use data in medical care (e.g., physicians, researchers, and managers) [32, 33].

4.3.1 Problems in the Input of Data

Data in health records should be accurate, complete, and up-to-date, in order to be useful, not only for healthcare practice (its main purpose) but also for further research activities. Paper-based medical records (PBMRs) are still an important foundation of information for healthcare, and are often considered the gold standards for the evaluation of EHR systems, as they represent the closest contact with the actual event they report. The bad reputation of PBMRs comes mostly from the fact that they require users to expend considerable time and effort to search for specific information, or to gather and obtain a general overview. Also, the input of information is performed by different persons, at different points in time, and is often done after the medical service has been administered, with main problems of poor handwriting, missing sheets, and imperfect documentation usually connected to the high workload of both physicians and nurses [34].

Over the past decades, a wide range of computer systems have been introduced to support clinical practice [35]. However, computerization does not necessarily help [12]. For example, Soto et al. [36] reported in their study on documentation quality that, despite the presence of an electronic medical record designed to facilitate documentation, rates of documentation of some domains fell below desirable levels. EHRs have been weakened by both misconceptions on the record design, and shallow (or nonexistent) research on the design of user interfaces used to fill in and extract data. To help clinicians find data faster and with less effort, everyone designing and writing in records needs to understand how and why we search records and the design features that make searching easier. On one hand, good record design can double the speed at which a practiced reader extracts information from a document, whereas poor design introduces an upper limit on speed that cannot be overcome by training [12]. On the other hand, the design of the user interface has a substantial influence on the usability of the system, and this plays an important role in the prevention of incomplete and incorrect data records [35]. Even considering perfect record and user interface designs, there is a high level of uncertainty in recorded data, some of it stemming from the fact that different users participate in data recording [36] and some stemming from the fact that data nowadays are being introduced in different record systems almost simultaneously or, at least, during the same patient's event, leading to record and event linkage problems [37].

4.3.2 Types of Errors

Arts et al. [38] reviewed the main conceptions about types of data errors, ranging from semantic specifications (e.g., interpretation, documentation, and coding errors) to underlying process definitions (e.g., systematic and random errors). Focus was given to the latter. Causes of systematic data errors include programming errors, unclear definitions for data items, or violation of the data collection protocol. Random data errors, for instance, can be caused by inaccurate data transcription and typing errors or illegible handwriting in the patient record [38]. They also conducted a simple case study to try to identify the main causes of data incompleteness and inaccuracy. They evaluated data recorded in two different intensive care units (ICUs), one using a PBMR and the other a patient data management system, both registering their own data into a central registry database at the National Institute for Health and Clinical Excellence coordinating center. The main sources of errors were searched for in the following three processes: local data recording, local data extraction, and central data transfer. From 20 randomly selected patients from each ICU, the overall evaluation resulted in the following: 2.0% inaccurate data (mostly for programming errors) and 6.0% incomplete data (mostly for poorly designed record, with missing variables) for the hospital using the automatic data collection; 4.6% inaccurate data (mostly for inaccurate transcription and/or calculations) and 5.0% incomplete data (almost evenly for the transcription from the PBMR and for programming errors in the data transfer process) for the hospital using manual data collection. Although this scenario is not one of the toughest ones regarding DQ, it revealed some interesting causes that need to be taken into account in EHR design. Tables 4.3 and 4.4 present the authors' overview of causes of insufficient DQ, in two different periods of a distributed EHR system implementation and deployment: registry setup and data collection.

We redirect the reader to the referred study for a thorough report on the causes of insufficient DQ. Nonetheless, we believe that the particular important causes that we should address in this chapter are poor interface design; lack of adherence to guidelines, protocols, and data definitions; and insufficient information on the collected data. A taxonomy of DQ problems (DQPs), organized by granularity level, is presented in Table 4.5 [39]. Next, we present a short definition for each DQP based on Oliveira et al. [39], and present some examples:

Missing values—a required attribute not filled, that is, the absence of value in a mandatory attribute (e.g., the gender of a patient is missing).

Syntax violation—attribute value violates the predefined syntax (e.g., birth_date is not in the correct date format).

Domain violation—attribute value violates the domain of valid values [e.g., length of stay (LOS) contains a negative value]. If the attribute

TABLE 4.3

Causes of Insufficient Data Quality during Setup and Organization of the Registry [38]

Problems at the Central Coordinating Center	Type of Error
Unclear/ambiguous data definitions	Systematic
Unclear data collection guidelines	Systematic
Poor case record form layout	Systematic/random
Poor interface design	Systematic/random
Data overload	Random
Programming errors	Systematic
Problems at the Local Sites	**Type of Error**
Illegible handwriting in data source	Random
Incompleteness of data source	Systematic
Unsuitable data format in source	Systematic
Data dictionary not available to data collectors	Systematic/random
Lack of motivation	Random
Frequent shift in personnel	Random
Programming errors	Systematic

TABLE 4.4

Causes of Insufficient Data Quality during Data Collection [38]

Problems at the Central Coordinating Center	Type of Error
No control over adherence to guidelines and data definitions	Systematic
Insufficient data checks	Systematic/Random
Problems at the Local Sites	**Type of Error**
Nonadherence to data definitions	Systematic
Nonadherence to guidelines	Systematic
Calculation errors	Systematic/Random
Typing errors	Random
Insufficient data checks at data entry	Systematic/Random
Transcription errors	Random
Incomplete transcription	Random
Confusing data corrections on case record form	Random

data type is string, this DQP can additionally be divided into the following:

- Overloaded attribute—attribute value partially violates the domain: a substring of it is valid, whereas the remaining substring is invalid (e.g., first_name contains all the names of the patient).

- Misspelling error—attribute value contains a misspelled error. A misspelling error can occur due to either typing errors or

TABLE 4.5

Data Quality Problems by Granularity Level [39]

Data Quality Problem	Attribute/Tuple			Single Relation	Multiple Relations	Multiple Sources
	Attribute	Column	Row			
Missing values	×					
Syntax violation	×					
Domain violation	×					
Overloaded attribute/invalid substring	×					
Misspelling error	×					
Ambiguous value	×					
Incorrect value	×					
Violation of business rule	×	×	×	×	×	×
Uniqueness violation		×				
Existence of synonyms		×			×	×
Violation of functional dependency				×		
Approximate duplicate tuples				×		×
Inconsistent duplicate tuples				×		×
Referential integrity violation					×	×
Incorrect reference					×	×
Heterogeneity of syntaxes					×	×
Heterogeneity of measure units					×	×
Heterogeneity of representation					×	×
Existence of homonyms						×

　　　　lack of knowledge of the correct spelling (e.g., prostate and prostrate).

－　Ambiguous value—the attribute value is an abbreviation or acronym (e.g., BPD can mean bronchopulmonary dysplasia or borderline personality disorder).

Incorrect value—attribute contains a value which is not the correct one, but the domain of valid values is not violated (e.g., age is 56 instead of 59).

Violation of business rule—this problem can happen at all granularity levels, when a given business domain rule is violated (e.g., patient_ name must have at least two words, but there is a tuple where this constraint is not respected).

Uniqueness violation—two (or more) tuples* have the same value in a unique value attribute (e.g., the same process_number for different patients).

Existence of synonyms—use of syntactically different values with the same meaning (within an attribute or among related attributes from multiple relations) (e.g., the use of gastric or stomach).

Violation of functional dependency—the value of a tuple violates an existing functional dependency among two or more attributes (e.g., in the same hospital, (dept_code = 40; dept_name = Gastroenterology) and (dept_code = 40; dept_name = Psychiatry)).

Approximate duplicate tuples—the same real-world entity is represented (equally or with minor differences) in more than one tuple [e.g., tuple department (Pneum, 8th floor, St. John Hospital) is an approximate duplicate of tuple department (Pneumology, eight floor, St. John Hospital)].

Inconsistent duplicate tuples—representation of the same real-world entity in more than one tuple but with inconsistencies between attribute values [e.g., address in duplicate tuples hospital (St. John Hospital, Great Ormond Street) and hospital (St. John Hospital, Saintfield Road) is inconsistent)].

Referential integrity violation—a value in a foreign key attribute does not exist in the related relation as a primary key value (e.g., principal diagnosis code 434.91 is not present in the diagnosis relation).

Incorrect reference—the referential integrity is respected but the foreign key contains a value, which is not the correct one (e.g., principal diagnosis coded as 434.10 instead of 434.11; both codes exists in the diagnosis relation).

Heterogeneity of syntaxes—existence of different representation syntaxes in related attributes, within a data source or among data sources (e.g., attribute admission_date has syntax dd/mm/yyyy, but attribute discharge_date has syntax yyyy/mm/dd).

Heterogeneity of measure units—use of different measure units in related attributes, within a data source or among data sources (e.g., in different data sources, the representation of attribute temperature in different scales (Celsius/Fahrenheit).

---

* In the text of relational databases, tuple is formally defined as a finite function that maps field names to values in the relational model.

Heterogeneity of representation—use of different sets of values to code the same real-world property, within a data source or among data sources (e.g., in one source, gender can be represented with values 1, 2 and, in another source, with values M, F).

Existence of homonyms—use of syntactically equal values with different meanings, among related attributes from multiple data sources (e.g., ventilation has at least two different meanings, one referring to the biological phenomenon of respiration, and the other referring to the environmental flow of air).

4.3.3 Data Cleansing

Outliers, inconsistencies, and errors can be included in the process of data cleansing [40]. Data cleansing consists of the exploration of data for possible problems and making an effort to correct errors. This is an essential step in the process of knowledge discovery in databases (KDD) [41]. There are many issues related to data cleansing that researchers are attempting to tackle, such as dealing with missing data and determining record usability and erroneous data [42]. There is no general definition for data cleansing as it is closely related with the area where it is applied, for example, in KDD, data warehousing, or total DQ management [40].

The subgroup of DQPs associated with database outliers, inconsistencies, and errors can be divided into semantic, syntactic, and referential integrity problems [43]. The characterization and systematization of these problems is very important. An object that does not comply with the general behavior of data is called an outlier [41]. Outliers can happen due to mechanical faults, changes in system behavior, fraudulent behavior, human errors, or instrument errors or faults [44]. They are, normally, very different from, or inconsistent with, the remaining data. An outlier can be an error but can also result from the natural variability of data, and can hold important hidden information. There is no universal technique for the detection of outliers; various factors have to be considered [18]. Statistics and machine learning contribute with important different methodologies for their analysis [41, 45–47]. Usually, computer-based outlier analysis methods follow a statistical, a distance-based, or a deviation-based approach [41]. Algorithms should be selected when they are suitable for the distribution model, the type of attributes, the speed, the scalability, and other specific domain characteristics [44].

The manner in which these potential DQPs are managed is also very important. It is necessary to analyze and define what to do in each situation (e.g., to delete or label an error). To facilitate outlier analysis, a probability can be assigned to each case. Issues related to data preprocessing are also essential for the reduction of computational efforts to achieve a faster domain comprehension and a faster implementation of methods.

4.3.4 Missing Values

Missing values can represent system-missing (e.g., resulting from not selecting any option) or user-missing (e.g., resulting from selecting an option named "unknown"). System-missing should be avoided and replaced by user-missing whenever possible. The main problem regarding system-missing values arises at analysis time, namely, by trying to find out what it means when a null or a blank value is stored in the database. To illustrate this problem, let us consider an example form for the introduction of information about an allergy. Usual forms consider only a simple checkbox.

Allergy to penicillin: [ ]
What does the blank value mean? Is the patient not allergic? The physician does not know? The question is not applicable in the current setting? The value has not yet been introduced, but will probably be in following iterations?
Clearer forms consider a yes/no radio button to force the user to give an answer, even if it is the default answer.

Allergy to penicillin: ( )Yes (*)No
But even this is not enough to clarify things for the analyst. More complex forms should consider other hypotheses (N/A means Not Applicable):

Allergy to penicillin:

```
( )Yes ( )No (*)Unknown
( )Yes ( )No (*)Unknown ( )N/A ( )Yes ( )No ( )Unknown ( )
    N/A (*)Never entered
( )Doctor says Yes ( )Doctor says No
( )Patient says Yes ( )Patient says No
( )Unknown (*)Never entered ( )N/A
```

A similar approach has been suggested in a study on demographic surveillance systems [48]. Aiming to improve data reliability, a set of standard values was defined to be used consistently throughout the database to indicate the status of a particular data value. The following standard values (and their meanings) were proposed:

"Never entered"—This is the default value for all data fields in a newly created record.

"Not applicable"—Given the data in related fields or records, a value for this data field is not applicable.

"Unknown"—The value is not known. Follow-up action yielded no better information or is not applicable.

"To be configured"—This indicates a need to query the value as it appears on the input document and to take follow-up action.

"Out of range"—The value on the input document is out of range and could not be entered. Follow-up action yielded no better information or is not applicable.

The last two standard values ("To be configured" and "Out of range") are more closely related to the demographic surveillance systems study, and therefore more difficult to generalize to other uses.

Moreover, software data entry programs requiring the user to enter a value into a field, regardless of whether an entry would be applicable, may find that a value has been entered merely to satisfy the requirements of the program rather than to record valid data. Having options related to missing data helps to solve these questions.

4.3.5 Default Values

Default values are preassigned content for a data container (e.g., form entry or table field). It is a value that is used when no value is provided. To increase simplicity of use, computer user interfaces often use default values. Default values are normally the most common value, and they are assumed to be true unless the user specifies otherwise. Such default assumptions are not appropriate for the entry of clinical data, for two reasons [49]:

1. They may bias the data, because they may appear to be the "expected" or "normal" value.
2. The user may simply miss a question if defaults are taken.

The alternative is to make all data entry fields blank or initially set to "unknown," so that each data point in the database represents an explicit input by the patient. Palmblad and Tiplady [49] stress that responses should always result from an action by the user—defaults should not be taken as data.

4.3.6 Clinical Concepts

There are several sources of problems when designing user interfaces, especially in the healthcare domain. In the study of Hyeoneui et al. [50], problems were found on an ICU nursing flow sheet related to data item labels. Some labels (e.g., "Status" and "Condition") were found to be vaguely defined. They did not convey sufficient semantic information about the data they contain, making it difficult to retrieve and perform inference on the data.

Coded data offer a possible way to apply statistics to the collected data. The advantages are obvious. Nevertheless, coded data always imply a simplification of the reality. Structured form is a model of the reality, and as such they aim to transform a complex reality in a simplified version. Since free text does not impose so many restrictions, information loss tends to be much lower. Also, when people are forced to select from a predetermined list of codes, they may discover that they cannot find the correct code and so they select a code that seems to be closest to, but does not truly represent, the real situation or observation [51].

For example, the accuracy of coded hospital information on a Patient Administration System of the Birmingham Women's Hospital was tested [52]. The accuracy of diagnosis, interventions, and diagnosis-intervention pairs on electronic records was low. The reported kappa (κ) agreement statistics were 0.39, 0.30, and 0.21, and the proportion of agreement was 69.69, 64.64, and 60.26, respectively [53]. It is important to note that these data had been previously used to measure the level of evidence-based healthcare [54]. The authors claim that a major source of error arose because the databases of maternities and surgical operations were not seamlessly linked to the Patient Administration System. This study concludes that a high degree of inaccuracy may exist in hospital electronic clinical data, and that researchers relying on hospital electronic data are advised to first check the level of accuracy.

In another example, the agreement on final diagnosis between two sources for pediatric emergency department (ED) visits in 19 U.S. institutions was recently studied [55]. Overall, 67% of diagnoses from the administrative and abstracted sources were within the same diagnosis group. Agreement varied by site, ranging from 54% to 77%. The authors concluded that the ED diagnoses retrieved from electronic administrative sources and manual chart review frequently disagreed. Agreement varied by institution and by diagnosis. Further work is recommended to improve the accuracy of diagnosis coding. Other studies have described misclassification issues in EHRs [56]. Coding problems increase when trying to integrate databases. Creating a common coding system from different sets of codes is complicated because it is probable that different processes for coding and different definitions were used. Below, four case studies related to coding issues are described.

Validation rule case study. In a central hospital discharges database, a simple validation tool, with domain rules defined by a specialist in medical codification, was implemented [57]. This tool periodically produces error reports and gives feedback to database administrators. With this feedback tool, and in only 7 months, critical errors decreased from 6% to 1% (from 173,795 to 27,218 cases). After that, critical errors continued to decrease and in 1 year were reduced to 0.13% (5.112 cases). This is a simple, yet very interesting, example on how simple procedures can clearly influence the quality of data and consequently the quality of any research using that data. Let us analyze an example of a validation rule (algorithm) for birth weight (see Figure 4.2). Newborns are coded by having the principal International Classification of Diseases, 9th revision, Clinical Modification (ICD-9-CM) diagnosis code starting with V3. In these cases, the birth weight attribute (BIRTH_WGT) cannot be missing.

Influenza coding among hospitals case study. More complete examples of erroneous data can be found in the same data. ICD-9-CM has diagnostic

> - Is the attribute filled?
>   - No → principal diagnosis has a code starting with V3?
>   - → Yes → output a critical error
>   - → No → ok
>   - Yes → principal diagnosis has a code starting with V3?
>   - → Yes → is BIRTH_WGT value between 400 and 9000?
>   - Yes → ok
>   - No → output a critical error
>   - → No → output a critical error

FIGURE 4.2
Example of validation rule for birth weight.

codes specific to influenza (487.0, 487.1, and 487.8) that can be easily retrieved from hospital discharge records. Although there have several successful ventures in the use of these codes [58], this specific codification is not uniformly done in different hospitals. In fact, using the previous national inpatient database, we can find substantial differences within different acute care hospitals (see Figure 4.3). The percentage of cases with influenza ranges from 1.77% to 0.00% of all hospitalizations in Portuguese hospitals. It is probable that most of the diagnoses of influenza were not introduced.

Ischemic stroke coding protocol case study. ICD-9-CM discharge data have also been used to identify patients with stroke for epidemiological, quality of care, and cost studies [59]. Nevertheless, for many years ischemic stroke (a poorly defined type of stroke) did not have a direct entry in the ICD-9-CM alphabetic index. In Portugal, due to an erroneous interpretation from an official entity, ischemic stroke was initially coded with 437.1 (other generalized ischemic cerebral-vascular disease), instead of the correct 436 code (acute but ill-defined cerebral-vascular disease). In October 2004, the Cooperating Parties and the Editorial Advisory Board for Coding Clinic for the ICD-9-CM clarified this situation and modified the classification system, pointing out the code 434.91 (cerebral artery occlusion unspecified with cerebral infarction) as the correct one for ischemic stroke. After a period of 2 to 3 years (time needed for the message to reach all medical coders in Portugal, because the use of the ICD-9-CM version is not up-to-date nor uniform), ischemic stroke coding started to be generally, and correctly, classified with 434.91. As shown in Figure 4.4, changes in the protocol for coding ischemic stroke clearly influenced ICD-9-CM discharge data: there is a clear reduction over years in episodes coded as 436 (not specified stroke) and a simultaneous increase in 434.91 (cerebral-vascular disease, including ischemic stroke).

Leukemia incidence decrease difficult to explain. Figure 4.5 shows the incidence (the number of new cases in a specified period) by year for leukemia,

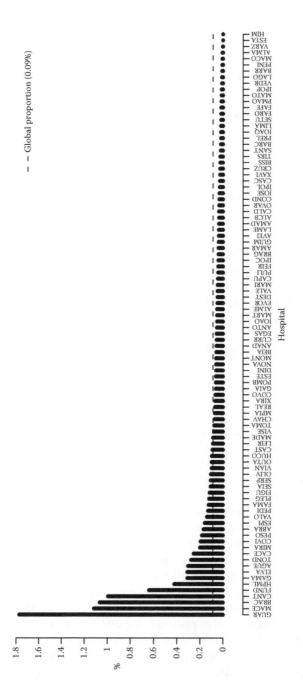

FIGURE 4.3
Influenza variation by hospital.

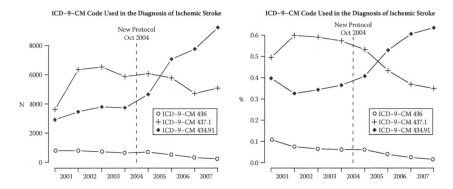

FIGURE 4.4
Evolution of ischemic cerebral-vascular disease coding.

calculated using the same national hospital discharge database. Medical specialists do not find a medical reason for such a decrease between years 1999 and 2001 (1183 to 770 cases). On the other hand, coding specialists suggest that perhaps a modification in coding policies could be the cause of this sudden decrease.

Unambiguous and consistent representation is the foundation of data reuse. Locally developed systems often fail to meet this requirement. There are methods to disambiguate concept representation [60]:

Top-down approach—identification of key concepts of a domain, which are then organized into a structure; then detailed concepts are filled into the structure.

Bottom-up approach—collection of all detailed concepts, which are then organized into a hierarchical structure.

In a 2008 study, Hyeoneui et al. [50] showed how these methods can be applied in a real-case scenario. A locally developed ICU nursing flow sheet was studied with the aim of extracting the conceptual model existing in the IS. Although a labor-intensive process, the disambiguation methods proved to be feasible in clarifying many ambiguous data representation in the local ICU nursing flow sheets.

4.3.7 Protocol of Data Collection

Pulling data elements out from the systems and environments that generate them also pulls them away from valuable information that gives them definition and structure. For example, for a single data element of blood pressure, its definition is fairly well understood. However, how one interprets blood pressure may differ with respect to: where it was measured (in the quiet confines

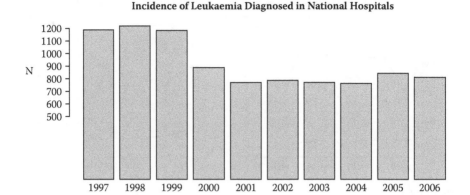

FIGURE 4.5
Incidence of leukemia in Portugal between 1997 and 2006, according to hospital coded data.

of a doctor's office or at the back of an ambulance); how it was measured; when it was measured (time and day); and who took the measurement.

Many questions may arise regarding data collection protocols:

Should it only store the data on blood pressure or should the protocol be also used to collect it?

Are values understandable without the protocol?

Can two temperatures, measured in different locations, represent the same variable?

Can two temperatures, measured with different devices, represent the same variable?

Savage [18] proposed that the following acquisition methods should be described in order to better understand the data:

- Business practices
- Measurement, observation, and assessment methods
- Recordkeeping practices
- Constraints and rules applied
- Changes in methods over time

In openEHR standard [61], special attention was given to the way health-related data are measured, so all the CARE ENTRY classes in the openEHR EHR Reference Model have a protocol section. This includes the OBSERVATION, EVALUATION, ACTION, and INSTRUCTION classes. The protocol section was added early in the design of openEHR based on research at the time demonstrating that computerization meant that a lot of details could be added to the documentation that could be of use in the future. This section is used to record information that is not critical, but may add value, to the interpretation of a measurement. This often includes information about the manner in which something was measured, such as the device or location of a measurement (when the measurement value is applied to the body—such as temperature).

A different illustrative example shows how differences in protocol have an important impact on data interpretation. In Portugal, LOS is calculated by subtracting the admission date from the discharge date. Same-day stays are consequently coded as 0. Leave days are not subtracted. Even considering admission and discharge time, the process of calculating LOS is not always the some among different hospitals throughout the country. For same-day stays we, find, in some cases, LOS with a value of 0 and, in other cases, with a value 1. Other national administrative/clinical applications do not use the standard definition and include the leave day. Consequently, an episode where the patient leaves in the day after admission is assigned 2 days for LOS.

4.3.8 Date and Time Issues

One important piece of information regarding clinical activities is the moment when they occurred. In many circumstances, the accuracy of time data has profound medical, medicolegal, and research consequences (e.g., child birth, death, surgery, anesthetics, or resuscitation). Regarding data mining, the analysis of time data allows users establish the order of events and the time lapse between each event, and thereby allow event linkage when integrating different databases or doing process mining on log data.

One of the problems stems from the fact that there are several unsynchronized mechanisms used to tell the time. There is an old saying, "A man with a watch knows what time it is. A man with two watches is never sure." During resuscitations, multiple timepieces are used, and many events occur within a short period. Inaccuracies make it impossible to accurately reconstruct the order of events, which increases liability risks in the event of a lawsuit [62]. Standard bodies of the medical informatics field have already proposed solutions, such as Consistent Time Integration Profile, although they were mainly intended to synchronize logs, authenticate users, and digitally sign documents.

Births per minute case study. Another problem is related to people rounding off the minutes (or seconds) of clinical events. To test this premise, the authors of this chapter have measured the frequency of births grouped by the minute of birth (0 to 59) in a central Portuguese hospital. The database used had more 10,000 births registered. Some of the calculated frequencies were as follows: 9.15% for 0 minutes, 4.94% for 30 minutes, 1.8% for 12 minutes, and 0.44% for 51 minutes (see Figure 4.6). The top 12 most frequent minutes were all multiples of 5. The chart clearly shows the health professional tendency to input minutes that are in multiples of 5. Today, it seems a nurse

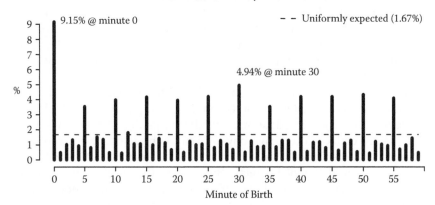

FIGURE 4.6
Frequency of births per minute.

with both a computer clock and a wall clock is never sure what time the birth really occurred. For several years now, nurses on the Perinatal Discussion List have questioned the dilemma of too many clocks ("Do you document the time from the wall clock, the electronic fetal monitor or the computerized medical record workstation clock?" "What if the times are discrepant?" "Where do you get standardized time?") [63].

A different study shows that 93% of cardiac arrest cases would contain a documentation error of 2 minutes (probably due to rounding off) or more and that 41% of cases would contain a documentation error of 5 minutes or more [64]. This value confirms the variation of critical timepiece settings in an urban emergency care system.

Kaye et al. [65] argue that the ability to use time intervals to evaluate resuscitation practice in the hospital is compromised by existing missing time data, negative calculated Utstein gold standard process intervals, unlikely intervals of 0 minute from arrest recognition to Advance Life Support interventions in units with cardiopulmonary resuscitation providers only, use of multiple timepieces for recording time data during the same event, and wide variation in coherence and precision of timepieces [65]. To detect such problems, the researcher should try to

Understand the protocol/policy used by the EHR users to record time.

Find out how the different timepieces are synchronized.

Check if the devices and servers are similarly configured regarding time zones and daylight saving time.

Create algorithms to test the accuracy of data (e.g., the minute distribution of births should balanced).

In some clinical scenarios, there as been concern in solving this DQ issue. Ornato et al. [64] have documented that an attempted synchronization has cut a 2-minute documentation error rate in half and reduced the 5-minute documentation error rate by three-fourths. However, the error rates were predicted to return to baseline 4 months after the attempted synchronization [64]. They concluded that community synchronization of timepieces to an atomic clock can reduce the problem significantly, but the effects of a one-time attempted synchronization event are short-lived. In a more recent study, it was concluded that manually synchronizing timepieces to coordinated universal time improved accuracy for several weeks, but the feasibility of synchronizing all timepieces is undetermined [66].

Regarding the resuscitation clinical domain, Kaye et al. [65] argue that practitioners, researchers, and manufacturers of resuscitation equipment must come together to create a method to collect and document accurately essential resuscitation time elements.

Ideally, all devices and servers involved in the EHR should have their times synchronized (using Network Time Protocol). The researcher should also consider that in some countries, the official time changes twice a year (daylight saving time changes in summer and winter), complicating even further the analysis of data [67].

Births per day of month case study. It is also possible to find problems related to dates of events. The authors of this chapter have measured the frequency of births grouped by the day of the month (1 to 31) of a large database with all inpatient episodes of all Portuguese public hospitals. The values were adjusted according to the number of days. As shown in Figure 4.7, it is clear that the days of birth are also rounded to 1 or multiples of 5. A more detailed analysis allowed us to find higher differences among people born between 1918 and 1947 (range, 2.35–4.33%) and practically no differences among people born between 1978 and 2007 (range, 3.16–3.32%). This is probably related to the fact that people then used to register their children a few months after the actual birth, thereby increasing the possibility of rounding the registered day of birth.

4.4 Integration Issues of EHRs

Currently, people have more mobility and longer lives, and healthcare is more shared than ever. The need to integrate EHRs for healthcare delivery, management, or research is widely acknowledged. In its "Crossing the Quality Chasm" report, the Institute of Medicine [68] has documented the consequences of the absence of integration on the quality and costs of healthcare, and the need of "far greater than the current investments in information technology by most healthcare organizations." The main problem for the lack of

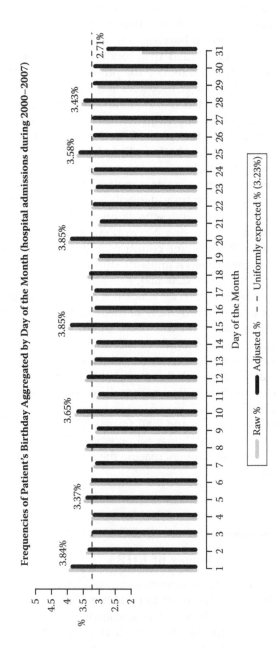

FIGURE 4.7

Frequency of births aggregated by day of the month. Data from 9 million records of all patients who had hospital admissions (inpatient episodes) in all Portuguese public hospitals between 2000 and 2007.

integration seems to be the poor incentive among healthcare institutions for overall integration [69]. Patients themselves, who have a strong incentive for integrated EHRs, are becoming the main drivers for the proliferation of the IS integration and Personal Health Records [70]. As patients become more aware and subsequently empowered in a patient-driven healthcare system, they will demand integrated EHRs as tools to help them manage their own health [71].

Clinical care increasingly requires healthcare professionals to access patient record information that may be distributed across multiple sites, held in a variety of paper and electronic formats, and represented as mixtures of narrative, structured, coded, and multimedia entries [72]. In hospitals, information technologies tend to combine different modules or subsystems, resulting in the coexistence of several IS aiming at a best-of-breed approach.

In a healthcare organization, processes are usually supported by several tools and there is a need to integrate these tools in order to achieve an integrated and seamless process [73]. Nevertheless, people will not willingly give up the stand-alone IS they use today because they fear data loss, loss of specific system functions customized to their needs, loss of control of their data (feeling that it represents their gold mine for research purposes), and they also have some pride about their own software implementation.

Integration of healthcare IS is essential to support shared care in hospitals, to provide proper care to mobile individuals, and to make regional healthcare systems more efficient. However, to integrate clinical IS in a manner that will improve communication and data use for healthcare delivery, research, and management, many different issues must be addressed [74–76]. Consistently combining data from heterogeneous sources takes substantial amounts of effort because the individual feeder systems usually differ in several aspects, such as functionality, presentation, terminology, data representation, and semantics [77]. It is still a challenge to make EHRs interoperable because good solutions to the preservation of clinical meaning across heterogeneous systems remain to be explored [72].

There are many standard bodies currently active in the formulation of international standards directly relating to EHRs. These are the International Organisation for Standardization (ISO), the European Committee for Standardization, and the Health Level Seven (HL7). Other organizations involved in the development of standards are the American Society for Testing and Materials, the Object Management Group, and the openEHR Foundation.

Over the years, different solutions to healthcare systems integration problems have been proposed and some have been applied. Many of these solutions coexist in today's healthcare settings and are influenced by technology innovation and changes in healthcare delivery. It should be noted that regarding standards in health informatics, there is the danger of confirming the ironic remark about the existence of so many of options that makes our choice difficult. The fact that there are many solutions to health systems integration using different standards and data architectures may prove to be the greatest obstacle to semantic interoperability [78].

Lately, there has been an increasing number of publications describing projects, that integrate data from multiple IS [79]. This is in agreement with the assumption about the interest in improving the communication of health-related data to support person-centered healthcare. As the number of heterogeneous health IS grows, their integration becomes a priority. Moreover, we may be witnessing an increasing interest in regional integration among heterogeneous healthcare IS across different institutions, to bolster communication between the different stakeholders (primary and secondary care doctors, nurses, and patients). This is also supported by the increasing communication of referral letters. It is noteworthy that efforts are being expended toward integration in countries such as Germany, Greece, and Denmark, which are trying to implement nationwide healthcare integrated networks fed by heterogeneous IS.

Messaging technologies (in particular, HL7) are more used than middleware solutions (e.g., DICOM or CORBA). Web-based technologies (web services and web browsers) support most of the projects, indicating that new technologies are quickly adopted in healthcare institutions. Nevertheless, it is obvious that many distinct technological solutions coexist to integrate patient data.

The lowest semantics is about data values. There are several data types (e.g., text and numeric) that are supported universally on all major computing platforms. The use of standardized or common agreed data types (e.g., ISO data types) could further enhance the interoperability of low-level data semantics across systems. Based on that, certain ways of expressing value constraints for validation could enhance DQ and thus yield more reliable research.

On a higher level is the semantics of EHR information models based on which EHR systems are built. These EHR models provide the sense of structures in the EHR so that data entries can be locally grouped to meet clinical recording requirements, for example, outpatient encounter or inpatient admission screen forms. Occasionally, parts of the structures are also rendered on the screen in the form of headings, rubrics, and panels for easy navigation and usability. With modern EHRs, users have the choice to define their own particular structures to satisfy their clinical recording needs. Such mechanism is sometimes known as EHR templates [80–82]. Latest EHR interoperability technology even goes further to standardize the base EHR information models and allow these models to be further customized to meet volatile clinical requirements. ISO/EN 13606, openEHR archetypes/templates, and HL7 CDA templates are examples of these.

The use of standardized terminologies, medical vocabularies, and classifications in EHR provides the links between the data and externally defined concept models. Such links, sometimes known as terminology bindings, are crucial to communicate the intended meaning of recorded data using concepts fully defined elsewhere. Such separation is necessary due to practical reasons. Concepts from terminology systems are universal and cover wide range from virus, bacteria, symptoms, to human anatomy, disease, and medical products. Authoring, managing, and maintaining these concepts and their relationships require access to experts from different domains of medicine, an effort that is only sustainable via international collaboration in order to achieve quality over long periods. This is exactly why international collaborations are now common (e.g., International Health Terminology Standards Development Organization). The rate of the change and the manner in which changes occur in these concept systems are quite different from those of the information models behind EHRs. The EHR information models are primarily designed for data recording to support care. Because of the changes in care protocols and processes, and the need for supporting *ad hoc* documentation, these EHR models are more volatile than the terminology systems and need to be close to where recording occurs.

4.4.1 Differences in Users

The users of EHRs are not all the same. They are different in terms of their background (e.g., medical doctors, nurses, radiology and laboratory technicians, and even patients), professional experience (e.g., young doctors doing their internship vs. senior specialists), or their computer experience (e.g., users typing long texts very fast vs. users having difficulties navigating through the IS). Physicians themselves enter the majority of data, either by populating specific fields or by keyboard entry of free text. Moreover, the exact time of entering data by physicians is also an issue, as most of the time this occurs immediately upon completion of the office visit; occasionally, this occurs during the visit in the presence of the patient, and sometimes at the end of a clinical session [36]. There are even cultural differences, which cannot be modeled by prior knowledge, that introduce high levels of uncertainty in the recorded data and the corresponding DQ.

A study that tried to unveil associations among users' clinical experience and DQ has been conducted by Soto et al. [36] in the ambulatory care setting. The study included primary care physicians (internists and pediatricians) and explored differences in the quality of medical records documentation according to several dimensions, including gender (both for physicians and patients), years since medical school, teaching status, and practice site (inside or outside the city). The objective was to measure the documentation of the patient's smoking history, drug allergies, medications, screening guidelines, and immunizations. Study results are paradigmatic of the type of (unexpected) differences that could rise in similar scenarios. Pediatricians and internists mainly differed in their patterns of documenting smoking status, which was expected as smoking status may be considered a more appropriate measure of quality for internal medicine than for pediatrics. However, although pediatricians were more likely to document smoking status for their older patients, internists were less likely to document smoking status with increasing age of the patient, suggesting biased focus of smoking documentation on adolescents and young adults. The study also revealed differences in documentation regarding gender and experience. A sample of some of the probably less expected results for the internists group include: female internists were more likely than male internists to document smoking history, but less likely to document drug allergies; with increasing number of years since completing medical school, internists were less likely to document drug allergies and immunizations, whereas the increase in clinical time was associated with better documentation for smoking history. Overall, if some of the differences were somehow expected due to experience and clinical practice, gender had a priori unpredictable effects on the documentation quality. The authors concluded that no consistent pattern of correlates of medical record documentation quality emerged from the study, which might reinforce our view that there is a high randomness factor associated with differences among users.

Differences between users case study. A different setting arises when two or more users record a single event, especially if they belong to different professional groups. Consider the following example where both the emergency team and the firemen record the time at which an emergency team arrives at the event scene assigned to the event (in this scenario, the fire department is responsible for patient transportation). We gathered the time of arrival of the emergency team recorded by themselves and by the firefighters for 235 different events. The reader should recall that there is no "gold standard" in this problem; we can only make relative comparisons, and without any quality assessment of each group's record. Most of the time (60%), firemen recorded later times than those recorded by the emergency team, whereas only in 20.4% of cases did both teams agree on the arrival time. Figure 4.8 shows the distribution of the differences between recording times in the two groups, for all events. One event was recorded with a 54-minute (negative) difference between the two groups, and as a difference of more than 30 minutes seems more like recording error than a disagreement, we considered it an outlier and discarded this record. The remaining 234 records follow a symmetric distribution, with mean = 2.21 and standard deviation = 5.028 minutes of difference between the two record types. Assuming this sample is representative of the population of events occurring in similar scenarios, and that the mean is significantly above zero (99% confidence interval, 1.36–3.06), we could conclude that firemen tend to record later times than the emergency team. In this scenario, none of the teams has access to a "correct" time, each one using their own clock and way of registration (at the time or retrospectively), and yet the emergency team records arrivals as having occurred 2 minutes (median) earlier than firemen do. Moreover, the distribution of absolute differences when the emergency team reports later arrival times than firemen is also different from the distribution of events when firemen report

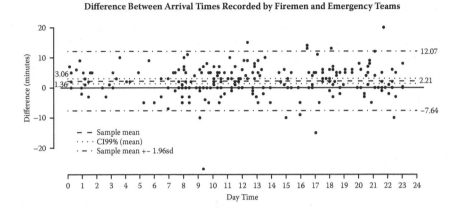

FIGURE 4.8
Differences between arrival times recorded by firemen and emergency teams.

later times (Mann-Whitney test, $p = 0.002$), with median values of 3 and 5 minutes (either by rounding or truncating the values), respectively, reinforcing the differences among the two groups of users. However, an important feature could be the basis of these differences: emergency teams have always registered event time in multiples of 5 minutes, whereas firemen have done it only around 45% of the times (nonetheless above the uniformly expected frequency of 20%).

4.4.2 Record and Event Linkage

One of the main challenges of health IS or networks is to be able to gather the different parts of the medical record of a patient without any risk of mixing them with those of another patient [83, 84]. Erroneous patient identification also has an impact on research and on hospital charging, as subsidiary partners refuse to pay for misidentified medical procedures. Record linkage between different IS is a risk but also an opportunity, because cross-checking between integrated distributed systems may be used to guarantee global patient DQ [85].

Patient identification errors case study. Cruz-Correia et al. [85] have studied the frequency of patients identification errors on clinical reports from four departmental IS and the hospital administrative database in a central Portuguese hospital. Table 4.6 presents the number of identification errors found as a new algorithm to cross-check data in different IS was being introduced. Furthermore, the assessment of the correctness of collected patient data is a difficult process even when we are familiar with the system under which it was collected [16].

Generally, record linkage refers to the task of finding entries or records that refer to the same entity (e.g., patient) in two or more files or databases. It

TABLE 4.6

Frequency of Patient's Identification Errors on Clinical Reports from Four Departmental Information Systems and the Hospital Administrative Database between July and December 2005

Information System	Total	Jul	Aug	Sep	Oct	Nov	Dec
System A	374	102	219	10	26	12	5
System B	44	12	7	5	5	11	4
System C	2					1	1
System D	1				1		
Hospital administrative system	2	2					
Total errors found	423	116	226	15	32	24	10
Total reports checked	391.258	62.455	61.810	66.737	67.267	67.680	65.309

is an appropriate technique when the user needs to join data that are spread over more than one database. Record linkage is a useful tool when performing data mining. One typical use involves joining records of persons based on name when no national identification number or similar information is recorded in the data. The term record linkage was initially coined in 1946 by Dunn [86], who used it to designate the linking of various records of a person's life. As an example, record linkage could be used in mortality data sets in a cohort study, to determine who has (or has not) died [87]. The methods used in record linkage can be deterministic or probabilistic.

They are deterministic when they are based on defined identifiers for each individual that are usually assigned centrally and used in any records that are kept for that individual. It can be undertaken whenever there is a unique identifier, such as a personal identification number. A critique of the deterministic match rules is that they do not adequately reflect the uncertainty that may exist for some potential links [88].

They are probabilistic when they are based on combinations of nonunique characteristics of each individual, such as name, date of birth, or gender. It uses probabilities to determine whether a pair of records refers to the same individual. Patterns of agreement and disagreement between identifying characteristics are translated into quantitative scores, which are then used to predict whether the two records should be linked [89]. Statistics are calculated from the agreement of fields on matching and differing records to determine weights on each field. During execution, the agreement or disagreement weight for each field is added to obtain a combined score representing the probability that the records refer to the same entity. Often, there is one threshold above which a pair is considered a match, and another threshold below which it is considered not to be a match. Between the two thresholds, a pair is considered to be "possibly a match," and dealt with accordingly (e.g., human reviewed, linked, or not linked, depending on the application).

Regardless of the record linkage technique used, data normalization is always very important. Heterogeneity can be found in the formats of dates, people names, organizations, or department names, etc. By normalizing these data into a common format and using comparison techniques that handle additional variation, a much higher consistency can be achieved, resulting in higher accuracy in any record linkage technique.

An extension of patient record linkage based on health-related events (event linkage) is currently being studied [90]. This technique uses some demographic data in conjunction with event dates to match events in two data sets providing a possible method for linking related events.

4.5 Discussion

Imperfect data have a strong negative effect on the quality of knowledge discovery results. In this chapter, we focus on DQ issues that mainly depend on confounding causes, not necessarily visible (or even imaginable) to the data analyst. The main "take-away message" we intend to pass is that the data analyst should also consider expert knowledge about the overall setting, and about the data themselves—how it was collected, processed, and analyzed.

The data recorded on EHRs is the result of the processes of healthcare delivery. For the data to be fully understood, it is essential for the researcher to know such processes. The authors of this chapter argue that blindly analyzing EHR data without understanding the data collection process will probably lead to erroneous conclusions. Unfortunately, proper documentation on the data collection process is rarely forthcoming, and so the responsibility is left to the researcher to perform this task.

Regarding DQ, many different issues must be tackled with in EHR data (e.g., missing values, erroneous clinical coding, time synchronization). Currently, it is still very difficult to guarantee that EHR data are accurate, complete, relevant, timely, sufficiently detailed, and appropriately represented, and that they retain sufficient contextual information to support decision-making.

The integration of different EHRs further increases the difficulty of performing information extraction from EHRs. Due to the development of both EHR models and terminology systems, there is a growing overlapping of semantics that could be possibly represented using one technology over another. The best approach to perform terminology bindings between common EHR models and standardized terminology systems is still under intensive research, and the topic is probably beyond the scope of this chapter. It is nonetheless important to recognize such a need, the ongoing efforts, and what has already been established as recommendations in the field.

Once the important role of reference terminologies (e.g., SNOMED Clinical Terms), common concept models (EN-13940: CONTsys), and EHR interoperability standards (e.g., EN/ISO-13606, openEHR) have been fully recognized, it will be possible to share detailed and machine-interpretable care plans [91] not only to support continuity of care, but also to facilitate clinical research. In such scenario, care plans are instantiated from commonly agreed and/or evidence-based clinical guidelines, and can be communicated and understood by different EHR systems to provide guideline-based decision support to care providers across different organizations over potentially long periods. Because the care plans are based on guidelines and fully computerized [92], it would be feasible to check the guideline compliance of the care provided. Noncompliance treatment would either be followed up as quality issues or serve as input into clinical research for discovery of new knowledge.

Research on as well as other uses of EHRs are not likely reach their full potential before reference terminologies, common concept models, and EHR interoperability standards have been widely adopted. The challenge is still considerable, but with the recent EHR R&D projects [93] taking place in the academia, standardization bodies, and industry, what was deemed "an impossible task before is now a very difficult one."

In conclusion, although much research is still needed to improve DQ in some areas (e.g., semantic interoperability), there are already simple techniques available that should be made mandatory in EHR implementation to improve the quality of research and reduce misconceptions (e.g., time synchronization, proper database documentation, version control of data, and registration of all protocol changes). Meanwhile, researchers analyzing EHR data should be very careful with the interpretation on the retrieved results.

4.6 Related Work and Further Readings

Data anomalies can take a number of different forms, each with a different range of analytical consequences [94], focusing on outliers (definition of which is several times subjective), missing data, misalignments (strongly connected with time-related data problems), and unexpected structure (mostly appearing as multivariate outliers). Most research topics dealing with imperfect records consider statistical approaches to detect and correct these imperfections [95]. The impact of imperfect data on healthcare domains is enhanced by the fact that in many medical studies, particularly (prospective) studies of ongoing events, the patient group whose health is most threatened is represented by rather small numbers of subjects [96]. In a seminal data mining book, Breiman et al. [84] presented several examples of medical studies, where the use of decision trees proved to be helpful, but not without inspecting DQ. For example, when studying the diagnosis of heart attacks, 3.6% of cases had to be excluded due to data incompleteness. Most of the works actually rely on this a priori analysis of anomalies to assure the quality of results. However, although all studies presented in the book reported missing data in the included cases, its impact on the results was not clearly discussed. Moreover, even if the protocol is followed "by the book," and no significant anomaly exists, there is also uncertainty in the data (e.g., if a sensor reads 100, most of times the real value is around 100—it could be 99 or 101), which should be taken into account.

A "good" data analysis result should be insensitive to small changes in either the methods or the data sets on which the analysis is based [94]. To produce robust and reliable results from such uncertain data sets, care has to be taken regarding the inferred conclusions. This idea is the mote for the *generalized sensitivity analysis* metaheuristic. A good introductory presentation on this procedure is presented by Pearson (Chapter 6) [94]. Basically, research has followed the path of a group of approaches that generate perturbations of initial learning set to assess the reliability of final models [97]. The bootstrap method [98] is a general tool for assessing statistical accuracy [99]. The main idea is to randomly draw data sets with replacement from the original data set, each of which has the same size as the original, and perform the analysis on all samples, and examine the fit of our model over the replications. *Bagging* [100] and *boosting* [101] are well known and possibly the most popular derivatives in the knowledge discovery field. They have been shown to improve generalization performance compared to individual models. Although *bagging* works by learning different models in different regions of the input space (by sampling original data set using specific bootstrap parameters), *boosting* focuses on those regions that are not so well covered by the learned model. These techniques perturb the entire learning data set that is fed to individual models, thus operating by creating different learning models [97].

Another related field deals with change mining, in the sense that data are not static and changes might occur and should be mined. When data are collected for long periods, the assumption that the process that is producing the examples is static does not hold. As seen in some of the examples we present in this chapter, such as the results on leukemia incidence and ischemic stroke coding, time matters. Stream mining and concept drift detection have been widely studied to implement such detection mechanisms [102]. In stream mining, data are processed as an open-ended continuous flow, where no (or little) storage is available [19, 103], so models should evolve with time. On one hand, mechanisms are necessary to detect changes in the underlying process producing the data stream [104]. On the other hand, change mining aims at identifying changes in an evolving domain by analyzing how models and patterns change [105]. This last subject is a hot topic in current data mining research, and their benefits to knowledge extraction from EHRs are clear, as the data in these changes are usually time-dependent. Further work should be considered in this field.

Acknowledgments

The authors would like to acknowledge the support given by the research project HR-QoD (outliers, inconsistencies, and errors) in hospital inpatient databases: methods and implications for data modeling, cleansing, and analysis (project PTDC/SAU-ESA/75660/2006). Also, the work of Pedro P. Rodrigues is supported by the Portuguese Foundation for Science and Technology (FCT) under PhD Grant SFRH/BD/29219/2006 and FCTs Plurianual financial support attributed to Laboratório de Inteligência Artificial e Apoio à Decisão. Finally, some of Rong Chen's work is part of NovaMedTech funded by Nutek, the Swedish Agency for Economic and Regional Growth, and the European Union Structural Funds.

References

1. Komaroff, A. L. 1979. The variability and inaccuracy of medical data. *Proceedings of the IEEE* 67(9):1196–1207.
2. Hogan, W. R., and Wagner, M. M. 1997. Accuracy of data in computer-based patient records. *Journal of the American Medical Informatics Association* 4(5):342–355.
3. Wyatt, J. C., and Wright, P. 1998. Design should help use of patients' data. *Lancet (British edition)* 352(9137):1375–1378.
4. Coiera, E. 2003. *Guide to Health Informatics*. London: Arnold London.
5. Barnett, O. 1990. Computers in medicine. *JAMA* 263(19):2631.
6. Richart, R. H. 1970. Evaluation of a medical data system. *Computers and Biomedical Research* 3(5):415.
7. Audit Commission. 1995. For your information: a study of information management and systems in the acute hospital. London: HMSO.
8. Mamlin, J. J., and Baker, D. H. 1973. Combined time-motion and work sampling study in a general medicine clinic. *Medical Care* 11:449–456.
9. Korpman, R. A., and Lincoln. T. L. 1998. The computer-stored medical record: for whom? *Journal of the American Medical Informatics Association* 259:3454–3456.
10. Wyatt, J. C. 1994. Clinical data systems: Part 1. Data and medical records. *The Lancet* 344:1543–1547.
11. Dick, R. S., and Steen, E. B., eds. 1977. *The Computer-based Patient Record: An Essential Technology for HealthCare*. Washington, D.C.: National Academy Press.
12. Nygren, E., Wyatt, J. C., and Wright, P. 1998. Helping clinicians to find data and avoid delays. *The Lancet*, 352:1462–1466.
13. Hammond, K.W., Helbig, S. T., Benson, C. C., and Brathwaite-Sketoe, B. M. 2003. Are electronic medical records trustworthy? Observations on copying, pasting and duplication. In *AMIA Annual Symposium Proceedings*, pp. 269–73.

14. Hohnloser, J. H., Fischer, M. R., Konig, A., and Emmerich, B. 1994. Data quality in computerized patient records. Analysis of a haematology biopsy report database. *International Journal of Clinical Monitoring and computing* 11(4):233–240.
15. Weir, C. R., Hurdle, J. F., Felgar, M. A., Hoffman, J. M., Roth, B., and Nebeker, J. R. 2003. Direct text entry in electronic progress notes—an evaluation of input errors. *Methods of Information in Medicine* 42(1):61–67.
16. Berner, E., and Moss, J. 2005. Informatics challenges for the impending patient information explosion. *Journal of the American Medical Informatics Association* 12(6):614–617.
17. Hogan, W. R., and Wagner, M. M. 1997. Accuracy of data in computer-based patient records. *Journal of the American Medical Informatics Association* 4(5):342–355.
18. Savage, A. M. 1999. Framework for characterizing data and identifying anomalies in health care databases. In *Proceedings of the AMIA Symposium*, p. 374. American Medical Informatics Association.
19. Muthukrishnan, S. 2005. *Data streams: Algorithms and Applications*. New York, NY: Now Publishers Inc.
20. Johnson, S. B. 1996. Generic data modeling for clinical repositories. *Journal of the American Medical Informatics Association* 3(5):328–339.
21. Van Ginneken, A. M., Stam, H., and Duisterhout, J. S. 1994. A powerful macro-model for the computer patient record. In *Proceedings of the Annual Symposium on Computer Application in Medical Care*, p. 496. American Medical Informatics Association.
22. Los, R. K. 2006. Supporting Uniform Representation of Data. PhD thesis, Department of Medical Informatics, Erasmus Medical Center, Rotterdam, the Netherlands.
23. Shortliffe, E. H., and Cimino, J. J. 2006. *Biomedical Informatics—Computer Applications in Health Care and Biomedicine*, 3rd edn. New York, NY: Springer.
24. Shortliffe, E. H., Perreault, L. E., Wiederhold, G., and Fagan, L. M. 1990. *Medical Informatics: Computer Applications in Health Care*. Boston, MA: Addison-Wesley Longman Publishing Co.
25. Wyatt, J. C., and Sullivan, F. 2005. *ABC of Health Informatics*. Blackwell Publishing, Malden, MA: BMJ Books.
26. Riva, G. 2003. Ambient intelligence in health care. *Cyberpsychology & Behavior* 6(3):295–300.
27. Anfindsen, O. J. 2000. Database management system and method for combining meta-data of varying degrees of reliability. US Patent 6,044,370.
28. Tayi, G. K., and Ballou, D. P. 1998. Examining data quality. *Communications of the ACM* 41(2):54–57.
29. Wyatt, J. C., and Liu, J. L. Y. 2002. Basic concepts in medical informatics. *British Medical Journal* 56(11):808–812.
30. Wang, R. Y. 1998. Total data quality. *Communications of the ACM* 41(2):58–65.
31. Gertz, M., Ozsu, T., Saake, G., and Sattler, K. 2003. Data quality on the Web. In *Dagstuhl Seminar*, Dagstuhl, Germany.
32. Strong, D. M. Lee, Y. W., and Wang, R. Y. 1997. Data quality in context. *Communications of the ACM* 40(5):103–110.
33. Orr, K. 1998. Data quality and systems theory. *Communications of the ACM* 41(2):66–71

34. Pourasghar, F., Malekafzali, H., Kazemi, A., Ellenius, J., and Fors, U. 2008. What they fill in today, may not be useful tomorrow: lessons learned from studying medical records at the women's hospital in Tabriz, Iran. *BMC Public Health* 8(1):139.

35. Jaspers, M. W., Knaup, P., and Schmidt, D. 2006. The computerized patient record: where do we stand. *Methods of Information in Med*, 45(Suppl 1):29–39.

36. Soto, C. M., Kleinman, K. P., and Simon, S. R. 2002. Quality and correlates of medical record documentation in the ambulatory care setting. *BMC Health Services Research* 2(1):22.

37. Roberts, C. L., Algert, C. S., and Ford, J. B. 2007. Methods for dealing with discrepant records in linked population health datasets: a cross-sectional study. *BMC Health Services Research* 7:12.

38. Arts, D. G. T., de Keizer, N. F., and Scheffer, G. J. 2002. Defining and improving data quality in medical registries: a literature review, case study, and generic framework. *Journal of the American Medical Informatics Association* 9(6):600–611.

39. Oliveira, P., Rodrigues, F., and Henriques, P. 2005. A formal definition of data quality problems. In *IQ*, F. Naumann, M. Gertz, and S. Madnick, eds. Cambridge, MA: MIT Press.

40. Maletic, J. I., and Marcus, A. 2000. Data cleansing: beyond integrity analysis. In *Proceedings of the Conference on Information Quality*, pp. 200–209.

41. Kamber, M., and Han, J. 2001. *Data Mining: Concepts and Techniques*. San Francisco, CA: Morgan Kaufmann Publishers.

42. Koh, H. C., and Tan, G. 2005. Data mining applications in healthcare. *Journal of Healthcare Information Management* 19(2):64–72.

43. Na, K. S., Baik, D. K., and Kim, P. K. 2001. A practical approach for modeling the quality of multimedia data. In *Proceedings of the 9th ACM international conference on Multimedia*, pp. 516–518. New York, NY: ACM Press.

44. Hodge, V., and Austin, J. 2004. A survey of outlier detection methodologies. *Artificial Intelligence Review* 22(2):85–126.

45. Lee, A. H., Xiao, J., Vemuri, S. R., and Zhao, Y. 1998. A discordancy test approach to identify outliers of length of hospital stay. *Statistics in Medicine*, 17(19):2199–2206.

46. Podgorelec, V., Hericko, M., and Rozman, I. 2005. Improving mining of medical data by outliers prediction. In *18th IEEE Symposium on Computer-Based Medical Systems, 2005. Proceedings*, pp. 91–96.

47. Ramaswamy, S., Rastogi, R., and Shim, K. 2000. Efficient algorithms for mining outliers from large data sets. In *Proceedings of the 2000 ACM SIGMOD International Conference on Management of data*, pp. 427–438. New York, NY: ACM Press.

48. Network, I. 2002. Population and health in developing countries: volume 1. *Population, Health, and Survival at INDEPTH sites*. IDRC, Ottawa, ON, CA.

49. Palmblad, M., and Tiplady, B. 2004. Electronic diaries and questionnaires: designing user interfaces that are easy for all patients to use. *Quality of Life Research* 13(7):1199–1207.

50. Hyeoneui, K., Harris, M. R., Savova, G. K., and Chute, C. G. 2008. The first step toward data reuse: disambiguating concept representation of the locally developed ICU nursing flowsheets. *Computers, Informatics, Nursing* 26(5):282.

51. Connell, F. A., Diehr, P., and Hart, L. G. 1987. The use of large data bases in health care studies. *Annual Review of Public Health* 8(1):51–74.

52. Ola, B., Khan, K. S., Gaynor, A. M., and Bowcock, M. E. 2001. Information derived from hospital coded data is inaccurate: the Birmingham Women's Hospital experience. *Journal of Obstetrics and Gynaecology* 21(2):112–113.
53. Cohen, J. 1960. A coefficient of agreement for nominal scales. *Educational and Psychological Measurement* 20(1):37.
54. Ellis, J., Mulligan, I., Rowe, J., and Sackett, D. L. 1995. Inpatient general medicine is evidence based. A-team, Nuffield Department of Clinical Medicine. *Lancet* 346(8972):407.
55. Gorelick, M. H., Knight, S., Alessandrini, E. A., Stanley, R. M., Chamberlain, J. M., Kuppermann, N., and Alpern, E. R. 2007. Lack of agreement in pediatric emergency department discharge diagnoses from clinical and administrative data sources. *Academic Emergency Medicine* 14(7):646–652.
56. Icen, M., Crowson, C. S., McEvoy, M. T., Gabriel, S. E., and Kremers, H. M. 2008. Potential misclassification of patients with psoriasis in electronic databases. *Journal of the American Academy of Dermatology* 59(6):981–985.
57. Silva-Costa, T., Freitas, A., Jácome, J., Lopes, F., and Costa-Pereira, A. 2007. A eficicia de uma ferramenta de validao na melhoria da qualidade de dados hospitalares. In *CISTI 2007—2 Conferncia Ibrica de Sistemas e Tecnologias de Informao*, Portugal, June.
58. Keren, R., Wheeler, A., Coffin, S. E., Zaoutis, T., Hodinka, R., and Heydon, K. 2006. ICD-9 codes for identifying influenza hospitalizations in children. *Emerging Infectious Disease* 12(10):1603–1604.
59. Goldstein, L. B. 1998. Accuracy of ICD-9-CM coding for the identification of patients with acute ischemic stroke: effect of modifier codes. *Stroke* 29(8):1602–1604.
60. Rassinoux, A. M., Miller, R. A., Baud, R. H., and Scherrer, J. R. Modeling concepts in medicine for medical language understanding. *Methods of Information in Medicine* 37(4–5):361–372.
61. Kalra, D., Beale, T., and Heard, S. 2005. The openEHR Foundation. *Studies in Health Technology and Informatics* 115:153.
62. Synchronize timepieces in your trauma room. 2000. *ED Management*, 12(2):23–24.
63. McCartney, P. R. 2003. Synchronizing with standard time and atomic clocks. *MCN: The American Journal of Maternal Child Nursing* 28(1):51.
64. Ornato, J. P., Doctor, M. L., Harbour, L. F., Peberdy, M. A., Overton, J., Racht, E. M., Zauhar, W. G., Smith, A. P., and Ryan, K. A. 1998. Synchronization of timepieces to the atomic clock in an urban emergency medical services system. *Annals of Emergency Medicine* 31(4):483–487.
65. Kaye, W., Mancini, M. E., and Truitt, T. L. 2005. When minutes count: the fallacy of accurate time documentation during in-hospital resuscitation. *Resuscitation* 65(3):285–290.
66. Ferguson, E. A., Bayer, C. R., Fronzeo, S., Tuckerman, C., Hutchins, L., Roberts, K., Verger, J., Nadkarni, V., and Lin, R. 2005. Time out! Is timepiece variability a factor in critical care? *American Journal of Critical Care* 14(2):113.
67. Neumann, P. 1995. *Computer-Related Risks.* New York, NY: ACM Press.
68. Institute of Medicine. 2001. *Crossing the Quality Chasm: A New Health System for the 21st Century.* Washington, D. C.: National Academy Press.
69. Herzlinger, R. E. 2004. *Consumer-Driven Health Care: Implications for Providers, Payers, and Policy-Makers.* San Francisco, CA: Jossey-Bass.

70. MacStravic, S. 2004. What good is an EMR without a PHR? *HealthLeaders,* September 3.

71. Kukafka, R., and Morrison, F. 2006. Patients' needs. In *Aspects of Electronic Health Record Systems,* H. P. Lehmann et al., eds. pp. 47–64. Calgary: Springer.

72. Kalra, D. 2006. Electronic health record standards. *Methods of Information in Medicine* 45(1):136–144.

73. Land, R., and Crnkovic, I. 2003. Software systems integration and architectural analysis—a case study. In *Proceedings of the International Conference on Software Maintenance, ICSM 2003,* pp. 338–347.

74. Heathfield, H., Pitty, D., and Hanka, R. 1998. Evaluating information technology in health care: barriers and challenges. *British Medical Journal* 316:1959–1961.

75. Berg, M. 2001. Implementing information systems in health care organizations: myths and challenges. *International Journal of Medical Informatics* 64(2–3):143–156.

76. Littlejohns, P., Wyatt, J. C., and Garvican, L. 2003. Evaluating computerised health information systems: hard lessons still to be learnt. *British Medical Journal* 326:860–863.

77. Lenz, R., and Kuhn, K. A. 2002. Integration of heterogeneous and autonomous systems in hospitals. *Business Briefing: Data management & Storage Technology.*

78. Ferranti, J., Musser, C., Kawamoto, K., and Hammon, E. 2006. The clinical document architecture and the continuity of care record: a critical analysis. *Journal of the American Medical Informatics Association* 13(3):245–252.

79. Cruz-Correia, R. J., Vieira-Marques, P., Ferreira, A., Almeida, F., Wyatt, J. C., and Costa-Pereira, A. 2007. Reviewing the integration of patient data: how systems are evolving in practice to meet patient needs. *BMC Medical Informatics and Decision Making* 7(1):14.

80. Chen, R., Enberg, G., and Klein, G. O. 2007. Julius—a template based supplementary electronic health record system. *BMC Medical Informatics and Decision Making* 7(1):10.

81. Los, R. K., van Ginneken, A. M., and van der Lei, J. 2005. OpenSDE: a strategy for expressive and flexible structured data entry. *International Journal of Medical Informatics* 74(6):481–490.

82. Hoya, D., Hardikerb, N. R., McNicollc, I. T., Westwelld, P., and Bryana, A. 2008. Collaborative development of clinical templates as a national resource. *Internation Journal of Medical Informatics* 78(1):95–100.

83. Quantin, C., Binquet, C., Bourquard, K., Pattisina, R., Gouyon-Cornet, B., Ferdynus, C., Gouyon, J. B., and Allaert, F. A. 2004. A peculiar aspect of patients' safety: the discriminating power of identifiers for record linkage. *Studies in Health Technology and Informatics* 103:400–406.

84. Arellano, M. G., and Weber, G. I. 1998. Issues in identification and linkage of patient records across an integrated delivery system. *Journal of Healthcare Information Management* 12(3):43–52.

85. Cruz-Correia, R., Vieira-Marques, P., Ferreira, A., Oliveira-Palhares, E., Costa, P., and Costa-Pereira, A. 2006. Monitoring the integration of hospital information systems: how it may ensure and improve the quality of data. *Studies in Health Technology and Informatics* 121:176–82.

86. Dunn, H. L. 1946. Record linkage. *American Journal of Public Health* 36(12):1412.

87. Blakely, T., and Salmond, C. 2002. Probabilistic record linkage and a method to calculate the positive predictive value. *International Journal of Epidemiology* 31(6):1246–1252.

88. Scheuren, F. 1997. Linking health records: human rights concerns. In *Record Linkage Techniques—1997: Proceedings of an International Workshop and Exposition*, March 20–21, 1997, Arlington, VA, p. 404. Federal Committee on Statistical Methodology, Office of Management and Budget.

89. Evans, J. M. M., and MacDonald, T. M. 1999. Record-linkage for pharmacovigilance in Scotland. *British Journal of Clinical Pharmacology* 47(1):105–110.

90. Karmel, R., and Gibson, D. 2007. Event-based record linkage in health and aged care services data: a methodological innovation. *BMC Health Services Research* 7(1):154.

91. Hägglund, M., Chen, R., Scandurra, I., and Koch, S. 2009. Modeling shared care plans using CONTsys and openEHR to support shared homecare of elderly. Submitted.

92. Chen, R., Hemming, G., and Åhlfeldt, H. 2009. Representing a chemotherapy guideline using openEHR and rules. *Studies in Health Technology and Informatics* 150: 653–657.

93. Chen, R., Klein, G., Sundvall, E., Karlsson, D., and Å hlfeldt, H. 2009, July. Archetype-based import and export of EHR content models: pilot experience with a regional EHR system. *BMC Medical Informatics and Decision Making* 9:33.

94. Pearson, R. K. 2005. *Mining Imperfect Data: Dealing with Contamination and Incomplete Records*. Philadelphia, PA: Society for Industrial and Applied Mathematics.

95. Hawkins, D. M. 1980. *Identification of Outliers*. London: Chapman and Hall.

96. Breiman, L., Friedman, J. H., Olshen, R. A., and Stone. C. J. 1984. *Classification and Regression Trees*. New York, NY: Chapman and Hall/CRC.

97. Rodrigues, P. P., Gama, J., and Bosnizć, Z. 2008. Online reliability estimates for individual predictions in data streams. In *Proceedings of the 8th International Conference on Data Mining Workshops (ICDM Workshops'08)*, pp. 36–45. Pisa, Italy, December, IEEE Computer Society Press.

98. Efron, B. 1979. Bootstrap methods: another look at the jackknife. *Annals of Statistics* 7:1–26.

99. Hastie, T., Tibshirani, R., and Friedman, J. 2000. *The Elements of Statistical Learning: Data Mining, Inference and Prediction*. New York, NY: Springer Verlag.

100. Breiman, L. 1996. Bagging predictors. *Machine Learning* 24:123–140.

101. Drucker, H. 1997. Improving regressors using boosting techniques. In *Machine Learning: Proceedings of the 14th International Conference*, pp. 107–115.

102. Gama, J., and Rodrigues, P. P. 2007. Data stream processing. In *Learning from Data Streams—Processing Techniques in Sensor Networks*, J. Gama and M. Gaber, eds., chapter 3, pp. 25–39. Berlin: Springer Verlag.

103. Gama, J., and Gaber, M., eds. 2007. *Learning from Data Streams—Processing Techniques in Sensor Networks*. Berlin: Springer Verlag.

104. Gama, J., Medas, P., Castillo, G., and Rodrigues, P. P. 2004. Learning with drift detection. In *Proceedings of the 17th Brazilian Symposium on Artificial Intelligence (SBIA 2004)*, volume 3171 of *Lecture Notes in Artificial Intelligence*, A. L. C. Bazzan and S. Labidi, eds., pp. 286–295, São Luiz, Maranhão, Brazil, October 2004. Springer Verlag.

105. Böttcher, M., Höppner, F., and Spiliopoulou, M. 2008. On exploiting the power of time in data mining. *SIGKDD Explorations* 10(2):3–11.

5

Ethical, Legal, and Social Issues for EHR Data Protection

Reid Cushman

CONTENTS

5.1 Introduction

In the U.S., privacy protections for health information are required by federal laws, such as the Health Insurance Portability and Accountability Act (HIPAA), and by most states' statutes as well. Private organizations certifying healthcare facilities, such as the Joint Commission on Accreditation of Healthcare Organizations (also known as Joint Commission), also require data privacy protections, and almost all health professional organizations have provisions about privacy in their codes of ethics. Together, these comprise the protections for health information in general, and for the content of electronic health records (EHRs) in particular. Reflecting the U.S.'s "federalist" approach—in the classic sense of that term, a mixture of protections from various levels of governance—the sum of the parts yields a complex landscape. Even an overview of the ethical, legal, and social issues associated with EHR privacy, such as presented here, can be complex.

Healthcare in the U.S. has long been the most technologically advanced on the planet. (That is why it is also the most expensive.) Thus, it seems surprising to some that the U.S. health sector has been a technological laggard with respect to information technology—arguably slower to adopt electronic record-keeping via EHRs than most other industrialized nations' health systems, and certainly slower when compared to other sectors of the U.S. economy. Even today, with EHRs ever more common, the computer-based records systems in use are often unstandardized, and so have trouble "talking" to each other. It is not efficient. And, in many cases, it is not very secure either. It is against this background that public- and private-sector protections for EHRs must be understood. Just as the technological applications are relatively new, so are the protective approaches. All of them should be viewed as works in progress. Even as this chapter is being written, major changes are being contemplated for HIPAA, which was passed in 1996 but not implemented until 2003. Other recent federal legislation, such as the Genetic Information Nondiscrimination Act of 2007, adds to the complex health privacy landscape.

Understanding the ethical, legal, and social issues requires an understanding of the concepts that underlie privacy itself. Hence, it is necessary to differentiate between such terms as privacy and confidentiality, data privacy and data security, data subject and data owner, even if their meaning seems self-evident. It is to such matters that the first part of this chapter attends. We examine what it means to be "fair" with respect to information use and disclosure, including generally understood components of fairness such as openness, access, security, and minimalism. The principle of consent, which lies at the very foundation of democracy, must also be examined in detail in the context of information systems.

From these general ethical dictates, one must move to the specifics embedded in professional norms and codes, national laws and regulations, and, in a federalist system such as the U.S. has, the additional legal-regulatory provisions of the states. Finally, one arrives at HIPAA, the central legal-regulatory apparatus for health privacy in the U.S. HIPAA's structure can only be understood well when accompanied by a glance at prior health privacy efforts.

The structure of HIPAA is examined in depth here, both its general provisions and those that apply specifically to research. Investigators contemplating EHR projects do not necessarily need to memorize the complexities, which may be changed by new legislation as well as amendments to HIPAA and updated interpretations of its existing regulations. Luckily for the investigator, most organizations that provide data for a research protocol will have specialists who can clarify the terms of research or other types of data used as of that moment. However, one must at least understand that there are complexities inherent in a law such as HIPAA, and have a sense of what those complexities entail. It is precisely because a legal-regulatory structure must balance conflicting ethical and social goals in a wide range of specific contexts that complexity cannot be ignored. Whatever HIPAA evolves into, or is replaced by, a research protocol using health information will have to navigate the particulars of notice and consent, audit trails, etc., or it cannot be true to the goals of privacy.

It is now common to criticize HIPAA as a mishmash of confusing require-ments that has failed to strike an appropriate balance, particularly with respect to research (e.g., Ness, 2007). No one who has read HIPAA's provisions in depth will defend them as a masterpiece of logic or of literature, and even a summary such as presented in this chapter may leave the reader in a cogni-tive fog. Yet, it is strikingly hard to write a set of specific regulatory provisions that stand up to the range of real-world conditions presented by an activity as complex as healthcare research, in a sector as dynamic as U.S. healthcare.

This chapter focuses on the privacy protections erected by legal-regulatory structures. Chapter 8 discusses potential protections available via computa-tional techniques to anonymize data that can enable information discovery on EHRs without implicating individual privacy.

5.2 Related Work and Further Readings

Although the public and private protections may be relatively new, and in the eyes of privacy advocates still relatively limited, that is not true of the literature on privacy and the related topic of information security. Many books and important articles are available, from which it is possible only to summarize a limited few.

Works on privacy. Records, Computers and the Rights of Citizens (Advisory Committee on Automated Personal Data Systems, 1973) still provides one of the classic discussions of the government's role in data protection in a democracy. *Databanks in a Free Society: Computers, Record-Keeping, and Privacy* (National Research Council, 1972) and *Computers, Health Records and Citizen's Rights* (Westin, 1977) are also classics worth revisiting. So is the government report "Personal Privacy in an Information Society" (Privacy Protection Study Commission, 1977).

For an excellent introduction to the history and philosophy of privacy laws in the U.S., see *Legislating Privacy: Technology, Social Values and Public Policy* (Regan, 1995). For contrasting views, compare *The Privacy Advocates: Resisting the Spread of Surveillance* (Bennett, 2008) with *The Limits of Privacy* (Etzioni, 2000). The latter takes the "communitarian" (and somewhat contrarian) stance that we worry too much about the loss of privacy. For a more academic treatment of privacy issues, *Engaging Privacy and Information Technology in a Digital Age* (Waldo et al., 2007) covers the landscape of privacy issues includ-ing health and medical privacy. *Understanding Privacy* (Solove, 2008) focuses more on history and legal-social institutions, and also offers an excellent overview of the topic.

Health information and health privacy. The Computer-Based Patient Record: An Essential Technology for Health Care (Dick et al., 1991) is one of the most com-prehensive studies of the benefits of computerizing health records. *Health*

Records: Social Needs and Personal Privacy (Department of Health and Human Services, 1993) is a classic statement on the benefits and risks. *Protecting Privacy in Computerized Medical Information* (Office of Technology Assessment, 1993) and *Bringing Health Care Online: The Role of Information Technologies* (Office of Technology Assessment, 1995) provide a thorough analysis of the issues in a pre-HIPAA world. *Health Data in the Information Age: Use, Disclosure and Privacy* (Donaldson and Lohr, 1994) is another excellent summary of the pre-HIPAA environment. (See Barrows and Clayton, 1996, for a shorter treatment of the issues.) *Privacy and Health Care* (Humbler and Almeder, 2001) also provides a collection of articles on these issues.

Health privacy and research. *Protecting Data Privacy in Health Services Research* (Committee on the Role of IRBs, 2000) provides an overview of research privacy issues for anyone involved in health services research, while focusing on the role of the institutional review board (IRB). *Beyond the HIPAA Privacy Rule: Enhancing Privacy, Improving Health Through Research* (Nass et al., 2009) also offers a comprehensive examination of the issues. *Searching Eyes: Privacy, the State and Disease Surveillance in America* (Fairchild et al., 2007) discusses the tensions between privacy and public health research in particular.

Information security. Although somewhat dated, *Computers at Risk: Safe Computing in the Information Age* (National Research Council, 1991) provides a comprehensive analysis of computer security issues. *Security Engineering: A Guide to Building Dependable Distributed Systems* (Anderson, 2001) provides an excellent, if somewhat idiosyncratic, look at computer security issues. *Computer Security Basics* (Russell and Gangemi, 1991) is a very good basic text. *Computer Security* (Gollman, 1999) and *Computer Security: Art and Science* (Bishop, 2003) also offer very good coverage of the topic, but are not for the beginner.

For the Record: Protecting Electronic Health Information (National Research Council, 1997) provides a comprehensive study of healthcare privacy practices, but also focuses on security issues; it provides an understanding of the foundation for the information security provisions adopted in HIPAA. The essence of security is the evaluation of risks, and *Computer-Related Risks* (Neumann, 1995) is a classic treatment of the topic. *Secrets and Lies: Digital Security in a Networked World* (Schneier, 2000) and *Beyond Fear: Thinking Sensibly about Security in an Uncertain World* (Schneier, 2003) are excellent layperson's introductions to the theory and practice of security, including the evaluation of risk.

Information technology ethics. Information privacy and security measures stand, even if unknowingly, atop a considerable philosophical base. *Ethics and Information Technology* (Anderson and Goodman, 2002) and *Ethics, Computing and Medicine* (Goodman, 1998) provide an overview of the application of moral philosophy to information technology issues. *Information Technology and Moral Philosophy: Philosophical Explorations in Computer Ethics* (van den Hoven, 1995) does the same, but from a more theoretical perspective.

5.3 Data Protection: Theory and Practice

5.3.1 Concepts and Terminology

To have a productive discussion of the issues, it is first necessary to clarify the concepts in use. Because concepts such as privacy are part of everyday life, they bring with them a range of meanings that can sometimes confuse as much as clarify. Less familiar concepts, such as "fair information practices," which include specific rights and duties with respect to personal data, can then be set against the background of more familiar terminology.

What does "privacy" mean? The concepts associated with *privacy* comprise a complex set of considerations, definitions, and expectations. In the terse legal maxim from the nineteenth century, privacy is simply "the right to be left alone" (Warren and Brandeis, 1890). More expansively, privacy can be thought of as describing conditions of limited accessibility to various aspects of an individual. These limitations embrace a range of social institutions and interactions, yielding varying capacities for solitude and bodily inviolability (physical privacy), as well as anonymity and secrecy (informational privacy) (see, e.g., Prosser, 1960; Gavison, 1984.) Regardless of how one slices the conceptual cake, of relevance here is the capacity of electronic record-keeping technologies to reset the parameters of the latter: the ability of persons to determine what, how, and when information about themselves is to be communicated to others, in matters related to health and in other areas of private life, or for research or for other public purposes.

What about "confidentiality"? Although sometimes used as a synonym for privacy, *confidentiality* formally refers to the obligations of individuals and institutions to appropriately use information under their control once it has been disclosed to them. Disclosures customarily come in the context of a particular relationship, with implicit or explicit "contractual" parameters, such as that between doctor and patient. Custom and professional, legal, and regulatory strictures set the terms of the contract.

The principle of *autonomy* dictates respect for each individual's choices about uses and disclosures of his/her own information, as it does for privacy in general. But individual control must obviously be weighed against other goals achievable only by limits on autonomy. Privacy and confidentiality may be "traded" for truly collective goods—such as, in the present context, use of individual data for healthcare research, or to protect unknowable others by mandating reporting of certain diseases in the context of public health measures. Trade-offs may also be presented to each individual—for example, the ability to secure appropriate medical treatment (requiring disclosure of symptoms and behavior), or obtain reimbursement from third-party payers for that treatment, may require disclosures that a person would otherwise prefer not to occur.

Data security versus privacy issues. Security refers to the range of technical and procedural mechanisms that aim to preserve confidentiality, restricting information access to authorized "knowers" for authorized purposes. Security modalities also have the goal of assuring the accuracy and timely accessibility of data for the legitimate user set, as well as promoting failure resistance in the electronic systems overall. This set of goals is sometimes referenced by the abbreviation "CIA"—short for confidentiality, integrity, and availability.

As in physical contexts, increased information security raises costs. The explicit expense comes in outlays for additional computer and telecommunications hardware, associated software and personnel, etc. The implicit cost stems from the time and inconvenience to legitimate users as they navigate across protective barriers (such as logging in and presenting passwords), and endure the strictures of security-enhancing administrative procedures.

The balance is in part an engineering question of costs and system capabilities given available technologies, a trade-off that is ever-shifting. It is also, fundamentally, a political question: How much privacy and confidentiality does a society want? What will it "trade" for it? Certainly, life in small town America offered less privacy in the sense of anonymity than does contemporary urban life (Regan, 1995). But in many other ways, new data technologies leave us potentially exposed to the world in unprecedented ways, with a limited vocabulary to articulate the trade-offs (see, e.g., Holtzman, 2006).

Other "data" terms. Terms such as privacy, confidentiality, and security often bring more confusion than clarity, given the range of meanings in play. Helpfully or not, the label *data protection* has been coined to encompass the range of legal, regulatory, and institutional mechanisms to structure collection, use, and disclosure of information. Up to now, it has been much more commonly used in international information policy than in the U.S. (Bainbridge, 2005; Room, 2007).

It is common to refer to the object or referent of personal data in an information system as the *data subject*. In turn, the *data controller* is the natural or legal person (department or other administrative unit of a private organization, public authority, or public agency) that determines the purposes and means of processing the data within an information system (ISO, 2005). It is also common to use the term *data owner* as a synonym for data controller. Since ownership can imply a property right, one also sees the terms *data steward* and *data custodian*. For some, these better state a relationship where the data ultimately belongs to the data subject, but has been loaned to a system for specific purposes. Whether such terminological niceties actually result in better data protection is not clear.

Institutional versus extrainstitutional records. Traditionally, "records" refer to official documents, "committed to writing as authentic evidence of a matter... evidence which is thus preserved, and may be appealed to in case of dispute" (*Oxford English Dictionary*, 1989). For most of the history of healthcare record-keeping, a person's health record has been entrusted to care providers or the institutions of which they are a part. Almost all of the legal-regulatory protections for health information assume such a structure, and accordingly place requirements on healthcare providers and institutions (e.g., "covered entities" in HIPAA terminology). Recent developments in personal health records (PHRs) challenge this traditional arrangement.

PHRs are now sponsored by a broad range of institutions, from healthcare providers to insurance companies to substantial players previously operating outside the health sector, such as Google and Microsoft. Individuals have long kept personal medical histories on pieces of paper, filed away for future reference. Lists of medications, allergies, and major medical events are typical content. Putting the same information on an unstructured electronic file would change only the storage medium. However, today's PHRs are designed as structured electronic repositories by which individuals can capture and use their own health data. Behind that functionality stands the organization providing hardware, software, and expertise to support the PHR.

PHRs are thus a "personal" record in the sense of containing data related to the individual person (indeed, some of it may be from the person), and perhaps also in the customized presentation of that information. But the sponsorship of large organizations to enable personal record-keeping makes the PHR a curious hybrid. Legislative and regulatory attention to the data protection issues for PHRs has barely begun. At least for now, the data on PHRs is beyond the reach of any research effort, but someday that may change.

Information fairness. Particulars of terminology aside, in formulations around the world there is agreement on the broad principles of what can be called *information fairness*. In the U.S., the provisions of the federal Privacy Act of 1974 were built on a set of five "fair information practices," first published in a Department of Health, Education, and Welfare report (Advisory Committee on Automated Personal Data Systems, 1973). They are as follows:

1. There must be no personal data record-keeping systems whose existence is a secret.
2. There must be a way for individuals to find out what information about them is collected, and how it is used.
3. There must be a way for individuals to prevent information obtained for one purpose from being used for other purposes without consent.
4. There must be a way for individuals to correct or amend identifiable information about themselves.
5. Organizations creating, maintaining, using, or disseminating identifiable personal information must assure the reliability of the data for its intended use, and must take reasonable precautions to prevent misuse.

Similar enumerations can be found in declarations made in the 1970s in Britain, Canada, France, Germany, and Sweden, and in reports by the Council of Europe and the Organization for Economic Cooperation and Development (Flaherty, 1989; Bennett, 1992).

Following Bennett (1992), the various international renderings can be condensed into a generic four:

1. Openness (i.e., antisecrecy)
2. Access and correction (to/of information about oneself)
3. Security (anti-access protections appropriate to the data in the system)
4. Minimalism (no more collection, use, or disclosure of data than necessary to achieve the system's goals)

To these, one can add an overarching fifth principle that flows from democratic values: consent. Either individual data subjects must consent to practices that apply to them, or society as a whole must consent collectively, via a democratically approved regime of data protection legislation and regulation that sets the rules that will apply to all.

Fair information details. Rendered as generalities, the principles are unexceptionable; the specifics are obviously a different matter. The principles of openness and access/correction are perhaps the least controversial, but even they are not without disagreement. Prosecrecy arguments are commonly made to promote the public goals of law enforcement and national security. Some level of secrecy is also in the interests of private institutions, for whom the corporate data store has competitive value. In healthcare, secrecy is sometimes advocated to protect vulnerable patients (such as the mentally ill), innocent third parties (who may have contributed data on a patient, or are implicated by data the patient has provided), and on behalf of providers (who may come to fear making candid comments in a health record).

Security is harder still. "Appropriate" security controls require a clear sense of potential attackers and modes of attack, and of the abilities of various technologies to resist intrusions. It also requires a consensus on the "value" of keeping the data secure. Empirical data sufficient to articulate a clear threat model are often lacking; so is agreement on the precise value of confidentiality in particular settings, such as the delivery of healthcare. Security regimes also require a clear sense of the privileges appropriately accorded to various classes of users. It is precisely the demands for data made by large numbers of individuals, in large numbers of organizations not directly involved in the provision of care, that makes healthcare data policy so difficult (National Research Council, 1997). Even inside care-providing institutions, large numbers of persons may need access to records. Appropriately balancing security provisions against easy access for appropriate uses is a constant challenge.

Minimalism is perhaps the hardest principle of the four. It requires a clear sense of appropriate goals—and the link between particular data system practices and the achievement of those goals—to judge what is truly "minimal." The information systems goals for healthcare—for administration, clinical care, research, and public health—are quite expansive and open-ended. Read broadly, they would justify systems of almost any scale and intrusiveness to achieve socially valued ends.

Variations on consent. It is the conjunction of socially valued ends set against individual risk that forms the core problem of information fairness, particularly in healthcare and particularly in the U.S. Individuals may value privacy for its own sake, being loath to have intimate details of their lives available to any and all comers. This is particularly true of the intimate details contained in a health record. More critically, in a society where personal information disclosures may have adverse consequences, such as in loss of insurance or employment, privacy has a clear instrumental value. Beyond the narrow confines of clinical care, where an EHR system may improve the quality of care a patient receives, the benefits of health information technologies are society-wide, indeed intergenerational. Although research and public health surveillance may benefit particular individuals in the long run, the link is tenuous, and not nearly as compelling in a data subject's decision calculus as the individual risks. Given the structure of risks and rewards, attempting to "opt out"—and "free ride" on the data contributions of others—may be the only rational choice to make. Institutions must be set up to counter free-rider behavior, injecting coercion by design into a system ostensibly built on consent.

Modern western biomedical ethics is grounded on autonomy, and of consequence elevates a model of individual consent. It is the standard for the clinical setting, where a competent adult is presumed to direct the course of his or her care. It is the standard for research, with informed consent to experimental participation expected for all but situations involving minimal risk to the subject (Beauchamp and Childress, 1994). Only public health, with an orientation toward the welfare of groups, consciously rejects the individualized model.

Political philosophy affords a broader range of "social consent" models. In democratic models, a majority may consent for all. Depending on the issue, assent by a plurality (less than half) may be sufficient, or a "supermajority" (more than half) may be required, as for constitutional questions in the U.S. system. Although accidents of history may explain much of how issues are categorized and decided, the general democratic principle is that the more important, onerous, or burdensome a choice is for individuals, the more compelling it is to seek individual consent if it is practical to do so. Since data protection issues are relatively new ones, there is little social-historical guidance on how to categorize them to decide on an appropriate model of consent, and there is little empirical data to suggest the risks and benefits actually visited upon individuals, to know the degree of "burden" implied by such choices.

5.3.2 Normative, Legal, and Regulatory Protections

Professional norms and codes. Healthcare providers' "information obligations" are routinely traced back to the Hippocratic oath, constructed sometime between the sixth century BCE and the first century CE. It enjoins that what is seen or heard in the course of treatment be kept to oneself and not "spread abroad." Ethical codes of the nineteenth century such as Thomas Percival's continue the Hippocratic tradition, promulgating a physician's obligation of "secrecy and delicacy" regarding information obtained in the "familiar and confidential intercourse" of a professional visit (Etziony, 1973). The American Medical Association Code of Medical Ethics has required that patient disclosures be safeguarded "to the greatest possible degree"; confidential communications or information are not to be revealed "without the express written consent of the patient" unless required by law (American Medical Association, 2009). The American Hospital Association Patient Bill of Rights states that patients may expect "all communications and records" to be treated as confidential by the hospital "and any other parties entitled to review" such information (American Hospital Association, 1992).

Strictly speaking, the Hippocratic oath and its progeny apply only to physicians. Most of the other healthcare professions, however, such as nursing, have analogous professional norms and codes (see Etziony, 1973). Regardless of the specific formulation, in a world where medical information exchange is common, and providers have little control over downstream data uses, the difficulty lies in sorting out confidentiality rules in actual practice. Some areas of legally mandated disclosure are clear, particularly those related to public health and safety (e.g., communicable diseases, gunshot, and knife wounds). Ethical practices are less well defined for the vast array of disclosures to secondary users—such as managed care evaluators, insurance companies, and professional review bodies—who, by constraints of law, custom, or contractual arrangement, are "entitled to review." The uncertainties extend to the realm of research, where the complexities of the data protection requirements imposed on individual investigators under laws such as HIPAA (discussed below) are in no small part complex because of an attempt to balance competing dictates of ethics.

Given the individual practitioner's difficulties in controlling information practices, professional norms targeted at an institutional level have come to be ever more important. For example, the Joint Commission on the Accreditation of Healthcare Organizations has added an "Information Management" component to its certification processes (Joint Commission, 2005). The National Committee on Quality Assurance standards include evaluation of medical record documentation (NCQA, 2008). Whether such private standards are a credible substitute for government oversight remains to be seen.

State law and policy. Before the advent of HIPAA, the principal governmental protections for health data in the U.S. were at the state level. Unfortunately, these presented a variable and inconsistent patchwork, characterized by one federal study as "a morass of erratic law, both statutory and judicial" (Workgroup for Electronic Data Interchange, 1992). Although almost every state made some statutory provision for healthcare privacy, these protections were spread across medical and other professional practice acts, in hospital and other institutional licensure laws, and only rarely in comprehensive medical information statutes (Gostin et al., 1993). Coverage and sanctions varied widely across states. Statutory dictates, not uncommonly, conflicted even within the same state (Goldman, 1995). For example, a state's statutes might specify different levels of obligation and protection for data held by different classes of health provider, vary according to the institution or setting of treatment, and haphazardly mix disease- and condition-specific protections with mandatory reporting requirements.

Most states had long recognized a common law duty of confidentiality applying to health professionals. In some cases, this duty had been interpreted as extending to a direct nondisclosure requirement on the provider, and also as requiring institutional policies and procedures to prevent unauthorized disclosures by others (Gostin et al., 1993). Some state courts had been willing to enforce professional standards of confidentiality, such as those in the American Medical Association ethical code, as part of the contractual relationship between physicians and patients (Office of Technology Assessment, 1993). But even in the rare instances where duties of one class of provider were clearly established, and extended consistently to other types of health professional, important gaps could remain. Obligations of nonpractitioners—such as researchers, insurance and other payers' employees, and provider institutions' own administrative staff—were often considerably more vague, if addressed directly at all. In particular, the minimal regulation of the information practices of insurers was inadequate to the evolving information strategies of managed care.

In this pre-HIPAA world, only about two thirds of U.S. states allowed patients access to their medical records, with varying provisions for what could be withheld. Many of those laws did not specify the ability to copy one's records or procedures to submit amendments or corrections (Bennett, 1995). Although they provided inadequate confidentiality and security specifications, many state laws also created obstacles to legitimate sharing of health information. For example, some limited the use of computerized record systems by requiring that orders be written in ink (referred to as "quill pen" laws), or restricted the permissible "official" health records storage media to paper or microform (Roberts, 1995). The protections and status afforded to electronic records in such jurisdictions were very uncertain, given that EHRs were relatively new and poorly understood by the officials responsible for regulating them. Such state legal deficiencies were widely perceived by proponents of EHRs as slowing the development of both healthcare information systems and the networks necessary to link them. Conflicting state laws were particularly problematic where large populations received care in states different from the ones in which they worked or resided (see, e.g., CDC, 1996).

Federal law and policy, pre-HIPAA. Until the advent of HIPAA, health privacy protections at the federal level were very limited in their reach. The landmark Privacy Act of 1974 protected individuals against disclosure of information held by federal agencies in any "system of records," including limits on data collection to objects "relevant and necessary" to the agency mission(s). Under the Act, release of personally identifiable data required consent, unless the disclosure was "compatible" with the purposes for which it was collected or served a public policy need for which statutory authority existed. Over the years since the measure's enactment, the notions of compatibility and public policy need had been expanded to justify a very broad range of uses and transfers of information, particularly in areas such as law enforcement (Schwartz, 1995a). Under the Privacy Act, agencies must permit individuals to determine what records are kept on them, and must provide a procedure whereby inaccurate information can be corrected or amended. However, individuals are in general poorly positioned to police the myriad government information practices affecting them, and this was particularly true of availing themselves of Privacy Act protections (Flaherty, 1989).

In the 1988 Computer Matching and Privacy Protection Act, which amended the 1974 Act, Congress addressed federal agency data sharing for purposes of comparing and linking records. The amendment required agencies to formulate procedural agreements to control information exchange. It also mandated establishment of new bodies, Data Integrity Boards, to oversee information practices. However, weak supervision by Data Integrity Boards and agency use of "routine practice" exemptions limited the amendment's effects (Schwartz, 1995a).

In general, the protective regime was a patchwork. Other federal legislation was extended to narrow categories of data in the private sector—such as education and credit records. There was, however, no extension to private organizations' collections of health records, leaving whatever protections existed in state law as the primary constraints.

Hospitals operated by the federal government were subject to the Privacy Act, as were a small number of private healthcare and research facilities maintaining medical records under federal contracts (Office of Technology Assessment, 1993). Federal statutes and regulations also prescribed confidentiality rules for patient records at federally funded drug and alcohol treatment facilities, providing a greater degree of protection than the 1974 Privacy Act's general coverage. Section 1106 of the Social Security Act, covering records held by the U.S. Department of Health and Human Services, provided additional protection for information derived from Medicare and Medicaid participation. But no federal statute before HIPAA defined an individual's rights regarding personally identifiable health information held by state and local governments (although there are some restrictions on the use of social security numbers). Private sector healthcare entities not under federal contract were also largely beyond the reach of these federal laws. It is against this backdrop that the protections of HIPAA, discussed in the next section, must be compared.

International codes. Before moving on to HIPAA, it is worthwhile to consider the influence of international data protection efforts. International convention has not commonly proved a strong constraint on national conduct, and data protection so far provides no exception to the rule. However, several international conventions are of interest, if only for indications of the promise and limits of such approaches.

Most industrialized nations around the world have or are moving toward comprehensive data protection legislation that reaches to both the public and private sectors. There are several important transnational agreements of historical interest in this regard. The Council of Europe "Convention for the Protection of Individuals with Regard to Automatic Processing of Personal Data" (Council of Europe, 1981) and the Organization for Economic Cooperation and Development (OECD, 1980) "Guidelines Governing the Protection of Privacy and Transborder Flows of Personal Data" both emerged in the late 1970s. As they were developed in concert, there are strong similarities, although the former is, by virtue of the membership body, "Euro-centric," and, as its title implies, applies only to automated data. The European Union adopted its "Directive on the Protection of Individuals With Regard to the Processing of Personal Data" (European Union, 1995), intended to harmonize existing European data laws and provide a common level of protection while removing obstacles to intermember data flows (Schwartz, 1995b).

Both the Council of Europe Convention and the OECD Guidelines are based on the general principles of "fair information practices" discussed earlier. Both operate at a fairly high level of generality, and neither provides specific details on application of standards or provisions for enforcement. The Council of Europe Convention is binding on its signatories, who are required to establish compliant data protection legislation, including appropriate procedural remedies and sanctions for violations. The OECD Guidelines are, as its name implies, voluntary. The U.S. is a member of the OECD, and since the Reagan administration voluntary adoption of it by American corporations has been encouraged from time to time. However, despite endorsement by hundreds of U.S. multinationals and trade associations, there is little evidence that U.S. information practices have changed as a result of conventions such as these. It has taken the sanctions of U.S. law to motivate change (Gellman, 1996).

Privacy laws continue to evolve around the world, although whether they lag ever farther behind technological developments is in the eye of the beholder (Agre and Rotenberg, 1997). The range of approaches defies summary here, but offer instructive alternatives for jurisdictions contemplating their own approaches. (For a summary of privacy laws around the world, see Electronic Privacy Information Center and Privacy International, 2006.)

5.4 The Federal Health Privacy Law: HIPAA

The Health Insurance Portability and Accountability Act of 1996 is the federal law that establishes standards for the privacy and security of health information, as well as standards for electronic data interchange of health information. Despite what many believe, the "P" in HIPAA has never stood for privacy, although many now see privacy as this legislation's main legacy. Its two main goals at the time of drafting, as its name implies, are

1. Make health insurance more portable when persons change employers
2. Make the healthcare system more accountable for costs—trying especially to reduce waste and fraud

It was understood by the law's supporters that cost accountability would require greater use of computerized information systems—still something of a rarity in the 1990s in the U.S.—and that, in turn, would raise the stakes for information privacy and security. Thus, came the privacy and security provisions of HIPAA, essentially as an afterthought. HIPAA's protections now supplement those of the states, as well as those imposed by private certification organizations such as Joint Commission on Accreditation of Healthcare Organizations, which have been discussed in earlier sections. HIPAA's regulations add a floor (minimum level) of safeguards to these other requirements. But state or private health privacy protections that are more stringent than HIPAA's generally remain in effect.

Regulations constructed under the authority of HIPAA provide a set of national "information rights" to all patients: access, amendment, disclosure accounting, restriction requests, confidential communications, and access to local and federal "complaint" resources, all of which are discussed in detail later. HIPAA also requires a Notice about those rights, which is why the law is more familiar (at least as far as its abbreviation) than most federal laws. HIPAA imposes a parallel set of "information duties" on entities covered by it, and on the persons who work in/for them. Everyone who handles health information is obligated to understand the specific rules that apply to their setting, and follow them in daily practice.

5.4.1 HIPAA in General

HIPAA has four parts—called "Rules" in regulatory parlance—that set standards for health information. Two of the four rules focus on technical specifications: the *Transactions and Code Sets Rule* mandates standard formats and coding for health data; the *Identifier Rule* sets standards for unique identifiers for health plans, employers, health practitioners, and patients. We will not cover the Transactions and Code Sets and Identifier rules here, but instead concentrate on the other two rules—the *Privacy Rule* and the *Security Rule*—which focus on just what their names suggest. (HIPAA regulations for the four Rules are codified in the Code of Federal Regulations, Title 45.)

Who and what is covered by HIPAA? Almost every U.S. organization that provides or pays for health services, or exchanges health data of any type, is within the reach of HIPAA. Healthcare providers (physicians, nurses, allied health practitioners); healthcare facilities (hospitals, clinics); health plans (health maintenance organizations, insurers); and health information clearinghouses are what HIPAA calls *covered entities*. HIPAA extends rights to every patient whose information is collected, used, or disclosed by such covered entities. It imposes duties on covered entities—and, by extension, on persons who work in or for covered entities—in order to secure those rights. HIPAA also reaches to the *business associates* of health institutions—that is, to companies that handle health data on a covered entity's behalf.

Under HIPAA, any information that is, or reasonably could be, linked to an individual is protected health information (PHI). HIPAA defines PHI very broadly: It is anything related to the "past, present or future physical or mental health condition" of a person. Only fully deidentified health information is excluded—where every explicit identifier of a person has been removed, as well as data that could potentially establish a link via statistical techniques. (For a discussion of de-identification, see Chapter 8.) HIPAA's Privacy Rule provisions apply to PHI held by covered entities in "any form or medium." That means *everything* containing PHI: paper records as well as electronic ones, faxes, emails, exchanges in telephone conversations, and even just talking face to face. (As discussed above, the relatively new repository options afforded by PHR providers are not yet clearly addressed by HIPAA or any other law.)

Persons versed in the nuances of HIPAA know that although its Privacy Rule applies to information in any form or medium, the Security Rule applies only to electronic form information. The latter rule requires conventional information security measures ranging from passwords to audit trails, itemized in Rule sections devoted to physical, technical, and administrative security. This coverage distinction between the two rules grows ever less important in a world where every important piece of information spends most of its life in electronic form. Moreover, it is well understood that information privacy exists only on a foundation of good information security, so covered entities are not free to neglect safeguards for any nonelectronic information collections they may have. As discussed in the sections on research information below, an investigator must be mindful of the security measures required by the Security Rule as well as the use and disclosure constraints imposed by the Privacy Rule.

Notification and acknowledgment. HIPAA's most visible change comes from its requirement that patients be given a *Notice of Privacy Practices*. This notice must describe, in general terms, how the covered entity will protect health information, and it must clearly specify the patient's rights under the law—both federal HIPAA rights and any stricter state protections in that jurisdiction. A copy of the Notice must be provided the first time a patient sees a direct treatment provider—that is, any provider that directly interacts with the patient—and any time thereafter when requested by the patient or when the Notice materially changes. Health plans and insurers must also provide periodic Notices to their customers.

Direct treatment providers must make a good faith effort to obtain an *acknowledgment*—by the patient's signature—confirming that a copy of the Privacy Notice was received. The signature does not affirm that the patient understands what is in the Notice, or even that he/she has read it, just receipt of it. (In emergency situations, getting an acknowledgment can be deferred.) In addition to affirming that a patient has been made aware of his or her rights, this step was designed to provide an opportunity for discussion of patients' privacy questions and concerns. Covered entities are obligated to have an adequate number of persons at their facilities who are knowledge-able enough to provide answers. However, in practice it is not clear that the communication envisaged by the regulatory writers occurs very often. Often the HIPAA Notice is just another in a stack of papers presented to patients on a first clinical encounter. (In a research setting, as discussed below, the dynamics are usually different.)

General HIPAA rights. Patients have a set of specific rights with respect to their health records, which are listed below. Beyond those, patients have a general right to appropriate privacy and security practices by any covered entity that uses or stores health information about them. If patients believe that their pri-vacy rights have been violated, they may file a complaint with the facility's *pri-vacy official*—a new position that HIPAA requires. (Every covered entity, even the smallest clinic, must have someone designated to fill this role.) If unsatis-fied with a local response, patients can also take their complaints to the federal agency charged with administering HIPAA: the U.S. Department of Health and Human Services' Office of Civil Rights (DHHS OCR). Usually, there is also a state-level agency to which privacy complaints may be directed.

HIPAA's specific protections with respect to patients' health records include

- A right to gain access to and obtain a copy of all one's health records (with some exceptions, such as psychotherapy notes)
- A right to request corrections of errors found in those records—or, alternatively, to include a statement of disagreement if the institu-tion believes the information is correct (sometimes called the "right of amendment")
- A right to receive an accounting of how one's health information has been used—that is, a list of the persons and institutions to whom/ which it has been disclosed
- A right to request restrictions on access to, and additional protec-tions for, particularly sensitive information

- A right to request confidential communications (by alternative means or at alternative locations) of particularly sensitive information
- A right to prevent certain "additional" types of use and disclosure—such as fundraising, marketing, and research—unless specific *authorization* is granted

A right to access and copy one's records had existed in most states, but not all. However, even where it existed it was often neither well understood by patients nor particularly easy to exercise in practice. HIPAA sets limits on the amount of time a covered entity may take to respond to such requests, so this is not a right to instant access.

The right to an accounting of disclosures is considerably less expansive than it might first appear. Disclosures for the very broad categories of *treatment*, *payment*, and *healthcare operations* do not need to be part of the accounting. Neither do disclosures that the patient has specifically *authorized*. (More about each of these terms is provided below.) It should be noted that many states have also mandated some form of disclosure accounting, and many of those do not provide the same broad exceptions as HIPAA. As with the other records rights, it is important to learn the rules that apply to the jurisdiction in which your organization operates if you have any responsibilities for preparing a disclosure accounting.

Covered entities are not required to honor requests for additional restrictions/protections on sensitive information—although they must abide by any extra provisions to which they agree. (What is sensitive? Whatever the individual patient considers so.) By contrast, covered entities are bound to honor "reasonable requests" for confidential communications.

Finally, note that not all fundraising, marketing, and research requires authorization—but much of it does. (We discuss the details of authorizations for research below.)

HIPAA's information categories. It may help to clarify HIPAA's protections if you also understand that it divides up health information uses and disclosures into three major categories:

1. Those that can occur without any specific permission from the patient
2. Those that are allowed (or prohibited) simply on the basis of an oral assent (or refusal)
3. Those that require specific, written permission

The first category is the largest one. HIPAA requires no permission from the patient to use or disclose information for "basic" functions, including treatment, payment, and a broad range of other core healthcare operations. Neither does HIPAA require specific permission for a broad range of activities required by law, including (but not limited to) public health and health system oversight activities; reporting about victims of abuse, neglect, or domestic violence; judicial and administrative proceedings; certain "specialized government functions" such as national security, military, and veterans activities; corrections and law enforcement; or to avert a serious, imminent threat to public safety. Be aware, however, that many states' laws do require explicit consent from the patient for some of these types of use or disclosure. (As noted, such "more restrictive" state laws remain in force. Where required by state law, the consent for information use or disclosure is often paired with the consent to be treated, and will include such details.)

Even if you are not a health data expert, you probably would have recognized that the vast majority of uses and disclosures fall into the first category. The second category is a much smaller one: Inclusion or exclusion from facility directories, and uses and disclosures to friends and family members involved in a person's care, can be permitted or limited based on oral agreement. Many organizations will still choose to get the patient to sign something about this. But HIPAA requires only that the patient be asked orally.

Finally, in the third category, HIPAA does require that patients sign a specific authorization before information can be used or disclosed for some types of research, marketing, and fundraising. Healthcare institutions cannot condition treatment or payment for healthcare services on receiving a patient's authorization for things in this third category.

Information decision makers and information types. For those circumstances where the patient does retain control, HIPAA's general rule is a simple one: If a person has a right to make a healthcare decision, then he/she has a right to control information associated with that decision. Minor children and those who are not competent may have their health information decisions made by a *personal representative.* Typically, that will be a parent in the case of a child. (But be advised that states' rules for minors can be particularly complex. Consult with a local expert if you have questions about a minor's health information rights.)

As you have just read, however, patients remain in control of relatively few information uses and disclosures once they have entered the healthcare system. What about all the areas where no consent or authorization from the patient is required? It is the covered entity's responsibility to have policies in place that comply with HIPAA's rules. (And, of course, the covered entity must follow them.) A patient's most important protection is responsible, safe use of health information by the healthcare professionals who have access to it. That was true before HIPAA and remains so now. In the terms of the previous section, individual consent for a range of practices has been replaced by collective consent to a regulatory regime.

Although the HIPAA restrictions on health information access depend primarily on the purposes for that access, the type of information itself can also be relevant. Beyond any information for which the patient makes a special confidentiality request, HIPAA currently extends extra protection to one type of information: psychotherapy notes. Separate authorization for release is required, and patients' access to this type of information may sometimes be restricted. By contrast, states' laws commonly extend special protection to many types of information—for example, data related to mental health, acquired immunodeficiency syndrome/human immunodeficiency virus, sexually transmitted diseases, genetic tests, and substance abuse. In such cases, separate authorization is usually required. The complexities and variability of state law preclude any summary here. (Once again, you will need to consult a local expert for the details in your jurisdiction.)

Covered entities' and workers' obligations. The privacy obligations of covered entities are, unsurprisingly, a mirror of patients' rights. Privacy Notices must be created and distributed. Direct treatment providers must attempt to obtain a signed acknowledgment of receipt of the Notice. One or more privacy officials must be appointed to answer questions, handle complaints, and administer all the paperwork associated with access, correction, accounting, etc. Most critically, privacy (and security) policies that reflect federal and state laws must be put in place. The organization's workers must be trained on those policies and procedures.

If you work in a covered entity—or are, as a healthcare provider, one yourself—you have personal obligations under the law. The big three are as follows:

- Use or disclose PHI only for work-related purposes
- Limit uses and disclosures of PHI to the minimum necessary to achieve the work purposes
- Otherwise, exercise reasonable and appropriate caution to protect all the PHI under your control

Use or disclosure of health information must be reasonably related to a legitimate work task. That means, for example, that one cannot access health information to satisfy curiosity about a colleague or about that famous patient who just checked in. (This may seem obvious, but it is one of the top HIPAA complaints filed with the DHHS OCR.) HIPAA provides severe sanctions for deliberate misuse of PHI, particularly where there is any intent to harm others or achieve personal financial gain. States' statutes also commonly provide for penalties.

HIPAA's *minimum necessary* rule requires that uses and disclosures of PHI should be what is reasonably required to get the job done under the circumstances, and no more. The minimum necessary rule tolerates reasonable errors. It requires care and exercise of reasonable restraint, but not perfection. It is understood that accidents happen—or, to use HIPAA's terminology, *incidental uses and disclosures* happen. Such accidents do not constitute violations of HIPAA as long as the excessive use or disclosure was not intentional, or a result of failure to exercise reasonable caution.

HIPAA forbids *intimidation or retaliation* against both patients and workers for reporting a problem or filing a complaint. Anyone who lacks confidence in his or her organization's ability or inclination to prevent harm to can report concerns anonymously—either to the local privacy official or to the DHHS OCR.

5.4.2 HIPAA and Research

Most healthcare researchers are already familiar with meeting federal standards for the protection of human subjects. The majority of biomedical and behavioral research in the U.S. is subject to the DHHS-codified "Common Rule" (45 CFR 46) and/or the analogous regulations of the Food and Drug Administration (FDA) (21 CFR 50, 56). The Common Rule and FDA protections focus on the rights, safety, and welfare of research subjects, including such matters as informed consent and appropriateness of risks relative to benefits. They also include attention to subjects' privacy and the confidentiality of information.

Protocol reviews using Common Rule/FDA criteria by IRBs are *per se* unaffected by HIPAA. That is, HIPAA's health information–focused protections are *in addition* to these venerable requirements, not a replacement. Where state laws and regulations are also in place to protect research subjects, these too remain in effect. As discussed above, HIPAA generally defers to state protections that are more stringent with respect to privacy.

Enforcement of HIPAA's research protections. HIPAA provisions state that covered entities may create a new body, called a *Privacy Board*, to handle local enforcement of HIPAA's rules. Alternatively, a covered entity may choose to rely on an IRB to assess compliance with both the FDA/Common Rule requirements and the HIPAA research requirements. Membership requirements for a privacy board are very similar to those for IRBs—for example, diversity, outside membership, avoidance of conflicts of interest.

A covered entity may also leave some decisions about compliance with the research provisions of HIPAA to its privacy official, such as determinations about whether a particular use or disclosure application needs privacy board/IRB review. Research subjects such as patients, in general, have recourse to the DHHS OCR in the event that they are not satisfied with the local bodies' protective efforts.

HIPAA defines research as any "systematic investigation, including research development, testing, and evaluation, designed to develop and contribute to *generalizable knowledge*." Not all types of research-like activities are included in this definition, however:

- *Quality assessment and improvement* activities, including outcomes evaluation and development of clinical guidelines or protocols, fall under the category of healthcare operations—provided the primary aim is not to obtain generalizable knowledge.
- Activities that aim primarily for generalizable knowledge of population health can fall into the category of *public health* activity.

Usually, a determination by at least the organization's privacy official is required to designate an activity as "not research."

Authorization and waivers. HIPAA generally requires separate, explicit *authorization* from patients to use their PHI for research activities. By contrast, as noted above, HIPAA's "big three"—treatment, payment, and healthcare operations—require no separate authorization. Neither does public health. As with any other planned information activity, however, research must be mentioned in the entity's Privacy Notice as a possible use for information.

An authorization, however, is not always required. HIPAA provides the following pathways for research uses and disclosures of PHI, each branch of which is explained further below. Authorization is required, unless

- A *waiver* of the authorization requirement is granted by the privacy board/IRB.
- The research meets *exceptions* to the authorization requirement for
  - Activities preparatory to research
  - Use of decedents' information
  - Other disclosures required by law
- The research is conducted with *limited data set* (LDS) under a *data use agreement* (DUA).
- Only *deidentified data* are involved.

An organization's IRB or a privacy board may determine that a waiver of the authorization requirement is appropriate, if the following criteria are met. (These will be familiar to anyone versed in the Common Rule.)

- Use or disclosure of the PHI involves no more than *minimal risk* to privacy of the research subjects, based on the following elements:
  - An adequate plan to protect data identifiers from improper use and disclosure
  - An adequate plan to destroy data identifiers at the earliest opportunity consistent with conduct of the research (unless there is a health or research justification for retaining the identifiers, or such retention is otherwise required by law)
  - Adequate written assurances that the PHI will not be reused or disclosed to any other person or entity, except as required by law, for authorized oversight of the research project, or for other research for which the use or disclosure of PHI would be permitted by the HIPAA
- The research could not practicably be conducted without the PHI.
- The research could not practicably be conducted without the waiver.

More about what counts as a "data identifier" is provided in the section below on LDSs and deidentified data, and in Chapter 8.

Alternatively, criteria are provided for three types of exceptions to the authorization requirement:

- Where the PHI will not leave the covered entity, will be used solely for reviews preparatory to research (e.g., for protocol development), and the researcher represents that such access is essential
- Where the PHI refers solely to deceased persons (the covered entity may ask for documentation of death), and the researcher again asserts that such access is essential for the research
- Where a PHI disclosure is required by state or other federal laws

Covered entities may determine their own processes for approval of these "representations" by an investigator. This may involve a submission to the organization's privacy official or such requests may go to a privacy board or IRB, as with an application for a waiver. In the latter case, the evaluation process will typically be analogous to "expedited review" under the FDA/Common Rule.

Finally, there are two ways for researchers to entirely bypass these authorization issues.

First, a covered entity may disclose PHI in an LDS to a researcher who has entered into an appropriate DUA. LDSs must have all direct identifiers removed; they may still include information that could "indirectly" identify the subject using statistical methods. A DUA must delineate the permitted uses and disclosures of such information by the recipient, consistent with the purposes of research; it must limit who can use or receive the data; and finally, it must require the recipient to agree not to reidentify the data or contact the individuals.

Second, a researcher may use PHI contained in fully *deidentified information*. As the name implies, deidentified information must have all direct and indirect identifiers removed, to eliminate—or at least make highly improbable—reidentification using statistical techniques. (These issues are discussed extensively in Chapter 8.) LDSs and deidentified data use are exempt from the disclosure accounting requirements. However, they are still subject to the minimum necessary standard.

Minimum necessary. Information uses and disclosures for research that finds a way to bypass the authorization requirement are subject to the minimum necessary standard. A covered entity may rely on a researcher's documentation—or the assessment of a privacy board or IRB—that the requested information is the minimum necessary for the research purpose.

By contrast, research information obtained using an authorization is *not* bound by the minimum necessary standard—on the theory that the research subject has given explicit permission for whatever information access the research team deems to be necessary, even if it is arguably "excessive."

(We do not think this makes ethical sense, but it is the HIPAA rule. IRBs may take a stricter stance about information that seems excessive to the research purpose, unless it appears impractical to collect a lesser amount.)

Disclosure accounting. Disclosures for research operating under a waiver/exception to the authorization requirement are subject to accounting requirements. Where the study involves more than 50 records, the accounting of disclosures can be met by providing individual research subjects with

- A list of all protocols for which their PHI may have been disclosed, along with the time frame for those disclosures
- The purpose of those protocols, and the types of PHI sought
- The researcher's name and contact information for each study

Covered entities must assist subjects in contacting researchers when they have questions about a disclosure or any other aspects of the protocol.

Where fewer than 50 records are involved, the listing must be more specific and detailed, commensurate with the requirements for other types of PHI disclosure accounting. Covered entities may still choose to impose more detailed reporting requirements for research, even on larger studies. (DHHS "encourages" providing more details, but does not require it.) Disclosure accounting is *not* required for data disclosures made under the authority of an authorization by the subject himself/herself, or, as noted, for disclosures that are part of an LDS or deidentified data. As with the waiver of the minimum necessary standard, the rationale for the first of these is that the research subject has given specific permission for the use of his/her data in a study, and thus needs no notification of that activity; for the latter, the reasoning is that the quasi-identification or full de-identification is protection enough.

Characteristics of authorizations. When they are required, HIPAA research authorizations must be executed in writing and signed by the research subject. The authorization must be "in plain language so that individuals can understand the information contained in the form, and thus be able to make an informed decision." HIPAA authorizations are normally required to have an explicit expiration date. In the context of research, however, it is sufficient to specify an expiration event—such as "the end of the study" or a research authorization can have no expiration date at all, although this absence must be clearly indicated to the data subject.

As with FDA/Common Rule requirements for informed consent, there are many format and content specifications for an HIPAA research authorization. (We cover only the highlights here. See Privacy/Data Protection Project, 2005, for detail.) Researchers probably should rely on standard models rather than create their own authorizations or other documents—particularly if their organization's IRB or privacy board has already designated a standard.

Normally, HIPAA authorizations cannot be combined with other types of documents (such as a Privacy Notice). However, research authorizations can be combined with any other legal permission related to the study, including another authorization or a Common Rule/FDA informed consent. If there are multiple documents associated with a research protocol that limit information use or disclosure, the most restrictive one applies.

DHHS has noted that it may be advisable—although not required—to include the following in the research authorization:

- How PHI obtained for a research study may be used and disclosed for treatment, payment, and healthcare operations. (Note that research-related treatment can be conditioned on provision of a research authorization. However, treatment unrelated to the research cannot.)

- Information about sources of funding for the study and payment arrangements for investigators. Consistent with general recommendations about informed consent, the view is that any information that might be "material to the potential subject's decision-making" should be included.

Like other types of HIPAA authorizations, those for research may be revoked by the subject at any time, provided that the revocation is done in writing. Revocation of an authorization is not valid to the extent that the covered entity has taken actions relying on it, such as in the provision of prior treatment, and such revocations may be limited "as necessary to maintain the integrity of the research study." The latter qualification would, for example, permit the continued use and disclosure of already-gathered PHI (e.g., for subsequent statistical analyses and reporting). It would not allow new data to be collected or used.

Recruiting and retrospective analyses. It is still permissible under HIPAA to discuss recruitment into research with patients for whom such involvement might be appropriate. This common practice is considered to fall within the definition of treatment. Typically, such a conversation would be undertaken by one of the patient's regular healthcare providers. By contrast, a patient's information cannot be disclosed to a third party (even another care provider) for purposes of recruitment into a research study without an authorization from the individual or an approved waiver/exception of authorization.

Because of conflict of interest issues, organizations may choose to place limits on recruitment where a regular treatment provider is also an investigator for the protocol into which the patient is being recruited. HIPAA, however, does not cover this circumstance.

Recruiting looks toward future research participation and data generation. It has also been a common practice to "browse"—or "data mine"—collections of health data from past encounters, looking for interesting patterns that could translate into research possibilities. DHHS has reiterated in its

HIPAA commentary that use or disclosure of PHI for retrospective research studies may be done only with patient authorization or a waiver/exception from an IRB or privacy board. It should not be difficult to meet one of the waiver/exception criteria for most efforts of this type (e.g., in-house examinations may be qualified as "preparatory to research"). This, however, is considered research—even if one is "just looking around" in a casual manner. Researchers can no longer proceed on their own without any permission.

What does HIPAA really add? Although the specifics are lengthy, the net administrative burden that HIPAA adds to existing Common Rule/FDA regulations is generally not a large one. Compared to protocol approval generally—and the details of informed consent particularly—an HIPAA authorization is a relatively easy addition. To approve a study under the Common Rule/FDA requirements, IRBs must already determine that there are adequate provisions to protect the privacy of subjects and to maintain the confidentiality of data. Where researchers are meeting those requirements, HIPAA changes very little. But it undoubtedly does add more "paperwork."

Security also matters. Efforts to meet the Common Rule, FDA, and HIPAA regulations' privacy requirements do not complete an investigator's data protection tasks. Research data collections must receive appropriate security protections for as long as they exist, to meet the requirements of HIPAA's Security Rule. Clinical data typically enjoy the security of an organized medical records system with institutionally funded safeguards. Research data are more often stored in hodgepodges of computer- and paper-based records maintained by the investigator with limited attention to security. HIPAA's rule, simply put, is: Whatever you collect, you must protect. Research activities are not subject to a lesser standard for data protection than clinical data under the HIPAA regulations.

5.5 Chapter Summary

Gostin (1994) notes that, given the magnitude of the social benefits, "[i]t is not surprising...to find that many advocates of a health information infrastructure simply assume that collection of ever-increasing health information, in ever more efficient ways, is inherently a social good." About 15 years later, the claims for the potential of networked electronic health data systems are still touted—and the gap between aspirations and reality still lamented, albeit with considerable uncertainties about how far behind the U.S. lags (Jha et al., 2006). But few doubt that increasing use of EHRs will improve quality in the long run.

Given the magnitude of the personal costs that can attach to information abuses, and the strong value that U.S. citizens place on privacy, it is also not surprising to find many privacy advocates who are deeply skeptical of healthcare's information aspirations. Yet, progress in medicine, for both personal and public health, has always depended critically on information from and about individuals. It is safe to assume that it will continue to be essential to the evaluation of new technologies and treatments, and to identify and respond to new health threats. Decisions about information policy are thus critical ones, both for the health of the U.S. population and that of populations around the world who leverage the contributions of U.S. biomedical research.

Almost all the various interests agree that federal legislation has been needed, to bring uniformity of protections and standardize practices, lest we build a health information infrastructure that is neither fair in its impact nor efficient in its functioning. However, differences remain about what should be the details of the evolving laws and associated regulations that balance individual privacy and social goals. It is in the nature of crafting policy in a Madisonian system such as that of the U.S. that a proposal capable of satisfying the majority must often contain elements unsatisfactory to each of the competing interests. For health information policy, legislative success requires a willingness to compromise on the details of preemption, the precise structure of consent, the procedural hurdles that attach to information access of various types, and a hundred other lesser elements that condition the day-to-day flows of information within the healthcare system.

It is worthwhile to remember that despite all the legislative accomplishments, substantial numbers of Americans still have serious reservations about the confidentiality and security of their health information, to the point where one in six reports withholding information from their health providers due to such worries (Harris Interactive, 2007). These fears mirror those heard during testimony on the implementation of HIPAA more than a decade ago (National Committee on Vital and Health Statistics, 1997). Inattention to the ethical and social issues associated with healthcare information will only perpetuate those fears, and undermine the flow of information on which all of us depend.

Acknowledgments

The author is indebted to many colleagues with whom he has collaborated on privacy-related research, including Patricia Abril, Anita Cava, Don Detmer, Michael Froomkin, Kenneth Goodman, and Jeroen van den Hoven. Some materials in this chapter were initially developed during projects supported by the Collaborative Institutional Training Initiative, the University of Miami Ethics Programs, the University of Miami Health System and School of Medicine, the Robert Wood Johnson Foundation, and the Milbank Memorial Fund.

References

Advisory Committee on Automated Personal Data Systems. 1973. *Records, Computers, and the Rights of Citizens*. Washington, DC: US Government Printing Office.

Agre, P. E., and Rotenberg, M. 1997. *Technology and Privacy: The New Landscape*. Cambridge: MIT Press.

American Hospital Association. 1992. *A Patient's Bill of Rights*. Chicago IL: American Hospital Association.

American Medical Association. 2009. *Code of Medical Ethics: Current Opinions with Annotations, 2008–2009*. Chicago IL: American Medical Association.

Anderson, J. G., and Goodman, K. W. 2002. *Ethics and Information Technology*. New York: Springer-Verlag.

Anderson, R. 2001. *Security Engineering: A Guide to Building Dependable Distributed Systems*. Indianapolis, IN: John Wiley and Sons, Inc.

Bainbridge, D. 2005. *Data Protection Law*. St. Albans, UK: XPL Publishing.

Barrows, R., and Clayton, P. 1996. Privacy, confidentiality and electronic medical records. *Journal of the American Medical Informatics Association* 3:139–148.

Beauchamp, T. L., and Childress, J. F. 1994. *Principles of Biomedical Ethics*, 4th edn. New York NY: Oxford University Press.

Bennett, B. 1995. *Medical Records: Sweeping Reforms to Ensure Privacy of Personal Medical Records*. Washington, DC: Federal Document Clearinghouse Press, Release, 24 October.

Bennett, C. J. 1992. *Regulating Privacy: Data Protection and Public Policy in Europe and the United States*. Ithaca NY: Cornell University Press.

Bennett, C. J. 2008. *The Privacy Advocates: Resisting the Spread of Surveillance*. Cambridge: Massachusetts Institute of Technology Press.

Bishop, M. 2003. *Computer Security: Art and Science*. London, UK: Pearson Education, Inc.

Centers for Disease Control and Prevention. 1996. Legislative Survey of State Confidentiality Laws, with Specific Emphasis on HIV and Immunization.

Code of Federal Regulations, Current Titles. U.S. Government Printing Office. http://www.gpoaccess.gov/cfr/.

Committee on the Role of Institutional Review Boards in Health Services Research Data Privacy Protection. 2000. *Protecting Data Privacy in Health Services Research*. Institute of Medicine. Washington, DC: National Academy Press.

Council of Europe. 1981. Convention for the Protection of Individuals with regard to Automatic Processing of Personal Data.

Department of Health and Human Services. 1993. *Health Records: Social Needs and Personal Privacy*. Washington, DC: US Government Printing Office.

Dick, R. S., Steen, E. B., and Detmer, D. E. (eds.) 1991. *The Computer-Based Patient Record: An Essential Technology for Health Care*. Institute of Medicine. Washington, DC: National Academy Press.

Donaldson, M. S., and Lohr, K. (eds). 1994. *Health Data in the Information Age: Use, Disclosure and Privacy*. Institute of Medicine. Washington, DC: National Academy Press.

Electronic Privacy Information Center and Privacy International. 2006. *Privacy and Human Rights 2006: An International Survey of Privacy Laws and Developments*. Washington, DC: EPIC.

Etzioni, A. 2000. *The Limits of Privacy*. New York, NY: Basic Books.

Etziony, M. B. 1973. *The Physician's Creed: An Anthology of Medical Prayers, Oaths and Codes of Ethics Written and Recited by Medical Practitioners through the Ages*. Springfield, IL: Charles C. Thomas.

European Union. 1995. Directive 95/46/EC on the Protection of Individuals With Regard to the Processing of Personal Data.

Fairchild, A. L., Bayer, R., and Colgrove, J. 2007. *Privacy, the State and Disease Surveillance in America*. Berkeley, CA: Milbank Foundation.

Flaherty, D. H. 1989. *Protecting Privacy in Surveillance Societies: The Federal Republic of Germany, Sweden, France, Canada, and the United States*. Chapel Hill, NC: University of North Carolina Press.

Gavison, R. 1984. Privacy and the limits of law. In Schoeman, F. (ed), *Philosophical Dimensions of Privacy: An Anthology*. Cambridge UK: Cambridge University Press.

Gellman, R. M. 1996. Can privacy be regulated effectively on a national level? Thoughts on the possible need for international privacy rules. *Villanova Law Review* 41(1):129–165.

Goldman, J. 1995. Statement before the Senate Committee on Labor and Human Resources on S.1360. Federal Document Clearinghouse Congressional Testimony, 14 November.

Gollmann, D. 1999. Computer Security. New York, NY: John Wiley and Sons, Inc.

Goodman, K. W. 1998. *Ethics, Computing and Medicine*. Cambridge UK: Cambridge University Press.

Gostin, L. O. et al. 1993. Privacy and security of personal information in a new health care system. *Journal of the American Medical Association* 270:2487–2493.

Gostin, L. O. 1994. Health information privacy. *Cornell Law Review* 80:101–132.

Harris Interactive. 2007. Harris Poll #127—Health Information Privacy Survey, http://www.harrisinteractive.com.

Holtzman, D. H. 2006. *Privacy Lost: How Technology Is Endangering Your Privacy*. San Francisco, CA: Jossey-Bass.

Humbler, J. M., and Almeder, R. F. (eds.) 2001. *Privacy and Health Care (Biomedical Ethics Reviews)*. Totowa, NJ: Humana Press.

International Organization for Standardization (ISO). 2005. *Information Technology—Security Techniques—Code of Practice for Information Security Management*. Geneva: ISO Publications.

Jha, As. K., Ferris, T. G., Donelan, K. et al. 2006. How common are electronic health records in the United States? A summary of the evidence. *Health Affairs* 25(6):496–507.

Joint Commission. 2005. *Comprehensive Accreditation Manual for Hospitals*. Oakbrook Terrace, IL: Joint Commission on Accreditation of Healthcare Organizations.

Nass, S. J., Levit, L. A., and Gostin, L. G. (eds.) 2009. *Committee on Health Research and the Privacy of Health Information: Beyond the HIPAA Privacy Rule—Enhancing Privacy, Improving Health through Research*. Institute of Medicine. Washington, DC: National Academy Press.

Ness, R. B., for the Joint Policy Committee, Societies of Epidemiology. 2007. Influence of the HIPAA privacy rule on health research. *JAMA* 298:2164–2170.

National Committee on Vital and Health Statistics (NCVHS). 1997. Hearings of the Subcommittee on Health Data Needs, Standards and Security, and of the Subcommittee on Privacy and Confidentiality, under the Health Insurance Portability and Accountability Act (PL 104–191).

NCQA. 2008. Physician and Hospital Quality Standards and Guidelines.

National Research Council. 1972. *Databanks in a Free Society: Computers, Record-Keeping, and Privacy*. Washington, DC: National Academy Press.

National Research Council. 1991. *Computers at Risk: Safe Computing in the Information Age*. Washington, DC: National Academy Press.

National Research Council. 1997. *For the Record: Protecting Electronic Health Information*. Washington, DC: National Academy Press.

Neumann, P. 1995. *Computer-Related Risks*. Reading, MA: Addison-Wesley.

Office of Technology Assessment. 1993. *Protecting Privacy in Computerized Medical Information*. Washington, DC: US Government Printing Office.

Office of Technology Assessment. 1995. *Bringing Health Care Online: The Role of Information Technologies*. Washington, DC: US Government Printing Office.

Organization for Economic Cooperation and Development. 1980. Guidelines on the Protection of Privacy and Transborder Flows of Personal Data.

Oxford English Dictionary, 2nd edn. 1989. Oxford, UK: Oxford University Press.

Privacy/Data Protection Project. 2005. University of Miami School of Medicine and University of Miami Ethics Programs. http://privacy.med.miami.edu.

Privacy Protection Study Commission. 1977. *Personal Privacy in an Information Society*. Washington, DC: US Government Printing Office.

Prosser, W. O. 1960. Privacy. *California Law Review* 48(3):383–423.

Regan, P. M. 1995. *Legislating Privacy: Technology, Social Values and Public Policy*. Chapel Hill, NC: University of North Carolina Press.

Roberts, C. 1995. Statement before the Senate Committee on Labor and Human Resources on S.1360. Federal Document Clearinghouse Congressional Testimony, 14 November.

Room, S. 2007. *Data Protection and Compliance in Context*. Swindon, UK: British Computer Society.

Russell, D., and Gangemi, G. T., Sr. 1991. *Computer Security Basics*. Sebastopol, CA: O'Reilly and Associates.

Schneier, B. 2000. *Secrets and Lies: Digital Security in a Networked World*. New York, NY: Wiley Computer Publishing.

Schneier, B. 2003. *Beyond Fear: Thinking Sensibly About Security in an Uncertain World*. New York, NY: Copernicus Books.

Schwartz, P. 1995a. Privacy and participation: personal information and public sector regulation in the United States. *Iowa Law Review* 80:553–618.

Schwartz, P. 1995b. European data protection law and restrictions on international data flows. *Iowa Law Review* 80:471–499.

Solove, D. J. 2008. *Understanding Privacy*. Cambridge, MA: Harvard University Press.

van den Hoven, M. J. 1995. *Information Technology and Moral Philosophy: Philosophical Explorations in Computer Ethics*. Rotterdam, Netherlands: Ridderprint BV.

Waldo, J., Lin, H. S., and Millet, L. I. 2007. *Engaging Privacy and Information Technology in a Digital Age. National Research Council*. Washington, DC: National Academy Press.

Warren, S. D., and Brandeis, L. D. 1890. The right to privacy. *Harvard Law Review* 4:193.

Westin, A. F. 1977. *Computers Health Records and Citizen's Rights*. New York, NY: Petrocelli Books.

Workgroup for Electronic Data Interchange. 1992. *Report to the Secretary of the Department of Health and Human Services*. Washington, DC: US Government Printing Office.

6

Searching Electronic Health Records

Ramakrishna Varadarajan, Vagelis Hristidis,
Fernando Farfán, and Redmond Burke

CONTENTS

6.1 Introduction

The National Health Information Network and its data-sharing building blocks, Regional Health Information Organizations, are encouraging the widespread adoption of electronic health records (EHR) for all hospitals within the next 5 years. To date, there has been little or no effort to define methods or approaches to rapidly search such documents and return meaningful results. As the use of EHRs becomes more widespread, so does the need to search and provide effective information discovery on them. Information discovery methods will allow practitioners and other healthcare stakeholders to locate relevant pieces of information in the growing corpus of available EHRs.

Before going into the details and specific challenges of searching EHRs, we provide an overview on searching documents, which is the focus of the Computer Science discipline of information retrieval (IR). In particular, the key focus of IR is how to rank the documents of a collection according to their "goodness" with respect to a query. The "goodness" of a result depends on factors such as relatedness to the query, specificity, and importance. The relevance is a subjective judgment and may include the following: being on the proper subject, being timely (recent information), being authoritative (from a trusted source), and satisfying the goals of the user and his/her intended use of the information (information need). The simplest notion of relevance is that the query string appears verbatim in the document. A slightly less strict notion is that the words in the query appear frequently in the document, in any order (bag of words). The query is usually expressed as a list of keywords, similarly to the case of Web search. Other types of queries are possible; however, we assume keyword queries throughout this chapter unless we specify otherwise. The ranking factors in IR are generally combined using a ranking function in order to assign a score to each document. The documents are then output in decreasing order of their IR score.

An intelligent IR system would take into account the *meaning* of the query words, the order of words in the query, and the authority of the information source. It should also adapt to the user based on direct or indirect feedback. The user interface of an IR system typically manages the interaction with the user by providing (1) query input and document output, (2) visualization of results, and (3) relevance feedback.

Special characteristics of EHR documents. Extensible Markup Language (XML) has emerged as the de facto standard format to represent and exchange data through the World Wide Web and other heterogeneous environments, spanning a wide variety of domains and applications. The increased popularity of XML repositories and XML documents in general must be accompanied by effective ways to retrieve the information stored in this format. One of the most promising standards for EHR manipulation and exchange is the XML-based Health Level 7's [1] Clinical Document Architecture (CDA) [2], which was introduced in Chapter 2. The definition and adoption of this standard presents new challenges for effective IR over the EHR corpus.

We present a series of challenges that have to be addressed to effectively perform information discovery on a corpus of CDA documents. For simplicity, we focus on plain keyword queries, although the same challenges are valid for semistructured queries as well—a semistructured query is a query where partial information about the structure of the results is provided. We discuss why the general work on information discovery on XML documents is not adequate to provide quality information discovery on CDA XML documents. The key reasons are the complex and domain-specific semantics and the frequent references to external information sources such as dictionaries and ontologies.

Exploit the link structure. As discussed in Chapter 1, an XML document can be viewed as a tree of nodes, where each XML element is seen as a node in the tree and ID-IDREF as edges. The collection of EHR documents can be viewed as a graph of interconnected entities—for example, an entity may be a doctor, a medication, a patient, and so on. The links are the associations between them. The keyword proximity concept in general text or Hypertext Markup Language (HTML) documents involve computing the physical distance between the keywords present in the document (the closer the keywords are to one another, the better). A document is ranked high if it contains all keywords of the query in close proximity. This concept of keyword proximity cannot be directly applied to XML, since the hierarchical tree structure of the document overrules traditional keyword proximity as handled in text documents or HTML documents. Two keywords that may appear physically proximal in the XML file may be distant or unrelated in the tree-structured XML document. XML keyword proximity search systems are designed to tackle this problem. Whereas keyword proximity search systems exploit this structure in computing results for queries, the authority flow systems exploit the link structure of the XML documents and go beyond traditional IR ranking techniques by providing high-quality authoritative and relevance ranking of the computed results.

Exploit health ontologies. Chapter 2 describes the key standards, dictionaries, and ontologies that are currently used in CDA: the Reference Information Model [3], the model from which the CDA documents derive their meaning. Three popular clinical dictionaries/ontologies referred to in CDA documents are presented—the Systematized Nomenclature of Human and Veterinary Medicine [4], the Logical Observation Identifiers Names and Codes [5], and RxNorm [6].

In this chapter, we discuss how these artifacts can be used to enhance the search quality. As an example, CDA documents routinely contain references to external dictionary and ontology sources through numeric codes. Hence, it is no longer enough to answer a query considering the CDA document in isolation, as is done by most previous works on searching text or XML documents.

A key message of this chapter is that computing the "best" results for a query, that is, the quality of the answer, can improve as more factors are considered. For instance, by exploiting the associations between the entities—for example, two patients are associated through a common medication—we gain useful information that can improve the quality of the answer. Similarly, exploiting health ontology can enhance the quality of the search engine.

The rest of the chapter is organized as follows. Section 6.2 discusses the related work. Section 6.3 reviews various traditional IR techniques. Section 6.4 describes the naïve techniques in searching EHRs. Section 6.5 describes the unique domain characteristics of EHRs that are relevant to search and retrieval. Section 6.6 describes how EHR document structure can be exploited in producing high-quality retrieval and ranking, whereas Section 6.7 describes how health ontologies and thesaurus can be exploited for searching purposes. Section 6.8 describes query models other than the popular keyword search paradigm. Section 6.9 describes measures for retrieval quality evaluation.

6.2 Related Work and Further Readings

IR is the science of searching relevant information from a collection of documents. An IR process begins with a user submitting a query to the IR system, which matches the user query to documents and returns a ranked list of relevant documents. Several key developments in this field happened in the 1960s. The System for the Mechanical Analysis and Retrieval of Text (SMART) Information Retrieval System [7–11] is an IR system developed in 1960s with many important concepts in IR developed as part of research on the SMART system, including the vector space model and relevance feedback. Later on, various models of document retrieval—basic Boolean model, extended Boolean, vector space [10], and probabilistic [12] models— were developed (we describe them in more detail in Section 6.3). These new models/techniques were experimentally proven to be effective on small text collections (several thousand articles) available to researchers at the time. The lack of availability of large text collections was changed in 1992 with the inception of Text Retrieval Conference, or TREC1 [13]. TREC is a series of evaluation conferences sponsored by various U.S. government agencies under the auspices of the National Institute of Standards and Technology, which aims at encouraging research in IR from large text collections.

For an overview of modern IR techniques, we refer to [14]. For a more detailed discussion on modern IR techniques, the readers are referred to [15]. Any state-of-the-art IR ranking function is based on the *tf-idf* principle [14]. The shortcoming of these semantics is that they miss objects that are very much related to the keywords although they do not contain the terms. The most popular specificity metric in IR is the document length (dl). The relevance information is hidden in the link structure of the data graph, which is largely ignored by the traditional IR techniques. Searching for pages on the World Wide Web is the most recent important IR application. Savoy [16] was the first to use the link structure of the Web to discover relevant pages. This idea became more popular with PageRank [17], where a global (query independent) score is assigned to each Web page. Haveliwala [18] proposed a topic-sensitive PageRank, where the topic-specific PageRanks for each page are precomputed and the PageRank value of the most relevant topic is used for each query. HITS [19] use mutually dependent computation of two values for each Web page: hub value and authority. Recently, the idea of PageRank has been applied to structured databases [20–22]. Balmin et al. [20] introduced the ObjectRank metric. In contrast to PageRank, ObjectRank is able to find relevant pages that do not contain the keyword, if they are directly pointed by pages that do. Huang et al. [22] proposed a way to rank the tuples of a relational database using PageRank, where connections are dynamically determined by the query workload and not statically by the schema. For XRANK, Guo et al. [21] proposed a way to rank XML elements using the link structure of the database. Furthermore, they introduced a notion similar to

ObjectRank transfer edge bounds, to distinguish between containment and IDREF edges.

Since XML has become a convenient format to represent EHRs, it is important to highlight the work conducted on searching text over XML documents. Many directions have been evaluated, from specific XML query languages—such as XPath, XQuery, etc.—to IR techniques.

There is a large corpus of work [21, 23–29] regarding the application of the popular keyword search paradigm on XML documents, where the query keywords are matched to XML nodes and a minimal tree containing these nodes is returned. A variety of ranking techniques are used ranging from the size of the result trees to IR scoring adaptations. XRANK [21] deals with keyword proximity, taking the proximity of the query keywords into account. The authors realize that a result can have high keyword proximity and low specificity, and vice versa. Also, by defining a ranking function similar to PageRank [17], they take into consideration the hyperlink structure of the document, exploiting this hyperlinked structure for their ranking function. XSEarch [30] ranks the results by taking into consideration both the degrees of the semantic relationship and the relevance of the keyword. Cohen et al. [31] present an extended framework to specify the semantic relationship of XML elements, providing a variety of interconnection semantics based on the XML schema, thereby improving the quality of the ranking of XSEarch. XIRQL (an XML query language) [25] uses a different strategy to compute its ranking, defining index units, which are specific entity types that can be indexed and used for tf-idf computation. Schema-free XQuery [28] refines the work of XSEarch by using meaningful lowest common ancestors instead of the concept of interconnected nodes. Cohen et al. [31] improve this approach even further by including the schema into the framework and discovering interconnection information. Xu and Papakonstantinou [29] define a result as a "smallest" tree, that is, a subtree that does not contain any subtree that also contains all keywords. Hristidis et al. [26] group structurally similar tree results to avoid overwhelming the user. XKeyword [27] operates on an XML graph (with ID-IDREF edges) and returns subtrees of minimum size. Recently, Li et al. [31a] proposed an efficient and adaptive keyword search method, called Ease, for indexing and querying large collections of heterogeneous data.

Work has also been done on integrating keyword search with structured XML querying [32–35]. Schmidt et al. [36] introduce a specific operator for XML, *meet*, which is similar to returning the most specific result. They also present efficient algorithms for computing *meet* using relational style joins and indices. Christophides et al. [37], Dao et al. [38], and Lee et al. [39] present systems for querying structured documents. However, the above systems do not consider ranking, two-dimensional keyword proximity, rank-based query processing algorithms, inverted lists, or integration with hyperlinked HTML keyword search, all of which are central to XRANK.

DBXplorer [40] and DISCOVER [41] support keyword search over relational databases, but do not support IR-style ranking. Furthermore, they are not directly applicable to XML and HTML documents, which cannot always be mapped to a rigid relational schema. BANKS [42], DataSpot [43], and Lore [44] support keyword search over graph-structured data. Some of these systems use hyperlinked structure (BANKS), and simple proximity (BANKS, Lore) for ranking. However, these systems do not generalize HTML search engines nor exploit the two-dimensional proximity inherent in XML. Furthermore, DataSpot does not present any query evaluation algorithms, and Lore [44] can only support keyword searches where the result type is known. BANKS requires that all the data edges fit in memory, which is not feasible for large datasets. Chakrabarti et al. [45] use nested HTML tag and hyperlink information to compute ranks at the granularity of a document.

The EquiX [23] language is a simple extension of a search engine for XML documents. However, EquiX can only deal with documents with a Document Type Definition (DTD), similar to the work of Carmel et al. [24]. In the study of Barg and Wong [46] and Hristidis et al. [27], it is suggested to rank query answers according to the distance in the document between the different document elements that satisfy a query. Closer elements would receive a higher ranking. XSEarch also uses this measure for its ranking, but it is only one of several measures. In the work of Hristidis et al. [27], efficient algorithms to compute the top k answers are presented. However, these algorithms are based on the assumption that each document has a schema, which may not necessarily hold. A theoretical treatment of the problem of flexibly matching a query to a document was presented by Kanza and Sagiv [47]. However, their approach did not include keyword searching.

Myaeng et al. [48] use term occurrences to compute the ranked results over Standard Generalized Markup Language Documents. XXL (a flexible XML search language) [49] uses term occurrences and ontological similarity for ranking. Luk et al. [50] survey commercial XML search engines. We are not aware of any system that uses hyperlink structure, a two-dimensional proximity metric, specializing on ranked inverted indices and query processing techniques for efficient XML and HTML keyword search.

As will be presented in Section 6.7, the use of medical ontologies, thesaurus, and dictionaries in EHRs constitutes an important mechanism to standardize nomenclature and to introduce semantics to the EHRs. Searching ontologies or using ontologies to improve search has also be an active topic in the research community. Various ontology query languages such as OWL-QL (a formal language and protocol using knowledge represented in the ontology web language) [50a] and SPARQL (a resource description framework language) [50b] have been proposed. These languages are used to query an ontology (expressed in formalism such as Resource Descriptor Framework or OWL) directly.

Pfeiffer et al. [51] present the need for intelligent search strategies and tools for healthcare. The expected functionalities from intelligent search engines in medicine are presented. The most important ones are as follows: (1) Extraction of the most important facts from an electronic healthcare record or personal healthcare record, which may be distributed across various types of databases at different locations; (2) expressing these facts as medical concepts and linking them using ontologies and specific medical grammar; (3) searching in quality-assured information systems for the latest information; (4) searching for the state-of-the-art treatment for a certain disease; (5) analyzing the outcomes of the latest clinical studies, etc. Inokuchi et al. [52] present an online analytical processing system that enables the interactive discovery of knowledge for clinical decision intelligence. It supports decision making by providing an in-depth analysis of clinical data from multiple sources.

6.3 Traditional IR

We briefly explain the evolution of modern textual IR system, that is, techniques to search text documents for relevant information given a query. Several IR models have been proposed in the literature. We briefly review them here.

Logical models. Traditionally, IR systems allowed users to specify their queries using complex Boolean expressions. The query terms were linked by the logical operators AND, OR, and NOT, and the search engine returned those documents that have combinations of terms satisfying the logical constraints of the query. For example, consider documents A and B in Figure 6.1 and a Boolean query—"tumor" and "symptoms." Both documents are returned as answers for this query since both contain the two terms. Similarly, for query "tumor" and "syndrome" only document B will be returned.

As a consequence, the Boolean model frequently returns either too few or too many documents in response to a user query. Even though the semantics are clear, there is no notion of document ranking. All of the retrieved documents are presumed to be of equal usefulness to the searcher. These limitations encouraged the development of fuzzy set models, which relaxed the strict constraints of the Boolean logic.

Unlike Boolean search systems, most IR systems assign a numeric score to every document and rank documents by this score. Several models were proposed for this process and the three most widely used models in IR research are the vector space models, the probabilistic models, and term weighting approaches, which are described below.

Vector space model. In the vector space model [10], a document is viewed as a set of terms and is represented by using a vector. The basic idea is that the terms are regarded as coordinates of a high dimensional information space. Terms, typically, are words or (and) phrases. If words are chosen as terms, then every word in the vocabulary becomes an independent dimension in a very high dimensional vector space. Hence, any text can then be represented by a vector in this high dimensional space. Both documents and queries are represented as vectors in which the ith element denotes the value of the ith term depending on the particular term weighting scheme that is being used.

To assign a numeric score to a document for a query, the *similarity* between the query vector and the document vector is measured. Typically, the angle between the two vectors is used as a measure of divergence between the vectors, and cosine of the angle is used as the numeric similarity. Several other alternatives are also possible. For example, the inner product or dot product can be used as a similarity measure. If $\vec{D}$ is the document vector of document D and $\vec{Q}$ is the query vector of query Q, then the dot product similarity between document D and query Q (or score of D for Q) can be represented as

$$\text{Sim}(\vec{D},\vec{Q}) = \sum_{t_i \in Q,D} w(t_i,D) \cdot w(t_i,Q) \qquad (6.1)$$

where $w(t_i,Q)$ is the weight of term t_i in the query vector $\vec{Q}$, and $w(t_i,D)$ is the weight of term t_i in the document vector $\vec{D}$. Since any word not present in either the query or the document has weight 0, we can do the summation only over the terms common in the query and the document.

Consider a query Q with keywords "tumor symptoms" over documents A and B in Figure 6.1. Assuming unit weights for terms in query vector, $\vec{Q}$, and term frequency (tf) as the term weight in the document vector $\vec{D}$, the dot product similarity for documents A and B can be calculated as

Document A

Lucy is a 34-year-old mother who is living with her husband and her 5-year-old son. Lucy was referred to a nearby Medical Center by her general practice with a 4-week history of headache, the *symptoms* of which were so bad that she forced to resign from work. She showed some behavioral *symptoms* that have become increasingly inappropriate, and she at times becomes belligerent and non-cooperative with all members of the family. A subsequent CT scan indicated the presence of a *tumor* in the right frontal lobe. Upon the CT diagnosis, Lucy experienced *symptoms* of depression and anxiety, which have progressively worsened. Later, a cranial biopsy was done to confirm the presence of the *tumor.*

Document B

Mrs. P., a 68-year-old married housewife, lives with her husband on a farm. She presented to the Emergency Department at a nearby Medical Center with *symptoms* of diarrhea and moderate dehydration following bowel resection two weeks earlier to remove carcinoid *tumor.* This follows a two-and-a-half year history of diarrhea and weight loss, which has seen Mrs. P. become increasingly housebound and more dependent on her husband, who suffers Tourrett's syndrome and depression, for care. Her current critical state follows closely on the suicide of her youngest daughter (aged 39 years) in March this year.

FIGURE 6.1
Two text documents with medical history content.

follows: $\text{Sim}(\vec{A},\vec{Q}) = \sum_{t_i \in Q, A} w(t_i, A) \cdot w(t_i, Q) = 2 \cdot 1 + 3 \cdot 1 = 5$, and $\text{Sim}(\vec{B},\vec{Q}) = \sum_{t_i \in Q, B} w(t_i, B) \cdot w(t_i, Q) = 1 \cdot 1 + 1 \cdot 1 = 2$. This shows that document A is more similar to query Q than document B.

Probabilistic models. Unlike database systems, where the information needed can be precisely represented as a structured query and results precisely computed (as the underlying data has structure), this situation is rather difficult in IR since the underlying data are mostly unstructured (English text) and the relevance judgments are subjective (user dependent). Hence, the IR process is intrinsically uncertain and probabilistic models are designed to cope up with this uncertainty. Given a document collection and a query, these models rank the documents in decreasing probability of their relevance to the query. This is often called the *probabilistic ranking principle* [12].

Since the relevance judgments are subjective, true probabilities are not available to an IR system. Hence, probabilistic IR models *estimate* the probability of relevance of documents for a query. This estimation is the key part of the model, and this is where most probabilistic models differ from one another. The initial idea of probabilistic retrieval was proposed by Maron and Kuhns [53]. Many probabilistic models have been proposed, each based on a different probability estimation technique.

Term weighting approaches in Modern IR [14]. The most common factors used in traditional IR to rank the documents are: (1) term frequency (tf)—words that repeat multiple times in a document are considered salient; (2) inverse document frequency (idf) [54]—words that appear in many documents are considered common and are not very indicative of document content (hence, we use the inverse of it); (3) document length (dl)—when collections have documents of varying lengths, longer documents tend to score higher since they contain more words and word repetitions. This effect is usually compensated for by normalizing for document lengths in the term weighting method.

Consider the query "tumor symptoms" on the documents in Figure 6.1. For document A, tf (tumor) = 2 and tf (symptoms) = 3. For document B, tf (tumor) = 1 and tf (symptoms) = 1. Although term frequency (tf) measures the frequency of a term in a document, the inverse document frequency (idf) estimates the importance of the term itself. The intuition behind idf is that infrequent keywords should be given a higher weight in the ranking. If a term appears in many documents, the general intuition is that, it is not so useful in differentiating relevant documents from irrelevant ones and is hence given a lower weight. For the current example, let us assume a collection of 10 medical documents in which the term "symptoms" appears in all 10 documents (hence, idf (symptoms) = 1/10 = 0.1) and "tumor" appears in five documents (hence, idf (tumor) = 1/5 = 0.2). The tf · idf weight of document A for query "tumor symptoms" is calculated as tf (tumor) · idf (tumor) + tf (symptoms) · idf (symptoms) = 2 · 0.2 + 3 · 0.1 = 0.7. Similarly, the tf · idf weight of document B for the query "tumor symptoms" is 0.3. Hence, document A is more relevant to the query than document B and shall be ranked higher than document B.

Many formulas have been proposed to combine tf, idf, and dl in order to assign a unique score to each document given a query. After several advancements in term weighting, two widely used weighting methods were introduced: (1) *Okapi weighting* (Equation 6.2) and (2) *pivoted normalization weighting* [55].

$$\text{Score}(D,Q) = \sum_{t \in Q, D} \ln \frac{N - df + 0.5}{df + 0.5} \frac{(k_1 + 1)tf}{\left(k_1(1-b) + b\dfrac{dl}{avdl}\right) + tf} \frac{(k_3 + 1)qtf}{k_3 + qtf} \tag{6.2}$$

where tf is the term's frequency in document (page), qtf is the term's frequency in query, N is the total number of documents in the collection, df is the number of documents that contain the term, dl is the document length (in words), avdl is the average document length, and k_1 (between 1.0 and 2.0), b (usually 0.75), and k_3 (between 0 and 1000) are constants.

Most IR researchers currently use some variant of these two weightings. Many studies have used the phrase *tf-idf weighting* to refer to any term weighting method that uses tf and idf, and do not differentiate between using a simple document scoring method and a state-of-the-art scoring method. A current state-of-the-art retrieval function used in document retrieval is Okapi BM25, which is a ranking function used by search engines to rank matching documents according to their relevance to a given search query.

Relevance feedback and query modification. Salton and Buckley [56] introduced the idea of using relevance feedback for improving search performance. Without sufficient knowledge of the document collection and the retrieval process, most users find it difficult to formulate effective initial search requests. This fact suggests that retrieval processes should start with a tentative initial query used to retrieve few useful items, which is later examined, and then a new improved query is constructed. The main idea consists of choosing important terms, or expressions, attached to certain previously retrieved documents that have been identified as relevant by the users, and enhancing the importance of these terms in a new query formulation. Relevance feedback covers a range of techniques intended to improve a user's query and facilitate retrieval of information relevant to a user's information need. In their work, Buckley et al. [57] showed that query expansion and query term reweighting are essential to relevance feedback. For a detailed survey of relevance feedback methods, we refer to Ruthven and Lalmas [58]. The basic approach of term selection, term reweighting, and query expansion using terms drawn from the relevant documents works well for traditional IR.

Inverted indexes. Thus far, we have focused on scores of documents, which determine the quality of a search engine. Next, we briefly discuss time performance, that is, how to answer queries with short response time. The most popular indexing mechanism in IR is the inverted index, which allows the user to efficiently retrieve all documents containing the query keywords. Indexing, in general, promotes efficiency in terms of time for retrieval by facilitating quick extraction of relevant documents. In particular, for each term occurring in the document collection, the inverted index stores a list of pointers to all occurrences of that term in the main text, sorted in some order (increasing document ID, decreasing document score for that term, etc.). This enables fast access to a list of documents containing a term. Since all documents are indexed by the terms they contain, the process of generating, building, and storing document representations is called *indexing* and the resulting inverted files are called the *inverted index*. Figure 6.2 shows inverted indexes for terms "tumor," "symptoms," and "biopsy" for documents shown in Figure 6.1.

6.4 Naïve Searching on EHRs

In the rest of the chapter, we assume that EHRs are represented in XML format (e.g., HL7 CDA) and queries are keyword queries. Most of the discussion below can be applied to other formats, as long as they represent the data in an EHR as a set of entities (e.g., XML elements) connected through associations (e.g., XML containment or ID-IDREF edges). Figure 6.3 shows a medical record in HL7 CDA format.

Unfortunately, the traditional and popular text-based search engines cannot deal efficiently with these documents, which may not fully exploit the added semantics of XML documents due to a series of limitations. First, search engines do not exploit the XML tags and nested hierarchical structure of the XML documents, omitting the semantic meaning of the tags or, even worse, simply ignoring them. Second, the whole XML document is treated as an integral unit. The main drawback here is that potentially large size documents may span to several megabytes or gigabytes, resulting in inappropriate and unmanageable results. Third, the granularity of the ranking is whole documents, since traditional search engines will assign a ranking to the whole document.

The naïve search strategy views the EHR XML document as a plain text document and applies traditional IR ranking techniques. For example, consider a query "chronic aspiration" over the medical document in Figure 6.3. Applying the tf·idf principle (assuming a collection of 10 HL7 CDA medical documents in which the term "chronic" appears in all the 10 documents (hence, idf (chronic) = (1/10) = 0.1) and "aspiration" appears in five documents (hence, idf (aspiration) = (1/5) = 0.2). The tf · idf weight of the document in Figure 6.3 is calculated as tf (chronic) · idf (chronic) + tf (aspiration) · idf

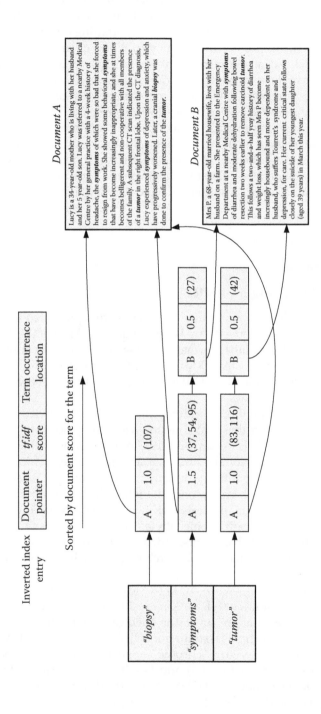

FIGURE 6.2
Inverted index for terms "biopsy," "symptoms," and "tumor" for documents *A* and *B*.

```
<?xml version="1.0" encoding="UTF-8" standalone="no" ?>
- <ClinicalDocument NS2:schemaLocation="urn:hl7-org:v3 CDA.ReleaseTwo.Committee.2004.xsd" templateId="2.16.840.1.113883.3.27.1776" xmlns="urn:hl7-org:v3"
  xmlns:NS2="http://www.w3.org/2001/XMLSchema-instance">
    <id extension="c266" root="2.16.840.1.113883.3.933" />
  - <recordTarget>
    - <patientRole>
        <id extension="49912" root="2.16.840.1.113883.3.933" />
      - <patientPatient>
        - <name>
            <given>FirstName</given>
            <family>LastName</family>
            <suffix>Jr.</suffix>
          </name>
        </patientPatient>
      </patientRole>
    </recordTarget>
  - <component>
    - <StructuredBody>
      - <section>
          <code code="10160-0" codeSystem="2.16.840.1.113883.6.1" codeSystemName="LOINC" />
          <title>Medications</title>
        - <Observation>
            <code code="84100007" codeSystem="2.16.840.1.113883.6.96" codeSystemName="SNOMED CT" displayName="Medications" />
          - <value NS2:type="CD" code="195967001" codeSystem="2.16.840.1.113883.6.96" codeSystemName="SNOMED CT" displayName="Asthma">
            - <originalText>
                <reference value="m1" />
              </originalText>
            </value>
          </Observation>
        - <Observation>
            <code code="84100007" codeSystem="2.16.840.1.113883.6.96" codeSystemName="SNOMED CT" displayName="Medications" />
          - <value NS2:type="CD" code="32398004" codeSystem="2.16.840.1.113883.6.96" codeSystemName="SNOMED CT" displayName="Bronchitis">
              <value NS2:type="CD" code="91143003" codeSystem="2.16.840.1.113883.6.96" codeSystemName="SNOMED CT" displayName="Albuterol" />
            </value>
          </Observation>
        - <SubstanceAdministration>
          - <text>
              <content ID="m1">Theophylline</content>
              20 mg every other day, alternating with 18 mg every other day, for 2 weeks. Stop if temperature is above 103F.
            </text>
          - <consumable>
            - <manufacturedProduct>
              - <manufacturedLabeledDrug>
                  <code code="66493003" codeSystem="2.16.840.1.113883.6.96" codeSystemName="SNOMED CT" displayName="Theophylline" />
                </manufacturedLabeledDrug>
              </manufacturedProduct>
            </consumable>
          </SubstanceAdministration>
        </section>
      - <component>
        - <section>
            <code code="10164-2" codeSystem="2.16.840.1.113883.6.1" codeSystemName="LOINC" />
            <title>History of Present Illness</title>
            <text>3 month old baby who has been transferred to MCH CICU for VSD repair. He was born FT, but had resp. distress requiring mehcanical ventilation for 3 days
            for ? pulmonary edema. He was diagnosed then to have a large VSD. He was admitted in the hospital for about a month for his resp. issues. He was sent home but
            after 3 weeks developed bronchiolitis and had been in the hospital since then. During this admission he was also diagnosed to have GE Reflux and Aspiration. He
            was also found to have Chronic lung disease --possibly due to aspiration. he also had complex partial seizures--?? due to resp. distress which were being treated
            with Phenobarb. For the last 4 days his feeds were switched to NJ-- He was now transferred to Miami for surgery on 11/15/06 to have the VSD closed.</text>
          </section>
        </component>
      </StructuredBody>
    </component>
  </ClinicalDocument>
```

FIGURE 6.3
An example HL7 CDA XML medical document.

(aspiration) $= (1) \cdot (0.2) + (2) \cdot (0.1) = 0.4$. The key drawbacks of this approach are as follows: (1) structure of the XML document is ignored, which leads to suboptimal ranking; (b) granularity of ranking is in document level and not in the entity level (XML element level); (c) the entire document is returned as a result (result specificity could be improved if document structure was considered). In Section 6.6, we show how this structure can be exploited to improve the results' ranking.

6.5 Unique Domain Characteristics

In the previous section, we described the basics of IR and explained how this process can be naïvely applied, as a general framework, over EHRs represented as XML documents. However, the complex and domain-specific semantics, and the frequent references to external information sources such as dictionaries and ontologies cause this general approach to be inadequate for providing high-quality information discovery on XML-based EHRs.

In this section, we briefly present a series of challenges that have to be addressed to effectively search a corpus of XML-based EHRs. For simplicity, we focus on plain keyword queries, although the same challenges are valid for semistructured queries as well—a semistructured query is a query where partial information about the structure of the results is provided. A more detailed discussion on these challenges can be found in the work of Hristidis et al. [59].

Structure and scope of results. In contrast to traditional Web search, where whole HTML documents are returned as query results, in the case of XML-based EHRs, we need to define what a meaningful query result is. The reason is that XML documents tend to be much larger than HTML documents. Previous work has studied different approaches to define the structure of results. Several studies [21, 25, 60] consider a whole subtree as a result, that is, a result is unambiguously defined by the lowest common ancestor (LCA) node of the keyword nodes. We refer to this approach as *subtree-as-result*. In contrast, a path as the result is proposed by Agrawal et al. [40], Bhalotia et al. [42], Hristidis and Papakonstantinou [41], Cohen et al. [30], and Hristidis et al. [27], where a minimal path of XML nodes is returned that collectively contain all the query keywords. We refer to this approach as *path-as-result*. Note that the term "path" is loosely used to differentiate it from the *subtree-as-result* approach, because it can be a collection of meeting paths (a tree) for more than two query keywords.

Minimal information unit. It is challenging to define the granularity of a piece of information in a manner that it is self-contained and meaningful, but at the same time specific. We may find out that very specific results are not meaningful to the user; on the other hand, some queries require some elements that do not contribute in connecting the query keywords or are part of the MIU of such a connecting node, to be included into the result.

Another issue is the static definition of an MIU. In XKeyword [27], a "target object" is the equivalent of an MIU and it is defined statically on the schema by a domain expert. Xu et al. [61] also define MIUs in a static manner. Such static MIU definitions may not be adequate for searching EHRs, since different queries and different users have different information and result presentation needs and preferences; there is a need to dynamically specify MIUs.

Semantics of node and edge types. It is challenging to incorporate the rich semantic information available for the clinical domain, and particularly for the elements of an EHR, in the results' ranking process. At the most basic, viewing an XML-based CDA as a tree of nodes and edges (as described in Chapter 1), a domain expert statically assigns a semantic weight to each node and edge type, as in BANKS [42]. In addition to that, we can assign relevance degrees to whole paths on the schema instead of single edges to improve ranking quality. Furthermore, it is desirable that the weights, that is, the degrees of semantic association, are adjusted dynamically exploiting relevance feedback [61a] and learning [62] techniques. Note that for relational (table-based) EHRs, the same principles apply, with the difference that the edges correspond to primary-to-foreign key relationships.

Access to dictionaries and ontologies. EHRs routinely contain references to external dictionary and ontology sources. Hence, it is no longer enough to answer a query considering the EHR in isolation, as is done by all previous work on searching XML documents. In this setting, the query keywords may refer to text in the EHR or an ontology that is connected to the EHR.

Also important are the different types of relations in the ontology. We need to assign an appropriate value to each of the relations present in the ontologies. Stricter and stronger relations in the ontology should intuitively have a higher weight. Furthermore, we need to take into consideration the direction of the edges. Specialization and generalization relations should be carefully treated to avoid imprecise results.

Free text embedded in EHRs. In some cases, plain text descriptions are added to certain sections to enrich the information about the record or to express a real life property not codified in dictionaries or ontologies. As a first measure, traditional text-based IR techniques [63, 64] should be included in the architecture to support such cases.

Another technique to address the coexistence of semistructured and unstructured data is presented by Hristidis et al. [65], wherein IR and proximity rankings are combined.

In addition to embedded plain text, HTML fragments can also be included to the EHRs, resulting in a mix of semantic mappings.

Special treatment of time and location attributes. Time and location may be critical attributes in some queries. For instance, for the query "drug-A drug-B," the doctor is probably looking for any conflict between these drugs, and hence the time interval between the prescriptions of these drugs for a patient is a critical piece of information. Location is also important since two patients located in nearby beds in the hospital should be viewed as associated because infections tend to transmit to neighboring beds. Clearly, it is challenging to standardize the representation of such location information within an EHR. Furthermore, time and location can lead to the definition of metrics similar to the idf in IR [63]. For instance, asthma is more common in summer; hence, a patient who has asthma in winter should be ranked higher for the query "asthma." Similarly, a patient who has the flu in a town where no one else has it should be ranked higher for the query "flu." Similarly, location relationships can be specified either within a hospital or across towns.

Finally, there should be a way to specify time intervals in the query, possibly using a calendar interface, and then use the specified time window as an answer's filter. Specifying the time-distance between the keywords can also be useful. For instance, the query "newborn heartblock," which is often needed at pediatric clinics, should not return a patient who had a heartblock when he/she was 60 years old but had the word "newborn" appearing in his/her EHR in a description field of his/her birthday.

Identity reconciliation and "value edges." A single real-life entity (e.g., a medication or a doctor) is duplicated every time it is used in an EHR. Hence, associating two records of the same author or two patients with the same medication is difficult. In contrast, in previous work on searching XML documents, a real-life entity is typically represented by a single XML element, which is linked using ID-IDREF edges where needed. For instance, in XKeyword [65] two articles of the same author have an IDREF to the same author element.

The problem of reference reconciliation has been tackled both in the context of structured databases [66–72] and in the context of free text document collections [69, 73–75]. However, focusing on the domain of EHRs allows a domain expert to manually specify rules on what types of elements are good candidates for referencing identical real-life objects, in case these elements have identical or "similar values.

EHR document-as-query. An alternative query type to the plain keyword query is using a whole (or part of) EHR as the query. This approach can be used to find similar EHRs, that is, EHRs of patients with similar history, demographic information, treatments, etc. The user should be able to customize and personalize such an information discovery tool to fit his or her needs. This issue is extended later in this section.

Handle negative statements. A substantial fraction of the clinical observations entered into patient records are expressed by means of negation. Elkin et al. [76] found SNOMED Clinical Terms (CT) to provide coverage for 14,792 concepts in 41 health records from Johns Hopkins University, of which 1823 (12.3%) were identified as negative by human review. This is because negative findings are as important as positive ones for accurate medical decision making. It is common in a medical document to list all the diagnoses that have been ruled out, for example, a note stating that "the patient does not have hypertension, gout, or diabetes." This creates a major problem when searching medical documents. Today, one has to examine the terms preceding a diagnosis to determine if this diagnosis was excluded or not. Ceusters and Smith [77] propose new ontological relationships to express "negative findings." It is challenging to handle such negative statements for an information discovery query in a manner that the user can specify whether negated concepts should be excluded from the search process.

Personalization. The information discovery engine should provide personalized results depending on the preferences of each user. For example, for different doctors, different entities and relationships in the EHR components are more important. For some healthcare providers, the medication may be more relevant than the observation, or the medication may be more relevant than the doctor's name. In addition, the relationships in ontologies may be viewed differently.

Furthermore, depending on whether a user is a nurse, a pharmacist, a technician, or a physician, the system could automatically assign different weights on edges and nodes of the EHR model, to facilitate the information needs of the users.

6.6 Exploit Structure

In this section, we describe techniques exploiting the structure of an XML-based HL7 CDA medical document for the purpose of providing sophisticated ranking and high-quality search results. Two main techniques are proposed in the literature as described below.

6.6.1 Keyword Proximity Search

A query language for XML, such as XQuery, can be used to extract data from XML documents. However, such a query language is not an alternative to a keyword-based XML search engine for several reasons. First, the syntax of XQuery is too complicated, and hence inappropriate, for a naïve user. Second, rather extensive knowledge of the document structure (its XML schema) is required in order to correctly formulate a query. Thus, queries must be formulated on a per document basis. Finally, XQuery lacks any mechanism for ranking answers—an essential feature, since there are likely to be many answers when querying large XML documents.

Keyword search has emerged as the most popular information discovery because the user does not need to know either a query language or the underlying structure of the data being queried. Any XML document can be viewed as a tree of nodes where each XML element is seen as a node in the tree and ID-IDREF as edges, as shown in Figure 6.4. The keyword proximity concept in general text or HTML documents involves computing the physical distance in number of words between the query keywords present in the document (the closer the keywords are to one another, the better). A document is ranked high if it contains all keywords of the query in close proximity. This concept of keyword proximity cannot be directly applied to XML, since the hierarchical tree structure of the document overrules traditional keyword proximity as handled in text documents or HTML documents. Two keywords that may appear physically proximal in the XML file may be distant or unrelated in the tree-structured XML document. XML keyword proximity search systems are designed to tackle this problem.

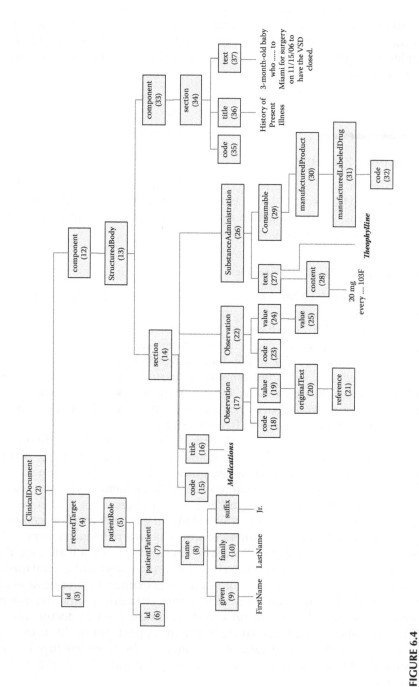

FIGURE 6.4
Tree representation of HL7 CDA XML medical document shown in Figure 6.3.

A *keyword proximity XML search system* exploits this structure to retrieve and rank high-quality search results. A *keyword proximity query* is a set of query keywords and the results are trees of XML fragments containing all the keywords and are ranked according to some parameters. For example, consider the keyword proximity query "theophylline medications" on the XML tree shown in Figure 6.4.

Several XML keyword proximity search systems have been proposed in the literature. Some of the most popular ones are XRANK [21], XSEarch [30], and XKeyword [27]. All three systems differ in the manner in which they compute a result and also in the way in they rank them. We briefly describe the differences below.

An important requirement for keyword search is to rank the query results so that the most relevant results appear first. This score value has to reflect the relevance of an answer regarding a user query. A higher score will imply a higher degree of relevance for that answer. Also, the query will generally return an XML document fragment, which implies that the granularity of the returned results will affect the scoring.

XRANK [21] processes XML keyword proximity queries by computing the LCAs containing all the query keywords specified in the query, in ranked order. XRANK computes rankings at the granularity of an element as it returns XML elements as results for keyword search queries. A corpus of works including XRANK [21, 25, 60] consider a whole subtree as result, that is, a result is unambiguously defined by the LCA node of the keyword nodes. Figure 6.5a presents an example of this approach. When ranking elements, XRANK considers element-to-element links (containment edges) in addition to document-to-document links (ID-IDREF edges). XRANK ranks the elements of an XML document by generalizing the PageRank algorithm of Google [17] and applying it to semistructured data (XML in particular). For the purpose of ranking, it also considers result specificity (specific results are ranked higher than less specific ones) and XML keyword proximity. For more details on XRANK ranking, please refer to Section 6.6, which presents the authority flow search techniques.

XKeyword [27], in contrast to XRANK, returns a minimal path of XML nodes that collectively contain all the query keywords as the result. This approach has been used in several systems [30, 40–42]. Figure 6.5b presents an example of this approach. XKeyword [27] ranks results according to their size. Trees of smaller sizes denote higher association between the keywords, which is generally true for reasonable XML schema designs.

XSEarch [30] serves as a semantic search engine for XML documents that has the ability to specify the tags in which the keywords must appear. Carmel et al. [24] present an approach to represent information units as XML fragments of the same nature as the documents that are being searched, using an extension to the vector space model to perform the search and rank the results by relevance.

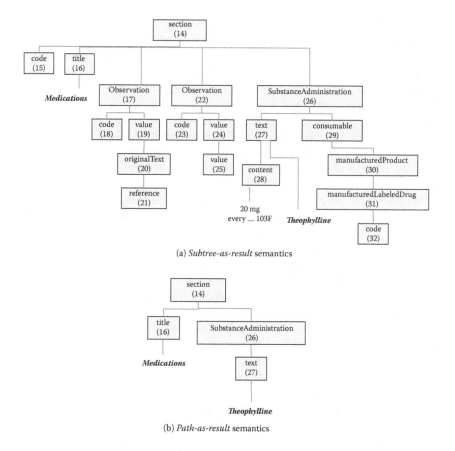

(a) *Subtree-as-result* semantics

(b) *Path-as-result* semantics

FIGURE 6.5
Output for query "theophylline medications" over XML document in Figure 6.3.

In addition to keyword search languages, several XML search systems proposed in the literature implement different query interfaces. Note that keyword search has the advantage of simplicity and ease of use. The user need not learn a query language or have a detailed knowledge of the underlying data. This provides great flexibility and added advantage especially to the novice users of the system. Other query language approaches proposed for XML are (1) tags and keyword query search, (2) path expression and keyword query search, and (3) XQuery and complex full-text search. The first class of languages adds semantic meaning. In addition to specify keywords, the user can specify labels and keyword-label combinations to be the input query. XSEarch [30] presents these same features. A second category of languages combines the use of path expressions with an extension to allow key search. This class is represented by XIRQL [25] and XXL [49]. The third class of languages extends XQuery to empower it with complex full-text search capabilities. TeXQuery [60], Schema-free XQuery [78], and XQuery Full Text [79] are implementations of this class.

6.6.2 Authority Flow Search

As described before, any XML document can be viewed as a tree of nodes with containment and ID-IDREFs as edges (links) as shown in Figure 6.4. Note that when ID-IDREFs edges are present in an XML document, the XML tree becomes a graph. In the previous section, we showed how this structure can be exploited in computing query results that tightly related the query keywords. In this section, we explain how the structure of EHR documents can be used to produce high-quality ranking of those results, that is, to find the most relevant elements of one or many EHRs given a query (typically, keyword query).

Note that the techniques we describe here exploit the link structure of the XML documents and go beyond traditional IR ranking techniques. The idea of using link structure was first applied on the Web (viewed as a graph with pages viewed as nodes and hyperlinks as edges) to discover relevant pages. Savoy [16] was the first to use the link structure of the Web to discover relevant pages. A simple example of this type of ranking used in the academic domain (where publications are regarded as nodes and citations as edges) for ranking publications is to take into account the number of citations of a publication. Publications that have several papers citing them would get a higher rank, which would intuitively seem correct. However, there is a minor problem in this type of ranking. For example, if we assume that Publication A is cited by ten low-quality papers and Publication B is cited by five high-quality papers, with this method Publication A would be ranked higher than B. This example illustrates the fact that not only the number of citations but also the importance of each citation should be taken in to account for ranking. Computing the importance of a citation would involve computing the importance of the paper that cites, whose importance in turn is determined by the papers that cite it. This leads to a recursive definition giving rise to a chain of computations. This idea became more popular with PageRank [17], where a global score is assigned to each Web page as we explain next.

We next describe the essentials of PageRank algorithm, which performs authority-based search, and the random surfer intuition. Let (V,E) be a graph, with a set of nodes $V = \{v_1, ..., v_n\}$ and a set of edges E. A surfer starts from a random node (Web page) v_i of V and at each step, he/she follows a hyperlink with probability d or gets bored and jumps to a random node with probability $1 - d$. The PageRank value of v_i is the probability $r(v_i)$ that at a given point in time, the surfer is at v_i. If we denote by r the vector $[r(v_1), ..., r(v_i), ..., r(v_n)]^T$, then we have

$$r = dAr + \frac{(1-d)}{|V|} e \qquad (6.3)$$

where A is a $n \times n$ matrix with $A_{ij} = 1/\text{Out Deg}(v_j)$ if there is an edge $v_j \rightarrow v_i$ in E and 0 otherwise, in which $\text{OutDeg}(v_j)$ is the outgoing degree of node v_j. Also, $e = [1, ..., 1]^T$. Note that vector e acts as a rank source (the set of nodes where the surfer jumps when bored). In the original PageRank [17], all pages in the Web graph act as rank sources.

PageRank measures the global importance of the pages, independently of a keyword query. The above PageRank equation is typically precomputed before the queries arrive and provides a global, keyword-independent ranking of the pages. Brin and Page [17] also proposed the idea of computing personalized rankings by using bookmarks of the user as rank sources. More recent papers [18, 80] exploit this idea and apply PageRank to estimate the relevance of pages to a keyword query. Haveliwala [18] computes topic-specific PageRank on the Web. ObjectRank [20, 81] appropriately extends and modifies PageRank to perform keyword search in databases and provide authority-based ranking. Given a keyword query, it ranks the results according to three factors: (1) relevance to the query, (2) specificity, and (3) global importance of the result. All factors are handled using authority flow techniques exploiting the link structure of the data graph, in contrast to traditional IR. The relevance is computed using the ObjectRank metric, which is a keyword-specific adaptation of PageRank to databases. The specificity is computed using Inverse ObjectRank metric and the global importance is computed using Global ObjectRank, which is the keyword-independent version of ObjectRank. In addition, ObjectRank introduces authority transfer edge bounds to differentiate authority flow in different types of database edges.

In ObjectRank, instead of using the whole set of nodes V as rank sources (called *base set S* in ObjectRank), that is, the set of nodes where the surfer jumps when bored, they use an arbitrary subset S of nodes, thereby increasing the authority associated with the nodes of S and the ones most closely associated with them. The base set is set to contain the nodes that contain at least one of the query keywords. In particular, they define a base vector $s = [s_0, \ldots, s_i, \ldots, s_n]^T$, where s_i is 1 if $v_i \in S$ and 0 otherwise. The PageRank equation is then

$$r = \mathrm{d}Ar + \frac{(1-d)}{|S|}s \qquad (6.4)$$

Regardless of whether one uses Equation (6.3) or Equation (6.4), the PageRank algorithm solves this fixpoint equation using a simple iterative method, where the values of the $(k + 1)$-th execution are calculated as follows:

$$r^{(k+1)} = \mathrm{d}Ar^k + \frac{(1-d)}{|S|}s \qquad (6.5)$$

The algorithm terminates when r converges, which is guaranteed to happen under very common conditions [82]. In particular, the authority flow graph needs to be irreducible (i.e., (V,E) should be strongly connected) and aperiodic. The former is true due to the damping factor d, whereas the latter happens in practice. Another work closely similar to ObjectRank was conducted by Huang et al. [22], who propose a way to rank the tuples of a relational database using PageRank; here, connections are determined dynamically by the query workload and not statically by the schema. Figure 6.6 shows a subset of the "anonymized" Miami Children's Hospital dataset with edges annotated with authority transfer rates.

Consider the damping factor $d = 0.85$ and query $Q = ["pericardial effusion"]$ on the clinical data subset shown in Figure 6.6. Note that in ObjectRank, the base set $S = \{v_1, v_4, v_5\}$ has all objects containing "pericardial effusion." In this example,

$$A = \begin{bmatrix} 0.0 & 0.0 & 0.0 & 0.0 & 0.0 & 0.0 & 0.0 \\ 0.0 & 0.0 & 0.5 & 0.0 & 0.0 & 0.0 & 0.0 \\ 0.0 & 0.0 & 0.0 & 0.0 & 0.0 & 0.0 & 0.0 \\ 0.0 & 0.0 & 0.0 & 0.0 & 0.0 & 0.0 & 0.0 \\ 0.0 & 0.0 & 0.0 & 0.0 & 0.0 & 0.0 & 0.0 \\ 0.0 & 0.0 & 0.5 & 0.5 & 1.0 & 0.0 & 0.0 \\ 1.0 & 0.0 & 0.0 & 0.5 & 0.0 & 1.0 & 0.0 \end{bmatrix} \text{ and } s = [1, 0, 0, 1, 1, 0, 0]^T |S| = 3$$

The computed ObjectRank scores vector $r = [0.05, 0.00, 0.00, 0.05, 0.05, 0.063, 0.117]^T$ after one iteration. This technique can also be applied to XML-based CDA documents given that links are containment and ID-IDREF edges. A big challenge in applying ObjectRank to EHRs is selecting the right semantic edge weights. For instance, the hospitalization-to-patient edge should have higher weight than the hospitalization-to-nurse edge. Varadarajan et al. [83] describe a novel technique to exploit user feedback to adjust the semantic

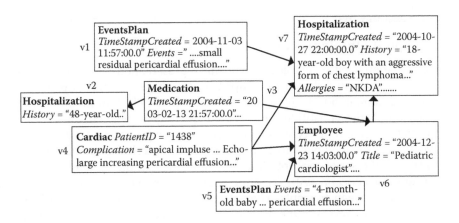

FIGURE 6.6
A subset of the clinical dataset.

edge weights, when ranking techniques based on authority-flow propagation are used.

We are now going back to XRANK, which performs proximity search. XRANK uses authority flow ranking as a component of its ranking function. In particular, the authors propose ElemRank, which is an adaptation of the idea of PageRank, to assign scores to individual nodes of the XML tree. Next, these scores are combined to compute the score of a result subtree. ElemRank extends PageRank (1) to consider bidirectional transfer of authority between elements due to tighter coupling of XML elements through containment edges and (2) to discriminate between containment and hyperlink(ID-IDREF) edges. ElemRank is a measure of the objective importance of an XML element, and is computed based on the hyperlinked structure of the XML documents. The ElemRank formula is presented by Guo et al. [23] as follows:

$$e(v) = \frac{1-d_1-d_2-d_3}{N_d \times N_{de}(v)} + d_1 \cdot \sum_{(u,v)\in HE} \frac{e(u)}{N_h(u)} + d_2 \cdot \sum_{(u,v)\in CE} \frac{e(u)}{N_c(u)} + d_3 \cdot \sum_{(u,v)\in CE^{-1}} e(u)$$

(6.6)

where $e(v)$ is used to denote the ElemRank of an element v (for notational convenience, we set $e(v)$ of a value node v to be 0). d_1, d_2, and d_3 are the probabilities of navigating through hyperlinks, forward containment edges, and reverse containment edges, respectively. $N_{de}(v)$ is the number of elements in the XML documents containing the element v. N_e is the total number of XML elements, $N_c(u)$ is the number of subelements of u, and $E = HE \cup CE \cup CE^{-1}$, where CE^{-1} is the set of reverse containment edges.

6.7 Exploit Ontologies and Thesaurus

In information sciences, ontology is a formal representation of a set of concepts within a domain and the relationships between those concepts. It is used to define the domain and to reason about its properties [84]. In medical informatics, ontologies constitute a structured list of concepts and the relationships between concepts, typically prepared by an expert or panel of experts.

Medical ontologies play an important role in describing the domain, by identifying the set of concepts that belong to the specific domain and connecting these concepts with semantic relationships that clearly describe the interaction between concepts. They also help in the process of term disambiguation. Many terms in the domain are used to refer to the same concept, and the use of ontologies leverages this problem by establishing relationships that can clarify ambiguity conflicts.

A sample ontology fragment is depicted in Figure 6.7. This fragment from the SNOMED CT [4] ontology captures the concept "Asthma" and some of the other concepts that are associated (related) to it in this domain.

In terms of IR, ontologies, dictionaries, and thesauri can be used to improve the quality of the results in several ways. A common technique is to perform query expansion using the information described in the ontology to find related concepts to reformulate the original query. Various query expansion strategies (e.g., [85]) have been proposed for general as well as biological documents search. For instance, the Query Execution Engine Framework [86] uses the unified medical language system (UMLS) ontology to suggest additional terms. Theobald [87], and Schenkel et al. [88, 89] propose a method to assign weights on the ontology edges by comparing the distributions of the contents of the two nodes and of their combination on a very large dataset such as the Web, where the ontological associations are exploited by expanding the XXL query. Kim and Kong [90] and Kim et al. [91] expand the query by matching the ontology to the document DTD. The above techniques are proposed for structured XML queries.

The Essie search engine [92] also performs query expansion based on domain ontologies. This search engine uses query expansion to produce a set of search phrases that are used later to identify potentially relevant documents. It is noteworthy that, in general, query expansion techniques increase the recall of IR systems, but may sacrifice the precision.

In the specific case of EHRs, unique opportunities arise since EHR documents routinely contain references to external dictionary and ontology sources through numeric codes, as shown in Figure 6.3. Hence, it is no longer enough to answer a query considering the EHR in isolation, as is done by all previous work on information discovery on XML documents. In this setting, the query keywords may refer to text in the EHR or an ontology that is connected to the EHR through a code reference. For example, the query keyword "appendicitis" may not be present in the document but its code might be present, so we need to go to the ontology and search for the query keyword there.

A novel related technique presented by Farfán et al. [93, 94] makes use of ontological definitions to allow the execution of semantic search on the XML EHR documents. By doing so, it is no longer required to have an exact match between keywords in the query and in the document, but it can make use of the domain ontology to infer a semantic relationship between keywords in the query and terms in the document. This allows returning more results that would otherwise not be returned with an exact match requirement. In this case, it is important to assign an appropriate value to each of the relations present in the ontologies. Stricter and stronger relations in the ontology should intuitively have a higher weight. Likewise, the direction of the edges has to be taken into consideration. For instance, following "Is A" edges specializes and restricts the search on one direction, but generalize in the other direction, with the risk of returning imprecise terms.

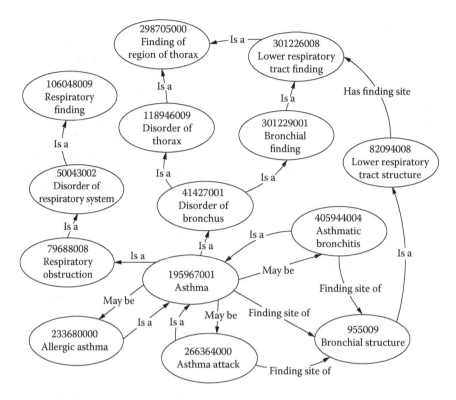

FIGURE 6.7
Ontology fragment sample. This image depicts the concepts associated with the term "Asthma" in the SNOMED CT ontology.

6.8 Other Query Models

Thus far, we have assumed that the query is expressed as a list of keywords. However, there are also other interesting query models in the health domain. These querying paradigms are still in their infancy and further research is necessary.

6.8.1 EHR as Query—Find Similar EHRs

An interesting problem for the health sciences is to measure the similarity between patients. A practitioner or researcher may use the data on closely related patients in order to better understand the situation of a current patient. Furthermore, patients could be clustered into groups for various purposes. This alternative query type—using a whole (or part of) EHR document as the query—can be used to find similar EHRs, that is, EHRs of patients with similar history, demographic information, treatments, etc.

To measure the semantic distance between two EHRs, which represent two patients, EHRs must be modeled in a manner that allows distance calculations. For instance, we could view each EHR as a vector, where a dimension is created for each attribute such as gender, age, height, diabetes, blood pressure, etc. Then traditional distance functions such as Euclidean distance (square root of sum of squares of differences of each coordinate) can be applied, after the dimensions have been appropriately normalized. A more elaborate solution could examine the time series and event correlations that may be represented in an EHR. For instance, the hourly temperature reading of a patient can be viewed as a time series. Time series comparison methodologies (e.g., [95]) may be applied.

6.8.2 EHR as Query—Find Relevant Literature

Another important use for the document-as-query paradigm could be to locate medical literature relevant to the current patient. In this scenario, the EHR application could have a button named "relevant literature" that invokes an information discovery algorithm on PubMed or other medical sources. Price et al. [96] present a first attempt toward this direction, where they extract all MeSH terms (MeSH refers to the U.S. National Library of Medicine's controlled vocabulary used for indexing articles for MEDLINE/PubMed) from an EHR and then query MEDLINE using these terms. The structured format of XML-based EHRs can potentially allow more elaborate searching algorithms where multiple terms that are structurally correlated can construct a single and more focused query on medical literature sources.

Reichert et al. [97] introduce the concept of "infobutton," which links EHRs to bibliographic resources. The laboratory tests or medications are manually annotated with LOINC terms and then linked with electronic medical records using these LOINC terms. SmartQuery [96] extract MeSH terms from an electronic medical record and presents them to the user. The user can mark which of these terms he/she thinks are important and then a query is generated and submitted to multiple content sources such as PubMed. The top answers from each source are returned.

The early work of Cimino [97] identifies three subproblems in order to link patient records to bibliographic resources: (1) identify the user's question, (2) identify the appropriate information source, and (3) compose retrieval strategy. They manually build a set of predefined generic queries and instantiate using the MeSH (or other UMLS) terms found at the EHR. Then, each type of query is manually mapped to an information source.

The above systems do not support an automatic way to select which are the most appropriate (important) keywords for this patient, as opposed to other similar patients. Also, if a user selects a particular portion of an EHR, the rest of the EHR could be used as the query context.

6.9 Evaluation of Quality

To evaluate the quality of the results of a search engine, precision and recall are the most popular metrics. The quality of the results is evaluated based on the relevancy of the retrieved items. Evaluating IR systems is inherently difficult because *relevancy* of the retrieved documents from a human stand-point is (1) *subjective* (depends on the specific user's judgment), (2) *situational* (relates to the user's needs), (3) *cognitive* (depends on human perception and behavior), and (4) *dynamic* (changes over time). Evaluating IR systems generally requires one or more human experts to exhaustively label the relevant documents in the document collection for each query being evaluated. We next present the precision and recall metrics.

Precision is the fraction of the documents retrieved that are relevant to the user's information need.

$$\text{Precision} = \frac{\text{No. of relevant documents retrieved}}{\text{Total no. of retrieved documents}}$$

Recall is the fraction of relevant documents that are successfully retrieved.

$$\text{Recall} = \frac{\text{No. of relevant documents retrieved}}{\text{Total no. of relevant documents}}$$

A search engine with both high precision and high recall is considered good. It is trivial to achieve a recall rate of 100% by returning all documents in response to any query. Therefore, recall alone is not enough; however, one also needs to measure the number of nonrelevant documents, for example, by computing the precision.

Precision/recall measures have a few drawbacks. The number of irrelevant documents in the collection is not taken into account. Recall is undefined when there are no relevant documents in the collection and precision is undefined when no document is retrieved by the IR system. There is another measure, called *fallout*, which addresses these drawbacks by measuring the proportion of nonrelevant documents that are retrieved, out of all available nonrelevant documents.

$$\text{Fallout rate} = \frac{\text{No. of nonrelevant documents retrieved}}{\text{Total no. of nonrelevant documents}}$$

In binary classification, fallout is closely related to specificity. More precisely, fallout = 1 − specificity.

Fallout can be viewed as the probability that a nonrelevant document is retrieved by the query. It is trivial to achieve a fallout rate of 0% by returning zero documents in response to any query.

In the case of XML documents, where a fragment is returned as an answer instead of the whole document, the precision/recall metrics need to be adjusted to penalize search systems that output exceedingly large (and hence, not specific) XML fragments. Furthermore, the overlap between the returned XML fragments must be taken into consideration. Kazai et al. [98] present precision/recall metrics for XML fragments, wherein a system is penalized if it outputs the same (relevant) XML element in multiple result fragments.

Accuracy [99] is the degree of closeness of a measured or calculated quantity to its actual (true) value. Accuracy indicates proximity to the true value, precision to the repeatability or reproducibility of the measurement. Accuracy is closely related to precision, also called reproducibility or repeatability, the degree to which further measurements or calculations show the same or similar results. Accuracy is the proportion of true results (both true positives and true negatives) in a population.

$$\text{Accuracy} = (\text{No. of true positives} + \text{No. of true negatives}) /$$

$$(\text{No. of true positives} + \text{No. of false positives}$$

$$+ \text{No. of true negatives} + \text{No. of false negatives})$$

An accuracy of 100% means that the test correctly identifies all sick and healthy people.

Precision and recall are popular in IR, but are not common in other sciences such as medicine. Instead, in medicine we use specificity and sensitivity, which are related to precision and recall.

Sensitivity [100] measures the proportion of actual positives that are correctly identified as such (i.e., the percentage of sick people who are identified as having the condition). In binary classification, recall is called sensitivity. Thus, it can be viewed as the probability that a relevant document is retrieved by the query. Specificity measures the proportion of negatives that are correctly identified (i.e., the percentage of healthy people who are identified as not having the condition). Specificity is sometimes confused with precision, because both terms refer to the fraction of returned positives that are true positives. The distinction is critical when the classes are of different sizes. A test with very high specificity can have very low precision if there are far more true negatives than true positives, and vice versa. Sensitivity (also called recall rate) and specificity are statistical measures of the performance of a binary classification test.

$$\text{Sensitivity} = (\text{No. of true positives})/(\text{No. of true positives} + \text{No. of false negatives})$$

$$\text{Specificity} = (\text{No. of true negatives})/(\text{No. of true negatives} + \text{No. of false positives})$$

For clarity, the following table and the quality evaluation measures are rewritten.

	Relevant Documents	Irrelevant Documents
Retrieved documents	A (true positives)	B (false positives)
Not retrieved documents	C (false negatives)	D (true negatives)

$$\text{Recall} = \text{Sensitivity} = (A)/(A + C)$$

$$\text{Specificity} = (D)/(D + B); \text{Precision} = (A)/(A + B)$$

$$\text{Accuracy} = (A + D)/(A + B + C + D)$$

Ranked lists. The above metrics assume that the answer of a query is a set of results. In reality, since searching is a fuzzy process, the results are a ranked list. Two ranked lists—for example, the returned list to the user's ideal list—are typically compared using list distance metrics such as Kendall tau or Spearman's footrule [101, 102]. These measures are 0 when the two lists are identical and take their maximum value if the two lists have the elements in reverse order. Recently, these measures have been extended for top k lists, which may not contain the same set of results [103].

6.10 Chapter Summary

In this chapter, we introduced the problem of effectively searching EHRs. We discuss the key challenges in searching EHRs in XML format introduced by the unique domain characteristics of EHRs. We present the concepts of proximity search and authority flow search, which discover how the query keywords are associated in an EHR and what elements are most relevant to the query keywords, respectively. The role of biomedical ontologies is also discussed as well as the opportunities they present to improve the quality of EHR search. Finally, we discussed query models other than the standard keyword retrieval models and presented several quality evaluation measures.

References

1. Health Level Seven Group. http://www.hl7.org/, 2007.
2. HL7 Clinical Document Architecture, Release 2.0. http://lists.hl7.org/read/attachment/61225/1/CDA-doc%20version.pdf, 2007.
3. HL7 Reference Information Model. 2007. http://www.hl7.org/library/data-model/RIM/C30204/rim.htm.
4. U.S. National Library of Medicine. 2004. SNOMED Clinical Terms® (SNOMED CT). http://www.nlm.nih.gov/research/umls/Snomed/snomed_main.html.
5. Logical Observation Identifiers Names and Codes (LOINC). http://www.regenstrief.org/medinformatics/loinc/, 2006.
6. RxNorm. 2007. United States National Library of Medicine. http://www.nlm.nih.gov/research/umls/rxnorm/index.html.
7. Buckley, C., Salton, G., and Allan, J. 1993. Automatic retrieval with locality information using SMART. In *Proceedings of the First Text REtrieval Conference (TREC-1)*, pp. 59–72. NIST Special Publication, 500-207.
8. Rocchio, J. J. 1971. Relevance feedback in information retrieval. In *The SMART Retrieval System—Experiments in Automatic Document Processing*, G. Salton, ed., pp. 313–323, Englewood Cliffs, NJ: Prentice Hall.
9. Salton, G., ed. 1971. *The SMART Retrieval System—Experiments in Automatic Document Retrieval*. Englewood Cliffs, NJ: Prentice Hall.
10. Salton, G., Wong, A., and Yang, C. S. 1975. A vector space model for information retrieval. *Communications of the ACM*, 18(11):613–620.
11. Salton, G., and Buckley, C. 1988. Term-weighting approaches in automatic text retrieval. *Information Processing and Management* 24(5):513–523.
12. Robertson, S. E. 1997. The probabilistic ranking principle in IR. *Journal of Documentation* 33:294–304.
13. Harman, D. K. 1993. Overview of the first Text REtrieval Conference (TREC-1). In *Proceedings of the First Text REtrieval Conference (TREC-1)*, pp. 1–20. NIST Special Publication 500-207, March.
14. Singhal, A. 2001. Modern information retrieval: a brief overview. Google. *IEEE Data Engineering Bulletin* 24(4):35–43.
15. Salton, G., and McGill, M. J. 1983. *Introduction to Modern Information Retrieval*. New York, NY: McGraw Hill Book Co.
16. Savoy, J. 1992. Bayesian inference networks and spreading activation in hypertext systems. *Information Processing and Management* 28(3):389–406.
17. Brin, S., and Page, L. 1998. The anatomy of a large-scale hypertextual web search engine. *Computer Networks* 30(1–7):107–117.
18. Haveliwala, T. 2002. Topic-sensitive PageRank. In *Proceedings of the 11th World Wide Web Conference (WWW)*, Honolulu, ACM Press.
19. Kleinberg, J. M. 1999. Authoritative sources in a hyperlinked environment. *Journal of the ACM* 46(5):604–632.
20. Balmin, A., Hristidis, V., and Papakonstantinou, Y. 2004. ObjectRank: authority-based keyword search in databases. In *Proceedings of the 30th international conference on Very Large Data Bases*.

21. Guo, L., Shao, F., Botev, C., and Shanmugasundaram, J. 2003. XRANK: ranked keyword search over XML documents. In *Proceedings of ACM SIGMOD International Conference on Management of Data*.

22. Huang, A., Xue, Q., and Yang, J. 2003. TupleRank and implicit relationship discovery in relational databases. In *Proceedings of the International Conference on Web-Age Information Management*, pp. 445–457.

23. Cohen, S., Kanza, Y., Kogan, Y., Nutt, W., Sagiv, Y., and Serebrenik, A. 2002. EquiX: a search and query language for XML. *Journal of the American Society for Information Science and Technology*, 53(6):454–466.

24. Carmel, D., Maarek, Y. S., Mandelbrod, M., Mass, Y., and Soffer, A. 2003. Searching XML documents via XML fragments. In *Proceedings of SIGIR*, CACM, pp. 151–158.

25. Fuhr, N., and Großjohann, K. 2001. XIRQL: a query language for information retrieval in XML documents. In *Proceedings of the 24th Annual International ACM SIGIR Conference on Research and Development in Information Retrieval*.

26. Hristidis, V., Koudas, N., Papakonstantinou, Y., and Srivastava, D. 2006. Keyword proximity search in XML trees. *IEEE Transactions on Knowledge and Data Engineering* 18(4):525–539.

27. Hristidis, V., Papakonstantinou, Y., and Balmin, A. 2003. Keyword proximity search on XML graphs. In *Proceedings of the 19th International Conference on Data Engineering ICDE*.

28. Li, Y., Yu, C., and Jagadish, H. V. 2004. Schema-free XQuery. In *Proceedings of the Conference on Very Large Data Bases Conference*.

29. Xu, Y., and Papakonstantinou, Y. 2005. Efficient keyword search for smallest LCAs in XML databases. In *Proceedings of SIGMOD 2005*.

30. Cohen, S., Mamou, J., Kanza, Y., and Sagiv, Y. 2003. XSEarch: a semantic search engine for XML. In *Proceedings of the 29th International Conference on Very Large Data Bases*.

31. Cohen, S., Kanza, Y., and Kimelfeld, B. 2005. Interconnection semantics for keyword search in XML. In *Proceedings of the CIKM*, pp. 389–396.

31a. Li, G., Ooi, B. C., Feng, J., Wang, J., and Zhou, L. 2008. EASE: efficient and adaptive keyword search on unstructured, semi-structured and structured data. In *Proceedings of the 35th SIGMOD International Conference on Management of Data*, pp. 681–694.

32. Aguilera, V., Cluet, S., and Wattez, F. 2001. Xyleme query architecture. In *Proceedings of the 10th World Wide Web Conference*, Hong Kong.

33. Bohm, K., Aberer, K., Neuhold, E. J., and Yang, X. 1997. Structured document storage and refined declarative and navigational access mechanisms in HyperStorM. *VLDB Journal* 6(4):296–311.

34. Brown, L. J., Consens, M. P., Davis, I. J., Palmer, C. R., and Tompa, F. W. 1998. A structured text ADT for object-relational databases. *Theory and Practice of Object Systems* 4(4):227–244.

35. Florescu, D., Kossmann, D., and Manolescu, I. 2000. Integrating keyword search into XML query processing. *International Journal of Computer and Telecommunications Networking* 33(1):119–135.

36. Schmidt, A., Kersten, M., and Windhouwer, M. 2001. Querying XML documents made easy: nearest concept queries. In *Proceedings of the ICDE Conference*.

37. Christophides, V., Abiteboul, S., Cluet, S., and Schollt, M. 1994. From structured documents to novel query facilities. In *Proceedings of the 1994 ACM SIGMOD Conference*, Minneapolis, MN.

38. Dao, T., Sacks-Davis, R., and Thom, J. 1997. An indexing scheme for structured documents and their implementation. *Conference on Database Systems for Advanced Applications*.

39. Lee, Y. K., Yoo, S. J., Yoon, K., and Berra, P. B. 1996. Index structures for structured documents. In *Proceedings of the 1st ACM International Conference on Digital Libraries*, pp. 91–99.

40. Agrawal, S., Chaudhuri, S., and Das, G. 2002. DBXplorer: A System for Keyword-Based Search over Relational Databases. In *Proceedings of the 18th International Conference on Data Engineering ICDE*.

41. Hristidis, V., and Papakonstantinou, Y. 2002. DISCOVER: keyword search in relational databases. In *Proceedings of the 28th international conference on Very Large Data Bases*.

42. Bhalotia, G., Nakhe, C., Hulgeri, A., Chakrabarti, S., and Sudarshan, S. 2002. Keyword searching and browsing in databases using BANKS. In *Proceedings of the 18th International Conference on Data Engineering ICDE*.

43. Dar, S., Entin, G., Geva, S., and Palmon, E. 1998. DTL's DataSpot: database exploration using plain language. In *Proceedings of the VLDB Conference*, pp. 645–649.

44. Goldman, R., Shivakumar, N., Venkatasubramanian, S., and Garcia-Molina, H. 1998. Proximity search in databases. In *Proceedings of the 24th International Conference on Very Large Data Bases*, New York, NY, pp. 26–37.

45. Chakrabarti, S., Joshi, M., and Tawde, V. 2001. Enhanced topic distillation using text, markup, tags and hyperlinks. In *Proceedings of the SIGIR Conference*, pp. 208–216.

46. Barg, M., and Wong, R. 2001. Structural proximity searching for large collections of semi-structured data. In *Proceedings of the 2001 ACM CIKM International Conference on Information and Knowledge Management*, pp. 175–182, Atlanta, GA, USA: ACM Press.

47. Kanza, Y., and Sagiv, Y. 2001. Flexible queries over semistructured data. In *Proceedings of the 20th Symposium on Principles of Database Systems*, pp. 40–51, Santa Barbara, California, USA: ACM Press, May.

48. Myaeng, S. H., Jang, D. H., Kim, M. S., and Zhoo, Z. C. 1998. A flexible model for retrieval of SGML documents. In *Proceedings of the SIGIR Conference*.

49. Theobald, A., and Weikum, G. 2002. The index-based XXL search engine for querying XML data with relevance ranking. In *Proceedings of the 8th International Conference on Extending Database Technology, EDBT 2002*, pp. 477–495, Prague, Czech Republic, Springer-Verlag.

50. Luk, R., Chan, A., Dillon, T., and Leong, H. V. 2000. A survey of search engines for XML documents. In *Proceedings of the SIGIR Workshop on XML and IR*, Athens.

50a. Fikes, R., Hayes, P. J., and Horrocks, I. 2004. OWL-QL—A language for deductive query answering on the semantic web. *Journal of Web Semantics*, 2(1): 19–29.

50b. Prud'Hommeaux, E. and Seaborne, A. 2006. SPARQL Query Language for RDF, W3C Working Draft. http://www.w3.org/TR/rdf-sparq-l-query/

51. Pfeiffer, K. P., Göbel, G., and Leitner, K. 2003. Demand for intelligent search tools in medicine and health care. In *Intelligent Search on XML Data*, LNCS 2818, pp. 5–18. Berlin: Springer-Verlag, 2003.

52. Inokuchi, A., Takeda, K., Inaoka, N., and Wakao, F. 2007. MedTAKMI-CDI: interactive knowledge discovery for clinical decision intelligence. *IBM Systems Journal* 46(1):115–134.

53. Maron, M. E., and Kuhns, J. L. 1960. On relevance, probabilistic indexing and information retrieval. *Journal of the ACM* 7:216–244.

54. Sparck Jones, K. 1972. A statistical interpretation of term specificity and its application in retrieval. *Journal of Documentation* 28:11–21.

55. Singhal, A., Buckley, C., and Mitra, M. 1996. Pivoted document length normalization. In *Proceedings of ACM SIGIR'96*, New York: Association for Computing Machinery, pp. 21–29.

56. Salton, G., and Buckley, C. 1999. Improving retrieval performance by relevance feedback. *Journal of the American Society for Information Science* 41(4):288–297.

57. Buckley, C., Salton, G., and Allan, J. 1994. The effect of adding relevance information in a relevance feedback environment. In *Proceedings of the 17th International Conference on Research and Development in Information Retrieval SIGIR*.

58. Ruthven, I., and Lalmas, M. 2003. A survey on the use of relevance feedback for information access systems. *The Knowledge Engineering Review* 18(2):94–145.

59. Hristidis, V., Farfán, F., Burke, R. P., Rossi, A. F., and White, J. A. 2008. Challenges for information discovery on electronic medical records. In *Next Generation of Data Mining*, ed. H. Kargupta, J. Han, P. S. Yu, R. Motwani, and V. Kumar, Chapman & Hall/CRC Data Mining, and Knowledge Discovery Series.

60. Amer-Yahia, S., Botev, C., and Shanmugasundaram, J. 2004. TeXQuery: a full-text search extension to XQuery. In *Proceedings of the 13th International Conference on World Wide Web*.

61. Xu, J., Lu, J., Wang, W., and Shi, B. 2006. Effective keyword search in XML documents based on MIU. In *Proceedings of the 11th International Conference of Database Systems for Advanced Applications DASFAA*.

61a. Salton, G. and Buckley, C. 1995. Optimization of relevance feedback weights. In *Proceedings of ACM Special Interest Group in Information Retrieval (SIGIR)*.

62. Mitchell, T. M. 1997. *Machine Learning*. New York, NY: McGraw-Hill Higher Education.

63. Salton, G. 1989. *Automatic Text Processing: The Transformation, Analysis, and Retrieval of Information by Computer*. Reading, MA: Addison Wesley.

64. Baeza-Yates, R., and Ribeiro-Neto, B. 1999. *Modern Information Retrieval*. New York, NY: ACM Press.

65. Hristidis, V., Gravano, L., and Papakonstantinou, Y. 2003. Efficient IR-style keyword search over relational databases. In *Proceedings of the 29th International Conference on Very Large Data Bases*.

66. Dong, X., Halevy, A., and Madhavan, J. 2005. Reference reconciliation in complex information spaces. In *Proceedings of the 2005 ACM SIGMOD International Conference on Management of Data*.

67. Hernández, M. A., and Stolfo, S. J. 1995. The merge/purge problem for large databases. In *Proceedings of the 1995 ACM SIGMOD International Conference on Management of Data SIGMOD*, 1995.

68. McCallum, A. K., Nigam, K., and Ungar, L. H. 2000. Efficient clustering of High-dimensional data sets with application to reference matching. In *Proceedings of the Sixth ACM SIGKDD International Conference on Knowledge Discovery and Data Mining*.

69. McCallum, A., and Wellner, B. 2003. Toward conditional models of identity uncertainty with application to proper noun coreference. In *IJCAI Workshop on Information Integration on the Web IIWEB*.

70. Sarawagi, S., and Bhamidipaty, A. 2002. Interactive deduplication using active learning. In *Proceedings of the 8th ACM SIGKDD International Conference on Knowledge Discovery and Data Mining SIGKDD*.

71. Tejada, S., Knoblock, C., and Minton, S. 2002. Learning domain-independent string transformation weights for high accuracy object identification. In *Proceedings of the 8th ACM SIGKDD International Conference on Knowledge Discovery and Data Mining KDD*.

72. Winkler, W. E. 1999. The State of Record Linkage and Current Research Problems. Technical report, U.S. Bureau of the Census, Washington, DC, 1999.

73. McCarthy, J. F., and Lehnert, W. G. 1995. Using decision trees for coreference resolution. In *Proceedings of the International Joint Conference on Artificial Intelligence IJCAI*.

74. Ng, V., and Cardie, C. 2002. Improving machine learning approaches to coreference resolution. In *Proceedings of the 40th Annual Meeting of the Association for Computational Linguistics ACL*.

75. Zelenko, D., Aone, C., and Richardella, A. 2003. Kernel methods for relation extraction. *Journal of Machine Learning Research* 3:1083–1106.

76. Elkin, P. L., Brown, S. H., Bauer, B. A. et al. 2005. A controlled trial of automated classification of negation from clinical notes. *BMC Medical Informatics and Decision Making* 5:13.

77. Ceusters, W., and Smith, B. 2005. Tracking referents in electronic health records. In *Proceedings of the 19th International Congress of the European Federation for Medical Informatics MIE*.

78. Li, Y., Yu, C., and Jagadish, H. V. 2004. Schema-Free XQuery. In *Proceedings of the 30th International Conference on Very Large Data Bases*.

79. World Wide Web Consortium. 2006. XQuery and XPath Full-Text Requirements. W3C Working Draft. http://www.w3.org/TR/xmlquery-full-text-requirements/.

80. Richardson, M., and Domingos, P. 2002. The intelligent surfer: probabilistic combination of link and content information in PageRank. *Advances in Neural Information Processing Systems 14*. Cambridge, MA: MIT Press.

81. Hristidis, V., Hwang, H., and Papakonstantinou, Y. 2008. Authority-based keyword search in databases. *ACM Transactions on Database Systems (TODS)* 33(1):1–40.

82. Motwani, R., and Raghavan, P. 1995. *Randomized Algorithms*. London: Cambridge University Press, 1995.

83. Varadarajan, R., Hristidis, V., and Raschid, L. 2008. Explaining and reformulating authority flow queries. In *Proceedings of the 24th International Conference on Engineering, ICDE*, pp. 883–892.

84. Uschold, N. and Gruninger, M. 1996. Ontologies: Principles, methods, and applications. *The Knowledge Engineering Review*, 11, 93–136.
85. Xu, J., and Croft, W. B. 1996. Query expansion using local and global document analysis. In *Proceedings of the Annual ACM SIGIR International Conference on Research and Development in Information Retrieval SIGIR*.
86. Wollersheim, D., and Rahayu, W. J. 2005. Using medical test collection relevance judgements to identify ontological relationships useful for query expansion. In *ICDEW '05: Proceedings of the 21st International Conference on Data Engineering Workshops*, Washington, DC, USA: IEEE Computer Society, p. 1160.
87. Theobald, A. 2003. An ontology for domain-oriented semantic similarity search on XML data. In *BTW, ser. LNI*, G. Weikum, H. Schoning, and E. Rahm, eds., vol. 26. GI, pp. 217–226.
88. Schenkel, R., Theobald, A., and Weikum, G. 2003. Ontology-enabled XML Search. In *Intelligent Search on XML Data, Ser. Lecture Notes in Computer Science*, H. M. Blanken, T. Grabs, H.-J. Schek, R. Schenkel, and G. Weikum, eds., vol. 2818, pp. 119–131. Berlin: Springer.
89. Schenkel, R., Theobald, A., and Weikum, G. 2005. Semantic similarity search on semistructured data with the XXL search engine. *Information Retrieval* 8(4):521–545.
90. Kim, M. S., and Kong, Y.-H. 2005. Ontology-DTD matching algorithm for efficient XML query. In *FSKD (2), Series Lecture Notes in Computer Science*, L. Wang and Y. Jin, eds., vol. 3614. Springer, pp. 1093–1102, 2005.
91. Kim, M. S., Kong, Y.-H., and Jeon, C. W. 2006. Remote-specific XML query mobile agents. In *DEECS, Series Lecture Notes in Computer Science*, J. Lee, J. Shim, S. Goo Lee, C. Bussler, and S. S. Y. Shim, eds., vol. 4055. Springer, pp. 143–151, 2006.
92. Ide, N. C., Loane, R. F., and Demner-Fushman, D. 2007. Essie: a concept-based search engine for structured biomedical text. *Journal of the American Medical Informatics Association* 14(3):253–263.
93. Farfán, F., Hristidis, V., Ranganathan, A., and Burke, R. P. 2008. Ontology-aware search on XML-based electronic medical records. In *Proceedings of the IEEE International Conference on Data Engineering ICDE*, Poster paper.
94. Farfán, F., Hristidis, V., Ranganathan, A., and Weiner, M. 2009. XOntoRank: ontology-aware search of electronic medical records. In *Proceedings of the IEEE International Conference on Data Engineering (ICDE)*.
95. Kalpakis, K., Gada, D., and Puttagunta, V. 2001. Distance measures for effective clustering of ARIMA time-series. In *Proceedings of the IEEE International Conference on Data Mining ICDM*.
96. Price, S. L., Hersh, W. R., Olson, D. D., and Embi, P. J. 2002. SmartQuery: context-sensitive links to medical knowledge sources from the electronic patient record. In *Proceedings of the 2002 Annual AMIA Symposium*, pp. 627–631.
97. Reichert, J. C., Glasgow, M., Narus, S. P., and Clayton, P. D. 2002. Using LOINC to link an EMR to the pertinent paragraph in a structured reference knowledge base. In *Proceedings of the AMIA Symposium*.
97. Cimino, J. J. 1996. Linking patient information systems to bibliographic resources. *Methods of Information in Medicine* 35:122–126.

98. Kazai, G., Lalmas, M., and de Vries, A. P. 2004. The overlap problem in content-oriented XML retrieval evaluation. In *Proceedings of the 27th Annual International ACM SIGIR Conference on Research and Development in Information Retrieval SIGIR.*

99. Taylor, J. R. 1982. *An Introduction to Error Analysis: The Study of Uncertainties in Physical Measurements.* University Science Books, pp. 128–129.

100. Altman, D. G. and Bland, J. M. 1994. Statistics notes: Diagnostic tests 1: Sensitivity and specificity. *British Medical Journal*, 308: 1552.

101. Fagin, R., Kumar, R., Mahdian, M., Sivakumar, D., and Vee, E. 2004. Comparing and aggregating rankings with ties. *ACM Symposium on Principles on Database Systems (PODS '04)*, pp. 47–58.

102. Fagin, R., Kumar, R. Mahdian, M., Sivakumar, D., and Vee, E. 2006. Comparing partial rankings. *SIAM Journal on Discrete Mathematics* 20(3):628–648.

103. Fagin, R., Kumar, R., and Sivakumar, D. 2003. Comparing Top-*k* lists. *SIAM Journal on Discrete Mathematics* 17:134–160.

7

Data Mining and Knowledge Discovery on EHRs

Donald J. Berndt, Monica Chiarini Tremblay, and Stephen L. Luther

CONTENTS

7.1 Introduction

Data mining, also referred to as knowledge discovery from data, is a multidisciplinary field. The concepts and techniques used in data mining are a convergence of machine learning (ML) and artificial intelligence, database systems, and statistics (we describe this in more detail in the next section). This chapter focuses on the application of data mining techniques to the electronic health record (EHR). These techniques are characterized by an inductive approach to uncovering patterns in data and are examples of ML, or—more specifically—techniques for knowledge discovery in databases.

Knowledge discovery and ML approaches are often referred to as "discovery science" and have shifted the traditional scientific model from hypothesis testing to hypothesis generation. The traditional investigative cycle starts with hypothesis formulation and proceeds through data collection, experimentation, and analysis (with any findings guiding subsequent work). Knowledge discovery is largely data-driven, starting with the many existing large-scale data collections such as EHRs. The process continues through experimentation or model building within a space of possible hypotheses, instantiation of a hypothesis, and verification of the results.

Although biologists have historically relied on testable and falsifiable scientific hypotheses for empirical evidence, the abundance of digital information has allowed for the emergence of new approaches for generating and testing hypotheses. Developments in text mining and hypothesis discovery systems are based on the early work of Swanson, a mathematician and information scientist. In the 1980s, Don Swanson developed the concept of "undiscovered public knowledge":

> Imagine that the pieces of a puzzle are independently designed and created, and that, when retrieved and assembled, they then reveal a pattern—undesigned, unintended, and never before seen, yet a pattern that commands interest and invites interpretation. So it is, I claim, that independently created pieces of knowledge can harbor an unseen, unknown, and unintended pattern, and so it is that the world of recorded knowledge can yield genuinely new discoveries. (Swanson, 1986b)

Swanson went on to publish several examples in which two disjoint literatures (i.e., sets of articles having no papers in common, no authors in common, and few cross citations) nevertheless held complementary pieces of knowledge that, when brought together, made compelling and testable predictions about potential therapies for human disorders (Swanson, 1986b, 1988). Besides publishing more predictions arising from this data mining approach (Swanson, 1993; Smalheiser and Swanson, 1994, 1996a, 1996b, 1998a), Swanson and his colleague, Neil Smalheiser, partially automated a systematic computer-assisted search strategy method called "Arrowsmith" (Swanson and Smalheiser, 1997, 1999; Smalheiser and Swanson, 1998b). This approach is credited with moving biology to a data-driven "big science" and for driving discoveries in climatology and astronomy (Smalheiser et al., 2006).

The potential of knowledge discovery in clinical science is already widely recognized. In this chapter, we illustrate several classification and predictive data mining techniques applied to the EHR, and we include examples from recent studies:

- Naïve Bayes classifier applied to the problem of embryo selection (Morales et al., 2008)
- Decision tree techniques to develop and validate a measure of risk stratification for in-hospital mortality due to acute decomposition heart failure (ADHF) (Fonarow et al., 2005)
- Neural networks to predict which patients would experience early failure of peritoneal dialysis (Tangri et al., 2008)
- Support vector machines (SVMs) to predict the bleeding source and identify the cohort among patients with acute gastrointestinal bleeding (GIB) who required urgent intervention, including endoscopy (Chu et al., 2008)
- Association rule mining to create rules about the co-occurrence of pathology tests in data collected in the health insurance industry, specifically, an episode (claims) database (Viveros et al., 1996)
- Association rule mining used to confirm rules used by an expert system that aided in heart disease diagnosis and to discover new rules in order to enrich the expert system's knowledge (Ordonez et al., 2000)
- Clustering as a data preprocessing step
- Text mining to identify fall-related injuries in the elderly (Tremblay et al., 2005)

7.2 Related Work and Further Readings

Data mining's foundation is provided by statistics, and has been driven by the natural evolution of information technologies. In this section, we describe the disciplines from which data mining has evolved.

7.2.1 Machine Learning

Learning by machines is defined by Mitchell (1997) as

> A computer program is said to *learn* from experience E with respect to some class of tasks T and performance measure P, if its performance at tasks in T, as measured by P, improves with experience E.

A less theoretical, but easier to understand definition can be found in Wikipedia (http://en.wikipedia.org/wiki/Machine_learning):

> As a broad subfield of artificial intelligence, machine learning is concerned with the design and development of algorithms and techniques that allow computers to 'learn.' At a general level, there are two types of learning: inductive and deductive. Inductive machine learning methods extract rules and patterns out of massive data sets.

In other words, inductive ML methods do not assume fixed theories, or rule sets, but rather rely on data—preferably massive volumes of data—to induce patterns, mappings, classifications, clusters, and other useful analyses, complementing traditional deductive approaches. In essence, ML algorithms search for mapping functions that relate a set of input data elements (typically called a feature set) to corresponding output variables while minimizing prediction errors (Bishop, 2006).

ML algorithms can be used to accomplish a variety of tasks including clustering, classification, and prediction. Often, the precise boundaries are blurred, but it is useful to consider several points along a task continuum. Classification tasks try to place cases into a known set of categories, with the simplest situation being a binary classification. A clinical example would be to classify patients as having a specific mental illness, such as posttraumatic stress disorder, or not. A multicategory classification might focus on a more complex task, such as assessing the severity level or stage of an illness. Finally, predictive tasks look into the future, applying a model to new data and making a qualitative classification or even a quantitative estimation. For instance, given training data on healthcare utilization or cost, a predictive task may seek to estimate utilization rates for future patients receiving specific treatments. ML algorithms provide inductive, data-driven approaches to a wide variety of tasks.

7.2.2 Statistics

For some time, statisticians equated data mining and ML to data dredging or fishing, noting that if sufficient time was spent trawling through data, patterns could be found, but the patterns would be due to random fluctuations in the data (Hand, 1998). This initial hesitation by statisticians is understandable. Statisticians usually concern themselves with analyzing small amounts of primary data, which they have collected with an objective in mind (hypothesis testing and probabilistic inference). Data mining, on the other hand, generally analyzes large amounts of secondary data, which from a statistician's perspective amounts to exploratory data analysis (Hand, 1998).

However, statisticians such as Hand (1998) and Friedman et al. (1997) contended about the importance of recognizing data mining as a field and the possibility that statisticians could make tremendous contributions to the data mining field. Today, many researchers in statistics are deeply involved in the development and improvement of data mining techniques. In fact, the fields of data mining, inference, and prediction are often coupled together and referred to as "statistical learning" by statistics scholars (Hastie et al., 2003). In industry, the job title "statistician" and "data mining analyst" are often synonymous.

Modern data mining incorporates many statistical techniques. The feature selection and extraction task, which includes the visualization of data, the selection of attributes, and the investigation of outliers, takes advantage of techniques originating in statistics such as correlation analysis, histograms, and principal component analysis. Additionally, statistical tests are often used in many ML algorithms to correct models so they do not "over fit" the data, and finally, statistical techniques are used to evaluate data mining models and to express their significance (Witten and Frank, 2005).

7.2.3 Databases and Data Warehouses

Advanced data analytics have been largely driven by the systematic evolution that has occurred in database systems since the 1960s. Originally, a database system's main role was that of data collection and database creation. Database systems continued to grow in both size and sophistication, and the focus shifted toward improved data management. Database systems included not only data storage and retrieval, but also sophisticated transaction processing techniques and technologies. One of the most important technological advances was the move from programming-intensive database systems to the relational model that provided an elegant theoretical foundation for fundamental database operations (Codd, 1983; Date, 2000). Relational database systems support declarative query languages such as the structured query language (SQL), making databases much easier to use for many data management tasks. Today, powerful and affordable computer hardware technologies are used to house large data warehouses that are populated with data from multiple heterogeneous sources, such as data repositories from transactional systems and the Internet. Data warehousing technologies include processes to clean the data, integrate it, and analyze it with online analytical processing (OLAP) tools.

OLAP is a technology designed to support browsing through large volumes of cases in a data warehouse environment (Kimball et al., 2008). This is human-in-the-loop data mining and pattern discovery, rather than the more automated ML techniques that are covered in the remainder of the chapter. However, data mining projects typically span a wide range of activities, from writing simple SQL queries to applying advanced ML algorithms. Understanding the data is one of the most important early activities, and the ability to quickly look through data with a pivot table-style interface, instead of writing individual queries, allows a data miner to consider many simple patterns and learn the idiosyncrasies of the data. Data warehousing tools and OLAP interfaces are fairly mature technologies that provide the infrastructure for subsequent data mining projects. Making use of this infrastructure by navigating and visualizing the data can be an excellent first step in building predictive models, but may also be an appropriate stand-alone technology for decision support. In the healthcare industry, data warehousing and OLAP tools have been successfully applied for planning and decision support in both the private and public sector (Berndt et al., 2003; Tremblay et al., 2007).

7.3 Supervised and Unsupervised Learning

ML algorithms learn by example, using large numbers of individual cases to iteratively construct models. Typically, ML algorithms are characterized as supervised or unsupervised learning methods. Supervised learning approaches use training cases that are labeled with the correct outcome or target variable. A good example would be decision tree algorithms that consider many cases while inductively constructing a decision tree (or rule set) that models patterns in the data (Berry and Linoff, 2004). The requirement for large numbers of correctly labeled training cases can be a challenge in the healthcare sector. At times, the only method of obtaining data sets with adequate quality levels is to pursue expensive and time-consuming medical chart reviews, often with multiple coders. Once a large collection of correctly labeled training cases is available, supervised ML algorithms look at differences between classes, building models that can automatically discriminate among several outcomes. Again, using decision trees as an example, the task might be to classify patients into four risk categories for heart disease. The training cases would need correctly assigned risk categories and the decision tree algorithm would consider each attribute or data element, such as patient age, gender, or laboratory test results, and decide on which element divides the cases into better (more uniform) subgroups with respect to risk. The typical decision tree algorithm makes successive splits, iteratively constructing a complete model as a decision tree.

Unsupervised learning approaches do not require target variables and include methods such as clustering algorithms or association rule mining. These types of ML algorithms simply look for order or patterns in a collection of data elements and are often used to gain some understanding of complex data sets, or even as preprocessing steps in a larger data mining project. Clustering seeks to group similar cases together, while keeping dissimilar cases apart (as defined by quantitative distance measures). Association rule mining (called market basket analysis in the business sector) is used to discover patterns or rules in cases that have many possible data elements (with or without some type of target). These techniques are often applied in the consumer product arena, mining the many baskets of items purchased during store visits. For an EHR-related example, consider a collection of medications for each patient. Are there common patterns in the many groups of medications being prescribed to patients with similar diagnoses?

7.4 Feature Sets and Data Quality

It is useful to consider the type of data available in a typical EHR, including structured data such as administrative items, standardized coding schemes such as the International Classification of Disease Clinical Modifications 9th revision or Diagnostic Related Groups, pharmacy data, laboratory results, as well as unstructured narratives from progress notes and other free text entries. Along with the standardized coding systems themselves, it is also necessary to maintain cross walks that allow users to substitute different hierarchical perspectives. The medical field is one of the few areas to make sustained investments in the development of controlled vocabularies and medical language resources. For instance, the Unified Medical Language System (http://www.nlm.nih.gov/research/umls/) is comprised of a unified vocabulary, metathesaurus, semantic network, and tools to manipulate these resources to foster the development of systems that can utilize medical texts (see the National Library of Medicine). Other resources include medical terminologies such as the Systematized Nomenclature of Medicine and coding systems such as the Logical Observation Identifiers Names and Codes for clinical observations and laboratory results. As a result of these long-term efforts, the medical body of knowledge includes some very interesting resources for use in ML. For many clinical tasks, the best approach is to combine these heterogeneous inputs or feature sets for a single classification or predictive task.

Healthcare data are used for a variety of purposes, administrative data are a central part of the billing process, and detailed patient data are, of course, used for treatment decisions, whereas aggregated data are used for business planning, policy formulation, government regulation, and healthcare research. Not all of these missions are equally well served by data collection efforts. The involvement of clinicians in maintaining and using the electronic medical record directly supports high-quality data collection efforts and effective user interfaces for the delivery of care. The billing requirements associated with specific treatments and procedures, with a direct financial incentive, means these data are also carefully vetted. However, additional information that does not directly relate to billing or may not be critical to short-term clinical decisions is likely to be of lower quality. For instance, some clinically relevant information may be embedded in textual components of the electronic medical record, accessible to clinicians at the point of care, but not easily used in aggregated form for business decisions or healthcare research. In these situations, text mining provides an alternative mechanism for uncovering information that can be explicitly coded, or otherwise included in database queries that aggregate information in support of analysis and decision making.

7.5 The Knowledge Discovery Process

Data mining and knowledge discovery projects involve a complex process of identifying, understanding, and transforming data modeling and evaluation efforts. Naturally, any models that are useful would need to be deployed before making an impact in practice. There are several data mining process frameworks that seek to organize these activities (Fayyad et al., 1996). A widely cited industry framework is the Cross-Industry Standard Process for Data Mining (CRISP-DM; http://www.crisp-dm.org) model. CRISP-DM offers a general model for data/text mining projects, highlighting the key tasks involved. According to the CRISP-DM framework, the life cycle of a knowledge discovery project consists of six phases, but the sequence of the phases is not strictly applied. Moving back and forth between different phases is always required. The process is iterative because the choice of subsequent phases often depends on the outcome of preceding phases. The life cycle begins with business understanding to ground the overall aims of the project, and then moves to data understanding to identify potential inputs and outputs, data quality issues, and potential privacy or security concerns. The third phase, data preparation, involves the extraction of relevant data for a particular modeling effort, data quality assurance, and any transformations required for specific modeling techniques. Typically, the data preparation tasks account for the majority of effort in a data mining project. The fourth phase, data modeling, is the central focus of any knowledge discovery effort and consists of the construction of models based on a variety of techniques, with evaluations (the fifth phase) conducted for all modeling techniques. The final step is deployment so that useful models can be embedded in information systems to support decision-making activities. Although the details of these phases are not crucial to understanding individual ML algorithms, it is important to understand that modeling is only a small, but interesting, part of a data mining project. Many of the most critical challenges involve selecting and formulating an appropriate task, and understanding and preparing the data assets available.

7.6 Data Mining Techniques

In the following section, we outline some of the most widely used supervised and unsupervised data mining techniques. In each section, we use recent examples in the medical informatics area.

7.6.1 Bayes' Theorem and the Naïve Bayes Classifier

One of the most straightforward data mining techniques rests on a foundation of Bayesian reasoning (and the eighteenth century work of Reverend Thomas Bayes). Bayes' theorem provides a method for assessing the likelihood of a hypothesis or outcome based on the prior probability of that outcome, along with the probabilities associated with a series of observations or cases. The cases can be viewed as pieces of evidence that incrementally contribute to the support of alternative hypotheses. This evidence-based perspective makes Bayesian reasoning a natural fit for medical decision making.

Bayes' theorem forms the basis for several ML approaches and provides a more general perspective for understanding other algorithms (see the equation below). The theorem yields a posterior probability $P(h|D)$ given the evidence provided by training data $P(D|h)$ and the prior probability of the hypothesis $P(h)$ for each hypothesis h. Posterior probabilities are statements regarding the most probable hypotheses. The prior probabilities $P(h)$ are statements made using only background knowledge regarding the occurrences of outcomes, or any of the training data items $P(D)$. The conditional probabilities, such as $P(D|h)$, consider the probabilities of the evidentiary data items given a hypothesis.

$$P(h|D) = \frac{P(D|h)P(h)}{P(D)}$$

A helpful exercise is to reflect on the effects of varying the terms in Bayes' theorem. The posterior probability $P(h|D)$ increases as $P(h)$ increases, that is, h is a more commonly occurring hypothesis apart from any supporting data. In addition, increasing the strength of any evidence in the training data $P(D|h)$ will also boost the posterior probability of h given data D. Finally, if the prior probability of the evidence provided by the training data $P(D)$ is fairly common (a high probability value), then it provides a weak case and decreases the posterior probability $P(h|D)$. The term $P(D)$ is independent of hypothesis h and acts as a constant that is omitted (see below).

Consider an example based on a simple medical diagnosis problem (following Mitchell, 1997). There are two competing hypotheses: the patient has cancer or the patient does not have cancer. The data or evidence comes from a laboratory test with either a positive or negative result with respect to the presence of the disease. Assume that the prior probability of invasive cancer is rare at 2.04% from birth to age 39 years for females (as reported in *Cancer Facts & Figures 2008* by the American Cancer Society). The fictitious laboratory test sensitivity and specificity rates result in the following probabilities.

Test/Condition (Diagnosis)	Positive (Cancer)	Negative (Not Cancer)
Positive test	0.98	0.03
Negative test	0.02	0.97

What conclusion should we draw if a patient receives a positive laboratory test result? Applying Bayes' theorem leads to the following two prior probabilities for the diagnostic hypotheses. Despite the positive test, the negative diagnosis is more highly supported using Bayesian reasoning. The posterior probabilities can be normalized so they sum to 1, yielding a 46% (0.1999/(0.1999 + 0.02388) probability of cancer given the positive test and 54% probability of no cancer. This example serves to illustrate the heavy reliance on prior probabilities—in this case, the relative rarity of cancer in young women. Naturally, in a diagnostic situation many pieces of evidence are brought together. In this example, a second positive laboratory test with similar sensitivity and specificity would dramatically change the conclusion, yielding a 96% posterior probability of cancer.

$$P \text{ (Cancer|Postive test)} = (0.98) (0.0204) = 0.01999$$
$$P \text{ (Not cancer|Postive test)} = (0.03) (0.796) = 0.02388$$

The naïve Bayes classifier is a very practical application of Bayes' theorem. The approach is useful whenever the task involves learning from a set of cases described by a conjunction of attribute values and labeled with an outcome (a fairly common problem structure). Despite the simplicity of the approach, naïve Bayes classifiers have compared favorably with techniques such as decision trees and neural networks across a wide range of tasks (Friedman et al., 1997). The naïve or simplifying assumption echoed in the name of the approach is that the probabilities associated with data items in a case can be considered independent. This assumption of conditional independence allows the probability of each data item to be calculated separately and all attribute probabilities to be multiplied together. The assumption of independence also avoids a pitfall with regard to data coverage since there would need to be a very large training data set to reliably represent all the unique attribute value combinations!

Although naïve Bayes classifiers are reasonable data mining methods, they find equal use as data exploration tools. Since the approach considers all pairwise combinations of attribute and target values, the results can be viewed in a number of ways to uncover useful insights. For example, a simple reporting tool can present the correspondence between each input attribute and output attribute. Alternatively, attribute values can be used to filter the data and look at constellations of remaining attributes that describe particular types of cases. Similar attribute selection strategies can be used to investigate the factors differentiating a group of cases from the larger population. Both tabular and graphical exploratory capabilities are often supported. The naïve Bayes classifier algorithms do not require much parameter setting, since the technique requires only basic attribute value counts. Typically, there are a few threshold parameters related to the number of input or output attributes to be considered; the number represents values or states, or some probability cutoffs.

7.6.1.1 An Example of Bayesian Classifiers

Assistive reproductive techniques often result in the development of multiple embryos. For various medical and legal reasons, it may be advisable or necessary to select fewer embryos for transfer and implantation. Typically, this process involves inspection of microscopic embryo images and selection by a clinician based on several somewhat subjective factors. Recasting the problem as a supervised learning task, the data might include embryonic images, possibly preprocessed by a variety of techniques, along with class labels indicating whether the implantation was successful (Morales et al., 2008). Morales et al. (2008) report on the use of Bayesian classifiers applied to the problem of embryo selection. Using an existing image analysis approach, the shape and textural features were extracted from the embryo images based on central moments (invariant with respect to rotation and scaling), yielding 10 image features plus the class label. The resulting data includes 249 cases, with 35 examples of successful implantation and 214 unsuccessful cases. Skewed or unbalanced data sets are quite common and can be handled by stratified sampling to create a more balanced set of cases.

In this study, the authors use receiver operating characteristic (ROC) curves to analyze the performance of several Bayesian classifiers. Naïve Bayes and selective naïve Bayes classifiers, which apply feature selection to remove problematic predictors, rely directly on Bayes' theorem and an assumption of independence. Other algorithms such as seminaïve Bayes, tree augmented naïve (TAN) Bayes, and *k*DB (k-dependence) Bayes consider some dependencies between variables. In all, the authors compared seven different Bayesian classifiers with accuracies from 79% to 91%, finding that the tree augmented naïve and *k*DB Bayesian classifiers topped the list. Finally, the Bayesian classifiers compared favorably with a baseline logistic regression (LG) model. As such, the authors suggest that Bayeisan classifiers might be a useful technology for decision support systems to assist clinicians in the embryo selection process.

7.6.2 Decision Tree Induction

Decision tree induction algorithms are among the most widely used supervised learning techniques. These algorithms construct decision trees by scanning a set of correctly labeled training cases and evaluating each split or decision node based on the available input variables or features. In addition, any resulting tree-based models are easily converted into rule sets. These algorithms are very efficient and produce models in the form of decision trees that are easily interpreted by humans, as well as quickly executed by machines. Basically, a decision tree is a simple flowchart for making a decision with each internal node representing a test on a specific data item or attribute, such as blood pressure, and each leaf node a particular classification or outcome. To arrive at a decision for any unseen case requires the traversal of a single branch or path through the tree starting from the root node and applying each test until a leaf node (and associated outcome) is reached.

There are several widely available implementations of decision tree induction algorithms based on measures of diversity (e.g., Gini index), entropy, or information gain (Quinlan, 1993). These algorithms are available in commercial tools such as SAS Enterprise Miner, as well as open sources tools such as WEKA (Witten and Frank, 2005). Most decision tree induction algorithms are "greedy" algorithms that construct the tree in a recursive top-down approach. At each step, the data item that best divides the cases along a given branch is selected until a leaf node with a known outcome is reached. Some attribute selection measure must be used to pick the "best" attribute at each node and therein lies the major difference between the various induction algorithms. Left unconstrained, the algorithms might keep elongating the branches, dividing the cases into successively smaller subsets, and producing very complex trees. Such complex trees typically overfit the data and are not very good predictors on unseen data. Therefore, several methods of stopping tree construction are used to arrive at reasonably sized trees that are good predictors, such as tree pruning, or stopping rules based on minimum thresholds for leaf node sizes.

As nodes are added to the tree during the induction process, the "best" test or split must be selected from the available data items. This attribute selection measure determines, in large part, the behavior of a decision tree induction algorithm. What are some of the available attribute selection measures? Most of the common attribute selection measures attempt to quantify the disorder or purity of the resulting subsets after a decision node, with respect to the outcomes. Thus, if you are trying to classify severity of illness into one of five categories, the fraction of cases that fall into a subset (or potential leaf node) for a given category is indicative of the quality of the proposed test. If the resulting subset contains a mixture of cases with 95% drawn from a single outcome, it is easy to say with some confidence that cases arriving at such a leaf node should be classified accordingly. However, if the case mixture is muddier, say 50% each of two categories, further tests might be in order. One of the widely used measures is based on information theory (Shannon, 1948) and the insight that it takes more information (or bits) to describe a disorderly situation. Quinlan used this theory to form the basis for attribute selection in the ID3 and subsequent C4.5 (or C5) tree induction algorithms (Quinlan, 1993).

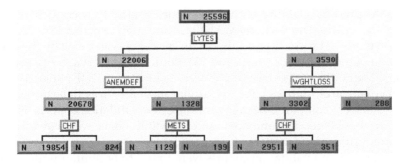

FIGURE 7.1
Example of a decision tree to predict length of stay.

An example decision tree is shown in Figure 7.1. This figure shows the first few levels of a decision tree used to predict length of stay (LOS) in the area of digestive system surgery (Tremblay et al., 2006). For this example, 30 comorbidities were fed into a decision tree using an F test splitting criterion (using SAS Enterprise Miner). The resulting splits select several comorbidity features, including LYTES (fluid and electrolyte disorders), ANEDEF (anemia), WGHTLOSS (weight loss), CHF (congestive heart failure), METS (metastatic cancer), as important attributes in predicting LOS for a patient with a digestive system surgery.

7.6.2.1 An Example of Decision Tree Analysis

Fonarow et al. (2005) used classification and regression tree techniques (CARTs) to develop and validate a measure of risk stratification for in-hospital mortality due to ADHF, a condition that is responsible for morbidity and mortality in the healthcare system (Fonarow et al., 2005). Data used in the analysis were taken from the Acute Decompensated Heart Failure Registry, which collects and stores detailed hospitalization data from 263 hospitals based on initial presentation in the hospital to discharge, transfer, or in-hospital death in an electronic database. A total of 65,275 patient records were divided into training ($n = 33,046$) and validation ($n = 32,229$) cohorts. There were 39 predictor variables entered into the model including demographics (e.g., age, gender, and race/ethnicity), primary insurance, heart failure history, medical history, laboratory values, and initial vital signs that were shown to be predictive of in-hospital mortality on univariate analysis* or in previously published studies.

Nodes in the CART tree were constrained to have a minimum size of 800 records in the parent nodes and 400 records in the final child or leaf nodes (a strategy for controlling tree size). A 10-fold cross validation was used to

---

* This type of analysis considers independently for each variable how well that variable predicts in-hospital mortality.

assess the predictive ability of the tree model. Mortality was calculated for each of the terminal nodes in the CART tree and used to generate a risk stratification model. The predictive value of the model was assessed by the determination of mortality odds ratio and 95% confidence intervals between risk groups. The ability of the derived risk trees to identify ADHF patients at low, intermediate, and high risk for in-hospital mortality was determined and the results were compared between training and validation cohorts. Finally, multivariable LG models and area under the ROC curve were calculated to compare results of the model in both groups.

The training and validation cohorts were found to be similar with respect to the variable in the analysis. The CART method identified three variables—dichotomized values for blood urea nitrogen at admission, systolic blood pressure, and serum creatinine levels—that stratified the patients into five risk categories. Models including additional nodes only slightly improved the prediction of in-hospital mortality. Multivariate LG models identified the three variables as being the most highly predictive of in-hospital mortality. Based on the area under the ROC curve, the accuracy of the CART models was 68.7% in the training cohort and 66.8% in the validation cohort. More complicated LG models improved prediction only marginally.

The authors emphasize that one of the important advantages of CART analyses over LG is that CART yields a decision tree that is relatively easy to apply at the bedside, which increases the likelihood that results can be implemented in a wide variety of clinical settings. The results of this CART analysis identified a simple three-step process (dichotomous interpretation of each clinical variable) that identifies patients as being at low, intermediate, or high risk for in-hospital mortality with accuracy near that of complex regression models. Patients at higher risk may receive higher-level monitoring and earlier, more intensive treatment for ADHF.

7.6.3 Neural Networks

Artificial neural networks (ANNs) are biologically inspired computational methods for pattern discovery (Hopfield and Tank, 1985; Hinton, 1989). Neural networks are another class of supervised learning algorithms requiring a large number of labeled training cases and typically more computational effort than decision tree induction (Berry and Linoff, 2004). The original focus of ANN research, pioneered by McCulloch and Pitts starting in the 1940s, was to model brain anatomy using computers (McCulloch and Pitts, 1943). However, the ideas gave rise to a new computing method for pattern detection and other challenges across a variety of application areas. As computer technology rapidly improved in the 1960s through the 1980s, many experimental neural network ideas were revisited and applied. This renewed interest was fostered by thorough theoretical foundations laid by Rosenblatt and other researchers (Rosenblatt, 1962; Minsky and Papert, 1969). Today, these techniques are very useful in classification, regression, and prediction tasks, supporting both discrete and continuous outputs (Haykin, 1999). In fact, traditional regression techniques can be formulated as special cases of neural networks. Complex neural networks are considered universal function approximators and can model continuous nonlinearities, rather than the discontinuous relationships modeled by decision trees. However, neural network representations are typically viewed as a matrix of weights and are not easily interpreted like decision trees or rules.

Neural networks are composed of self-contained computing elements or nodes, sometimes called neurodes, which are loosely modeled on neurons (see Figure 7.2). These computing elements aggregate a set of weighted inputs and apply a function to determine whether to "fire" or emit a signal to subsequent levels in the network. By adjusting the interaction of many simple elements, neural networks are able to model complex phenomena. There are two main features of these computing elements: a set of weighted input edges or links (mirroring the biological role of dendrites and synapses), and an activation function, which combines the inputs and controls the signaling behavior, akin to an axon in a real pyramidal cell. The activation function can be further decomposed into two separate functions: a combination function that aggregates the inputs into a single value and a transfer function that controls the output signal. For instance, the sigmoid transfer function is a commonly used rule for triggering a node, feeding an output signal to other nodes in the network. The sigmoid function, as well as other firing rules, has a steep midrange segment where small changes in the input can have a large impact on the output signal (see Figure 7.3). The transfer function is substantially less sensitive to changes when input values are near the tails of the function. These nonlinear functions mimic the complexity of biological systems, amplifying slight input variations near such thresholds, possibly causing a cascade of signals that significantly affects the final output behavior.

The inputs themselves are weighted and combined to form a single parameter to the transfer function. Each input to the neuron is paired with a weight that conveys a relative importance when combined with other inputs. The inputs are also normalized to avoid any bias due to differences in magnitude

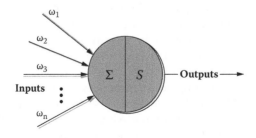

FIGURE 7.2
A neural network node.

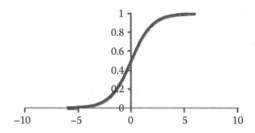

FIGURE 7.3
A sigmoid transfer function.

(often using a −1.0 to 1.0 range or a similar restriction). The weights provide the primary mechanism for learning as they are adjusted during the training process to reflect new information from each case. All other components, such as the functions within a node or the connections between nodes, usually remain fixed. A combination function aggregates the weighted inputs before the application of the transfer function. The most common combination function sums each of the inputs multiplied by the associated weights, although functions based on the mean or maximum input values are also used. Thus, each neuron is a simple stand-alone processing element that combines a set of inputs, weighted by a learning algorithm, and forwards an output signal to adjacent nodes in the network.

The individual neurons are assembled to form an ANN that can model complex, nonlinear functions. The most common neural network architecture arranges the simple computational nodes into three layers: an input layer, a hidden layer, and an output layer (see Figure 7.4). A feedforward neural network restricts the information flow, so that signals move from the input layer toward the output layer during the execution of a model, making the application of neural networks fairly efficient. As discussed below, the actual training process can be computationally demanding and involves the feedback and adjustment of the many input weights at each layer. The neurons may vary within a single network, for instance, different activation functions might be used for the input, hidden, or output layer. Another architectural characteristic is the connectivity between nodes. Although this used to be a parameter for tuning networks, most networks are now implemented as fully connected, with each node's output serving as an input to all nodes in the next layer. It is also possible to have more than three layers, with multiple hidden layers sandwiched between the input and output nodes. The number of hidden layers and hidden nodes within those layers affects the power of the network. Again, most neural networks are simply implemented using three layers. More hidden layer nodes are added to allow the network to model more complex phenomena. Although most neural network tools have reasonable default values, it can be important to match the size of the neural network, especially the number of hidden layer nodes, to the problem at hand. For example, a network might have a node for each input, one

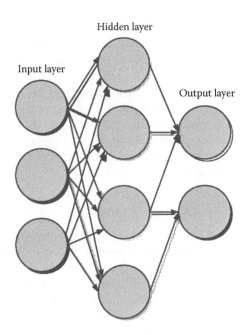

Hidden layer

Input layer

Output layer

FIGURE 7.4
A three-layer neural network.

to two times as many nodes in the hidden layer, and a set of output nodes that depend on the type of result. However, simple patterns can be modeled with smaller networks. An excessive number of neurons may allow a neural network to model unwanted idiosyncratic patterns in the training data. Therefore, it is always important to evaluate any model on unseen data and possibly to adjust the number of hidden layer neurons to reflect the nature of any patterns being learned.

ANNs are typically trained using an iterative learning algorithm that makes small adjustments to each of the input weights on a case-by-case basis, depending on the difference between the actual and predicted result. Since neural networks are a supervised learning method, each training case includes a correctly assigned result. The most widely studied learning method is the back-propagation algorithm. Although there have been many improvements and more efficient alternatives developed, the back-propagation algorithm is a very useful conceptualization of the learning process. The process begins with an initial assignment of randomly generated weights (typically in the range −1.0 to 1.0). This randomized starting point does mean that any particular training process can lead to markedly different models, with individual neurons playing different roles. The back-propagation algorithm then iteratively considers each training case in a two-phase process. First, the case is processed in a forward direction, with the inputs flowing through the neurons using the existing weights to arrive at a result. The second phase reverses the flow of information from output nodes toward input nodes, propagating the prediction errors throughout the network and adjusting the weights accordingly. The goal is to not to remove all errors seen in the training data, thereby overfitting the model. The goal is to arrive at a set of weights that embody more general patterns. In general, the learning process can be viewed as an optimization problem, concerned with finding an appropriate set of weights in an immense search space. Among the most widely used learning algorithms is the conjugate gradient method, which draws on multidimensional geometry to arrive more quickly at a satisfactory set of weights (although still using an iterative process) (Fletcher, 1987).

7.6.3.1 Example of Neural Network Analysis

Tangri et al. (2008) used data from a large, multicenter, prospective database to determine the ability of ANNs to predict which patients would experience early failure of peritoneal dialysis (PD). Results of the ANN were compared with the results of the more commonly used statistical method, LG. A total of 3269 patients were eligible for the study. The primary outcome variable was peritoneal dialysis technique failure defined as change in dialysis modality to hemodialysis for a period exceeding 1 month. Potential predictor variables included demographics, cause of end-stage renal disease (ESRD) comorbid conditions, physical examination, and laboratory data. A dummy variable was also created indicating centers with fewer than 20 patients in the study.

Multilayer perceptron ANNs with 40-80-1 modal architectures were constructed and trained using the back-propagation approach. Predictive performance was determined with bootstrap iterations; 75% of the data (approximately 2450 cases) were randomly selected and used to train the network with the validation set consisting of the remaining cases. Twenty random training and validation sets and ANNs were created. The accuracy of the 20 sets of predictions was each assessed using area under the ROC curve analysis. A similar strategy was used for the LG analysis with 20 random samples of 75% of cases being selected, regression models being developed, and then the model coefficients were used to predict cases in the remaining 25% of the sample. The 20 ROC curves from the ANN bootstrap were compared with 20 counterparts from the logistic bootstrap that yielded 400 pairs of comparisons. For each comparison, the ratio of the difference in the areas of the ANN and logistic ROC curves to the standard error of the difference yielded a normally distributed z-statistic and a two-sided p value. The overall significance of the difference in the area under the ROC curve for the ANN and logistic bootstrap was taken as the average of the p values for the 400 pairs.

The average area under the ROC curve for the ANN bootstrap was 0.760 [standard error (SE) = 0.0167], whereas the average area under the ROC curve for LG was 0.709 (SE = 0.0208). Overall, the ANN models preformed better that the LG models. The average difference in the area under the ROC curve values for the ANN and LG models was 0.0512 with an average p value = 0.0164.

The authors suggest that ANN analysis has distinct advantages compared to the more familiar LG models. Logistic models assume linearity; however, nonlinear, "u-shaped" relationships have been found between predictor variables and outcome variables in a number of areas of nephrology. Although LG models can handle these types of data through logarithmic or polynomial transformation, the analyst must know a priori that the relationship exists and which transformation to use.

7.6.4 Support Vector Machines

SVMs are a recent newcomer in the data mining and ML discipline. SVMs are learning machines that can perform binary classification (pattern recognition), multiclass classification, and regression estimation tasks. SVMs have proven to be a powerful method that is both easy to apply and capable of excellent results in comparison with other methods (Lovell and Walder, 2006). An SVM can be a robust classifier with the capacity to handle noisy and high dimensional data.

SVMs have been successfully used in image processing (Decoste and Schölkopf, 2002) and facial recognition (Osuna et al., 1997). In healthcare, SVMs have been primarily used for the characterization of digital medical images (Maglogiannis and Zafiropoulos, 2004), for example, computer-aided diagnosis of ultrasonographic images of the breast (Chen et al., 2003) and investigation of high-resolution imaging in ophthalmology (Medeiros et al., 2004a, 2004b; Gerth et al., 2008; Marmor et al., 2008). There are also several examples where SVMs were successfully used for classification of EHRs (Goodwin et al., 2003; Chu et al., 2008; Uzuner et al., 2008). These studies will be discussed after a brief explanation of SVM technologies.

The underlying idea of SVM methods is the process of finding a decision function that creates a hyperplane separating the data (in the case of a two-dimensional plane, this hyperplane is a line). Additionally, the selected hyperplane should not only correctly separate the classes but should also maximize the margin between the hyperplane and the nearest training data (Kecman, 2001; Hastie et al., 2003; Lovell and Walder, 2006). Figure 7.5 illustrates a binary classification task, where a line separates the two classes and the margins maximize the space between the line and the nearest sample data. Those margins are referred to as the "support vectors." In the SVM algorithm, an optimization is used to find the support vectors.

Several approaches exist for cases where the data are not linearly separable. In one approach, the constraints can be "softened," thus allowing for some errors. This is carried out by adding an error term to the original objective function of the optimization, and minimizing the error term as well as the margin. Another approach is to find a mapping of the data that

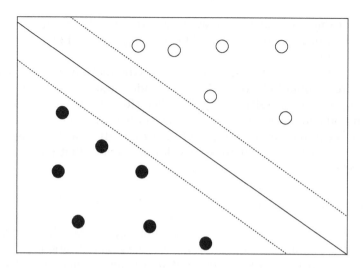

FIGURE 7.5
Support vectors for a binary classification task.

transforms the data to a new, higher-dimensional space (the "feature space") in which the data are linearly separable, and then proceeds with regular SVM classification. This, however, introduces a mathematical dilemma. By mapping the data into feature space, the dimensionality of the data is increased (the so-called "curse of dimensionality"), and mathematically there may not be enough data to find a classifier. In 1995, Vapnik introduced a method to convert the original SVM to the Lagrangian dual problem, which, in very simple terms, finds a kernel function that allows for linear separation (also referred to as the "kernel trick"; Vapnik, 1996). The two most common kernel functions are the polynomial kernel and the Gaussian kernel (Lovell and Walder, 2006). The kernel function is one of the settings that must be chosen when using SVM data mining tools.

7.6.4.1 Examples of SVMs

Two exemplars of SVM methods used on EHRs are discussed by Chu et al. (2008) and Uzuner et al. (2008). Chu et al. (2008) developed a model to predict the bleeding source and identify the cohort among patients with acute GIB who required urgent intervention, including endoscopy. Using ICD-9 codes for acute GIB, 189 patients with acute GIB and all available data variables required to develop and test models were identified from a hospital medical records database. Clinical data such as presenting signs and symptoms, demographic data, presence of comorbidities, laboratory data, and corresponding endoscopic diagnosis and outcomes were collected. Clinical data and endoscopic diagnosis collected for each patient were used to retrospectively ascertain optimal management for each patient. Clinical presentations and corresponding treatment were utilized as training examples. The authors trained and compared eight mathematical models: ANN, SVM, *k*-nearest neighbor, linear discriminant analysis, shrunken centroid, random forest, LG, and boosting. In this study, the random forest model outperformed SVM, but SVM was a close second.

7.6.5 Association Rule Mining

Association rule mining, or market basket analysis as it is commonly referred to in the business sector, is an unsupervised learning technique that searches for patterns in databases of transactions, such as sets of purchased items in the consumer products domain. These transactions need not include any outcome labels for training as in supervised learning approaches. The large numbers of transactions collected via point-of-sale systems provide an easily accessible infrastructure for association rule mining. The patterns discovered typically focus on which items are purchased together or how likely some items are to be purchased with others. Coupled with customer information via loyalty programs, patterns that highlight different customer segments can also be discovered.

The association task has two goals: to find frequent itemsets (groups of items) and to find association rules. For association rule mining algorithms, each attribute/value pair is considered an item. Each itemset has a size, which corresponds to the number of items it contains. For example, for some demographic data, we could have a three-item itemset with a gender of "female," an age of "30," and a homeownership of "true." The coverage of this itemset is the number of times this combination occurs (thus, for our previous example, the coverage is 4). Support is coverage expressed as a percentage, and is often specified by the user ahead of time. For example, support = 4% means that the model analyzes only itemsets that appear in at least 4% of the cases.

The second goal of market basket analysis algorithms is to find rules. An association rule has the form A, B => C with a confidence measure (a probability measure that is also predefined by the user). Thus, if we had a confidence value of 60% for the rule if gender = female and age = 30 => homeowner = true, then there is a 60% chance that 30-year-old females in this data set are homeowners.

Some of the important issues to consider when using association rule mining in the EHR are

1. *Attribute selection.* An event will frequently have the choice of many dimensions or attributes. An important step is to limit the number of attributes used in order to generate a reasonable number of meaningful rules.

2. *Data preparation and transformation.* Most association rule mining algorithms require the data to be in a certain format, usually

requiring the user to pivot the data so that it is in a transaction ID, attribute format (one large case per record).

3. *Rule interpretation and selection.* Association rule mining algorithms will generate many rules. Some may be trivial patterns (such as pregnancy => female), others may be difficult to interpret by nonexpert audiences (e.g., a series of medications commonly prescribed for diabetes).

4. *Selecting and setting a support value.* Minimum support is applied to find all frequent itemsets in a database. These thresholds are critical in limiting the volume of resulting rules. The fundamental assumption used by most algorithms is that any nonfrequent itemset cannot be made frequent by the addition of an item, thereby pruning the search space.

5. *Selecting and setting a confidence value.* Frequent itemsets and the minimum confidence constraint are used to form rules and to rank them by interestingness.

The Apriori algorithm family (Agrawal and Srikant, 1994) includes some of the most widely used association rule mining techniques, taking advantage of several measures of rule coverage and certainty to quickly find strong rules. Many of these patterns could be uncovered using SQL, but might require writing thousands of queries rather than running an efficient ML algorithm. In the clinical domain, many problems can be recast as baskets of items, including groups of medications, comorbidities, or even trajectories of diseases over time.

7.6.5.1 Examples of Association Rule Mining

Viveros et al. (1996) apply association rule mining to data collected in the health insurance industry, specifically an episode (claims) database. In this study, a database tuple (or record) corresponds to a unique identifier and one or more medical tests (or services) taken at a given instance in time, with a maximum of 20 tests per episode. Since there was a possibility of an episode containing at least 20 interesting attributes, the researchers pivoted the data, such that the records were organized as a transaction ID-attribute pair. Association rules were obtained by using the Apriori algorithm presented by Agrawal and Srikant (1994). The authors experimented with three different values for minimum support: 1%, 0.5%, and 0.25% (there was a total of 6.8 million episodes for pathology services, so 1% represented 68,000 transactions). The experiments generated 24, 64, and 135 rules, respectively, for the support values listed above. An example of a rule is as follows:

> If Iron Studies and Thyroid Function Tests occur together then there is an 87% chance of Full Blood Examination occurring as well. This rule was found in 0.55% of transactions.

The authors were able to provide some interesting interpretations of the rules. For example, the researchers discovered that the most commonly ordered combination of tests occurred together in 10.9% of episodes. If test B was claimed with test C, there was a 92.8% chance that a test A would also be claimed. The authors thought that this rule could be indicative of different ordering habits for similar clinical situations. In fact, they found that a large proportion of pathology tests ordered were of a nonspecific screening nature rather than a more of planned approach.

In another interesting example (Ordonez et al., 2000), researchers investigated the use of association rule mining to confirm rules used by an expert system that aided in heart disease diagnosis. They also expected to discover new rules in order to enrich the expert system's knowledge. The researchers encountered similar challenges as those previously outlined: high dimensionality in medical data, content in many formats, noise, and the need to map transactional data into a format suitable for mining rules. They also made some interesting suggestions with regard to managing some of these difficulties. They suggest to constrain the rules to those in which specific items appear in a specific part of the rule (either the antecedent, the consequent, but not both) in order to minimize uninteresting rules. They also suggest limiting association size (itemset size) to improve algorithm performance and decrease the number of rules generated. With a data set of 655 records and 113 attributes, the researchers generated 27 rules, of which 3 were meaningful, and existed in the expert system, thus helping to validate previous knowledge.

In the final example (Delgado et al., 2001), researchers tried to improve the semantics of association rules by creating rules with qualitative values to mimic how humans would normally express these rules. They state:

> A physician will find it more appropriate to describe his/her knowledge by means of rules like 'if fever is high and cough is moderate then disease is X' than by using rules like 'if fever is 38.78°C and cough is 5 over 10 then disease is X'.

They accomplish this by finding a suitable representation for the imprecise terms that the users consider to be appropriate in the domain of each quantitative attribute—in essence, creating what they refer to as "fuzzy sets" or bins for quantitative variables (with the help of domain experts). For example, they may bin time into qualitative variables such as "early morning," "morning," "noon," "afternoon," and "night."

7.6.6 Clustering Data

Clustering algorithms find natural groupings within databases based on different types of similarity metrics, uncovering "hidden" attributes or features that nicely divide the cases. These divisions or groupings can often provide insights, such as understanding different types of customers or finding patient subpopulations. Gaining customer insights through segmentation makes clustering a popular tool in marketing (Berry and Linoff, 2004), but these techniques have also been widely used in science and medicine. Data clustering is a well-researched area of statistics with many very effective algorithms available, both in commercial packages and open source toolkits. These algorithms typically propose a candidate grouping criteria, assign cases, evaluate the cluster quality, and propose improved grouping criteria, iteratively searching the space of possible clusters. The process often starts with a random assignment of cases, with algorithms differing in the measures of similarity or how cases are assigned to clusters in subsequent passes over the data.

Among the most widely known methods for clustering data is the k-means algorithm (Jain and Dubes, 1988). This simple approach to forming clusters rests on a geometric interpretation of the data, with a fixed number (k) of clusters being formed based on the proximity of individual data points. Each point or case is represented as a multielement vector, and it is the selection of these dimensions or attributes that affects the quality and meaning of resulting clusters. The steps of the algorithm include the following.

1. The algorithm begins with the random selection of k points to serve as cluster centers (or centroids).
2. All remaining data points are then assigned to the "closest" centroids, forming the first clusters (with all points assigned to one and only one cluster).
3. Centroids are recalculated as the mean of all member data points along the vector of dimensions. A return to step 2 reassigns the data points to new centroids. Steps 2 and 3 are repeated until the cluster centroids and boundaries stop changing.

This elegant method constructs k clusters, but the interpretation of those clusters rests firmly in the eye of the beholder. Natuarally, the selection of k itself can be somewhat arbitrary, driven by a theory or simple intuition. Therefore, there is an implicit outer loop to the algorithm that might consider different values of k. In fact, there are many alternative methods of clustering that substitute for other mathematical foundations or pursue hierarchical clusters that construct a tree of groups and subgroups.

One of the most interesting applications of clustering for scientific discovery relates to the grouping of stars in astronomy (Kaufman and Rousseeuw, 1990). The Hertzsprung–Russell diagram (named for the two astronomers who independently arrived at the idea) arranges stars along the two dimensions of luminosity and temperature. Viewed as a scatter plot, the stars form easily identifiable groups representing main sequence dwarf stars, white dwarfs, red giants, and even supergiants. These clusters of stars highlight important aspects of the stellar life cycle and the underlying natural processes that generate energy. The challenge is to find those dimensions that uncover such natural groupings and then to interpret the resulting clusters in an insightful manner.

Although clustering methods can certainly serve as primary data mining techniques, these algorithms are often used during data preprocessing activities (Weiss and Indurkhya, 1998). It is widely recognized that data preparation usually accounts for the bulk of effort in any data mining project and can easily influence the ultimate results (Tremblay et al., 2006). In large and complex data sets, there may be many interesting patterns all vying for discovery, yet interacting in ways that create confusing signals and obstacles to interpretation. Clustering can be thought of as a data reduction technique that takes a vector of dimensions describing a set of data points and results in a single cluster label. This surrogate value representing a unique collection of individual data points can then be used in subsequent analyses and as input to other data mining techniques. For instance, a basic data reduction step might be to take a wide-ranging integer value for an input parameter and apply k-means clustering to find a small number of well-defined groupings that approximate the input. Since data mining projects often start with very large numbers of potential input variables that may vary over correspondingly large ranges of values, anything that can change the levels of abstraction might bring important patterns into sharper focus. Data transformation and reduction techniques are as critical as any modeling algorithms used in the final steps of an analysis.

7.6.7 Text Mining Clinical Narratives

Clinical notes are among the most interesting and challenging components of the EHR, requiring algorithms for text mining or information extraction. Any data extract from these free text components could then be combined with existing structured data as inputs to other ML algorithms. There are three fundamental approaches to information extraction from text: simple keyword or regular expression matching, natural language processing (NLP), and ML algorithms. Simple keyword or string matching approaches are typically not powerful enough for extracting information from clinical notes, although the approach can be very useful in constrained contexts. NLP approaches are deductive in nature, using clinical theory to construct controlled vocabularies and ontologies that underpin the text processing, with additional components to handle negation and temporal relationships. The vocabularies, standardized coding systems, and concept ontologies necessary for NLP approaches require significant investments. The medical domain is one of the few fields to make the decades-long investments required to construct these fundamental language processing resources and achieve reasonable results in a variety of applications. In contrast, ML algorithms are inductive, data-driven approaches to text mining that do not directly rely on controlled vocabularies or ontologies (Mitchell, 1997). These algorithms take a more statistical approach, calculating word frequencies and term weights to discriminate between or group documents using similarity measures.

ML seeks to discover the mappings between input data and output concepts, such as between words in free-text documents and the topics of the documents, or between words and phrases in symptom descriptions (possibly augmented with laboratory test results and other measurements) and canonical names of diseases in taxonomies. These mappings should be maximally accurate on training examples and generalize well to new instances (new documents, new patients, etc.). ML is applicable to a variety of important tasks in biomedical informatics, especially in medical text processing; these range from automated classification and extraction to hidden pattern detection and multitype predictions. Methods for ML-based text mining include latent semantic indexing, which uses a term-by-document matrix to discover latent connections among synonyms and related lexical variants and to enhance document retrieval performance (Deerwester, 1990; Yang and Chute, 1993), with variations on the approach such as probabilistic latent semantic indexing (Hofmann, 1999) and flexible latent variable models (Zhang et al., 2008). These techniques often derive vectors of weighted terms that summarize the unique characteristics of and allow cluster assignment. These same vectors and term frequencies can be fed into other modeling techniques, such as LG, for classification tasks and other predictive purposes.

7.6.7.1 Examples of Text Mining

The work done by Tremblay et al. (2005) is an example of using ML approaches for text mining to extract useful information from clinical notes that can be used in database queries and to create summary reports for business analysis and health research. The researchers used text mining techniques to study unintentional injury due to falls in the Veterans Health Administration ambulatory care setting. This study used data and text mining techniques to investigate electronic medical records in order to identify those records in the administrative data that should have been coded as fall-related injuries. The challenges highlighted by this study included data preparation from administrative sources and the electronic medical records, de-identification of the data (to assure HIPAA compliance), and the conducting of a chart review to construct a "gold standard" data set. Both supervised and unsupervised text mining techniques were run as comparison techniques to traditional medical chart review.

The researchers found that conducting text mining on electronic medical records was helpful in correctly identifying fall-related injuries.

7.7 Evaluating Accuracy of Data Mining Techniques

In the exemplars outlined above, researchers always discuss the accuracy of the models created. We briefly outline some of the accuracy and error measures used to estimate the fit quality for data mining models. Two different accuracy measures are discussed: those used for classification models and those used for predictor models.

In a classification model (e.g., when trying to classify medical data cases as "cancer" or "not cancer"), *accuracy* is the percentage of cases correctly classified by a model. Figure 7.6 illustrates some of the terms commonly used to describe the accuracy of a model. *True positives* are those cases where the positive cases are correctly labeled by the model. *True negatives* are the number of correctly labeled negative cases. *False positives* are those negative cases that were incorrectly labeled and *"false negatives* are the positive cases that were mislabeled. In our example of cancer classification, we are more interested in understanding the true positives and true negatives than the overall accuracy of the model. Therefore, *sensitivity* (proportion of true positives found), *specificity* (proportion of true negatives found), and *precision* (percentage of cases labeled as positives that are actually found) are used. Often, an ROC curve is used to visually compare two classification models. The ROC curve illustrates the trade-off between sensitivity and specificity. Figure 7.7 shows an example of an ROC curve.

Predicted Class

Actual Class	True positive	False negative
	False positive	True negative

FIGURE 7.6
Model accuracy terms.

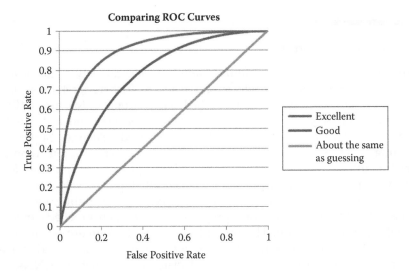

FIGURE 7.7
Comparing receiver operator characteristic curves.

In cases where the predicted variable is continuous (e.g., when predicting LOS), accuracy is evaluated by how close the predicted value is to the actual known values. Several error measures or rates exist that are based on a *loss function*, which measures the difference between the predicted value and the actual value.

In both the classification and the predictor models, there are two major challenges. One major challenge is that we may find very optimistic accuracy measures. This is generally due to "over-fitting" of the data mining model, which means the model overspecializes in the data used to train the model. Another challenge is that a randomized starting point used by learning models could mean that the training process can lead to markedly different models (as in neural networks). Several approaches are taken to minimize these problems. The *holdout method* randomly partitions the data set into a training and evaluation data set. *Training data* are used to train the model based on the known predictor variable. The models are then run on *evaluation data* (not used in the training process) and the predicted value is compared to the true value. Two other approaches are cross-validation and bootstrap methods. *Cross validation* approaches partition the data set into subsets of approximately equal size. The model is trained k times, each time leaving out one of the subsets from training, but using only the omitted subset to compute the error criterion of interest. *Bootstrapping* is an alternative to cross-validation (Efron and Tibshirani, 1993). In bootstrapping, instead of repeatedly analyzing subsets of the data, random subsamples (with replacement from the full sample) are repeatedly analyzed.

7.8 Chapter Summary

This chapter reviews the foundations of several key data mining technologies, including key reference disciplines such as database systems, artificial intelligence, and statistics. The basic concepts of ML are outlined, with their focus on data-driven inductive approaches, and a distinction is drawn between supervised and unsupervised learning. Supervised learning relies on cases that are correctly labeled with the outcomes, so that this information may be used in training processes. The knowledge discovery process itself is presented as a multistep life cycle that begins with problem and data understanding, explicitly highlights the considerable effort necessary for data preparation, and then proceeds through modeling and evaluation. The final phase is the deployment of predictive models into existing systems. The bulk of the chapter reviews widely used supervised learning methods such as decision tree induction, ANNs, and SVMs. In addition, unsupervised methods such as association rule mining and clustering are also discussed. These techniques are often used as part of the data preparation process, especially for data reduction by replacing multiple attributes or values with cluster identifiers. Finally, some basic text mining methods are discussed. Text mining can be used to extract information from unstructured components of the EHR such as progress notes. Again, these techniques can be used as precursor steps in developing new features for subsequent modeling steps. The last section discusses strategies for model assessment and techniques for ensuring that models do not result from good or bad luck, but provide the performance one would expect from the available data. All of these data mining techniques can be used to uncover interesting patterns in the EHR for a variety of clinically relevant purposes.

References

Agrawal, R., and Srikant, R. 1994. Fast algorithms for mining association rules in large databases. In *Proceedings of the 20th International Conference on Very Large Data Bases*, pp. 487–499, Santiago, Chile, Morgan Kaufmann Publishers Inc.

Berndt, D. J., Hevner, A. R. et al. 2003. The CATCH data warehouse: support for community health care decision-making. *Decision Support Systems* 35(3):367.

Berry, M. J. A., and Linoff, G. 2004. *Data mining Techniques: for Marketing, Sales, and Customer Relationship Management*. Indianapolis, IN: Wiley.

Bishop, C. M. 2006. *Pattern Recognition and Machine Learning*. New York, NY: Springer.

Chen, D.-R., Chang, R.- F. et al. 2003. Computer-aided diagnosis for 3-dimensional breast ultrasonography. *Archives of Surgery* 138(3):296–302.

Chu, A., Ahn, H. et al. 2008. A decision support system to facilitate management of patients with acute gastrointestinal bleeding. *Artificial Intelligence in Medicine* 42(3):247–259.

Codd, E. F. 1983. A relational model of data for large shared data banks. *Communications of the ACM* 26(1):64–69.

Date, C. J. 2000. *An Introduction to Database Systems*. Boston, MA: Addison Wesley Longman.

Decoste, D., and Schölkopf, B. 2002. Training invariant support vector machines. *Machine Learning Journal* 46(1–3):161–190.

Deerwester, S. 1990. Indexing by latent semantic analysis. *Journal of the American Society for Information Science* 41(6):391–407.

Delgado, M., Sanchez, D. et al. 2001. Mining association rules with improved semantics in medical databases. *Artificial Intelligence in Medicine* 21(1):241–245.

Efron, B., and Tibshirani, R. J. 1993. *An Introduction to the Bootstrap*. London: Chapman & Hall.

Fayyad, U., Piatetsky-Shapiro, G. et al. 1996. The KDD process for extracting useful knowledge from volumes of data. *Communications of the ACM* 39(11):27–34.

Fletcher, R. 1987. *Practical Methods of Optimization*. Chichester: Wiley.

Fonarow, G. C., Adams, K. F., Jr. et al. 2005. Risk stratification for in-hospital mortality in acutely decompensated heart failure: classification and regression tree analysis. *JAMA* 293(5):572–580.

Friedman, N., Geiger, D. et al. 1997. Bayesian network classifiers. *Machine Learning* 29:31–163.

Gerth, C., Zawadzki, R. J. et al. 2008. Retinal morphological changes of patients with x-linked retinoschisis evaluated by Fourier-domain optical coherence tomography. *Archives of Ophthalmology* 126(6):807–811.

Goodwin, L., Vandyne, M. et al. 2003. Data mining issues and opportunities for building nursing knowledge. *Journal of Biomedical Informatics* 36(4–5):379–388.

Hand, D. J. 1998. Data mining: statistics and more? *The American Statistician* 52(2):112.

Hastie, T., Tibshirani, R. et al. 2003. *The Elements of Statistical Learning*. New York, NY: Springer.

Haykin, S. S. 1999. *Neural Networks: a Comprehensive Foundation*. Upper Saddle River, NJ: Prentice Hall.

Hinton, G. E. 1989. Connectionist learning procedures. *Artificial Intelligence in Medicine* 40:185–234.

Hofmann, T. 1999. Probabilistic latent semantic indexing. In *Proceedings of the 22nd Annual International SIGIR Conference on Research and Development in Information Retrieval*, pp. 35–44.

Hopfield, J. J., and Tank, D. W. 1985. Computing with neural circuits: a model. *Science* 233:625–633.

Jain, A. K., and Dubes, R. C. 1988. *Algorithms for Clustering Data*. Englewood Cliffs, NJ: Prentice Hall.

Kaufman, L., and Rousseeuw, P. J. 1990. *Finding Groups in Data: An Introduction to Cluster Analysis*. New York, NY: John Wiley & Sons.

Kecman, V. 2001. *Learning and Soft Computing: Support Vector Machines, Neural Networks, and Fuzzy Logic Models*. Cambridge, MA: MIT Press.

Kimball, R., Ross, M. et al. 2008. *The Data Warehouse Lifecycle Toolkit*, 2nd edn. New York, NY: Wiley.

Lovell, B. C., and Walder, C. J. 2006. Support vector machines for business applications. In *Business Applications and Computational Intelligence*. K. Voges and N. Pope, eds. Hershey, PA: Idea Group Publishing.

Maglogiannis, I. G., and Zafiropoulos, E. P. 2004. Characterization of digital medical images utilizing support vector machines. *BMC Medical Informatics and Decision Making* 4(4).

Marmor, M. F., Choi, S. S. et al. 2008. Visual insignificance of the foveal pit: reassessment of foveal hypoplasia as fovea plana. *Archives of Ophthalmology* 126(7):907–913.

McCulloch, W. S., and Pitts, W. 1943. A logical calculus of the ideas of immanent in nervous activity. *Bulletin of Mathematical Biophysics* 5:115–133.

Medeiros, F. A., Zangwill, L. M. et al. 2004a. Comparison of scanning laser polarimetry using variable corneal compensation and retinal nerve fiber layer photography for detection of glaucoma. *Archives of Ophthalmology* 122(5):698–704.

Medeiros, F. A., Zangwill, L. M. et al. 2004b. Comparison of the GDx VCC scanning laser polarimeter, HRT II confocal scanning laser ophthalmoscope, and stratus OCT optical coherence tomograph for the detection of glaucoma. *Archives of Ophthalmology* 122(6):827–837.

Minsky, M. L., and Papert, S. 1969. *Perceptrons.* Cambridge, MA: MIT Press.

Mitchell, T. M. 1997. *Machine Learning.* New York, NY: McGraw-Hill.

Morales, D. A., Bengoetxea, E. et al. 2008. Selection of human embryos for transfer by Bayesian classifiers. *Computers in Biology and Medicine* 38(11–12):1177–1186.

Ordonez, C., Santana, C. A. et al. 2000. Discovering interesting association rules in medical data. In *ACM SIGMOD Workshop on Research Issues on Data Mining and Knowledge Discovery.*

Osuna, E., Freund, R. et al. 1997. Training support vector machines: an application to face detection. *In Proceedings of the IEEE Computer Society Conference on Computer Vision and Pattern Recognition (CVPR'97).*

Quinlan, J. R. 1993. *C4.5: Programs for Machine Learning.* San Mateo, CA: Morgan Kaufmann.

Rosenblatt, F. 1962. *Principles of Neurodynamics.* Washington, DC: Spartan Books.

Shannon, C. E. 1948. A mathematical theory of communication. *Bell System Technical Journal* 27:379–423, 623–656.

Smalheiser, N., Torvik, V. et al. 2006. Collaborative development of the Arrowsmith two node search interface designed for laboratory investigators. *Journal of Biomedical Discovery and Collaboration* 1(1):8.

Smalheiser, N. R., and Swanson, D. R. 1994. Assessing a gap in the biomedical literature: magnesium deficiency and neurologic disease. *Neuroscience Research Commun* 15:1–9.

Smalheiser, N. R., and Swanson, D. R. 1996a. Indomethacin and Alzheimer's disease. Neurology 46:583.

Smalheiser, N. R., and Swanson, D. R. 1996b. Linking estrogen to Alzheimer's disease: an informatics approach. *Neurology* 47:809–810.

Smalheiser, N. R., and Swanson, D. R. 1998a. Calcium-independent phospholipase A_2 and schizophrenia. *Archives of Geneonal Psychiatry* 55:752–753.

Smalheiser, N. R., and Swanson, D. R. 1998b. Using ARROWSMITH: a computer-assisted approach to formulating and assessing scientific hypotheses. *Computer Methods and Programs in Biomedicine* 57:149–153.

Swanson, D. R. 1986a. Fish oil, Raynaud's syndrome, and undiscovered public knowledge. *Perspectives in Biology and Medicine* 30:7–18.

Swanson, D. R. 1986b. Undiscovered public knowledge. *Library Quarterly* 56:103–118.

Swanson, D. R. 1988. Migraine and magnesium: eleven neglected connections. *Perspectives in Biology and Medicine* 31:526–557.

Swanson, D. R. 1993. Intervening in the life cycles of scientific knowledge. *Library Trends* 41:606–631.

Swanson, D. R., and Smalheiser, N. R. 1997. An interactive system for finding complementary literatures: a stimulus to scientific discovery. *Artificial Intelligence* 91:183–203.

Swanson, D. R., and Smalheiser, N. R. 1999. Implicit text linkages between Medline records: using Arrowsmith as an aid to scientific discovery. *Library Trends* 48:48–59.

Tangri, N., Ansell, D. et al. 2008. Predicting technique survival in peritoneal dialysis patients: comparing artificial neural networks and logistic regression. *Nephrology Dialysis Transplantation* 23(9):2972–2981.

Tremblay, M. C., Berndt, D. et al. 2005. Utilizing text mining techniques to identify fall related injuries. In *Proceedings of the 11th Americas Conference on Information Systems (AMCIS 2005)*, Omaha, NE.

Tremblay, M. C., Berndt, D. J. et al. 2006. Feature selection for predicting surgical outcomes. In *Proceedings of the 29th Annual Hawaii International Conference on System Sciences*, Hawaii.

Tremblay, M. C., Fuller, R. et al. 2007. Doing more with more information: changing healthcare planning with OLAP tools. *Decision Support Systems* 43(4):1305–1320.

Uzuner, Ö., Sibanda, T. C. et al. 2008. A de-identifier for medical discharge summaries. *Artificial Intelligence in Medicine* 42(1):13–35.

Vapnik, V. N. 1996. *The Nature of Statistical Learning Theory*. New York, NY: Springer-Verlag.

Viveros, M. S., Nearhos, J. P. et al. 1996. Applying data mining techniques to a health insurance information system. In *Proceedings of the 22th International Conference on Very Large Data Bases*, Morgan Kaufmann Publishers.

Weiss, S. M., and Indurkhya, N. 1998. *Predictive Data Mining: A Practical Guide*. San Francisco, CA: Morgan Kaufmann.

Witten, I. H., and Frank, E. 2005. *Data Mining: Practical Machine Learning Tools and Techniques*. San Francisco, CA: Morgan Kaufmann.

Yang, Y., and Chute, C. G. 1993. An application of least squares fit mapping to text information retrieval. In *Proceedings of the 16th Annual International ACM SIGIR Conference on Research and Development in Information Retrieval*, Pittsburgh, PA: ACM.

Zhang, J., Z. Ghahramani, et al. 2008. Flexible latent variable models for multitask learning. *Machine Learning* 73(3):221–242.

8

Privacy-Preserving Information Discovery on EHRs

Li Xiong, James Gardner, Pawel Jurczyk, and James J. Lu

CONTENTS

8.1 Introduction

Although there is an increasing need to release and share electronic health records (EHRs) for information discovery, such data release and sharing must be governed by data privacy requirements. One of the biggest challenges for information discovery on EHRs is allowing sharing and dissemination of EHRs while maintaining a commitment to patient privacy.

Chapter 5 discussed the philosophy and different dimensions of privacy for handling EHRs as well as privacy regulations such as Health Insurance Portability and Accountability Act (HIPAA). In this chapter, we will discuss the potential solutions and computational techniques that enable information discovery on EHRs while protecting individual privacy. The purpose of the protection is to ensure that the risk of disclosing confidential information about identifiable persons is very small.

We first consider a motivating scenario. Pathologists in the United States examine millions of tissue samples each year and a large proportion of recent samples have reports available in electronic format. Researchers need pathology-based data sets, annotated with clinical information, to discover and validate new diagnostic tests and therapies. The National Cancer Institute (NCI) proposed the development of the Shared Pathology Informatics Network (SPIN) recognizing the situation. The ultimate goal of the network is to provide researchers throughout the country access to tissue specimens. It is necessary to protect the data from disclosures before releasing the contents of the surgical pathology reports that form the core of the information network so that confidential information about patients is not disclosed.

Disclosure occurs when confidential information is revealed about individual data subjects. Several different definitions of disclosure have been proposed in the literature. A common definition distinguishes three types of disclosure: identity disclosure, attribute disclosure, and inferential disclosure.

Identity disclosure occurs if a third party can identify a subject or respondent from the released data. Revealing that an individual is a respondent or subject of a data collection may or may not violate confidentiality requirements. However, for released data containing additional confidential information, identification is generally regarded as disclosure, because identification will automatically reveal additional attribute information that was not used in identifying the record.

Attribute disclosure occurs when confidential information about a data subject is revealed and can be attributed to the subject. Thus, attribute disclosure comprises identification of the subject and divulging confidential information pertaining to the subject. Attribute disclosure is the primary concern for data owners. It is important to note that the release of sensitive attributes alone does not compromise privacy unless they are associated with an identifiable subject.

Inferential disclosure occurs when individual information can be inferred with high confidence from statistical properties of the released data. Inferential disclosure is of less concern in most cases as inferences are designed to predict aggregate behavior, not individual attributes, and thus are often poor predictors of individual data values.

In order to protect EHRs from the different types of disclosures, one or a combination of a few general methods can be used: restricted access,

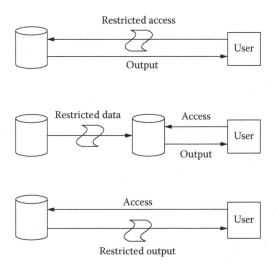

FIGURE 8.1
General methods for protecting confidential information.

restricted data, and restricted output. Figure 8.1 presents an illustration of each of the methods.

Restricted access approach imposes conditions on access to the data. For example, in many institutions, investigators wishing to use EHRs for research purposes have to obtain permission from the patients or obtain a waiver of informed consent from their institutional review boards (IRBs). A role-based access control mechanism can be implemented to assign different levels of access rights to different user roles (e.g., physician, researchers with patient permission or IRB approval, other researchers).

Restricted data approach restricts the amount of information or transforms the data to a modified data set, which is then made available to the researchers. For example, in some institutions, investigators wishing to use EHRs for research purposes can use a data set that has had all or most of protected health information (PHI) under HIPAA (identifying information) removed. Data can be also perturbed with random noise before being accessed by the users.

Restricted output approach restricts or transforms the results to user queries or mining tasks while leaving the data unchanged. An example of such techniques is association rule hiding methods, in which some of the association rules are suppressed in order to preserve privacy.

When data need to be shared in a large scale (such as for the SPIN initiative) for information discovery, the restricted data approach provides a scalable way for sharing EHRs while preserving privacy of patients. We will focus on the *restricted data* approach in this chapter and discuss privacy-preserving data publishing and mining techniques that allow release of a modified data set for queries and data mining tasks. Within the restricted data approach, we will consider two main problems: privacy-preserving data publishing and privacy-preserving data mining.

Privacy-preserving data publishing: Privacy-preserving data publishing is the problem of how a *data custodian* can distribute an anonymized view of the data that does not contain individually identifiable information to a *data recipient* for various information discovery tasks. The problem is also called *data anonymization* or *data de-identification*. It aims to protect the data from identity disclosure by removing or replacing identifying information in order to dissociate the individual from his or her EHR. The main techniques include generalization, suppression (removal), permutation, and swapping of certain data. It is often studied independent of specific information discovery tasks. The main goal is to guarantee that the released data do not contain individually identifiable information while preserving all the medically relevant information about the patient. Since the data cannot be associated with an identifiable subject, the data are protected from attribute disclosure as well.

PHI is defined by HIPAA* as individually identifiable health information (please refer to Chapter 5). Identifiable information refers to data explicitly linked to a particular individual as well with data that could enable individual identification. The HIPAA Privacy Rule specifies two ways in which information can be deidentified: statistical de-identification and full de-identification. It also includes a limited data set option that allows the use and disclosure of selected identifiers.

> *Statistical de-identification.* A person with appropriate expertise can render information "not identifiable" if she/he can determine that the risk is very small that the information could be used alone or in combination with other reasonably available information by an anticipated recipient to identify the individual.
>
> *Full de-identification.* Alternatively, HIPAA identifiers (direct and indirect) of the individual and his/her relatives, employers, or household members must be removed or coded. There is no actual knowledge that the information could be used alone or in combination with other information to identify the individual. This is also referred to as safe harbor method.
>
> *Limited data set.* The middle option allows the use and disclosure of selected identifiers with only limited Privacy Rule requirements. It can be used for research, healthcare operations, and public health purposes only. A Data Use Agreement must be signed by the covered

---

* HIPAA. http://healthcare.partners.org/phsirb/hrchipaa.htm.

entity and the recipient of the limited data set. For the limited data set, the direct identifiers of an individual or of relatives, employers, or household members of the individual must be removed. It can include the indirect identifiers including geographic data, dates, and other unique identifiers other than those that are expressly disallowed.

Disclosure can occur based on the released data alone, or may result from combining the released data with publicly available information. The accessing and/or linking by the public to electronic databases creates some degree of risk that disclosure of confidential information may occur even though personal identifiers are removed. The seminal work by Sweeney [1] shows that a data set that simply has identifiers removed is subject to linking attacks. For example, an individual who is the only Caucasian male born in 1925 living in a sparsely populated area could have his age, race, gender, and zip code joined with a voter registry from the area to obtain his name and mailing address.

A few *principles* have been proposed that serve as criteria for judging whether a published data set provides sufficient privacy protection [1–8]. The most well-known principle is k-anonymity [1], which requires that a set of k records (entities) be indistinguishable from each other based on a quasi-identifier set given other available data sources. Many techniques have been proposed to transform a data set that satisfies a given principle.

Privacy-preserving data mining. Privacy-preserving data mining is the problem of how a data custodian can distribute its data to a data recipient for mining without disclosing confidential information. It aims to protect the data from attribute disclosure while enabling data mining from the data. The problem is often studied in conjunction with specific data mining applications such as association rule mining or classification. The main technique being used is *data perturbation*, which perturbs sensitive attributes with random noise. The main notion of privacy studied in this context is data uncertainty as opposed to individual identifiability for data anonymization. The main goal is to guarantee that the exact data values of the sensitive attributes are not disclosed while the statistical properties of the data values are preserved can be reconstructed to allow the specific mining tasks to achieve accurate results.

The most basic form of disturbing continuous variables is the addition of, or multiplication by, random noise with a given distribution. This noise may be added to the data records in their original form or to some transformation of the data depending on the intended use of the file. The data custodian must decide whether to publish the distribution(s) used to add noise to the data. Publishing the distribution(s) could aid data users in their information discovery tasks but might also increase disclosure risk of the data.

Chapter organization. The rest of the chapter is organized as follows. Section 8.2 provides a brief overview of related work and further readings on the topic. Sections 8.3 and 8.4 discuss privacy-preserving data publishing and privacy-preserving data mining in detail. For each problem, we will first give an overview of the general techniques and state-of-the-art solutions from database research as well as medical informatics community. We then present a few representative algorithms in more detail to illustrate the techniques and give a flavor of the complexity of the solutions. Most of these techniques are developed for general domains and are applicable to EHRs. For privacy-preserving data publishing, there is a set of works specifically addressing the de-identification problem for EHRs and we will survey and discuss them in detail. At the end of each of these two sections, we also discuss the problem in the distributed setting for multiple distributed data sources and provide an overview of relevant solutions. The survey and discussion are not intended to be comprehensive. The objective is to highlight the representative approaches and software tools that can be used or adopted by practitioners and summarize the techniques and limitations of current work for researchers. Finally, we conclude the chapter and point out open problems and suggest a few directions for future research in the area.

8.2 Related Work and Further Readings

We briefly review the related work to the topic and provide pointers to further readings.

Privacy-preserving access control. Previous work on multilevel secure relational databases [9] provides many valuable insights for designing a fine-grained secure data model. In a multilevel relational database, each piece of information is classified into a security level, and every user is assigned a security clearance. Based on the access class, the system ensures that each user gains access to only the data for which (s)he has proper clearance, with no information flow from a higher security level to a lower security level. Hippocratic databases [10–12] incorporate privacy protection within relational database systems. Byun et al. [13] presented a comprehensive approach for privacy-preserving access control based on the notion of purpose. Purpose information associated with a given data element specifies the intended use of the data element. Although these mechanisms enable multilevel access of sensitive information through access control at a granularity level up to a single attribute value for a single tuple, microviews of the data are desired where even a single value of a tuple attribute may have different views [14].

Statistical databases. Research in statistical databases has focused on enabling queries on aggregate information (e.g., sum, count) from a database without revealing individual records [15]. The approaches can be broadly classified into data perturbation and query restriction. Data perturbation involves either altering the input databases or altering query results returned. Query restriction includes schemes that check for possible privacy breaches by keeping audit trails and controlling overlap of successive aggregate queries. The techniques developed have focused only on aggregate queries and relational data types.

Privacy-preserving data publishing. Privacy-preserving data publishing or data anonymization provides a microview of the data while preserving privacy of individuals [16]. The work in this area can be classified into a number of categories. The first one aims at devising generalization principles in that a generalized table is considered privacy preserving if it satisfies a *generalization principle* [1–8]. Another large body of work contributes to transforming a data set to meet a privacy principle (dominantly k-anonymity) using techniques such as generalization, suppression (removal), permutation, and swapping of certain data values [17–31].

EHR de-identification. In the medical informatics community, there are some efforts on deidentifying medical documents [32–38]. Some of them are specialized for specific document types (e.g., pathology reports [34, 36, 38]). Some of them focus on a subset of HIPAA identifiers (e.g., name only [34, 35]), and some focus on differentiating PHI from non-PHI [37]. We will discuss the representative ones in detail in this chapter.

Privacy-preserving data mining. One data sharing model is the mining-as-a-service model, in which data custodians submit the data to a data collector for mining or a data custodian outsources mining to an untrusted service provider. The main approach is data perturbation that transforms data by adding random noise in a principled manner [39, 40]. There are studies focusing on specific mining tasks such as decision tree [39, 41], association rule mining [42–44], and on disclosure analysis [41, 45–47].

Distributed privacy-preserving data sharing. Distributed privacy-preserving data sharing deals with data sharing for specific tasks across multiple data sources in a distributed manner [48–62]. The main goal is to ensure that data are not disclosed among participating parties. Common techniques include data approach that involves data perturbation and protocol approach that applies secure multiparty computation (MPC) protocols or random response techniques.

8.3 Privacy-Preserving Data Publishing

We discuss privacy-preserving data publishing in this section. We first introduce a few anonymization principles followed by the main techniques for anonymizing a data set guided by the principles. Most of the principles and algorithms apply exclusively to structured (relational) data. As a substantial amount of EHRs reside in textual forms, we devote a subsection to anonymization of EHRs, in particular, textual EHRs, to outline the challenges for deidentifying medical text. We survey a set of existing solutions designed specifically for deidentifying EHRs. Finally, we briefly discuss the problem of distributed data anonymization for multiple distributed data sources.

8.3.1 Anonymization Principles

Data anonymization aims to remove or replace personally identifiable information in order to protect the privacy of individuals. Since the accessing and/or linking of the anonymized data set with external data sources creates some degree of risk that a disclosure may occur even when personal identifiers are removed, we need *statistical criteria* or *principles* that can serve as a basis for judging whether a published data set provides sufficient privacy protection. Among the many privacy principles or criteria, k-anonymity [1] and its extension, l-diversity [2], are the two most widely accepted and serve as the basis for many others, and hence, will be used in our discussions and illustrations. Below, we introduce some terminologies and illustrate the basic ideas behind these principles.

Given a relational table T, the attributes are characterized into three types.

Unique identifiers are attributes that identify individuals. Known identifiers are typically removed entirely from released microdata.

Quasi-identifier set is a minimal set of attributes $(X_1, ..., X_d)$ that can be joined with external information to reidentify individual records. We assume that a quasi-identifier is recognized based on the domain knowledge.

Sensitive attributes are those attributes that an adversary should not be permitted to uniquely associate their values with a unique identifier.

Table 8.1a illustrates an original relational table of personal information. Among the attributes, *Name* is considered an identifier, (*Age, Gender, Zipcode*) is considered a quasi-identifer set, and *Diagnosis* is considered a sensitive attribute.

The k-anonymity model provides an intuitive requirement for privacy in stipulating that no individual record should be uniquely identifiable from a group of k with respect to the quasi-identifier set. The set of all tuples in T containing identical values for the quasi-identifier set $X_1, ..., X_d$ is referred to as an *Equivalence class*. T is k-anonymous with respect to $X_1, ..., X_d$ if every tuple is in an equivalence class of size at least k. A k-anonymization of T is a transformation or generalization of the data T such that the transformed data set is k-anonymous.

The l-diversity model provides a natural extension to incorporate a nominal sensitive attribute S. It requires that each equivalence class also contains at least l "well-represented" distinct values for s to avoid the homogeneous sensitive information revealed for the group. Table 8.1b illustrates one possible anonymization with respect to a quasi-identifier set (*Age, Gender, Zipcode*) using data generalization that satisfies 2-anonymity and 2-diversity.

TABLE 8.1

Illustration of Anonymization: Original Data and Anonymized Data

Name	Age (Years)	Gender	Zipcode	Diagnosis
(a) Original data				
Henr	25	Male	53710	Influenza
Irene	28	Female	53712	Lymphoma
Dan	28	Male	53711	Bronchitis
Erica	26	Female	53712	Influenza
(b) Anonymized data				
*	25–28	Male	[53710–53711]	Influenza
*	25–28	Female	53712	Lymphoma
*	25–28	Male	[53710–53711]	Bronchitis
*	25–28	Female	53712	Influenza

* Attribute value removed.

Following k-anonymity and l-diversity, t-closeness [5] is proposed to protect the numeric sensitive attributes that requires the distribution of sensitive values in each group to be analogous to the distribution of the entire data set. Aggarwal et al. [4] generalizes k-anonymity with clustering principles where quasi-identifiers of data records are first clustered and then cluster centers are published and each cluster must contain no fewer than a prespecified number of data records. δ-presence [8] is proposed to protect the presence of individuals in a published data set. A recent work [63] also considered *personalized anonymity* to guarantee minimum generalization for every individual in the data set. As these principles focus on "one-time" release of the data, m-invariance [6] is proposed to limit the risk of privacy disclosure in republication of the data.

8.3.2 Anonymization Techniques

In this subsection, we first give an overview of anonymization techniques, then introduce a few representative algorithms for anonymization based on the k-anonymity principle, followed by recent developments in the area.

Typical anonymization techniques for transforming a data set so that it does not contain individually identifiable information include data suppression, data generalization, data swapping, and microaggregation.

> *Data suppression.* The simplest method is data suppression, in which the value of the attribute is removed completely. The apparent drawback with this technique is the information loss associated with the attribute removal.

> *Data generalization.* The main approach for anonymization is generalization that reduces the granularity of the quasi-identifiers so that records are grouped into equivalence classes. For numeric

attributes, they are discretized to a range. For categorical attributes, they are generalized to a value higher in the concept hierarchy. For example, the date of birth could be generalized to a range such as year of birth, so as to reduce the risk of identification. A geographic attribute such as city could be generalized into the state that the city belongs to.

Data swapping. The basic idea of data swapping is to transform the database by switching a subset of attributes between selected pairs of records.

Microaggregation. In the method of microaggregation or clustering, clusters of records are constructed. For each cluster, the data values are replaced with a representative value that is typically the average value along each dimension in the cluster.

Applying the above techniques to find an optimal transformation of a data set in order to meet one of the privacy principles poses computational challenges. The reason is that we want an optimal solution that performs as little transformation as possible while meeting the privacy criteria so that we minimize the information loss and maintain as much useful information as possible.

A large body of work contributes to the algorithms for transforming a data set to one that meets a privacy principle and minimizes certain quality cost metrics. Most of them use k-anonymity or a variation as the privacy principle, and generalization and suppression as the main techniques. Several hardness results [19, 21] show the computational complexity of the problem of computing the optimal generalized table. Optimal solutions [20, 25] enumerate all possible generalized relations with certain constraints using heuristics to prune the search space. Greedy solutions [17, 18, 22–24, 26–28] are proposed to obtain a suboptimal solution much faster. We refer readers to the work of Fung et al. [16] for a survey of recent developments in this area.

A few recent works are suggesting new approaches, such as releasing marginals [29], anatomy technique [30], and permutation technique [31], to improve the utility of the anonymized data set. The marginals approach [29] releases marginals of the data set, each of which anonymizes the projection of the original microdata on a subset of the attributes. The anatomy technique [30] publishes quasi-identifiers and sensitive values in two separate tables. The permutation technique [31] permutates (instead of generalizing) the quasi-identifer and sensitive attributes after grouping the records.

8.3.3 Anonymization of EHRs

Although most of the principles and algorithms apply exclusively to structured (relational) data, a considerable amount of EHRs resides in

> **CLINICAL HISTORY:** **77-year-old female** with a history of B-cell lymphoma (Marginal zone, **SH-02-2222 2**, 6/22/01). Flow cytometry and molecular diagnostics drawn.

FIGURE 8.2
A sample pathology report section.

unstructured text forms such as clinical notes, SOAP (subjective, objective, assessment, patient care plan) notes, radiology and pathology reports, and discharge summaries. Although some identifying attributes can be clearly defined in structured data, an extensive set of identifying information is often hidden or have multiple and different references in the text. In this subsection, we discuss the specific challenges and solutions for anonymizing EHRs, in particular, textual EHRs, and survey a set of existing solutions and software tools for anonymization of EHRs.

We first consider a motivating example. Figure 8.2 shows a sample pathology report section with personally identifying information such as age and medical record number highlighted. It is necessary for the anonymization process to detect the personal identifiers from the text and replace or remove them.

The problem of de-identification of EHRs is primarily studied in the medical informatics community and mainly focuses on medical text only. The problem is recognized to have two subtasks: (1) the identification of personally identifying references within medical text; and (2) the masking, coding, or replacing of these references with irreversible values. Once the de-identification is done, the last step is to effectively evaluate the de-identification for quality control and further improvement. Most of these works rely on simple identifier removal or grouping techniques. They do not take advantage of the recent developments of anonymization principles and techniques that guarantee a more formalized notion of privacy while maximizing data utility.

To fill the above gap and to link the work of the data privacy community more closely with the medical informatics community, we have developed the system for Health Information DE-identification (HIDE) [64, 65]. The system anonymizes an integrated view of the EHRs consisting of both structured and unstructured data, and adopts the formal anonymization principles and techniques. Our conceptual framework consists of three components: identifying attribute extraction, attribute linking, and attribute anonymization.

Identifying and sensitive information extraction. Since an extensive set of identifying information is often hidden or have multiple and different references in the text portion of EHRs, the first subtask is to detect the personally identifying references and sensitive attributes from the textual EHRs.

Attribute linking. In relational data, we assume that each record corresponds to an individual entity. This mapping is not present in heterogeneous EHRs. For example, one patient may have multiple pathology and laboratory reports prepared at different times. An important task for anonymizing EHRs is to link relevant attributes (structured or extracted) to each individual entity and produce a person-centric representation of the data.

Anonymization. Once the identifying attributes are extracted and linked, anonymization techniques can be applied to generate anonymized EHRs.

Extracting identifiers from textual EHRs can be viewed as an application of named entity recognition (NER) problem. It is a subtask of information extraction that seeks to locate and classify atomic elements in text into predefined categories such as the names of persons, organizations, locations, expressions of times, quantities, monetary values, percentages, etc. NER systems can be roughly classified into two categories: grammar-based or rule-based techniques and statistical techniques.

The *grammar-based* or *rule-based* techniques rely heavily on hand-coded rules and dictionaries. Depending on the type of identifying information, there are common approaches that can be used. For identifiers that qualify as a *closed class* with an exhaustive list of values such as geographical locations and names, common knowledge bases such as lists for area codes, common names, words that sound like first names (Soundex) can be used for lookups. Local knowledge such as first names of all patients in a specific hospital can be also used for specific data set. For identifying information that follows certain *syntactic pattern* such as phone numbers and zip codes, regular expressions can be used to match the patterns. Common recording practices (templates) with respect to personal information can be used to build rules. For many cases, a mixture of semantic information including context such as prefix for a person name, syntactic features, dictionaries, and heuristics need to be considered.

Such hand-crafted systems typically obtain good results, but at the cost of months of work by experienced domain experts. In addition, the rules used for extracting identifying information will likely need to change for different types of records (radiology, surgical pathology, operative notes) and across organizations (hospital A formats, hospital B formats). The software will become increasingly complex and slow with growing rules and dictionaries.

The *statistical learning* approaches have been applied to the NER problem with remarkable success. They typically require a large amount of manually annotated training data with prelabeled identifiers. It can then use a list of feature attributes to train a classification model and classify the terms in new text as either identifier or nonidentifier. Typical feature sets include terms themselves, their local contexts (such as words before and after), global contexts (such as document characteristics), and dictionary-related features. The most frequently applied techniques were the maximum entropy model, hidden Markov model, and support vector machines (SVMs). It can be imported to other languages, domains, or genres of text much more rapidly and require less work overall.

Below, we discuss a few representative solutions and software tools for anonymizing EHRs. The objective is to highlight the representative approaches and tools for practitioners who are looking to adopt solutions. A summary of the surveyed systems is provided in Table 8.2 for a quick comparison. For the representative systems, we discuss and compare them along the following dimensions.

Document types that the approach is designed for. They can be general EHRs or specific document types such as pathology reports.

Methods that are used for extracting identifying information. Most of these systems use simple identifier removal technique.

TABLE 8.2

Comparison of EHR Anonymization Systems

Systems	HER Types	Methods	Data Set	Results
Scrub system [32]	General	Rule and dictionary based	3198 letters to referring physicians	Recall = 99–100%
Semantic Lexicon system [66]	General	Rule based	Unknown (40 rules used)	Precision =100% Recall = 96.8%
Concept-match system [67] (open source)	Pathology reports	Dictionary based (white list)	JHARCOLL (567,921 pathology phrases)	Recall = 100%
DE-ID [36] (Commercial)	General	Rule and dictionary based	1000 and 3000 pathology reports	Unknown
De-identification nursing notes [68] (open source)	Nursing notes	Rule and dictionary based	747 nursing notes (22 patients)	Precision = 43.5% Recall = 92%
HMS Scrubber [38] (open source)	Pathology reports	Rule and dictionary based	Test: 1800 pathology reports	Precision = 42.8% Recall = 98.3%
SVM-based System [37]	Discharge summaries	Statistical—SVM classifier	Reidentified data set: 2784 identifiers; authentic: 4194 identifiers	Precision = 92–97.7% Recall = 92.1–98.2%
HIDE [65] (open source)	General	Statistical—conditional random field	100 pathology reports	Precision = 98.2% Recall = 98.2%

Evaluation of the approach including the data sets being used and the results in terms of quality of de-identification and performance. The results are measured by precision (the number of correctly labeled identifying attributes over the total number of labeled identifying attributes) and recall (the number of correctly labeled identifying attributes over the total number of identifying attributes in the EHRs).

8.3.3.1 Scrub System

The scrub system [32], one of the earliest scrubbing systems, locates and replaces HIPAA-compliant personally identifying information for general medical records.

Methods. The system is an example of the rule-based and dictionary-based systems. It uses a set of detection algorithms competing in parallel to label text as being a name, an address, a phone number, and so forth. Each detection algorithm recognizes a specific entity such as first name, street address, and date. The entities may overlap. For example, there is a detection algorithm for first name, last name, and full name. The precedence is based on the number of entities that constitute the algorithm's assigned entity. For example, the location detection algorithm constitutes city, state, and country, and detecting location may make it possible to identify a city, state, and country. Therefore, location has a higher precedence than the latter three detection algorithms. Each algorithm tries to identify occurrences of its assigned entity, and reports a certainty score. The algorithm with the highest precedence and greatest certainty above a minimal threshold prevails.

In terms of anonymization technique, if the detected entity was a date, the replacement date may involve lumping days to the first of the nearest month or some other grouping. If the detected entity was a first name, the typical strategy is to perform a hash-table lookup using the original name as the key. The result of the lookup is the replacement text. This provides consistent replacement. In terms of the replacement content, several strategies are available including the use of orthographic rules that replace personally identifying information with fictitious names. The system also suggests a few strategies to combat the problem of reverse scrubbing, where a person with inside knowledge is able to identify the real person from scrubbed materials. One of them is to group fields together such as lumping dates by week. Although the work has a similar motivation as the k-anonymity approach of preventing record identification, it does not formally use a k-anonymity model in order to prevent identification through linkage attacks.

Data set and evaluations. A subset of pediatric medical record system consisting of 275 patient records and 3198 letters to referring physicians are used for evaluation. The reported recall achieves a rate of 99–100%. The precision is not reported.

8.3.3.2 Semantic Lexicon-Based System

The medical document anonymization system with a semantic lexicon [66] is another scrubbing system that locates and removes personally identifiable information in patient records. It removes explicit personally identifiable information such as name, address, phone number, and date of birth.

Methods. The system is rule based. It differentiates strict identity marker tokens always directly followed or preceded by identifiers, for example, Ms. and Dr., and tokens likely to refer to general persons (doctors, professors) and not necessarily followed or preceded by identifiers. Phone numbers and dates use explicit markers and well-defined patterns (exhaustively listed).

The system replaces each character of any confidential item by an "*x*," and respects the case and punctuation. Tractability is not allowed in the system, that is, P.Nertens, and W.Keuster are both replaced by X.Xxxxxx. The advantage of such a replacement strategy is that reverse scrubbing is impossible or more difficult. However, tractability is lost, which may be necessary for studies on genealogy.

Data set and evaluations. The evaluation involved tuning the system on 20% of the corpus (training set) and writing more than 40 rules to reach 100% success rate for the training set. It was then tested on 80% of the corpus (test set). It was reported that 96.8% (452 of 467) identifiers are correctly removed and 0 tokens removed that are not identifiers. This translates to a 100% precision and 96.8% recall. However, it is a very small data set. In addition, it is at the cost of 3 weeks to write all the rules. It is not clear how such a system would perform with a large volume of data.

8.3.3.3 Concept-Match Scrubber

The concept-match scrubber [67] provides an alternative to traditional de-identification systems by extracting and removing every word from the text except words from an approved list of nonidentifying words. It is designed for pathology reports.

Methods. The concept-match–based medical data scrubbing system uses a whitelist-based approach; in other words, it extracts every word as identifying information except words from an approved list of nonidentifying words such as the Unified Medical Language System (UMLS). When a medical term matching a standard nomenclature term is encountered, the term is replaced by a nomenclature code and a synonym for the original term. When a high-frequency stop word, such as "a," "an," "the," or "for," is encountered, it is left in place. When any other word is encountered, it is blocked and replaced by asterisks.

8.3.3.4 DE-ID

DE-ID [36] was developed at the University of Pittsburgh, where it is used as the de-identification standard for all clinical research approved by the IRB.

DE-ID's main function is to locate identifiable text, as defined by the HIPAA full de-identification or the limited data set, in the document in question. DE-ID Data Corp acquired the global rights to DE-ID Software in 2004 and, after a period of product development and refinements, launched DE-ID for commercial and academic license in March 2005. The NCI has licensed DE-ID to be used as a de-identification component of some of the software applications developed in the Tissue Banks and Pathology Workspace of the NCI-sponsored cancer Biomedical Informatics Grid (caBIG). As of the publication of this book, the NCI has purchased licenses through June 2010. After this date, the institutes are responsible for obtaining de-identification software for their systems.

Document types. DE-ID is designed to work with archives of all types of clinical documents. There had been an initial, limited evaluation of the software's performance on a variety of clinical documents (history and physical examination reports, operative notes, discharge summaries, and progress notes). However, the reported evaluation [36] only includes pathology reports. It supports multiple formats of input documents including Extensible Markup Language (XML)-formatted documents and tab-delimited documents (spreadsheets or relational databases).

Deidentified information. It includes the 17 (full-face photographic images not included) HIPAA-specified identifiers as well as potential identifiers not included in safe harbor, such as names of healthcare providers (physicians, laboratories, and hospitals), employers, and relatives.

Methods. DE-ID implements a set of rules and dictionaries designed to identify the identifying information. Examples of these rules include the examination of document headers for patient and provider names, use of the UMLS Metathesaurus for identification of medical phrases (such as the Gleason score) to retain in the document, pattern matching of numeric text to detect phone numbers and zip codes, the U.S. Census dictionary to aid in the identification of names, and a variety of user-customizable dictionaries for identifiers and healthcare providers unique to an institution.

DE-ID replaces identifiable text with deidentified but specific tags. Identifiers found multiple times in the report are replaced consistently with the same tag to improve continuity and readability of the report. Dates are replaced by tags, but date tags from two different dates retain the time interval between them.

Data set and evaluation. Gupta et al. [36] described the initial quality assurance evaluation of the DE-ID engine in the domain of surgical pathology reports and described a useful model for other testing and quality control of de-identification engines at other institutions and for identifying the unique challenges presented by pathology reports. Textual surgical pathology reports were randomly selected from the University of Pittsburgh Medical Center and processed by the DE-ID engine. The deidentified reports were distributed for evaluation to four pathologists. The de-identification engine was evaluated three times. Problems identified at each pass were discussed between evaluations to improve de-identification of pathology reports. A new set of 1000 reports was reviewed in a similar manner in the second evaluation and an additional 300 reports were evaluated in the third evaluation. Only a number of overmarking errors and itemized number of undermarking errors and total number of reports are reported. No precision or recall is reported or can be derived without the knowledge of the total number of marked identifiers.

8.3.3.5 HMS Scrubber

HMS Scrubber [38] is an open-source, HIPAA-compliant de-identification tool tailored for pathology reports.

Methods. HMS Scrubber performs a three-step process for removing potential identifiers. The pathology reports are first converted to an XML format. This format includes a header portion and a textual portion. The header portion contains demographic information about the patient such as name, medical record number, date of birth, and social security number; and information about the pathology report, such as the accession number and the pathology department. The first step of the extraction is to take advantage of identifying information that may be present in the header of the file such as name, medical record number, pathology accession number, etc., and remove them from the textual portion of the reports. The second step is to perform a series of pattern matches to look for predictable patterns likely to represent identifying data (e.g., dates, access numbers, addresses) as well as patient, institution, and physician names that can be found via markers such as Dr., MD, etc. The pattern searches are implemented as regular expressions. Finally, a database of proper names derived from publicly available census lists and geographic locations derived from a gazetteer file, which contains U.S. place names, is used. At one institution, the names were augmented with the names of pathologists who were active during the period from which the reports were drawn.

Data set and evaluation. Pathology reports from three institutions were used to design and test the algorithms. The software was trained on training sets until it exhibited good performance (the exact number of reports used as training set is not reported). A total of 1800 new pathology reports were used as a test set. It reported a recall of 98.3% (3439 of 3499 unique identifiers in the test set were removed). Although it achieved results similar to previous systems designed for pathology reports, the outcome also highlighted the wide variance in the number of identifiers between external consult and in-house cases as well as between different institutions. It also reported a precision of 42.8% (4671 over-scrubs) that is primarily related to the large number of words contained in names and places table. The reported performance is 47 cases per minute, which makes it suitable for high volume applications compared to other approaches.

8.3.3.6 SVM-Based System

An SVM-based system is proposed by Sibanda and Uzuner [37] for deidentifying medical discharge summaries using statistical SVM-based classification method.

Document types. The system has been designed and tested on discharge summaries. The authors argued that the medical discharge summaries are characterized by incomplete, fragmented sentences, and ad hoc language. Entity names can be misspelled or foreign words can include entity names that are ambiguous between PHI and non-PHI, etc. In addition, discharge summaries do not present information in the form of relations between entities, and many sentences contain only one entity. Given such situations, the local context (words before and after the entity to be classified) is more important than the global context (other sentences in the document) in learning the identifiers.

Methods. The system uses statistical learning, namely, an SVM-based classifier, to classify whether a target word (TW) was part of PHI. The feature set focuses on immediate context of the TW, paying particular attention to cues human annotators found useful for de-identification. The feature set included a total of 26 features, 12 of which were dictionary-related. Information gain showed that the most informative features were the TW, the bigram before and after the TW, the word before and after the TW.

Data set and evaluations. The evaluation used two corpora. One was previously deidentified where many PHI and some non-PHI had been replaced with the generic placeholder and then reidentified by replacing the placeholders with appropriate, fake PHI or non-PHI terms. The second corpus is a set of authentic discharge summaries. It reported a precision of 97.5% on authentic discharge summaries and 92–97.7% on reidentified data set including the corpus containing ambiguous data. The recall is 95% on authentic discharge summaries and 92.1–98.2% for the reidentified data set.

8.3.3.7 HIDE

HIDE [64, 65] is an open-source system* designed to integrate the de-identification process for both textual and structured health records and adopt formal anonymization principles and techniques for EHRs.

Methods. HIDE uses a statistical learning approach, in particular, a conditional random field (CRF)-based named entity recognizer, for extracting identifying and sensitive attributes. A CRF [69] is an advanced discriminative probabilistic model shown to be effective in labeling natural language text. A CRF takes as input a sequence of tokens from the text, where each token has a feature set based on the sequence. Given a token from

---

* http://www.mathcs.emory.edu/hide.

the sequence, it calculates the probabilities of the various possible labeling (whether it is a particular type of identifying or sensitive attribute) and chooses the one with maximum probability. The probability of each label is a function of the feature set associated with that token. More specifically, a CRF is an undirected graphical model that defines a single log-linear distribution function over label sequences given the observation sequence. The CRF is trained by maximizing the log-likelihood of the training data.

To facilitate the overall attribute extraction process, HIDE consists of (1) a tagging interface, which can be used to annotate data with identifying and sensitive attributes to build the training data set; (2) a CRF-based classifier to classify terms from the text into multiple classes (different types of identifiers and sensitive attributes); and (3) a set of data preprocessing and postprocessing strategies for extracting the features from text data for the classifier and feeding the classified data back to the tagging software for retagging and corrections. A unique feature of the approach is its iterative process for classifying and retagging that allows the construction of a large training data set without intensive human efforts in labeling the data from scratch.

Once the identifying attributes are extracted, HIDE offers several options for de-identification. It performs attribute removal (suppression) to allow full de-identification (as possible) and partial de-identification. It also allows statistical de-identification through attribute generalization that guarantees privacy based on k-anonymity.

Data set and evaluations. Our initial evaluation was conducted against a data set of 100 textual pathology reports containing 106,255 tokens. Most identifying attributes achieve nearly perfect performance in both precision and recall, whereas the name attribute has a precision and recall of about 97%. We plan to add new features such as part of speech tagging to further improve the performance.

Since our approach offers k-anonymization, we also evaluated and compared the data utility in terms of query precision of using k-anonymization and full de-identification. The results showed that k-anonymization offered a desirable trade-off that provides a guaranteed privacy level while offering a higher level data utility.

8.3.4 Distributed Anonymization

Our discussion so far deals with anonymizing a single database. In this subsection, we present the scenario of anonymizing and integrating EHRs from multiple distributed databases and discuss potential solutions.

We consider the SPIN scenario again. The problem of privacy-preserving data publishing for multiple distributed data sources is that multiple *data custodians* need to publish an anonymized and integrated view of the data that do not contain individually identifiable information. Such data sharing is subject to two constraints. The first constraint is the privacy of the individuals or the data subject (such as the patients). The second one is the data confidentiality of the data custodians (such as the institutions). Given a query spanning multiple databases, query results should not contain individually identifiable information. In addition, institutions should not reveal their databases to each other apart from the query results.

There are three major approaches that one may apply to enable privacy-preserving data publishing for multiple distributed databases: independent anonymization, trusted third party, and distributed anonymization.

Independent anonymization. One approach is for each data custodian to perform data anonymization independently. Data recipients or clients can query the individual anonymized databases and then integrate the results. One main drawback of this approach is that data are anonymized before the integration and hence will cause the data utility to suffer. In addition, individual databases reveal their ownership of the anonymized data records.

Trusted third party. An alternative approach assumes an existence of a third party that can be trusted by each of the data owners. In this scenario, data owners send their data to this third party, where data integration and anonymization are performed. Then, clients can query the centralized database. However, finding such a trusted third party is not always feasible. The level of trust required for the third party with respect to intent and competence against security breaches is very high. Compromise of the server by hackers could lead to a complete privacy loss for all participating parties.

Distributed anonymization. In this approach, data owners participate in distributed protocols to produce a *virtual* integrated and anonymized database that can be then queried by clients. It is important to note is that the anonymized data still reside at individual databases and the integration and anonymization of the data is performed through the distributed protocols.

The distributed anonymization approach has its roots in the secure MPC problem [70, 71]. In MPC, a given number of participants, each having a private data, wants to compute the value of a public function. An MPC protocol is secure if no participant can learn more from the description of the public function and the result of function. Although there are general secure MPC protocols, they incur substantial computation and communication costs and are impractical for multiparty large database problems.

There are some works that focus on data anonymization of distributed databases following the secure MPC model. Jiang and Clifton [72] presented a two-party framework along with an application that generates k-anonymous data from two vertically partitioned sources without disclosing data from one site to the other. Zhong et al. [73] proposed provably private solutions for k-anonymization in the distributed scenario by maintaining end-to-end privacy from the original customer data to the final k-anonymous results.

Our recent work [74] presents a distributed anonymization approach for multiple horizontally partitioned databases. It introduces a new notion, *l–site–diversity*, for data anonymization to ensure the anonymity of data providers in addition to that of data subjects. It includes two protocols: a *distributed anonymization protocol*, which allows multiple data providers with horizontally partitioned databases to build a virtual anonymized database based on the integration (or union) of the data, and a *distributed querying protocol*, which allows clients to query the virtual database. As the output of the distributed anonymization protocol, each database produces a local anonymized data set and their union forms a virtual database that guarantees the anonymity of both data subjects and data providers. When users query the virtual database, each database executes the query on its local anonymized data set, and then engage in the distributed querying protocol to assemble the results that preserve anonymity. Both protocols use multiparty protocols for suboperations such that information disclosure between individual databases is minimal. In contrast to previous work, the protocols are not based on heavy cryptographic primitives. They exploit the inherent anonymity of a large number of participating sites and utilize probabilistic methods to achieve minimal information disclosure and minimal overhead.

8.4 Privacy-Preserving Data Mining

In this section, we discuss the problem of privacy-preserving data mining. We first introduce the main randomization techniques for privacy-preserving data mining. We then discuss the scenario and solutions for distributed privacy-preserving data mining.

8.4.1 Randomization Techniques

The main technique being used for privacy-preserving data mining is data perturbation or data randomization, which adds certain noise to the sensitive attributes of the data. The challenge is to guarantee a certain level of privacy while allowing specific data mining tasks to be carried out on the perturbed data. There are two main approaches for data randomization: additive randomization and multiplicative randomization.

Additive randomization. The seminal work of Agrawal and Srikant [39] proposed an additive randomization–based privacy-preserving data mining solution for building decision trees. The method can be described as follows. Consider a set of sensitive data values, $x_1, \ldots, x_N$; given an original value x_i, the method returns a value $x_i + r$, where r is a random value drawn from some probability distribution such as uniform or Gaussian distribution. In general, it is assumed that the variance of the added noise is large enough, so that the original record values cannot be easily guessed from the distorted data. Although the individual original values cannot be recovered, the approach can accurately estimate the distribution of the original data values using a Bayesian procedure. Using the reconstructed distributions, it is able to build a decision tree classifier whose accuracy is comparable to the accuracy of classifiers built with the original data.

The randomization method has been studied for a variety of specific data mining problems such as classification [39, 41] and association rule mining [42–44]. The problem of association rules is especially challenging because of the discrete nature of the attributes corresponding to the presence or absence of items. To deal with this issue, the randomization technique needs to be slightly modified. Instead of adding quantitative noise, random items are dropped or included with a certain probability. The perturbed transactions are then used for aggregate association rule mining.

Multiplicative randomization. Two basic forms of multiplicative noise have been well studied in the statistics community. One is to multiply each data element by a random number that has a truncated Gaussian distribution with mean one and small variance. The other one is to take a logarithmic transformation of the data first, add predefined multivariate Gaussian noise, and then take the antilog of the noise-added data. In practice, the first method is good if the data disseminator only wants to make minor changes to the original data; the second method assures higher security than the first one, but maintains the data utility in the log scale. More recent work also studied multiplicative perturbation based on projection, rotation, and geometric perturbation [75].

Categorical data randomization. Additive and multiplicative perturbation usually deal with numeric data only. Perturbation for categorical data can be addressed using a randomized response method developed for the purpose of data collection through interviews. Given a certain randomization probability, a categorical attribute is reported either truthfully or falsely. Categorical data perturbation is also studied in the context of association rule mining. Instead of adding quantitative noise, random items are dropped or included with a certain probability.

Having discussed both data anonymization and data randomization methods, we briefly compare the two approaches. First, a main advantage of data anonymization is that the released data remain "truthful" instead of distorted although at a coarse level of granularity. This allows various information discovery tasks to be carried out using the data, including queries.

Second, a key advantage of the randomization method is that it is relatively simple, and does not require knowledge of the distribution of other records in the data. In contrast, most anonymization methods we discussed earlier require the knowledge of other records in the data. Therefore, the randomization method can be implemented at data collection time, and does not require the use of a trusted server containing all the original records in order to perform the anonymization process. Finally, randomization methods are subject to various attacks. For example, in the additive randomization method, since it treats all records equally irrespective of their local density, outlier records are more susceptible to adversarial attacks. To guard against this, one may need to be overly aggressive in adding noise to all the records in the data. This reduces the utility of the data for mining purposes.

8.4.2 Distributed Privacy-Preserving Data Mining

So far, we have considered privacy-preserving data mining for one data source. In the healthcare domain, each medical institution (hospitals, clinics, etc.) provides a database containing a complete (or almost complete) subset of EHRs. There is an increasing need and interest in sharing the data from all sources and learning data mining models that take into account all the available information without sharing explicitly private information among the sources. This can be considered as a privacy-preserving distributed data mining problem, where the ultimate goal is to perform similarly or identically to a model learned by having access to all the data at the same time.

The approach of protecting the privacy of distributed sources was first addressed by the seminal work of Lindell and Pinkas [48] on construction of decision trees. This work closely followed the traditional secure MPC approach and achieved perfect privacy. Since then, there has been work addressing association rules [49, 50], naive Bayes classification [51–53], and k-means clustering [54], as well as general tools for privacy-preserving data mining [76]. As a recent effort, there is also research on privacy-preserving top-k queries [57] and privacy-preserving distributed k-NN classifier [58], both across vertically partitioned data using k-anonymity privacy model. A few specialized protocols have been proposed, typically in a two-party setting, for example, for finding intersections [56], and the kth ranked element [55]. Wang et al. [77] studied the problem of integrating private data sources with vertically partitioned data while satisfying the k-anonymity of the data. Although still based on cryptographic primitives, they achieve better efficiency than traditional multiparty secure computation methods by allowing minimal information disclosure. In addition, data perturbation techniques are also used to achieve distributed privacy-preserving data mining [40, 78, 79].

8.5 Chapter Summary

We have discussed the problem of privacy-preserving information discovery on EHRs, in particular, privacy-preserving data publishing and privacy-preserving data mining. For each problem, we gave an overview of the general techniques and discussed the representative algorithms. We also surveyed the existing anonymization solutions developed for EHRs. We hope the discussion can provide some insights for practitioners who are looking to adopt solutions as well as for researchers who are looking to do research on the topic.

Although there have been extensive developments of data anonymization and privacy-preserving data mining technologies in general domains, its practical utilization in medical fields lags behind. Many of the techniques are certainly applicable, but it remains a challenge to adopt them in the context of EHRs. Below, we discuss some open problems in the context of EHRs and suggest directions for future research.

Indirect identifying information. Indirect identifying information such as unique medical or social history, sequence of events, or combinations are inherently difficult to detect in textual EHRs because they do not contain specific identifiers, but can effectively limit the number of possible individuals significantly. For example, the physician's note might describe a 46-year-old man with Addison's disease who received a fatal gunshot wound to the head. It is possible that people could identify this person despite the lack of identifiers such as name, address, or phone number. Currently, there is no good mechanism for any de-identification system to identify such unique combinations or sequences of events in textual information that has the potential for patient identification. Relationship extraction techniques can be explored in addition to entity extraction techniques to detect relationships and implicit identifying information.

Attack resistance. Many of the methods are still subject to adversary attacks. There is a recent survey of attack techniques on data perturbation based privacy-preserving data mining [75]. It remains an important challenge to develop privacy-preserving methods that are attack resilient.

Benchmark. Lack of publicly available and standardized data set has been one of the biggest barriers to privacy research on EHRs. It is a chicken-and-egg problem that researchers need clinical data to design and evaluate privacy-preserving algorithms but authentic clinical data are very difficult to obtain for privacy reasons without a good proven privacy-preserving system. In addition, without a common benchmark, it is extremely difficult to evaluate and compare various approaches. Uzuner et al. [80] took an important step toward this direction during their i2b2 workshop on natural language processing challenges for clinical records. They generated and released a set of fully deidentified medical discharge summaries that is reidentified with surrogate and ambiguous personal identifying information to the research community. One of the significant challenges for the workshop is automatic de-identification of the released data. The availability of clinical records will be a major resource for both medical informatics community and natural language processing community.

Easy deployment and continued quality assurance. Finally, it is important to have systems and techniques that can be easily deployed with minimal tuning. In addition, mechanisms and interfaces for continued monitoring will also prove extremely useful, especially when expanding the types or sources of data for information discovery purposes.

Acknowledgments

We would like to thank the editor of the book for providing us the opportunity to contribute this chapter and the anonymous reviewers for their valuable feedback that helped improve our work. Part of the presented work was supported by an Emory ITSC grant, an Emory URC grant, and a Woodrow Wilson Career Enhancement Fellowship.

References

1. Sweeney, L. 2002. *k*-Anonymity: a model for protecting privacy. *International Journal on Uncertainty, Fuzziness and Knowledge-Based Systems* 10(5):557–570.
2. Machanavajjhala, A., Gehrke, J., Kifer, D., and Venkitasubramaniam, M. 2006. *l*-Diversity: privacy beyond *k*-anonymity. In *Proceedings of the IEEE International Conference on Data Engineering*.
3. Truta, T. M., and Vinay, B. 2006. Privacy protection: *p*-sensitive *k*-anonymity property. In *Proceedings of the ICDE Workshops*.
4. Aggarwal, G., Feder, T., Kenthapadi, K., Khuller, S., Panigrahy, R., Thomas, D., and Zhu, A. 2006. Achieving anonymity via clustering. *In Proceedings of PODS*, pp. 153–162.
5. Li, N., and Li, T. 2007. *t*-Closeness: privacy beyond *k*-anonymity and *l*-diversity. In *Proceedings of the 23rd IEEE International Conference on Data Engineering (ICDE)*.
6. Xiao, X., and Tao, Y. 2007. *M*-invariance: towards privacy preserving republication of dynamic datasets. In *Proceedings of the SIGMOD Conference*, pp. 689–700.
7. Martin, D. J., Kifer, D., Machanavajjhala, A., Gehrke, J., and Halpern, J. Y. 2007. Worst-case background knowledge for privacy-preserving data publishing. In *Proceedings of the ICDE*.
8. Nergiz, M. E., Atzori, M., and Clifton, C. 2007. Hiding the presence of individuals from shared databases. In *Proceedings of the ACM SIGMOD*.

9. Jajodia, S., and Sandhu, R. 1991. Toward a multilevel secure relational data model. In *Proceedings of the ACM SIGMOD*.
10. Agrawal, R., Kieman, J., Srikant, R., and Xu, Y. 2002. Hippocratic databases. In *Proceedings of the 28th International Conference on Very Large Data Bases*.
11. LeFevre, K., Agrawal, R., Ercegovac, V., Ramakrishnan, R., Xu, Y., and DeWitt, D. 2004. Limiting disclosure in Hippocratic databases. In *Proceedings of the 30th International Conference on Very Large Data Bases*.
12. Agrawal, R., Bird, P., Grandison, T., Kieman, J., Logan, S., and Rjaibi, W. 2005. Extending relational database systems to automatically enforce privacy policies. In *Proceedings of the 21st IEEE International Conference on Data Engineering*.
13. Byun, J.-W., Bertino, E., and Li, N. 2005. Purpose based access control of complex data for privacy protection. In *ACM Symposium on Access Control Models, and Technologies (SACMAT)*.
14. Byun, J., and Bertino, E. 2006. Micro-views, or on how to protect privacy while enhancing data usability—concept and challenges. *SIGMOD Record* 35(1): 9–13.
15. Adams, N. R., and Wortman, J. C. 1989. Security-control methods for statistical databases: a comparative study. *ACM Computing Surveys* 21(4):515–556.
16. Fung, B. C. M., Wang, K., Chen, R., and Yu, P. S. 2010. Privacy-preserving data publishing: a survey on recent developments. *ACM Computing Surveys*, 42 (4).
17. Iyengar, V. S. 2002. Transforming data to satisfy privacy constraints. In *Proceedings of the 8th ACM International Conference on Knowledge Discovery and Data*, pp. 279–288.
18. Wang, K., Yu, P. S., and Chakraborty, S. 2004. Bottom-up generalization: a data mining solution to privacy protection. In *Proceedings of ICDM*.
19. Meyerson, A., and Williams, R. 2004. On the complexity of optimal *k*-anonymity. In *Proceedings of ACM Symposium on Principles of Database Systems*, pp. 223–228.
20. Bayardo, R. J., and Agrawal, R. 2005. Data privacy through optimal *k*-anonymization. In *Proceedings of the ICDE 2005*.
21. Aggarwal, C. C. 2005. On *k*-anonymity and the curse of dimensionality. In *Proceedings of the 31st International Conference Very Large Data Bases*, pp. 901–909.
22. Fung, B. C. M., Wang, K., and Yu, P. S. 2005. Top-down specialization for information and privacy preservation. In *Proceedings of ICDE*.
23. Bertino, E., Ooi, B. C., Yang, Y., and Deng, R. H. 2005. Privacy and ownership preserving of outsourced medical data. In *Proceedings of the ICDE 2005*.
24. Zhong, S., Yang, Z., and Wright, R. N. 2005. Privacy-enhancing *k*-anonymization of customer data. In *Proceedings of PODS*, pp. 139–147.
25. LeFevre, K., Dewitt, D., and Ramakrishnan, R. 2005. Incognito: efficient full-domain *k*-anonymity. In *Proceedings of the ACM SIGMOD International Conference on Management of Data*.
26. LeFevre, K., Dewitt, D., and Ramakrishnan, R. 2006. Mondrian multidimensional *k*-anonymity. In *Proceedings of the IEEE ICDE*.
27. LeFevre, K., Dewitt, D., and Ramakrishnan, R. 2006. Workload-aware anonymization. In *Proceedings of the ACM SIGKDD*.
28. Wang, K., and Fung, B. C. M. 2006. Anonymizing sequential releases. In *Proceedings of the ACM SIGKDD*.

29. Kifer, D., and Gehrke, J. 2006. Injecting utility into anonymized datasets. In *Proceedings of the SIGMOD Conference*, pp. 217–228.

30. Xiao, X., and Tao, Y. 2006. Anatomy: simple and effective privacy preservation. In *Proceedings of the 32nd International Conference on Very Large Data Bases*, pp. 139–150.

31. Zhang, Q., Koudas, N., Srivastava, D., and Yu, T. 2007. Aggregate query answering on anonymized tables. In *Proceedings of ICDE*.

32. Sweeney, L. 1996. Replacing personally-identifying information in medical records, the scrub system. *Journal of the American Informatics Association*, 333–337.

33. Sweeney, L. 1997. Guaranteeing anonymity when sharing medical data, the datafly system. In *Proceedings of AMIA Annual Fall Symposium*.

34. Thomas, S. M., Mamlin, B., Schadow, G., and McDonald, C. 2002. A successful technique for removing names in pathology reports. In *Proceedings of the Annual AMIA Symposium*, pp. 777–781.

35. Taira, R. K., Bui, A. A., and Kangarloo, H. 2002. Identification of patient name references within medical documents using semantic selectional restrictions. In *Proceedings of the AMIA Symposium*.

36. Gupta, D., Saul, M., and Gilbertson, J. 2004. Evaluation of a de-identification (De-id) software engine to share pathology reports and clinical documents for research. *American Journal of Clinical Pathology* 121(2):176–186.

37. Sibanda, T., and Uzuner, O. 2006. Role of local context in de-identification of ungrammatical fragmented text. In *Proceedings of the North American Chapter of Association for Computational Linguistics/Human Language Technology*.

38. Beckwith, B. A., Mahaadevan, R., Balis, U. J., and Kuo, F. 2006. Development and evaluation of an open source software tool for de-identification of pathology reports. *BMC Medical Informatics and Decision Making* 42(1):13–35.

39. Agrawal, R., and Srikant, R. 2000. Privacy-preserving data mining. In *Proceedings of the ACM SIGMOD Conference on Management of Data*, pp. 439–450.

40. Verykios, V. S., Bertino, E., Fovino, I.N., Provenza, L. P., Saygin, Y., and Theodoridis, Y. 2004. State-of-the-art in privacy preserving data mining. *ACM SIGMOD Record* 33(1):50–57.

41. Bu, S., Lakshmanan, L. V. S., Ng, R. T., and Ramesh, G. 2007. Preservation of patterns and input-output privacy. In *Proceedings of the ICDE*.

42. Rizvi, S., and Haritsa, J. R. 2002. Maintaining data privacy in association rule mining. In *Proceedings of the 28th International Conference on Very Large Data Bases*, pp. 682–693.

43. Evfimievski, A. V., Gehrke, J., and Srikant, R. 2003. Limiting privacy breaches in privacy preserving data mining. In *Proceedings of PODS*, pp. 211–222.

44. Evfimievski, A. V., Srikant, R., Agrawal, R., and Gehrke, J. 2004. Privacy preserving mining of association rules. *Information Systems* 29(4):343–364.

45. Kargupta, H., Datta, S., Wang, Q., and Sivakumar, K. 2003. On the privacy preserving properties of random data perturbation techniques. In *Proceedings of the ICDM*.

46. Huang, Z., Du, W., and Chen, B. 2005. Deriving private information from randomized data. In *Proceedings of the SIGMOD Conference*, pp. 37–48.

47. Teng, Z., and Du, W. 2006. Comparisons of k-anonymization and randomization schemes under linking attacks. In *Proceedings of the ICDM*.

48. Lindell, Y., and Pinkas, B. 2002. Privacy preserving data mining. *Journal of Cryptology* 15(3):177–206.

49. Vaidya, J., and Clifton, C. 2002. Privacy preserving association rule mining in vertically partitioned data. In *Proceedings of the 8th ACM International Conference on Knowledge Discovery and Data Mining.*

50. Kantarcioglu, M., and Clifton, C. 2004. Privacy preserving data mining of association rules on horizontally partitioned data. *IEEE Transactions on Knowledge and Data Engineering* 16(9):1026–1037.

51. Kantarcoglu, M., and Vaidya, J. 2003. Privacy preserving naive Bayes classifier for horizontally partitioned data. In *Proceedings of the ICDM Workshop on Privacy Preserving Data Mining.*

52. Vaidya, J., and Clifton, C. 2003. Privacy preserving naive Bayes classifier for vertically partitioned data. In *Proceedings of the 9th ACM International Conference on Knowledge Discovery and Data Mining.*

53. Yang, Z., Zhong, S., and Wright, R. N. 2005. Privacy-preserving classification of customer data without loss of accuracy. In *Proceedings of SIAM SDM.*

54. Vaidya, J., and Clifton, C. 2003. Privacy-preserving k-means clustering over vertically partitioned data. In *Proceedings of SIGKDD.*

55. Aggarwal, G., Mishra, N., and Pinkas, B. 2004. Secure computation of the kth ranked element. In *Proceedings of the IACR Conference on Eurocrypt.*

56. Agrawal, R., Evfimievski, A., and Srikant, R. 2003. Information sharing across private databases. In *Proceedings of SIGMOD.*

57. Vaidya, J., and Clifton, C. 2005. Privacy-preserving top-k queries. In *Proceedings of ICDE.*

58. Kantarcioglu, M., and Clifton, C. 2005. Privacy preserving k-NN classifier. In *Proceedings of the ICDE.*

59. Xiong, L., Chitti, S., and Liu, L. 2005. Top-k queries across multiple private databases. In *Proceedings of the 25th International Conference on Distributed Computing Systems (ICDCS 2005).*

60. Bhowmick, S. S., Gruenwald, L., Iwaihara, M., and Chatvichienchai, S. 2006. Private-iye: A framework for privacy preserving data integration. In *Proceedings of the ICDE Workshops.*

61. Xiong, L., Chitti, S., and Liu, L. 2007. Mining multiple private databases using a knn classifier. In *Proceedings of the ACM Symposium on Applied Computing (SAC),* pp. 435–440.

62. Xiong, L., Chitti, S., and Liu, L. 2007. Preserving data privacy for outsourcing data aggregation services. *ACM Transactions on Internet Technology (TOIT)* 7(3):17.

63. Xiao, X., and Tao, Y. 2006. Personalized privacy preservation. In *Proceedings of the 2006 ACM SIGMOD International Conference on Management of Data.*

64. Gardner, J., and Xiong, L. 2008. HIDE: an integrated system for health information de-identification. In *Proceedings of the IEEE CBMS.*

65. Gardner, J., and Xiong, L. 2009. An integrated framework for anonymizing unstructured medical data. *Data and Knowledge Engineering (DKE),* in press. Available online at doi:10.1016/j.datak.2009.07.006.

66. Ruch, P., Baud, R. H., Rassinoux, A. M., Bouillon, P., and Robert, G. 2000. Medical document anonymization with a semantic lexicon. In *Proceedings of the AMIA Symposium.*

67. Berman, J. J. 2003. Concept-match medical data scrubbing: how pathology text can be used in research. *Archives of Pathology and Laboratory Medicine* 127(66):680–686.

68. Douglass, M., Clifford, G. D., Reisner, A., Long, W. J., Moody, G. B., and Mark, R. G. 2005. De-identification algorithm for free-text nursing notes. *Computers in Cardiology* 32:331–334.

69. Lafferty, J., McCallum, A., and Pereira, F. 2001. Conditional random fields: probabilistic models for segmenting and labeling sequence data. In *Proceedings of the 18th International Conference on Machine Learning*.

70. Goldwasser, S. 1997. Multi-party computations: past and present. In *Proceedings of the ACM Symposium on Principles of Distributed Computing*.

71. Goldreich, O. 2001. Secure multi-party computation. Working Draft, Version 1.3.

72. Jiang, W., and Clifton, C. 2006. A secure distributed framework for achieving *k*-anonymity. *The VLDB Journal* 15(4):316–333.

73. Zhong, S., Yang, Z., and Wright, R. N. 2005. Privacy-enhancing *k*-anonymization of customer data. In *Proceedings of the 24th ACM SIGMOD-SIGACT-SIGART Symposium on Principles of Database Systems*, pp. 139–147. New York, NY: ACM Press.

74. Jurczyk, P., and Xiong, L. 2009. Distributed anonymization: achieving anonymity for both data subjects and data providers. In *Annual IFIP WG 11.3 Working Conference on Data and Applications Security (DBSec)*.

75. Aggarwal, C., and Yu, P. S., eds. 2008. *Privacy-Preserving Data Mining: Models and Algorithms*. New York, NY: Springer.

76. Clifton, C., Kantarcioglu, M., Lin, X., Vaidya, J., and Zhu, M. 2003. Tools for privacy preserving distributed data mining. In *Proceedings of SIGKDD Explorations*.

77. Wang, K., Fung, B. C. M., and Dong, G. 2005. Integrating private databases for data analysis. In *Proceedings of the IEEE ISI*.

78. Kargupta, H., Datta, S., Wang, Q., and Sivakumar, K. 2003. On the privacy preserving properties of random data perturbation techniques. In *Proceedings of the IEEE International Conference on Data Mining*, p. 99, Melbourne, FL, November.

79. Liu, K., Kargupta, H., and Ryan, J. 2006. Random projection-based multiplicative data perturbation for privacy preserving distributed data mining. *IEEE Transactions on Knowledge and Data Engineering* 18(1):92–106.

80. Uzuner, O., Szolovits, P., and Kohane, I. 2006. i2b2 Workshop on natural language processing challenges for clinical records. In *Fall Symposium of the American Medical Informatics Association (AMIA)*.

9

Real-Time and Mobile Physiological Data Analysis

Daniele Apiletti, Elena Baralis, Giulia Bruno,
Tania Cerquitelli, and Alessandro Fiori

CONTENTS

9.1 Introduction

In the past few years, the general population has grown steadily older and the number of people with physical or cognitive disabilities has been growing and will grow even more significantly in the future. Hence, supporting long-term patient healthcare needs requires comprehensive health monitoring solutions for nursing homes, hospitals, and homes [1].

With this goal in mind, the combination of information technologies and telecommunications has supported the developments of telematics technologies, which play a key role in the development of new healthcare applications. To make an effective use of the data and telematics technologies, intelligent approaches and architecture have been studied to help medical professionals fulfill their mission, by optimizing their medical processes and improving the quality of care and social welfare [2]. Healthcare telematics applications have been designed and developed for the continuity of care through all stages of care delivery, prevention, diagnoses, treatment, and rehabilitation. Telematics technologies have also improved services in all points of care (e.g., hospitals, rehabilitation centers, laboratories) to foster better management in the health sector and to improve the quality of care. However, the increasing cost of healthcare services has created several challenges for policy makers, healthcare providers, hospitals, insurance companies, and patients. A major challenge is how to provide better healthcare services to an increasing number of people using limited financial and human resources. To address this challenge, healthcare services have become more mobile, ubiquitous, and user-friendly through the use of wireless technologies. Wireless telemedicine, which exploits increasingly ubiquitous wireless infrastructures, allows monitoring of patients and intervention from healthcare professionals as and when required. Through wireless telemedicine applications, many treatments can be done at home with as little discomfort as possible and hospital length of stay is shortened. Hence, this technology reduces total healthcare costs by enabling better utilization of limited healthcare resources, and encouraging independent living for increasingly older individuals in most countries [3].

The first wireless patient monitoring devices recorded long-term activity as raw data from the patient and stored the information in a local storage device or sent the data to the medical center. In both cases, an offline analysis on a physician's desktop for the recorded period was required. It is clear, however, that offline analysis did not allow for immediate detection or prevention of unsafe situations. Hence, medical staff and patients could benefit from the monitoring process by applying automatic real-time analysis. Furthermore, with the increase in computational power of modern wireless technology, the mainstream of research has turned toward data-intensive approaches and intelligent systems, which are nowadays primarily used as tools for ubiquitous real-time monitoring of physiological signals.

Although data collection processes are well established in medicine and the amount of collected medical data is substantial, only limited success has been achieved so far in exploiting the knowledge hidden within data for improving medical processes and quality of care. Different mobile monitoring systems [4–6] have been proposed to enhance human comfort, efficiency of healthcare, and prevention of illness prevention [7]. In a mobile health system, the patient wears a set of sensors that monitor his/her physiological signals (e.g., temperature, heart rate, blood pressure, oxygen saturation, serum glucose). These sensors, which are integrated into noninvasive objects (e.g., watches [8]) transmit recorded signals to the user's device [e.g., a smart phone or a personal digital assistant (PDA)]. The user's device locally elaborates the incoming signals to detect life-threatening situations and when a risk situation is detected, an alert message is sent to the closest medical center to request prompt medical intervention. Furthermore, the user's mobile device can also send the recorded signals to the hospital for further analysis. Current applications of the described mobile health system include continuous monitoring as part of a diagnostic procedure, optimal maintenance of a chronic condition, and supervised recovery from an acute event or surgical procedure. Further developments and potential applications will exploit context awareness of the patient's current activity and physiological state (e.g., heart rate, oxygen saturation, blood pressure, body temperature), leading to significant improvements for the healthcare professional's decision-making process.

Many research activities have been focused on the architecture and connectivity among devices [9, 10], and less attention has been devoted to the design and development of analysis techniques to automatically detect unsafe situations in real time. The challenges in analyzing the monitored physiological signals include characterizing both common and uncommon clinical situations to learn patient behaviors. The extracted knowledge may be exploited to assess in real time the current state of the monitored patient in order to efficiently and effectively detect risk situations. The definition of efficient algorithms that automatically detect unsafe situations in real time is a very difficult task. Hence, different proposed techniques address this issue by relaxing some constraints, for example, by performing the real-time analysis task limited to a specific physiological signal [11], using some type of a priori information and fixed thresholds [12], or focusing on long-term trends [13].

This chapter is organized as follows. Section 9.2 presents related work. In Section 9.3, different architectures of health systems are presented and discussed, with a focus on the collected health measurements, transmission issues, and clinical data analysis performed on different devices (e.g., personal server as smart phone or mobile device, and remote centers). In Section 9.4, relevant knowledge discovery applications are described and discussed in detail. Among the different health applications, we focus on cardiovascular diseases, Alzheimer's disease, and intensive care applications. Experimental validation of different monitoring systems is presented. Section 0provides an in-depth description of different patient data modeling techniques proposed in the literature. Proposed techniques characterize common and uncommon behaviors of a specific patient to build a behavioral model tailored to him/her. The model is then exploited in real-time analysis to assess the instantaneous risk of monitored patients. Section 9.6 discusses several requirements (e.g., management of both routine and emergency vital signs, confidential and private transmission) and pitfalls (e.g., the reliability of message delivery to healthcare professionals) that mobile monitoring and analysis systems have to deal with. Section 9.7 draws conclusions and suggests research directions on mobile and ubiquitous healthcare systems to analyze physiological signals.

9.2 Related Work and Further Readings

Many research activities have been focused on the design of wearable medical systems [12,14] for home-based and ambulatory health monitoring, and the reduction of power consumption of medical body sensors [15, 16]. Wireless smart sensors with sensing and communication capabilities have been integrated into advanced wearable accessories (e.g., watches [8], gloves [14], T-shirts [17]). These sensors can measure physiological signals and transmit recorded data to a mobile device [10, 18].

Although considerable efforts have been dedicated to improve healthcare system architecture [16, 19], less research has been devoted to investigating analysis techniques to assess the current risk level of a patient. Furthermore, it should also be noted that real-time monitoring of human signals may provide information about people's activities.

Although body sensor networks have already found applications in healthcare, a new emerging area is sport activity monitoring [11, 20]. In the study conducted by Ermes et al. [20], different classifiers have been used for detecting sport activities by analyzing 3D accelerometer signals. The main focus was on the comparison of the activity recognition between supervised and unsupervised settings. A low-power mobile system to investigate long-term patterns and classify different activities (e.g., rest, postural orientation) is presented by Karantonis et al. [11]. Accelerometer signal processing is performed directly onboard of the wearable unit by satisfying memory and time constraints. Although body activity is a component of the health status, when using a single signal (e.g., the accelerometer) the physiological conditions of a patient cannot be properly analyzed. A future trend in sport activity analysis could be the joint analysis of physiological signals and technical performance parameters to provide a physiological and technical characterization of the monitored athlete, and to allow the timely identification of body stress conditions. This knowledge could support technical learning, enhance injury prevention, improve performance, and support rehabilitation (e.g., by tracking the progress of an individual with a disability).

A parallel effort has been devoted to support interoperability among healthcare informatics systems. In the past, clinical information such us observations, treatments, therapies, administered drugs, and allergies were stored in various proprietary formats. In 1998, Iakovidis [21] introduced the electronic health record (EHR) as a digitally stored healthcare information about an individual's lifetime to support continuity of care and ensure confidentiality at all times. Since medical data exchanged over healthcare systems are mostly elaborated in a distributed manner, by multiple autonomous and heterogeneous, but cooperating, information systems, EHR can be efficiently exploited to support interoperability in such systems by improving the data exchange. Real-time physiological data, collected via the technologies and architectures discussed in this chapter, can be summarized in EHRs to be more carefully analyzed offline and efficiently shared in heterogeneous information systems.

9.3 Health System Architectures

In the classical healthcare systems, patients are located in a medical center and connected with machinery that collects vital signs, or patients are subjected to isolated medical examinations.

Advances in information technology and telecommunications, and their combination (i.e., telematics technologies) lead to the development of different types of information infrastructures with the potential of supporting new and enhanced services. In recent years, different healthcare systems have been developed to improve the quality of care and patient comfort during treatment and rehabilitation.

Developments in sensing devices, miniaturization of low-power microelectronics, and wireless networks provide an opportunity to improve the quality of care services for both patients and health professionals, thus allowing patients to stay at home or at different locations outside hospitals.

Furthermore, a comprehensive health-monitoring system should be context aware, thereby enhancing healthcare professionals' decision-making process regarding patient conditions and healthcare needs.

Figure 9.1 shows the building blocks of a multitier system architecture. Each patient wears a set of sensors that monitor his/her physiological signals and activities. These sensors, which are integrated into noninvasive objects, are connected to a user's device (also called personal server, e.g., a smart phone or a PDA) through a short-range communication link in charge of transmitting recorded signals. The device may locally elaborate the incoming signals to immediately detect life-threatening situations. Communication

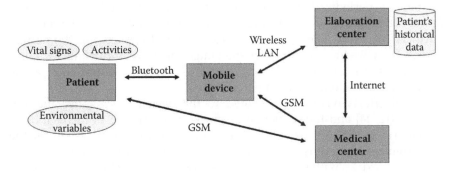

FIGURE 9.1
Architecture of mobile healthcare systems.

between the user's mobile device and the remote centers is made possible via an infrastructure of wired or wireless networks. Communication with remote centers may occur when recorded data are transferred to the system for offline analysis or for backup and/or gathering of historical data. Finally, an alert message may be sent, through the mobile phone network, to the closest medical center to request prompt medical intervention when a risk situation is detected. An alert message may also be sent by the patient herself/ himself if she/he happens to need physician intervention [22].

Each block represents a fairly complex subsystem used to ensure efficiency, portability, security, and reduced cost. A more detailed description of each subsystem is presented in the following sections.

9.3.1 Patient Health Measurement

Clinical data are gathered at the patient location via sensors or point-of-care testing (POCT) devices. The latter are portable instruments and test kits that allow diagnostic tests to be performed at the patient site. Examples of POCT devices include human immunodeficiency virus salivary assays and blood glucose meters. Even though use of POCT devices is spreading and becoming cost-effective for many diseases, when vital signs need to be continuously measured at the patient location, integrated sensors must be used. Sensors may be connected through a body sensor network.

A body sensor network consists of multiple sensing devices capable of sampling and processing one or more vital signs (e.g., heart rate, blood pressure, oxygen saturation, body temperature), patient activity, or environmental parameters (e.g., patient location, environment temperature, light). Furthermore, these devices are able to transfer relevant gathered information to a personal server (i.e., a mobile device such as PDA or a smart phone) through a wireless personal network implemented using ZigBee or Bluetooth technologies (see Section 9.3.2).

According to the type and nature of a healthcare application, the frequency of relevant events (e.g., sampling, processing, and communicating) is set. Sensors periodically transmit their status and gathered measurements. Power consumption–reducing strategies are exploited to extend battery life. Furthermore, since sensing devices are strategically placed on the human body, as tiny wearable accessories they must satisfy requirements for minimal weight, miniature form factor, and low power consumption to allow extended health monitoring time.

Several efforts have been devoted to the design of wearable medical systems [12, 14] and the reduction of power consumption of medical body sensors [15, 16, 23]. For example, Axisa et al. [14] describe a system for the measurement of nervous system activity via a smart shirt and a smart glove, which use textiles with sensors and wires for communication. Anliker et al. [23] describe several ways to reduce power consumption by choosing passive sensors, activating the display backlight only when the user presses a button, putting special care in the analog processing unit design, reducing clock frequency, and replacing a discrete analog board with an application-specific integrated circuit (ASIC). Meanwhile, Branche and Mendelson [16] describe a method to minimize light-emitting diode driving currents, which lowers the overall power requirement of a reflectance mode pulse oximeter.

9.3.2 Transmission of Clinical Data

Two main phases can be identified in clinical data transmission:

1. Once data have been collected by sensors, they must be transmitted to the local mobile device for real-time analysis, as depicted in Figure 9.2.
2. Next, data at patient location is transferred to the remote elaboration center or to the medical center for further analysis. This may be done via a scheduled background task (e.g., backup copy of daily measurements) or may be caused by triggered alarms, which require deeper investigation by medical staff.

Each phase involves different communication technologies. Local transmission is focused on short-range and low-power wireless networks, whereas remote communications are mainly based on existing mobile phone networks. However, new emerging technologies from computer networks can also be used for long-distance transmissions.

9.3.2.1 Local Transmission

The most popular wireless protocols for connections among local devices (sensors, smart phones, etc.) at the patient location are Bluetooth, defined in the IEEE 802.15.1 specifications [24], and ZigBee [25], based on the IEEE 802.15.4 standard. Bluetooth has been designed to exchange data among different devices (e.g., mobile phones, laptops, printers, cameras) in a wireless

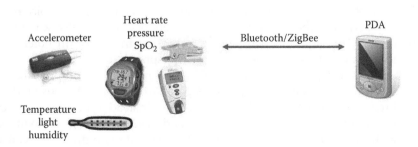

FIGURE 9.2
Patient health measurement and local transmission.

personal area network, that is, a network of computer-based devices spatially close to a person. The range of the network can vary from few meters to about 100 m depending on the power of the devices. Bluetooth focuses on low power consumption and low-cost transceivers (i.e., the microchip in charge of the radio transmission), which may cost less than $3. It enables equipped devices to communicate with each other when they are in range. Since the system is based on radio communications, devices do not have to be in line of sight; they can even be in different rooms, as long as the received transmission power is sufficient. Many versions of the protocol have been developed so far, but their analysis falls beyond the scope of this book. In our context, it is relevant to note that Bluetooth provides a high data rate (currently up to 3.0 Mbit/s), which is more than enough to exchange live measurements of physiological signals and audio streams. In contrast, it may be not be sufficient for video and high-resolution image transmissions, which may take tens of minutes to be accomplished. Bluetooth has a wide transmission range (up to 100 m), and uses an unlicensed radio band at the frequency of 2.4 GHz, which is free for use almost everywhere in the world, that is, no license is required to transmit at this frequency.

The ZigBee protocol is another choice for short-range communications. Compared to Bluetooth, although it provides a lower data rate (up to 250 kbit/s, i.e., about one-tenth of Bluetooth) and uses different radio frequency bands (868 MHz, 915 MHz, and 2.4 GHz), the data rate is still sufficient for most situations (e.g., live monitoring) and the frequencies are in unlicensed bands. It is unsuitable for audio and video streams, as well as for high-resolution image transmission, because of its low speed. Although ZigBee is geared toward even lower power consumption and cheaper devices, both protocols address security issues by providing data encryption and also more sophisticated security techniques, and they have similar transmission ranges. One key factor in favor of the Bluetooth protocol is the wider equipped base of consumer electronic devices, in particular, smart phones, whereas ZigBee may seem more suitable—thanks to its specific applications in industrial and home automation (e.g., centralized management of lighting, heating, cooling, and security) as well as personal healthcare (e.g., patient monitoring).

To complete the communication technology overview, a third choice must be mentioned. It is the wireless local area network (LAN), also known as WiFi or 802.11b/g standard [26], which is present in almost all notebooks and laptop computers, besides an increasing spread among smart phones, which makes it the most popular wireless technology for computer-based devices. However, in our context it is relegated to last resort because it does not address the low power and low cost issues. Instead, it provides a much higher data transmission rate (more than 10 times the Bluetooth maximum rate), with similar transmission ranges (i.e., 100 m). It main drawback is that WiFi has been designed to replace the typical office local networks, thus with very different aims in mind. Nevertheless, it can be used in semioffice environments, such as nursing homes, where patient mobility is restricted to delimited areas and a proper infrastructure can be deployed.

9.3.2.2 Remote Transmission

Connections between the mobile device (e.g., PDA) at the patient location and the remote centers require long-distance communications, as depicted in Figure 9.3. The main technologies involved are provided by phone networks, both in the wired and wireless implementations.

A wired network can be used to connect the local device at the patient location to the remote medical or elaboration center when such location has very limited changes over time. Despite the limitations in mobility, the wired connection offers the advantage of a very high availability, thanks to low interference and the privileged transmission channel provided by the dedicated cable, in contrast with the shared air channels when using radio communications. Furthermore, the available data rate with cable connections is higher in absolute value and also costs less on average, compared to wireless connections. The most popular data connection technology for fixed phone lines is the Digital Subscriber Line [27], which is available in many commercial packages in most countries, and provides speeds in the order of Mbit/s. An old-fashioned alternative could be the usage of computer modems between the two endpoints. This solution could be effective and costs less when transmissions take place rarely and involve very few data, since it is typically billed on the connection time and provides data rates up to 56 kbit/s. In contrast,

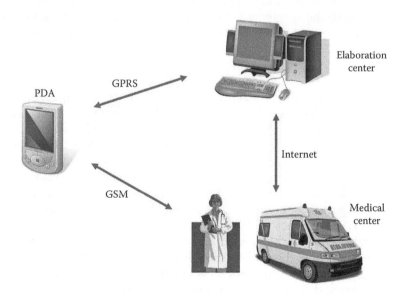

FIGURE 9.3
Transmission to remote centers.

optical fiber is a more advanced and faster alternative that may be available in some countries, but which could lead to higher costs.

That said, mobility remains crucial for monitoring patients who are not required to stay in bed. Thus, exploiting wireless phone networks is probably the most appropriate solution for transmitting local data to remote centers. Many technologies exist and others are emerging in this field. We briefly survey the most popular.

The most widespread technology is Global System for Mobile (GSM) communications [28], which covers 70–80% of the global mobile market [29]. Enhanced versions now exist, especially regarding data transfer. In fact, the original GSM specification allows data exchange at 14.4 kbit/s. General Packet Radio Service (GPRS) increased this limit to tens of kbit/s, and Enhanced Data rates for GSM Evolution (EDGE) provides up to 118.4 kbit/s of upload speed, even though further evolutions have higher peak values. These mobile communication protocols were developed as improvements of the GSM network. However, completely new technologies, the so-called 3G, third generation, have been introduced since 2001. They include Universal Mobile Telecommunications System (UMTS) and IS-2000 (also known as Code Division Multiple Access-2000) protocols [30], which are available in many countries worldwide. Evolutions of 3G networks can provide transfer data at speeds of tens of Mbit/s, which would satisfy any request in clinical data transmission.

Exploiting the phone network for remote connections enables the local mobile device and the elaboration or medical center to be placed virtually anywhere in the world, but requires the local mobile device to be capable of connecting to the specific wireless phone network. Characteristics of the mobile device are analyzed in Section 9.3.3.

9.3.3 Personal Server

The core of the overall architecture is a personal server, implemented by a mobile device that records physiological values from wearable sensors, transmits vital signs to the elaboration center, locally elaborates them to detect dangerous situations, and sends alert messages to request prompt medical intervention. Connectivity with other architectural components uses different technologies. Whereas the personal server interfaces to the body sensor network through a network coordinator that implements ZigBee or Bluetooth protocols, it exploits mobile telephone networks (e.g., GSM) or wireless WLANs to reach an Internet access point for communicating with the medical server (see Section 9.3.2). Furthermore, the personal server is also a critical point of the architecture. Since portable appliances work with different constraints (e.g., power consumption, memory, battery), the analysis of physiological signals performed on mobile devices requires optimized power consumption and short processing response times, which are important research topics in different computer science areas.

The development of analysis algorithms on mobile devices requires handling of some issues. First of all, in contrast to traditional personal computers, diverse operating systems are commonly used in a relevant percentage of devices in the market. The most popular are Symbian, Windows Mobile, BlackBerry, iPhone, and PalmOS. Since each operating system requires a specific version to be developed, the choice of the particular mobile device has to be considered carefully. Second, depending on the analysis performed, memory and processing resources are to be assessed. Typical available main memory for running programs in current smart phones is up to 256 MB, whereas storage memory can usually be expanded to a few gigabytes via additional memory cards. Processing resources depend on the installed central processing unit (CPU) and its speed, whose approximate value can be given by its frequency. Current CPUs have frequencies in the order of hundreds of MHz. Compared to traditional desktop PCs, resources of a mobile device can be estimated to be one-tenth, both in memory and processing power. Although this is not a pressing limitation, mobile devices suffer from another critical issue: battery life. Assessing the actual battery life is difficult because it strongly depends on the usage pattern. A continuous transmission over the phone network can make a device last only few hours, whereas in standby mode many days may pass before it powers off (i.e., without actually using it). Thus, only under a specific test scenario can the actual battery life of the involved mobile device be assessed, even though an approximate life of a few days can be reasonably expected.

9.3.4 Remote Centers

Once the physiological data have been collected via the body sensor network and transferred to the personal server, this device may send them to remote centers. Although there could be a single remote center (and it could even be the hospital itself, from a logical point of view), two remote centers can be identified: an elaboration center and a medical assistance center.

The former focuses on further analysis of collected clinical data, whereas the latter provides medical assistance to patients in need (e.g., rescue service, life-saving intervention).

The elaboration center is generally a computer system that stores historical physiological signals collected during daily monitoring, diagnostic test results, and other context information on the patient (e.g., age, sex, previous clinical history). It usually provides a powerful graphical user interface to show the time series of physiological data, allows physicians to analyze historical patient data, and performs further statistical analyses.

The medical center aims at providing prompt medical intervention to the patient; thus, the personal server may either contact this center in case of critical health situations or send collected data in real time. Many efforts have been devoted to the latter situation [5], where mobile devices (e.g., PDAs) transfer the patient's signals to a remote central management unit for access and analysis by medical staff. The framework proposed by Wu et al. [4] is focused on a medical mobile system that performs real-time telediagnosis and teleconsultation. Patient measures are collected by a digital signal processor–based hardware, compressed in real time, and sent to physicians in a hospital.

The two logical centers, when physically separated, may exchange data via an Internet connection, so that results of the refinement analyses performed at the elaboration center are sent to the medical center, which can decide whether intervention at the patient site is required.

9.4 Knowledge Discovery Applications

Knowledge discovery applications rely on intelligent systems that are capable of extracting relevant information from clinical data. Intelligent systems in medicine exploit two main technologies, both based on data processing and search: optimization and machine learning. Some data mining techniques are discussed in Chapter 7. They are used for different types of medical problems such as clinical data mining, diagnosing, medical imaging, and signal processing.

Application-specific algorithms mostly use digital signal preprocessing combined with a variety of artificial intelligence techniques to model users' states and activities in each state, including filters to resolve high and low frequency components of a signal, wavelet transform [31], power spectrum analysis and a Gaussian model to classify activity types [32], and fuzzy logic [33].

Most of the algorithms in the open literature are not executed in real time, or require powerful computing platforms for real-time analysis. Indeed, the definition of efficient algorithms that automatically detect unsafe situations in real-time is not a light task.

In the following, some specific application scenarios are described in detail, with relevant literature cited. Furthermore, a paramedical context in which intelligent systems have been applied is the sport field, where the monitoring of athletes' physiological parameters plays a key role in the training plan and the performance evaluation [34].

9.4.1 Activity Recognition

The ability to record and classify the movements of an individual is essential when attempting to determine his or her degree of functional ability and general level of activity. Furthermore, the real-time monitoring of human movement can provide an automated system for supervising functional statuses over extended periods.

User activity recognition fits into the bigger framework of context awareness. Ubiquitous computing is centered around the idea of provisioning

FIGURE 9.4
Sample architecture for activity recognition applications.

services to the user based on her/his location or activity. Signals for activity recognition can be obtained from different types of detectors. These include electromyography, audio sensors, image sensors, and accelerometers. Among them, accelerometers that can record acceleration data caused by movements and gravity have drawn much attention in the field of activity recognition; meanwhile, image processing techniques are discussed in Chapter 10.

An accelerometer is a sensor that returns a real valued estimate of acceleration along the x and y axes (including z if it is a triaxial accelerometer). Advances in miniaturization will permit accelerometers to be embedded within wrist bands, bracelets, and belts, and to wirelessly send data to a mobile computing device that can use the signals to make inferences. A sample architecture for activity recognition applications is depicted in Figure 9.4.

An important work in this field is the one discussed by Bao and Intille [35]. Subjects wore five biaxial accelerometers on different body parts as they performed a variety of activities such as walking, sitting, standing, watching TV, running, bicycling, eating, reading, etc. Data generated by the accelerometers was used to train a set of classifiers, which included decision trees, decision tables, naïve Bayes classifiers, and nearest-neighbor algorithms.

Ravi et al. [36] attempted to recognize activities by using a single triaxial accelerometer worn near the pelvic region. Activity recognition is formulated as a classification problem and, in addition to the base-level classifiers, their combination is exploited to achieve a higher accuracy. The advantages of combining classifiers are discussed, along with their most relevant features (such as mean, standard deviation, and correlation) and hardest-to-recognize activities (e.g., short activities).

Maurer et al. [37] also presented an activity recognition and monitoring system. The system identifies the user's activity in real time by using a biaxial accelerometer. They compared multiple features and sampling rates, and analyzed the trade-off between recognition accuracy and computational complexity. The variation of the classification accuracy is evaluated for different body positions used for wearing electronic devices.

In the work of Yang et al. [38], the focus is on the development of a neurofuzzy classifier for activity recognition using one triaxial accelerometer and feature reduction approaches. First, the raw acceleration sequences are cut into many overlapping windows of the same length and features are extracted from each window into a feature set. Then, feature extraction is performed among the computed features (such as mean, standard deviation, energy) by transforming original feature sets into a lower-dimensional feature space with class separability.

Tapia et al. [39] focus on the problem of recognizing not only the activities but also their intensities. They use five triaxial wireless accelerometers and a wireless heart rate monitor. A large data set consisting of 30 physical gymnasium activities collected from a total of 21 people is used.

Previously discussed works exploit classifiers because they have labeled data. Activity recognition is performed by comparing new and labeled data, measuring the similarity to assign the correct label to the new data.

In literature there are also techniques to determine the level of activity by exploiting thresholds. For example, Karantonis et al. [11] implemented a movement classification algorithm based on specific thresholds. They distinguished between periods of activity and rest, recognized the postural orientation of the wearer, and detected events such as walking and falling to a reasonable degree of accuracy, and also provide an estimation of metabolic energy expenditure. The problem of real-time classification has also been addressed.

9.4.2 Cardiovascular Diseases

Cardiovascular disease refers to the class of diseases that involve the heart or blood vessels (arteries and veins). Although the term technically refers to any disease affecting the cardiovascular system, it is usually used to refer to those related to atherosclerosis (arterial disease). They include coronary heart disease (heart attacks), cerebrovascular disease, raised blood pressure (hypertension), peripheral artery disease, rheumatic heart disease, congenital heart disease, and heart failure.

Such diseases can be effectively prevented and controlled only if the physiological parameters of the patient are constantly monitored, along with the full support of health education and professional medical care [40]. Physiological signals include arterial blood pressure, heart rate, saturation of hemoglobin, and electrocardiogram (ECG). A sample architecture for cardiovascular disease prevention and control, focusing on remote monitoring of heart rate, is depicted in Figure 9.5.

To allow continuous and ubiquitous monitoring, Lee et al. [40] proposed an intelligent mobile healthcare system providing an alert mechanism to automatically detect abnormal health conditions of a patient. To achieve this aim, considering hypertension and arrhythmia diseases, an in-depth analysis of the information exchanged between different players (e.g., patients, physicians, and care providers) is performed and physiological signal recognition algorithms are applied to blood pressure, pulse, and ECG signals. The proposed algorithms have been designed and developed for mobile devices, and their communication features were exploited to effectively support the monitoring of physiological signals without space constraints.

Heart rate   PDA   Medical center

Bluetooth   GSM

FIGURE 9.5
Sample architecture for cardiovascular disease applications.

The current healthcare for such diseases is still mainly from outpatient services. Due to the developments in information and communication technology, home telecare is now highly feasible.

Among the different devices and monitoring systems that are commercially available, there are some that only record data, and then the classification is made offline, such as the Holter monitors. To overcome this restriction, there are proposals where remote real-time classification is performed. For example, the MobiHealth project [10] has developed a vital sign monitoring system based on a platform that can transmit sensor measurements via UMTS or GPRS to a back-end system, where a remote detection of emergencies is performed. A similar architecture was also utilized by Dai and Zhang [41]. A further improvement of the analysis is the local real-time classification, which reduces communication costs and delays in alarm notification.

Rodriguez et al. [42] demonstrated the feasibility of achieving a good accuracy for classifying beats and rhythms, and of implementing real-time classification on a PDA.

Varady et al. [12] proposed an algorithm to discover physiological problems (e.g., cardiac arrhythmias) based on a priori medical knowledge. Physiological time series recorded through sensors may be exploited for learning usual behavioral patterns on a long time scale. Any deviation is considered an unexpected and possibly dangerous situation.

A system for out-of-hospital follow-up and monitoring of cardiac patients has been proposed by Sharshar et al. [43]. It has been developed to monitor physiological signals to prevent some cardiovascular risks (i.e., arterial hypertension, malignant arrhythmias, heart failure, and postinfarction rehabilitation) on patients with chronic heart diseases who are in stable conditions. A different set of heart and physiological parameters are monitored for each type of risk. For example, for the heart failure risk, blood pressure, pulse oximetry, and weight are monitored by appropriate wearable sensor equipment, whereas for malignant arrhythmias risk, ECG and blood pressure are monitored. Furthermore, each monitored patient needs to fill out a questionnaire in which the patient declares his/her physical conditions (e.g., fatigue, feel poorly). Collected data are summarized in a patient's electronic healthcare record and transmitted to the medical center for further analysis.

Lorenz and Oppermann [44] proposed a project for monitoring vital personal parameters specifically adapted to the needs of elderly who suffer from hypertension. Two services are described that allow continuous and context-aware access to the required information. First, a mobile setup collects the vital health data using an oxygen concentration measure (found in the blood) and a set of ECG sensors that are woven into a shirt. The system then analyzes and transmits the data to a mobile device, allowing the user to view and interact with the data. Second, a standard TV set allows elderly users to inspect numerical or graphical summaries of the data and possibly unusual events for specific periods. The combination of these two services goes beyond a mobile application on a dedicated portable device and includes access to the services from different places (inside or outside the home). The focus of the work includes both the design of a mobile device that is capable of receiving continuous data, small enough to be worn on a belt or in the pocket but large enough to provide a readable display, and the design of an interface for the TV that is familiar to elderly users.

9.4.3 Alzheimer's Disease

Alzheimer's disease is the most common form of dementia often diagnosed in people older than 65 years. Since Alzheimer's disease cannot be cured and is a degenerative and terminal disease, the management of patients is very important. Corchado et al. [45] proposed an intelligent environment for monitoring patients Alzheimer's disease in geriatric residences based on AGALZ (Autonomous aGent for monitoring ALZheimer patients) integrated within a multiagent system called ALZ-MAS (ALZheimer Multiagent System). The monitoring system exploits agent technology to improve the quality and efficiency of healthcare and the supervision of patients in geriatric residences, thereby providing efficient and dynamic working schedules for the staff. Each nurse and doctor has a mobile device on which an AGALZ agent runs. AGALZ agents are reasoning motors that provide information about patient locations, historical clinical data, and alarms. They generate working schedules based on past experiences and planning strategies. To easily locate the patients inside the geriatric residence, they must always wear a bracelet on wrist or ankle, with Radio Frequency Identification technology. This technology electronically identifies, tracks, and stores information about patient location, which is also sent to nurses and doctors.

The ALZ-MAS system has been validated in the Alzheimer Santisíma Trinidad Residence of Salamanca, which is a geriatric residence for 60 patients. The staff consists of an average of six nurses, one social worker, and five other employees with different responsibilities. The experimental validation has involved 30 patients and 6 nurses. The continuous monitoring of the environment and the patients has been performed by means of: 42 door readers, one for each door and elevator; 4 controllers, one for each exit; and 36 bracelets, one for each patient and nurse. The door readers obtain the ID number from the bracelets and send the data to the controllers, which trigger a notification to the manager agent. The ALZ-MAS system used in the experimental validation is composed of four different types of agents. (1) The patient agent manages the personal data and behavior for a single patient. Every hour, this agent validates the patient location, monitors the patient state, and sends a copy of its memory base (e.g., treatment, location, patient's profile, doctor prescriptions). (2) The manager agent controls the patients' locations and manages locks and alarms. (3) The nurse AGALZ agents dynamically generate working day schedules based on tasks needed for each assigned patient. The generated schedules guarantee that all the patients assigned to the nurse are given care. (4) The doctor AGALZ agent interacts with the patient agent to *order* treatments and receive periodic reports, with the Manager agent to *consult* medical records and assigned patients, and with the AGALZ agent to *ascertain* patient evolution. Manager and patient agents run in a central computer, whereas AGALZ agents run on mobile devices. The experimental validation highlighted the fact that the ALZ-MAS system resulted to increased time for direct patient care and reduced time spent for supervision and attending false alarms.

9.4.4 Intensive Care Context

In the intensive care context, there is a need for algorithms that automatically detect risk situations, because clinicians have to process large amounts of clinical data.

As discussed by Imhoff and Kuhls [46], the majority of alarms in critical care monitoring are false positives, which can compromise patient safety and the effectiveness of care, by leading to a dangerous desensitization of the intensive care staff toward true alarms. Approaches exploiting simple threshold alarms lead to many false positives without real clinical meaning. Hence, alarm generation algorithms should be improved by increasing the robustness against artifacts and missing values and by performing real-time analysis. However, clinicians are assisted in the decision-making process by medical informatics application recently developed, mainly with the function of storage and displaying patient information. Despite the potential of these systems, there are no comprehensive health technology assessments incorporating considerations of technical performance, clinical effectiveness, and economic implications [47].

Wu et al. [48] presented a mobile diagnostic method based on multiple wearable sensors. It is focused on the dynamic selection of the minimal set of sensors required to reach the right diagnosis. A single clustering algorithm is applied in the model building phase. The mobile intelligence that locally processes physiological measures aims at determining the optimal set of sensors, whereas the severity level evaluation of the physiological conditions is actually performed in a remote central server.

The intensive care unit (ICU) monitoring networks have been developed to an advanced level of Web-based representation. There are projects, such that described by Alves et al. [49], which develop Micro Web Servers (MWS), that is, embedded computer systems, in order to monitor physiological data and make them available via the Web. In particular, a model for patient monitoring in ICUs is presented. It uses a web application tool and an embedded computer system to monitor physiological data, such as body temperature, systolic blood pressure, diastolic blood pressure, cardiac frequency, and oximetry. Through MWS, data are acquired in real time and stored in an efficient manner, allowing both local and remote access. The proposed model is characterized by a client/server application. In the server side (the ICU), each bed will have an MWS receiving the signals from the patient sensors. MWS also features a data communication interface, allowing Internet connections. The client is simply any web browser supporting Java applets.

9.5 Patient Data Modeling Techniques

One important issue in mobile activity recognition systems is customization or personalization. High accuracy recognition of some activities may require an individual training phase. Monitoring physiological signals related to patients with different health conditions may require different behavioral models tailored to specific patients.

Patient data modeling techniques are especially useful to suit the characteristics of patients presenting particular conditions. By considering training data coming from patients affected by the same disease, a disease-specific model can be built. Furthermore, models may be trained by using measurements from a single patient, thus building a patient-specific model. A general model, which does not refer to a specific context, is needed in less-defined conditions. It can be built by considering records coming from patients affected by different diseases.

Given historical physiological data related to a single patient, the framework proposed by Apiletti et al. [22] automatically learns both common and uncommon behaviors and builds a behavioral model tailored to the specific patient. The model is then exploited in the real-time classification of vital signs to perform stream analysis of physiological data. The real-time analysis exploits data mining techniques [50] for assessing the instantaneous risk of monitored patients. To allow ubiquitous analysis, real-time analysis is performed on mobile devices (e.g., Pocket PCs, smart phones). When a dangerous situation is detected, an immediate intervention is requested by triggering an alarm (e.g., a phone call, a short message). Experimental validation reported by Apiletti et al. [22] has been performed on 64 patients affected by different critical illnesses [51], and demonstrates the effectiveness and flexibility of the framework in detecting different severity levels of monitored patients' clinical situation.

Another example of data modeling is presented by Shahar and Musen [52], in the context of patients with insulin-dependent diabetes. The authors exploited a temporal abstraction task to summarize large amounts of clinical data over time. It enables an assessment of a patient condition by abstracting high level features and states from raw numerical data (e.g., blood glucose values).

More recently, Sharshar et al. [13] proposed the extraction of temporal patterns from single or multiple physiological signals via statistical techniques (e.g., regression). Single signal analysis provides trend descriptions such as increasing, decreasing, constant, and transient. A machine learning process is utilized to discover pattern templates from sequences of trends related to specific clinical events.

9.6 Requirements and Pitfalls

As described by Varshney and Sneha [53], there are several requirements that patient monitoring systems have to deal with.

For example, due to potentially life-threatening situations, the reliability of message delivery to healthcare professionals is one of the most crucial requirements of patient monitoring. Among the influencing factors are device range and bit rate (see Section 9.3.2 for different transmission technologies), available power (see Section 9.3.3 for battery life of mobile devices), and any failure or uncooperative behavior of other devices. Furthermore, the network should deliver the messages carrying vital signs within a certain time depending on the level of emergency. It is necessary to contain the delays that could arise under frequent monitoring or for a large number of monitored patients.

Conserving device power while satisfying the reliability requirement of patient monitoring is also a serious problem. To be unobtrusive, the sensors must be lightweight with small form factor. The size and weight of sensors are dominated by the size and weight of batteries. Requirements for extended battery life directly oppose the requirement for small form factor and low weight. This implies that sensors have to be extremely power efficient, as frequent battery changes for multiple body area network sensors would likely hamper users' acceptance and increase the cost. In addition, low power consumption is very important as we move toward future generations of implantable sensors that would ideally be self-powered, using energy extracted from the environment.

Other issues related to requirements are the scalability in terms of the number of patients, the managing of both routine and emergency vital signs, and the manageable cognitive load for healthcare professionals. In fact, the monitoring system should not oppress healthcare professionals, but should make intelligent decisions about the patient condition and alerting only when an anomaly or emergency is detected.

Finally, there is a critical requirement for healthcare administrators and government regulators. As information is being transmitted over wireless networks, efforts should be made to keep it confidential and private. When dealing with the design of real-time monitoring systems, these requirements have to taken into consideration and evaluated in advance.

9.7 Chapter Summary

This chapter presented and discussed alternative designs of mobile healthcare systems to analyze physiological signals and for ubiquitous patient monitoring. Relevant literature on healthcare applications has been reviewed, along with advantages and disadvantages of proposed works.

To sum up, the combination of information technologies and telecommunications enables the design and exploitation of smart mobile devices, which are able to ubiquitously collect real-time streams of physiological signals. These devices, integrated in *ad hoc* health system architectures, can continuously evaluate patient health conditions by enhancing human comfort, efficiency of healthcare, and prevention of illness. Furthermore, mobile health applications play a key role in saving lives, by allowing timely assistance and by significantly cutting the cost of medical services.

Although many research efforts have been focused on improving health system architectures, the design and development of efficient analysis techniques for mobile platforms have received less attention. However, techniques exist to perform the analysis task in real time. Proposed approaches have been limited to specific physiological signals, utilize fixed thresholds, or use some type of a priori knowledge.

Moreover, a host of technical challenges remain for a better utilization of smart mobile devices into ubiquitous health applications. Power consumption, computational capabilities, and bandwidth constraints demand new approaches to software design in the mobile context. Although computational and memory resource limits are not pressing, battery life remains a strong issue, which current and future research should address.

References

1. Varshney, U. 2006. Managing wireless health monitoring for patients with disabilities. *IT Professional* 8(6):12–16.
2. Podgorelec Vili et al., 2005. Some applications of intelligent systems in medicine. In *Proceedings of the 3rd IEEE International Conference on Computational Cybernetics*, Budapest, Hungary.
3. Varshney, U., and Sneha, S. 2006. Patient monitoring using ad hoc wireless networks: reliability and power management. *IEEE Communications Magazine* 1:63–68.

4. Wu, H.-C. et al. 1999. A mobile system for real-time patient-monitoring with integrated physiological signal processing. In *Proceedings of the 1st Joint BMES/EMBS Conference*, p. 712.
5. Lin, Y.-H. et al. 2004. A wireless PDA-based physiological monitoring system for patient transport. *IEEE Transactions on Information Technology in Biomedicine* 8(4):439–447.
6. Lee, R.-G., Chen, K.-C., Hsiao, C.-C., and Tseng, C.-L. 2007. A mobile care system with alert mechanism. *IEEE Transactions on Information Technology in Biomedicine*, 11(5): 507–517.
7. Saranummi, N. 2002. Information technology in biomedicine. *IEEE Transactions on Biomedical Engineering* 49(12):1385–1386.
8. Skyaid Watch. Available at: http://Tinyurl.com/MXNTC9htm. (Accessed Sept. 23, 2009).
9. Lorincz, K. et al. 2004. Sensor networks for emergency response: challenges and opportunities. *IEEE Pervasive Computing* 3(4):16–23.
10. Jones, V. et al. 2006. Mobihealth: mobile health services based on body area networks. Technical Report TR-CTIT-06-37 Centre for Telematics and Information Technology, University of Twente, Enschede.
11. Karantonis, D. M., Narayanan, M. R., Mathie, M., Lovell, N. H., and Celler, B. G. 2006. Implementation of a real-time human movement classifier using a triaxial accelerometer for ambulatory monitoring. *IEEE Transactions on Information Technology in Biomedicine* 10:156–167.
12. Varady, P., Benyo, Z., and Benyo, B. 2002. An open architecture patient monitoring system using standard technologies. *IEEE Transactions on Information Technology in Biomedicine* 6:95–98.
13. Sharshar, S., Allart, L., and Chambrin. M. C. 2005. A new approach to the abstraction of monitoring data in intensive care. *Lecture Notes in Computer Science* 3581:13–22.
14. Axisa, F., Dittimar, A., and Delhomme, G. 2003. Smart clothes for the monitoring in real time and conditions of physiological, emotional and sensorial reaction of human. In *Proceedings of the 25th Conference IEEE Engineering Medicine and Biology Society*, pp. 3744–3747.
15. Cheng, P.-T., Tsai, L.-M., Lu, L.-W., and Yang, D.-L. 2004. The design of PDA-based biomedical data processing and analysis for intelligent wearable health monitoring systems. In *Proceedings of the 4th Conference on Computer and Information Technology*.
16. Branche, P., and Mendelson, Y. 2005. Signal quality and power consumption of a new prototype reflectance pulse oximeter sensor. In *Proceedings of the 31st Northeast Bioengineering Conference*, pp. 42–43.
17. Weber, J. L. et al. 2004. Telemonitoring of vital parameters with newly designed biomedical clothing. *Studies in Health Technology and Informatics* 108:260–265.
18. Manders, E., and Dawant, B. 1996. Data acquisition for an intelligent bedside monitoring system. In *Proceedings of the 18th Conference IEEE Engineering in Medicine and Biology Society*, 1987–1988.
19. Gupta, S., and Ganz, A. 2004. Design considerations and implementation of a cost-effective, portable remote monitoring unit using 3G wireless data networks. In *Proceedings of the 26th Conference IEEE Engineering in Medicine and Biology Society*, pp. 3286–3289.

20. Ermes, M., Pärkkä, J., Mäntyjärvi, J., and Korhonen, I. 2008. Detection of daily activities and sports with wearable sensors in controlled and uncontrolled conditions. *IEEE Transactions on Information Technology in Biomedicine* 12(1):20–26.

21. Iakovidis, I. 1998. Towards personal health record: current situation, obstacles and trends in implementation of electronic healthcare records in Europe. *International Journal of Medical Informatics* 52(128):105 –117.

22. Apiletti, D., Baralis, E., Bruno, G., and Cerquitelli, T. 2008. Real-time individuation of global unsafe anomalies and alarm activation. In *Intelligent Techniques and Tools for Novel System Architectures*, Vol. 109, P. Chountas, I. Petrounias, and J. Kacprzyk, Eds., Studies in Computational Intelligence. Springer Verlag. ISBN: 978-3-540-77621-5.

23. Anliker, U., et al. 2004. AMON: a wearable multiparameter medical monitoring and alert system. *IEEE Transactions on Information Technology in Biomedicine* 8(4):415–427.

24. IEEE 802.15 WPAN Task Group 1. Available at: http://www.ieee802.org/15/pub/TG1.html. (Accessed Sept. 23, 2009).

25. ZigBee Alliance. Available at: http://www.zigbee.org/.

26. IEEE 802.11 Wireless Local Area Networks. Available at: http://ieee802.org/11/. (Accessed Sept. 23, 2009).

27. ITU Recommendation (standard) ITU-T G.992.1. Available at: http://www.itu.int/rec/T-REC-G.992.1-200207-I!Cor2/en. (Accessed Sept. 23, 2009).

28. Global System for Mobile communications. Available at: http://www.gsmworld.com/. (Accessed Sept. 23, 2009).

29. GSM Facts and Figures. Available at: http://www.gsmworld.com/news/newsroom/marketdata/marketdata_summary.htm (Accessed Sept. 23, 2009).

30. Technical Specifications and Technical Reports for a UTRAN-based 3GPP system. Available at: http://www.3gpp.org/ftp/Specs/html-info/21101.htm. (Accessed Sept. 23, 2009).

31. Aminian, K., Najafi, B., Bla, C., Leyvraz, P. F., and Robert, P. 2001. Ambulatory gait analysis using gyroscopes. 25th Annual Meeting of the American Society of Biomechanics, San Diego, CA.

32. Pentland, A. 2004. Healthwear: medical technology becomes wearable. *Computer* 37(5):42–49.

33. Lee, S.-W., and Mase, K. 2002. Activity and location recognition using wearable sensors. *Pervasive Computing, IEEE* 1(3):24–32.

34. Apiletti, D., Baralis, E., Bruno, G., and Cerquitelli, T. 2007. SAPhyRA: stream analysis for physiological risk assessment. In *Proceedings of the IEEE CBMS*, pp. 193–198.

35. Bao, L., and Intille, S. S. 2004. Activity recognition from user-annotated acceleration data. In *Proceedings of the 2nd International Conference on Pervasive Computing*, pp. 1–17.

36. Ravi, N., Dandekar, N., Mysore, P., and Littman, M. L., 2005. Activity recognition from accelerometer data. In *Proceedings of the National Conference on Artificial Intelligence*, American Association for Artificial Intelligence, pp. 1541–1546.

37. Maurer, U., Smailagic, A., Siewiorek , D. P., and Deisher, M. 2006. Activity recognition and monitoring using multiple sensors on different body positions. In *Proceedings of the International Workshop on Wearable and Implantable Body Sensor Networks* (BSN'06).

38. Yang, J.-Y., Chen, Y.-P., Lee, G.-Y., Liou, S.-N., and Wang, J.-S. 2007. Activity recognition using one triaxial accelerometer: a neuro-fuzzy classifier with feature reduction. In *Proceedings of the ICEC 2007*, LNCS 4740, pp. 395–400.
39. Tapia, E. M., Intille, S. S., Haskell, W., Larson, K., Wright, J., King, A., and Friedman, R. 2007. Real-time recognition of physical activities and their intensities using wireless accelerometers and a heart rate monitor. In *Proceedings of the International Symposium on Wearable Computers*, IEEE Press, Boston, MA.
40. Lee, R.-G., Chen, K.-C., Hsiao, C.-C., and Tseng, C.-L. 2007. A mobile care system with alert mechanism. *IEEE Transactions on Information Technology in Biomedicine* 11(5):507–517.
41. Dai, S., and Zhang, Y. 2006. A wireless physiological multi-parameter monitoring system based on mobile communication networks. In *Proceedings of tthe IEEE CBMS'06*.
42. Rodriguez, J., Goi, A., and Illarramendi, A. 2005. Real-time classification of ECGs on a PDA. *IEEE Transactions on Information Technology in Biomedicine* 9(1):23–34.
43. Salvador, C. H., Carrasco, M. P., de Mingo, M. A. G., Carrero, A. M., Montes, J. M., Martin, L. S., Cavero, M. A., Lozano, I. F., and Monteagudo, J. L. 2005. Airmed-cardio: a GSM and Internet services-based system for out-of-hospital follow-up of cardiac patients. *IEEE Transactions on Information Technology in Biomedicine* 9(1):73–85.
44. Lorenz, A., and Oppermann, R., In press. Mobile health monitoring for elderly: design for diversity. *Pervasive and Mobile Computing*.
45. Corchado, J. M., Bajo, J., de Paz, Y., and Tapia, D. I. 2008. Intelligent environment for monitoring Alzheimer patients, agent technology for health care. *Decision Support Systems* 44(2):382–396.
46. Imhoff, M., and Kuhls, S. 2006. Alarm algorithms in critical care monitoring. *Anesthesia & Analgesia* 102:1525–1537.
47. Adhikari, N., and Lapinsky, S. E. 2003. Medical informatics in the intensive care unit: overview of technology assessment. *Journal of Critical Care* 18:41–47.
48. Wu, W. H., Bui, A. A. T., Batalin, M. A., Liu, D., and Kaiser, W. J. 2007. Incremental diagnosis method for intelligent wearable sensor systems. *IEEE Transactions on Information Technology in Biomedicine* 11(5):553–562.
49. Alves, J. B. M., da Silva, J. B., and Paladini, S. 2006. A low cost model for patient monitoring in intensive care unit using a micro web-server. IADIS Virtual Multi Conference on Computer Science and Information Systems, MCCSIS 2006.
50. Han, J., and Kamber, M. 2000. Data mining: concepts and techniques. *Morgan Kaufmann Series in Data Management Systems*. Morgan Kaufmann.
51. MIMICDB. Available at: http://www.physionet.org/physiobank/database/mimicdb.
52. Shahar, Y., and Musen, M. 1996. Knowledge-based temporal abstraction in clinical domains. *Artificial Intelligence in Medicine* 8(3):267–298.
53. Varshney, U., and Sneha, S. 2006. Patient monitoring using ad hoc wireless networks: reliability and power management. *IEEE Communications Magazine* 44:49–55.

10

Medical Image Segmentation

Xiaolei Huang and Gavriil Tsechpenakis

CONTENTS

10.1 Introduction

Recent advances in a wide range of medical imaging technologies have revolutionized how we view functional and pathological events in the human body and define anatomical structures in which these events take place.

X-ray, computed axial tomography, magnetic resonance imaging (MRI), ultrasound, nuclear medicine, among other medical imaging technologies, enable two-dimensional (2D) or tomographic 3D images to capture in vivo structural and functional information inside the body for diagnosis, prognosis, treatment planning, and other purposes.

To achieve compatibility and to improve workflow efficiency between imaging systems and other information systems in healthcare environments worldwide, the Digital Imaging and Communications in Medicine (DICOM) standard is created as a cooperative international standard for communication of biomedical diagnostic and therapeutic information in disciplines using digital images and associated data. The DICOM standard, which includes a file format definition and a network communications protocol, is used in handling, storing, printing, and transmitting information in medical imaging. DICOM files can be exchanged between two entities that are capable of receiving image and patient data in DICOM format. An example DICOM file header is shown in Figure 10.1a, and raw image intensities (Figure 10.1b) are stored following the header in the DICOM file. DICOM also addresses the integration of information produced by various specialty applications in the patient's electronic health record. It defines the network and media interchange services allowing storage and access to these DICOM objects for electronic health record systems. The National Electrical Manufacturers Association holds the copyright to the DICOM standard.

Medical images in their raw form are represented by arrays of numbers in the computer, with the numbers indicating the values of relevant physical quantities that show contrast between different types of body tissue. Processing and analysis of medical images are useful in transforming raw images into a quantifiable symbolic form for ease of searching and mining, in extracting meaningful quantitative information to aid diagnosis and in integrating complementary data from multiple imaging modalities.

One fundamental problem in medical image analysis is image segmentation, which identifies the boundaries of objects such as organs or abnormal regions (e.g., tumors) in images. Having the segmentation result makes it possible to perform shape analysis, to detect volume change and to make a precise radiation therapy treatment plan. In the literature of image processing and computer vision, various theoretical frameworks have been proposed for segmentation. Among some of the leading mathematical models are thresholding [1], region growing [2], edge detection and grouping [3], Markov random fields (MRFs) [4], active contour models (or deformable models) [5], Mumford-Shah functional based frame partition [6], level sets [7, 8], graph cut [9], and mean shift [10]. Significant extensions and integrations of these frameworks [11–17] have improved their efficiency, applicability, and accuracy.

Despite intensive research, however, segmentation remains a challenging problem due to the diverse image content, cluttered objects, occlusion, image noise, nonuniform object texture, and other factors. In particular, boundary insufficiencies [i.e., missing edges and/or lack of texture contrast between

```
0002,0000,File Meta Elements Group Len=196
0002,0001,File Meta Info Version=256
0002,0002,Media Storage SOP Class UID=1.2.840.10008.5.1.4.1.1.2.
0002,0003,Media Storage SOP Inst UID=1.3.12.2.1107.5.6.1.123.30150
0002,0010,Transfer Syntax UID=1.2.840.10008.1.2.1.
0002,0012,Implementation Class UID=1.3.12.2.1107.5.9.20000101
0002,0013,Implementation Version Name=SIEMENS.SWFVC20H
0008,0005,Specific Character Set=ISO.IR 100
0008,0008,Image Type=AXIAL
0008,0012,Instance Creation Date=20040123
0008,0013,Instance Creation Time=141428.000000
0008,0016,SOP Class UID=1.2.840.10008.5.1.4.1.1.2.
0008,0018,SOP Instance UID=1.3.12.2.1107.5.6.1.123.3015010402061805
0008,0020,Study Date=20040123
0008,0021,Series Date=20040123
0008,0022,Acquisition Date=20040123
0008,0023,Image Date=20040123
0008,0030,Study Time=140858.000000
0008,0031,Series Time=141102.000000
0008,0032,Acquisition Time=141121.000000
0008,0033,Image Time=141428.000000
0008,0050,Accession Number=
0008,0060,Modality=CT
0008,0070,Manufacturer=GE MEDICAL SYSTEMS
0008,0090,Referring Physician's Name=REF02062
0008,1010,Station Name=STA02062
0008,103E,Series Description=CT Atten Cor Head In 3.75 thk
0008,1070,Operator's Name=OPER02062
0008,1090,Manufacturer's Model Name=Discovery ST
0008,1140,7=..........P.UI..1.2.840.10008.5.1.4.1.1.2...U.UI6.1.3.1
```

(a)

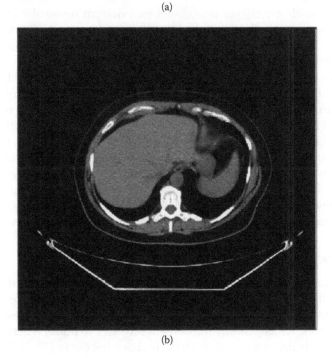

(b)

FIGURE 10.1

(a) Example DICOM header for a computed tomography (CT) medical image. (b) Display of one cross section slice of the CT volume.

regions of interest (ROIs) and background] are common in medical images. In this chapter, we focus on introducing two general categories of segmentation methods—the deformable models and the learning-based classification approaches—which incorporate high-level constraints and prior knowledge to address challenges in segmentation. In Section 10.2, we aim at giving the reader an intuitive description of the two categories of image segmentation approaches. We then provide details on two medical image segmentation methods, the Metamorphs and the conditional random field (CRF) geometric models, in Sections 10.3 and 10.4, respectively. We show additional medical image segmentation results in Section 10.5, and conclude our discussion in Section 10.6.

10.2 Related Work and Further Readings

10.2.1 Deformable Models for Segmentation

Deformable models are curves or surfaces that deform under the influence of internal (shape) smoothness and external image forces to delineate object boundary. Compared to local edge-based methods, deformable models have the advantage of estimating boundary with smooth curves or surfaces that bridge over boundary gaps. The model evolution is usually driven by a global energy minimization process, where the internal and external energies (corresponding to the smoothness and image forces) are integrated into a model total energy, and the optimal model position/configuration is the one with the minimum total energy. When initialized far away from object boundary, however, a model can be trapped in local energy minima caused by spurious edges and/or high noise. Deformable models are divided into two main categories: *parametric* and the *geometric* models. Among these two classes, there are methods that use edges as image features to drive the model toward the desired boundaries, and methods that exploit region information for the model evolution.

10.2.1.1 Parametric Deformable Models

The first class of deformable models is the *parametric* or *explicit* deformable models [5, 18–20], also known as active contours, which use parametric curves to represent the model shape. Edge-based parametric models use edges as image features, which usually make them sensitive to noise, whereas region-based methods use region information to drive the curve [17, 21, 22]. A limitation of the latter methods is that they do not update the region statistics during the model evolution, and therefore local feature variations are difficult to capture. Region updating is proposed in the study conducted by Florin et al. [23], where active contours with particle filtering are used for vascular segmentation.

Figure 10.2 illustrates two examples of medical image segmentation using a parametric deformable model. In the first example (Figure 10.2[a]), the goal is to segment the left and right ventricle (LV and RV, respectively) regions in an MR cardiac image. The leftmost image shows the original grayscale image, whereas the second from the left image shows the *ground truth*, that is, the actual boundaries of RV and LV, with two closed lines; these boundaries were obtained by manual segmentation. The third (from the left) image shows the image edges obtained with the canny edge detector; the closed contours superimposed on the edge image show the segmentation result of the deformable model (initialized around RV and LV), which, in this case, uses edge information as external image forces [5]. In the next image, we show both the ground truth and the estimated boundaries. In the rightmost image, which shows a magnification of the ventricles, one can observe that the deformable model converges to edges that do not correspond to the actual region boundaries, which is caused by a local minimum of the model's energy.

The second example in Figure 10.2(b) shows an ultrahigh resolution optical coherence tomography [24] cross-sectional image of a mouse retina (panel A): the region inside the box (dashed line) is a cross section of a retinal tumor, which is the slightly brighter region. In this example, one can understand that the tumor boundaries are not determined by edges, as in the previous example, but by the texture contrast. Therefore, the external forces driving the deformable model are defined by a region-based feature, namely, the intensity distribution. Panel B shows five instances of the model evolution, with the circle in the center of the tumor being the model initialization. Panel C shows the final solution, that is, the configuration/position where the model converges.

10.2.1.2 Geometric Models

The second class of deformable models is the *geometric* or *implicit* models [6, 8, 25], which use the level set–based shape representation, transforming the curves into higher-dimensional scalar functions, as shown in Figure 10.3. The 1D closed lines of (a) and (c) (evolving fronts) are transformed into the 2D surfaces of (b) and (d), respectively, using the scalar distance function that is mathematically defined in the following sections. According to this representation, the evolving front corresponds to the cross section of the 2D distance function with the zero level, shown with the gray-colored planes in (b) and (d). Moreover, the model interior, that is, the ROI, can be implicitly determined by the positive values of the distance surface, as described below. This distance-based shape representation has two main advantages: (1) the evolving interface can be described by a single function, even if it consists of more than one closed curves; (2) the model shape is formulated with a function of the same dimensionality with the data, that is, for the case of the image segmentation (2D data), the model shape is also a 2D quantity.

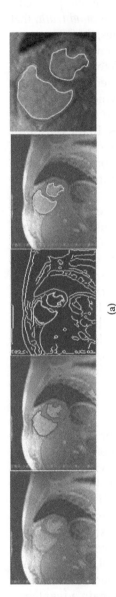

(a)

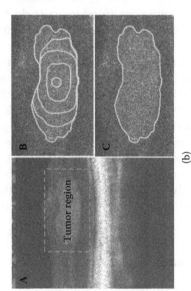

(b)

FIGURE 10.2

Two examples of segmentation using parametric deformable models (active contours). (a) Edge-based model for the segmentation of the left (LV) and right ventricles (RV) in a cardiac MRI. From left to right: original image, ground truth boundaries, edge map (canny edge detection) with the final model solution superimposed, ground truth and final solution superimposed on original image, magnified view of LV and RV along with the ground truth and the final solution. (b) Cross-sectional optical coherence tomography (OCT) image showing a tumor in a mouse retina. (A) Original image indicating the tumor inside the box (dashed line); (B) five instances of the evolution of a region-based deformable model; (C) the final segmentation result for the retinal tumor. (The OCT image is Courtesy of S. Jiao, Bascom Palmer Eye Institute, University of Miami.)

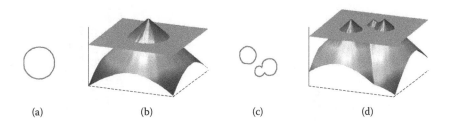

FIGURE 10.3
Deformable model shape representation using a distance transform. The shape of the 1D closed curves of (a) and (c), which are evolving in the image domain, can be implicitly described by the 2D distance functions of (b) and (d), respectively.

The latter, and in contrast to using 1D parametric curves, allows for a more direct mathematical description of a deformable model.

In the work of Mumford and Shah [6], the optimal function is the one that best fits the image data—it is piecewise smooth and presents discontinuities across the boundaries of different regions. Paragios and Deriche [25] proposed a variational framework integrating boundary and region-based information in partial differential equations (PDEs) that are implemented using a level set approach. These methods assume piecewise or Gaussian intensity distributions within each partitioned image region, which limits their ability to capture intensity inhomogeneities and complex intensity distributions.

Figure 10.4 illustrates an example of segmentation using a geometric deformable model [26]. The leftmost image (a) shows an *en face* fundus image of the human retina obtained with spectral domain optical coherence tomography [27]; the bright region in the center of the image is clinically called *geographic atrophy* [28], which corresponds to the atrophy of the retinal pigment epithelium, common in dry age-related macular degeneration. Figure 10.4(b) shows the result of the geographic atrophy segmentation; Figure 10.4(c) and (d) illustrates the distance function as shape representation of the deformable model, for the initialization and the final configuration of the model, respectively. The cross section of the surface with the image plane (zero level) is the evolving boundary. Panel (e) shows eight instances of the deformable model evolution: the grid points correspond to the model interior during the evolution [the leftmost image corresponds to the initialization shown in (c) and the rightmost image shows the final model interior corresponding to (d)].

10.2.1.3 Edge- versus Region-Based Image Features

Although the parametric and geometric deformable models differ in formulation and in implementation, traditionally both use primarily edge (or image gradient) information to derive external image forces that drive a

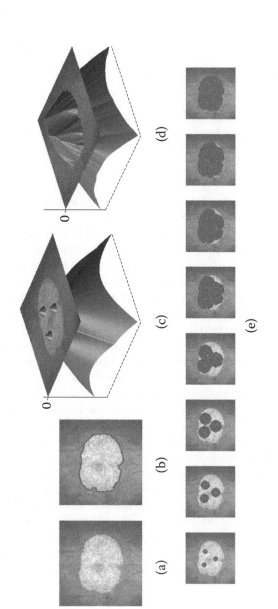

FIGURE 10.4

Segmentation of an *en face* fundus image of the human retina [26], obtained with spectral domain optical coherence tomography [27]: the bright region in the center is clinically called *geographic atrophy* [28], which corresponds to the atrophy of the retinal pigment epithelium, common in dry age-related macular degeneration. (a) Original *en face* image; (b) final position of the deformable model capturing the geographic atrophy boundaries; (c)–(d) model shape representation of the initialization and the final solution: the cross section of the surfaces with the image plane (zero plane) correspond to the model boundary in the image domain; (e) eight instances of the model interior during the evolution. (The OCT data are Courtesy of G. Gregori, B. Lujan, and P. J. Rosenfeld, Bascom Palmer Eye Institute, University of Miami.)

shape-based model. In parametric models, a typical formulation [5] for the energy term deriving the external image forces is as follows:

$$E_{\text{ext}}(C) = -\int_0^1 |\nabla \hat{I}(C(s))|\, ds \qquad (10.1)$$

Here, C represents the parametric curve model parameterized by curve length s, $\hat{I} = G_\sigma * I$ is the image I after smoothing with a Gaussian kernel of standard deviation σ, and $\nabla\hat{I}(C)$ is the image gradient along the curve. Basically, by minimizing this energy term, the accumulative image gradient along the curve is maximized, which means that the parametric model is attracted by strong edges that correspond to pixels with local-maxima image gradient values.

In geometric models, a typical objective function [7] that drives the front propagation of a level set (distance) function is

$$E(C) = \int_0^1 g\left(|\nabla\hat{I}(C(s))|\right)|C'(s)|ds, \quad \text{where } g\left(|\nabla\hat{I}|\right) = \frac{1}{1+|\nabla\hat{I}|^2} \qquad (10.2)$$

Here, C represents the front (i.e., zero level set) curve of the evolving level set function. To minimize the objective function, the front curve deforms along its normal direction $C''(s)$, and its speed is controlled by the speed function $g(|\nabla\hat{I}|)$. The speed function definition, $g(|\nabla\hat{I}|)$, depends on image gradient $\nabla\hat{I}$, and it is positive in homogeneous areas and zero at ideal edges. Hence, the curve moves at a velocity proportional to its curvature in homogeneous regions and stops at strong edges.

The reliance on image gradient information in both parametric and geometric deformable models, however, makes them sensitive to noise and spurious edges so that the models often need to be initialized close to the boundary to avoid getting stuck in local minima. Geometric models, in particular, may leak through boundary gaps or generate small holes/islands. To address the limitations in these deformable models, and develop more robust models for boundary extraction, there have been significant efforts to integrate region information into both parametric and geometric deformable models.

Along the line of parametric models, region analysis strategies have been proposed [17, 21, 22, 29, 30] to augment the "snake" (active contour) models. Assuming the partition of an image into an object region and a background region, a region-based energy criterion for active contours is introduced in the study of Ronfard [21], which includes photometric energy terms defined on the two regions. In the work of Zhu and Yuille [17], a generalized energy function that combines aspects of snakes/balloons and region growing is proposed and the minimization of the criterion is guaranteed to converge to a local minimum. However, this formulation still does not address the problem of unifying shape and appearance, because of the large difference in representation for shape and appearance. Although the model shape is represented using a parametric spline curve, the region intensity statistics are captured by parameters of a Gaussian distribution. This representation difference prevents the use of gradient descent methods to update both region parameters and shape parameters in a unified optimization process, so that the two sets of parameters are estimated in separate steps in the study conducted by Zhu and Yuille [17], and the overall energy function is minimized in an iterative manner. In other hybrid segmentation frameworks [29, 30], a region-based module is used to obtain a rough binary mask of the object of interest. Then, this rough boundary estimation serves as initialization for a deformable model, which will deform to fit edge features in the image using gradient information.

Along the line of geometric models, the integration of region and edge information [15, 16, 25, 31] has been mostly based on solving reduced cases of the minimal partition problem in the Mumford and Shah model for segmentation [6]. In the Mumford-Shah model, an optimal piecewise smooth function is pursued to approximate an observed image, such that the function varies smoothly within each region, and rapidly or discontinuously across the boundaries of different regions. The solution represents a partition of the image into several regions. A typical formulation of the framework is as follows:

$$F^{MS}(u,C) = \int_{\Omega} (u-u_0)^2 \, dxdy + a \int_{\Omega/C} |\nabla u|^2 \, dxdy + b|C| \qquad (10.3)$$

Here, u_0 is the observed, possibly noisy image, and u is the pursued "optimal" piecewise smooth approximation of u_0. Ω represents the image domain, ∇u is the gradient of u, and C are the boundary curves that approximate the edges in u_0. One can see that the first term of the function minimizes the difference between u and u_0, the second term pursues the smoothness within each region (i.e., outside the set C), and the third term constrains the boundary curves C to be smooth and have the shortest distance.

Although the above framework nicely incorporates gradient and region criteria into a single energy function, no practical globally optimal solution for the function is available, most notably because of the mathematical difficulties documented (e.g., [6]). In the past few years, progress has been made and solutions for several reduced cases of the Mumford-Shah functional have been proposed in the level set framework. One approach [15] is able to segment images consisting of several regions, each characterizable by a given statistics such as the mean intensity and variance. Nevertheless, the algorithm requires known a priori the number of segments in the image and its performance depends on the discriminating power of the chosen set of statistics. Another approach [31] applies a multiphase level set representation to segmentation, assuming piecewise constant intensity within one region. It is regarded as solving a classification problem because it assumes that the mean intensities of all region classes are known a priori, and only the set of boundaries between regions is unknown. In the work conducted by Vese and Chan [16] and Chan and Vese [32], piecewise constant and piecewise smooth approximations of the Mumford-Shah functional are derived for two-phase (i.e., two regions) [32] or multiphase (i.e., multiple regions) [16] cases in a variational level set framework. The optimization of the framework is based on an iterative algorithm that approximates the region mean intensities and level set shape in separate steps. Geodesic active region [25] is another method that integrates edge- and region-based modules in a level set framework. The algorithm consists of two stages: a modeling stage that constructs a likelihood map of edge pixels and approximates region/class statistics using mixture-of-Gaussian components, and a segmentation stage that uses level set techniques to solve for a set of smooth curves that are attracted to edge pixels and partition regions that have the expected properties of the associated classes. In summary, the approaches cited above all solve the frame partition problem, which can be computationally expensive when dealing with busy images containing many objects and clutter. Their assumptions of piecewise constant, piecewise smooth, Gaussian, or mixture-of-Gaussian intensity distributions within regions can also limit their effectiveness in segmenting objects whose interiors have textured appearance and/or complex multimodal intensity distributions.

10.2.2 Learning-Based Classification for Segmentation

Learning-based pixel and region classification is among the popular approaches for image segmentation. This type of methods exploit the advantages of supervised learning (training from examples) to assign probabilities of belonging to the ROI to image sites. Graphical models are commonly used to incorporate neighborhood interactions and contextual information, and they can be characterized as either *generative* or *discriminative*. Generative models are commonly used in segmentation/recognition problems where the neighboring property is well defined among the data, and they are robust to compositionality (variations in the input features), without having to see all possibilities during training. However, generative models can be computationally intractable because they require representations of multiple interacting features or long-range dependencies. On the other hand, discriminative models, such as support vector machines and logistic regression, infer model parameters from training data and directly calculate the class posterior given the data (mapping); they are usually very fast at making predictions, since they adjust the resulting classification boundary or function approximation accuracy, without the intermediate goal of forming a *generator* that models the underlying distributions during testing. However, discriminative models often need large training sets in order to make accurate predictions, and therefore they cannot be used for data with relatively high rates of ambiguities in a straightforward manner. To address this problem, some approaches integrate discriminative with generative models, where the parameters of a generative approach are modeled and trained in a discriminative manner. Also, for the same purpose, discriminative methods are used in active learning frameworks, to select the most descriptive examples for labeling, in order to minimize the model's entropy without increasing the size of the training set.

10.2.2.1 Markov Random Fields

A representative example of learning-based region classification is the Markov random fields (MRFs) [33]. In MRFs, the image is divided into *sites*, either at the pixel level or at the level of patches of predetermined spatial scale (size). Each site corresponds to (1) a hidden node, or label node, which is the desired label to be calculated for the specific site: in region segmentation, this label can be either *ROI* or *background*; (2) the observation, or feature node, which corresponds to the site's feature set directly estimated from the image.

Figure 10.5 illustrates the concept of learning-based classification of image sites using a common MRF. Panel (a) shows the original image of the example of Figure 10.2(b), and panel (b) shows the magnified view of the region indicated by the box in (a). The patches in (b) indicate the sites, which, in this case, correspond to single pixels. Figure 10.5(c) shows the graphical representation of the MRF. The upper level is the label field to be calculated, where each node corresponds to the (unknown) label of each pixel. The lower level is the observation set, where each node (usually indicated with a box) corresponds to the feature vector of each site; here, the feature vector contains a single value, which is the grayscale value of the pixel. Specifically in MRFs, the label of each site depends on (1) the corresponding observation and (2) the labels of its neighboring sites; we illustrate these dependencies with the solid and dashed lines. The segmentation result is obtained as

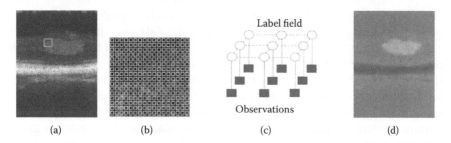

(a)   (b)   (c)   (d)

FIGURE 10.5
Image segmentation for the example shown in Figure 10.2(b); (a) probability field estimated by an MRF. (b) Magnification of the region inside the box in panel; the grid shows the image sites, which in this case correspond to pixels. (c) Graphical representation of the MRF, where each feature (gray box) corresponds to the intensity value of a pixel. (d) Probability field for the entire image: the bright regions indicate high probability of belonging to the ROI (tumor); by thresholding these probabilities, we obtain the ROI.

a global optimization problem—that is, estimating the optimal label field, given the observations. In contrast to traditional deformable models that follow deterministic energy minimization approaches, learning-based classification methods are usually based on a probabilistic solution, that is, they are driven by the maximization of a probability. Figure 10.5(d) illustrates the probabilities of all pixels belonging to the ROI, that is, the tumor: bright regions correspond to high probabilities, whereas darker regions denote the least likely sites to belong to the tumor. The label field of the image (tumor vs. background) is derived by thresholding these probability values.

10.2.2.2 *Conditional Random Fields*

Intuitively, the common MRF formulation assumes that neighboring image sites should have similar labels, and this (Markovian) property results in smooth probability fields. To obtain better probability smoothing, CRFs were introduced in computer vision by Lafferty et al. [34]. Although CRFs were first used to label sequential data, their extensions are used for image segmentation [26, 35–39]. The main advantage of CRFs is that they handle the known label bias problem [34], avoiding the conditional independence assumption among the features of neighboring sites (the labels neighboring property is driven by the corresponding features). Kumar and Hebert [35] reported on discriminative random fields (DRFs), which allow for computationally efficient maximum a posteriori probability (MAP) inference. In addition, He et al. [36] also used CRFs in different spatial scales to capture the dependencies between image regions of multiple sizes. A potential limitation of CRFs is that they do not provide robustness to unobserved or partially observed features, which is a common problem in most discriminative learning models.

10.2.3 Integration of Deformable Models with Learning-Based Classification

The integration of deformable models with learning-based classification is a recently introduced framework for propagating deformable models in a probabilistic manner, by formulating the *traditional* energy minimization as an *MAP* estimation problem. The main advantages of such integration are: (1) the model evolution provides a framework for updating the region statistics in a learning-based region classification; (2) the probabilistic formulation can provide the desired robustness to data (region) ambiguities; and (3) the final solution is a locally smooth boundary around the ROI, due to the deformable model formulation. In the survey of McInerney and Terzopoulos [19], methods that use probabilistic formulations are described. Huang et al. [22] proposed the integration of probabilistic active contours with MRFs in a graphical model framework to overcome the limitations of edge-based probabilistic active contours. Huang et al. [33] also proposed a framework that tightly couples 3D MRFs with deformable models for the 3D segmentation of medical images. To exploit the superiority of CRFs compared to common first-order MRFs, Tsechpenakis et al. [37, 39] proposed a coupling framework where a CRF and an implicit deformable model are integrated in a simple graphical model. More recently, Tsechpenakis et al. [26, 38] used the integration of geometric models with CRFs for medical image segmentation.

10.3 The Metamorphs Model

In this section, we describe a new class of deformable models, called Metamorphs, which integrates edge- and region-based image features for robust image segmentation. A Metamorphs model does not require *a priori* offline learning, yet enjoys the benefit of having appearance constraints by online adaptive learning of model-interior region intensity statistics. The basic framework of applying a Metamorphs model to boundary extraction is depicted in Figure 10.6. The object of interest in this example is the corpus callosum structure in an MRI image of the brain. First, a simple shape (e.g., circular) model is initialized inside the corpus callosum (see the circle in Figure 10.6[a]). Considering the model as a "disk," it has a shape and covers an area of the image that is the interior of the current model. The model then deforms toward edges as well as toward the boundary of a region that has similar intensity statistics as the model interior. Figure 10.6(b) shows the edges detected using a canny edge detector; note that the edge detector with automatically determined thresholds gives a result that has spurious edges and boundary gaps. To counter the effect of noise in edge detection, we estimate an ROI that has similar intensity statistics with the model interior. To find this region, we first estimate the model-interior probability density function (PDF) of intensity; next, a likelihood map is computed that specifies the likelihood of a pixel's intensity according to the model-

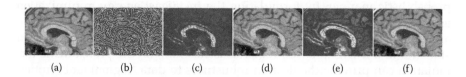

| (a) | (b) | (c) | (d) | (e) | (f) |

FIGURE 10.6

Metamorphs segmentation of a brain structure. (a) An MRI image of the brain; the initial circular model is drawn on top. (b) Edges detected using canny edge detector. (c) Intensity likelihood map computed according to the intensity PDF of the initial model interior. (d) Intermediate evolving model after 15 iterations. (e) Intensity likelihood map according to the intermediate model's interior statistics. (f) Final converged model after 38 iterations.

interior PDF. Figure 10.6(c) shows the likelihood map computed based on the initial model interior; then, we threshold the likelihood map to obtain the ROI. The evolution of the model is then derived using a gradient descent method from a unified variational framework consisting of energy terms defined on edges, the ROI boundary, and the likelihood map. Figure 10.6(d) shows the model after 15 iterations of deformation. As the model deforms, the model interior and its intensity statistics change, and the new statistics lead to the update of the likelihood map and the update of the ROI boundary for the model to deform toward. This online adaptive learning process empowers the model to find more robustly the boundary of objects with nonuniform appearance. Figure 10.6(e) shows the updated likelihood map given the evolved model in Figure 10.6(d). Finally, the model converges taking a balance between the edge and region influences, and the result is shown in Figure 10.6(f).

The key property of Metamorphs is that these new models have both shape and appearance, and they naturally integrate edge information with region statistics when applied to segmentation. By doing so, these new models generalize the two major classes of deformable models in the literature, parametric and geometric models, which are traditionally shape-based and take into account only edge or image gradient information.

10.3.1 The Metamorphs Shape Representation

The model's shape is implicitly embedded in a higher-dimensional space of distance transforms. The Euclidean distance transform is used to embed the boundary of an evolving model as the zero level set of a higher-dimensional distance function [40]. To facilitate notation, we consider the 2D case. Let $\Phi : \Omega \to R^+$ be a Lipschitz function that refers to the distance transform for the model shape $\mathcal{M}$. By definition, Ω is bounded since it refers to the image domain. The shape defines a partition of the domain: the region that is enclosed by $\mathcal{M}$, $[\mathcal{R}_\mathcal{M}]$, the background $[\Omega - \mathcal{R}_\mathcal{M}]$, and on the model, $[\partial \mathcal{R}_\mathcal{M}]$ (a very narrow band around the model shape $\mathcal{M}$). Given these definitions, the following implicit shape representation for $\mathcal{M}$ is considered:

$$\Phi_\mathcal{M}(\mathbf{x}) = \begin{cases} 0, & \mathbf{x} \in \partial \mathcal{R}_\mathcal{M} \\ +\mathcal{D}(x,\mathcal{M}), & \mathbf{x} \in \mathcal{R}_\mathcal{M} \\ -\mathcal{D}(x,\mathcal{M}), & \mathbf{x} \in [\Omega - \mathcal{R}_\mathcal{M}] \end{cases} \tag{10.4}$$

where $\mathcal{D}(\mathbf{x}, \mathcal{M})$ refers to the minimum Euclidean distance between the image pixel location $\mathbf{x} = (x, y)$ and the model $\mathcal{M}$.

Such implicit embedding makes the model shape representation a distance map "image," which significantly facilitates the integration of shape and appearance information. It also provides a feature space in which objective functions that are optimized using a gradient descent method can be conveniently used. A sufficient condition for convergence of gradient descent methods requires continuous first derivatives, and the considered implicit representation satisfies this condition. In fact, one can prove that the gradient of the distance function is a unit vector in the normal direction of the shape. This property will make our model evolution fast. Examples of the implicit representation can be found in Figures 10.3 and 10.4(c, d).

10.3.2 The Model's Deformations

The deformations that a Metamorphs model can undergo are defined using a space warping technique, the free form deformation (FFD) [41, 42], which is a popular approach in graphics and animation. The essence of FFD is to deform the shape of an object by manipulating a regular control lattice F overlaid on its volumetric embedding space. The deformation of the control lattice consists of displacements of all the control points in the lattice, and from these sparse displacements, a dense deformation field for every pixel in the embedding space can be acquired through interpolation using interpolating basis functions such as the cubic B-spline functions. One illustrative example is shown in Figure 10.7. A circular shape [Figure 10.7(1.a)] is implicitly embedded as the zero level set of a distance function [Figure 10.7(1.b)]. A

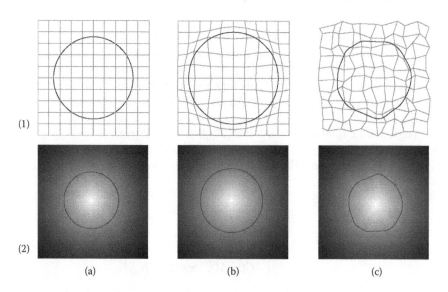

FIGURE 10.7
Shape representation and deformations of Metamorphs models. (1) The model shape. (2) The implicit distance map "image" representation of the model shape. (a) Initial model. (b) Example FFD control lattice deformation to expand the model. (c) Another example of the free-form model deformation given the control lattice deformation.

regular control lattice is overlaid on this embedding space. When the embedding space deforms due to the deformation of the FFD control lattice as shown in Figure 10.7(b), the shape undergoes an expansion. Figure 10.7(c) shows another example of free-form shape deformation given a particular FFD control lattice deformation. In Metamorphs, we consider an incremental free form deformations (IFFD) formulation using the cubic B-spline basis functions for interpolation [43].

Compared with optical flow type of deformation representation (i.e., pixelwise displacements in x and y directions) commonly used in the literature, the IFFD parameterization we use allows faster model evolution and convergence, because it has significantly fewer parameters. A hierarchical multilevel implementation of IFFD [43], which uses multiresolution control lattices according to a coarse-to-fine strategy, can account for deformations of both large and small scales. The advantages of coarse-to-fine optimization have been demonstrated in deformable contour frameworks in the literature [44]. Another property of IFFD is that it imposes implicit smoothness constraints, since it guarantees C^1 continuity at control points and C^2 continuity everywhere else. Therefore, there is no need to introduce computationally expensive regularization components on the deformed shapes. As a space warping technique, IFFD also integrates naturally with the implicit shape representation that embeds the model shape in a higher-dimensional space.

10.3.3 The Model's Texture

To approximate the intensity distribution of the model interior, we model the distribution using a nonparametric kernel-based density estimation method, also known as the Parzen windows technique [45], which is a popular nonparametric statistical method. Recently, this technique has been applied to imaging and computer vision, most notably in modeling the varying background in video sequences [46], and in approximating multimodal intensity density functions of color images [10]. In this work, we use this representation to approximate the intensity PDF of the model interior.

Suppose that the model is placed on an image I, and the image region bounded by current model Φ_M is $\mathcal{R}_M$, then the intensity PDF of the model interior region can be represented using a Gaussian kernel-based density estimation:

$$P(i|\Phi_M) = \frac{1}{V(\mathcal{R}_M)} \iint_{\mathcal{R}_M} \frac{1}{\sqrt{2\pi}\sigma} e^{\frac{-(i-I(\mathbf{y}))^2}{2\sigma^2}} d\mathbf{y} \tag{10.5}$$

where $i = 0, \ldots, 255$ denotes the pixel intensity values, $V(\mathcal{R}_M)$ denotes the volume of $\mathcal{R}_M$, $\mathbf{y}$ represents pixels in the region $\mathcal{R}_M$, and σ is a constant specifying the width of the Gaussian kernel.

One example of this nonparametric density estimation can be seen in Figure 10.8. The zero level set of the evolving models $\Phi_{\mathcal{M}}$ are drawn on top of the original image in Figure 10.8(a). The model interior regions $\mathcal{R}_{\mathcal{M}}$ are cropped and shown in Figure 10.8(b). Given the model interiors, their nonparametric intensity PDFs $\mathbf{P}(i \mid \Phi_{\mathcal{M}})$ are shown in Figure 10.8(c), where the horizontal axis denotes the intensity values $i = 0, ..., 255$, and the vertical axis denotes the probability values $P \in [0,1]$. Finally, over the entire image I, we evaluate the probability of every pixel's intensity, according to the model interior intensity PDF, and the resulting probability (or likelihood) map is shown in Figure 10.8(d).

Using this nonparametric estimation, the intensity distribution of the model interior gets automatically updated while the model deforms to cover a new set of interior pixels; and it avoids the need to estimate and keep a separate set of intensity parameters such as the mean and variance if a Gaussian or mixture-of-Gaussian model is used. Moreover, this kernel-based estimation in Equation (10.5) is a continuous function, which facilitates the computation of derivatives in a gradient descent–based optimization framework.

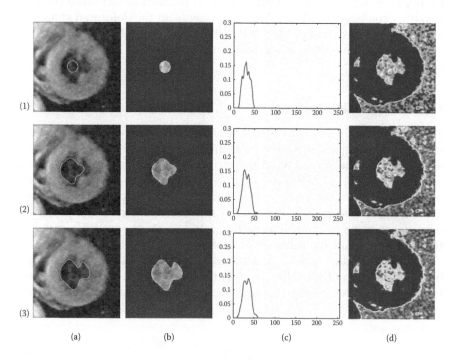

(a)   (b)   (c)   (d)

FIGURE 10.8

Left ventricle endocardium segmentation, demonstrating Metamorphs appearance representation. (1) Initial model. (2) Intermediate result after four iterations. (3) Final converged result after 10 iterations. (a) The evolving model drawn on original image. (b) Interior region of the evolving model. (c) Intensity PDF of the model interior. (d) Image intensity probability map according to the PDF of the model interior.

10.3.4 The Metamorphs' Dynamics

To fit to the boundary of an object, the motion of the model is driven by two types of energy terms derived from the image: the edge data terms, E_E, and the region data terms, E_R. Thus, the overall energy functional E is defined by [14]

$$E = E_E + kE_R \tag{10.6}$$

where k is a constant balancing the contributions from the two types of terms. In this formulation, we are able to omit the model smoothness term, since this smoothness is implicit by using FFDs.

10.3.4.1 The Edge Term, E_E

The Metamorphs model is attracted to edge features with high image gradient. We encode the edge information using a "shape image," Φ, which is the unsigned distance transform of the edge map of the image. The edge map is computed using canny edge detector with default parameter settings. In Figure 10.9c, we can see the "shape image" of an example MR heart image.

Intuitively, this edge term encourages deformations that map the model boundary pixels to image locations closer to edges, so that the underlying "shape image" values are as small (or as close to zero) as possible. During optimization, this term will deform the model along the gradient direction of the underlying "shape image" toward edges. Thus, it will expand or shrink the model accordingly, serving as a two-way balloon force implicitly and making the attraction range of the model large.

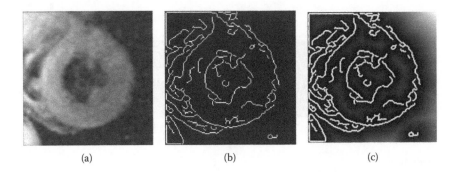

(a)   (b)   (c)

FIGURE 10.9
Effects of small spurious edges on the "shape image." (a) An MRI image of the heart; the object boundary is the endocardium of the left ventricle. (b) Edge map of the image. (c) The derived "shape image" (distance transform of the edge map), with edges drawn on top. Note how the small spurious edges affect the "shape image" values inside the object.

One additional advantage of this edge term is that, at an edge with small gaps, this term will constrain the model to go along the "geodesic" path on the "shape image," which coincides with the smooth shortest path connecting the two open ends of a gap. This behavior can be seen in Figure 10.10. Note that at a small gap on an edge, the edge term favors a path with the smallest accumulative distance values to the edge points.

10.3.4.2 The Region Data Term, E_R

An attractive aspect of the Metamorphs is that their interior intensity statistics are dynamically learned, and their deformations are influenced by forces derived from this dynamically changing region information. This region information is very important in helping the models out of local minima, and converge to the true object boundary. In Figure 10.9, the spurious edges both inside and around the object boundary degrade the reliability of the "shape image" and the edge data term. Yet, the intensity probability maps computed based on model interior intensity statistics, as shown in Figure 10.8(d), give a consistent and clear indication on where the rough boundary of the object is. In another MR heart image shown in Figure 10.11(1.a), a large portion of the object boundary (LV endocardium) is missing during computation of the edge map using default canny edge detector settings (Figure 10.11[1.b]). Relying solely on the "shape image" (Figure 10.11[1.c]) and the edge data term, a model would have leaked through the large gap and mistakenly converged to the outer epicardium boundary. In this situation, the probability maps (Figure 10.11[2–4.d]) computed based on model interior intensity statistics become the key to optimal model convergence.

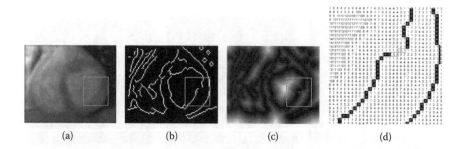

(a)　　　　　　　(b)　　　　　　　(c)　　　　　　　(d)

FIGURE 10.10

At a small gap in the edges, the edge data term constrains the model to go along a path that coincides with the smooth shortest path connecting the two open ends of the gap. (a) Original image. (b) The edge map (note the small gap inside the square). (c) The "shape image." (d) Zoom-in view of the region inside the square. The numbers are the "shape image" values at each pixel location. The dots are edge points; the small squares indicate a path favored by the edge term for a Metamorphs model.

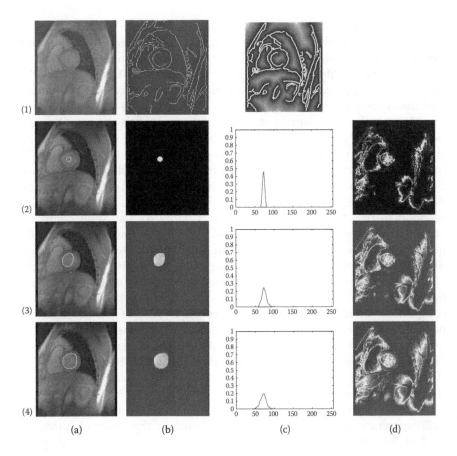

FIGURE 10.11

Segmentation of the left ventricle endocardium in an MRI image. (1.a) The original image. (1.b) The edge map; note that a large portion of the object boundary is missing in the edge map). (1.c) The "shape image." (2) Initial model. (3) Intermediate model. (4) Converged model. (a) Zero level set of the current model drawn on the image. (b) Model interiors. (c) The interior intensity PDFs. (d) Intensity probability maps.

In our framework, we define two region data terms—an ROI-based balloon term E_{R_l} and a maximum likelihood (ML) term E_{R_m}; thus, the overall region-based energy function E_R is:

$$E_R = E_{R_l} + bE_{R_m} \tag{10.7}$$

The ROI-based balloon term E_{R_l}. We determine the ROI as the largest possible region in the image that overlaps the model and has a consistent intensity distribution as the current model interior. The ROI-based balloon term is designed to efficiently evolve the model toward the boundary of the ROI.

Given a model $\mathcal{M}$ on image I (Figure 10.12[a]), we first compute the image intensity probability map P_I (Figure 10.12[b]), based on the model interior intensity statistics (see Equation 10.5). A threshold (typically the mean probability over the entire image domain) is applied on P_I to produce a binary image P_B. More specifically, those pixels that have probabilities higher than the threshold in P_I are given the value 1 in P_B, and all other pixels are assigned the value of 0 in P_B. We then apply a connected component analysis algorithm based on run-length encoding and scanning [47] on P_B to extract the connected component overlapping the model. Considering this connected component as a "disk" that we want the Metamorphs model to match, it is likely that this disk has small holes due to noise and intensity inhomogeneity, as well as large holes that correspond to real "holes" inside the object. How to deal with compound objects that potentially have holes using Metamorphs is an interesting question that we will briefly discuss in Section 10.6. Here, we assume the ROIs that we apply Metamorphs to segment are without interior holes. Under this assumption, the desired behavior of the model is to evolve toward the ROI border regardless of small holes in the ROI connected component. Hence, we take the outermost border of the selected connected component as the current ROI boundary. We encode this ROI boundary information by computing its "shape image," ϕ_r, which is its unsigned distance transform (Figure 10.12c). The ROI-based balloon term is then defined by multiplicately combining the ROI "shape image" ϕ_r and the model representation, ϕ_m [14].

Within the overall energy minimization framework, the ROI-based balloon term is the most effective in countering the effect of unregularized or inhomogeneous region intensities such as that caused by speckle noise and spurious edges inside the object of interest (e.g., in Figures 10.9 and 10.13). This is because the ROI term deforms the model toward the

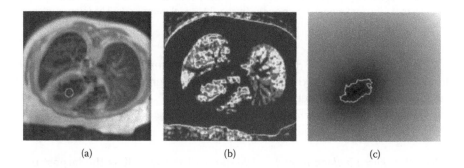

(a)   (b)   (c)

FIGURE 10.12
Deriving the ROI-based region data term. (a) The model shown on the original image. (b) The intensity probability map computed based on the model interior statistics. (c) The "shape image" encoding boundary information of the ROI.

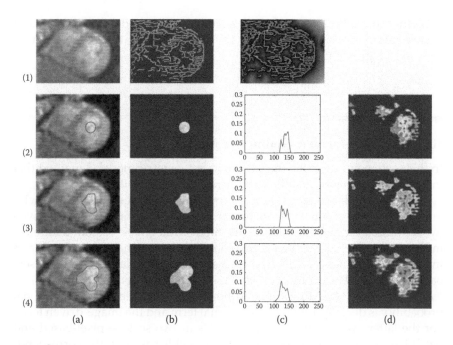

FIGURE 10.13
Tagged MRI heart image example. (1.a) Original image. (1.b) Edge map. (1.c) "Shape image" derived from the edge map. (2) Initial model. (3) Intermediate result. (4) Converged model (after 12 iterations). (2–4)(a) The evolving model. (2–4)(b) Model interior. (2–4)(c) Model interior intensity PDF. (2–4)(d) Intensity probability map according to the PDF in (c).

outermost boundary of the identified ROI, disregarding all small holes inside. Although this makes the assumption that the object to be segmented has no holes, it is a very effective measure to discard incoherent pixels, and ensure that noise and intensity inhomogeneity do not influence model convergence. Moreover, the ROI term generates adaptively changing balloon forces that expedite model convergence and improve convergence accuracy, especially when the object shape is elongated, or has salient protrusions or concavities.

The ML term E_{R_m}. The previous ROI term is efficient in deforming the model toward object boundary when the model is still far away. When the model gets close to the boundary, however, the ROI may become less reliable due to intensity changes in the boundary areas. To achieve better convergence, we design another ML region-based data term that constrains the model to deform toward areas where the pixel intensity probabilities of belonging to the model-interior intensity distribution are high. This ML term is formulated by maximizing the log-likelihood of pixel intensities in a narrow band around the model [14]. During model evolution, when the model is still far away from the object boundary, this ML term generates very little force to influence the model deformation. When the model gets close to the boundary, the ML term helps the model to converge and is particularly useful in preventing the model from leaking through large gaps (e.g., Figure 10.11).

10.4 The CRF-Driven Geometric Model

In this section, we describe the CRF-driven geometric model, a method that integrates deformable models with learning-based classification.

A topology-independent solution is presented for segmenting ROIs with texture patterns of any scale, using an implicit deformable model driven by conditional random fields. This model integrates region and edge information as image-driven terms, whereas the probabilistic shape and internal (smoothness) terms use representations similar to the level set–based methods. The evolution of the model is solved as an maximum *a posteriori* probability (MAP) estimation problem, where the target conditional probability is decomposed into the internal term and the image-driven term. For the latter, we use discriminative CRFs in two scales—pixel-based and patch-based—to obtain smooth probability fields based on the corresponding image features.

In this method, we (1) use the shape representation of known level set–based approaches, to achieve topology independence; (2) integrate edge and region information, which is being updated during the model evolution, to handle local feature variations; (3) avoid the problem of getting trapped in local minima, which hounds most of the energy minimization-driven models; (4) exploit the superiority of CRFs compared to MRFs for image segmentation, coupling a CRF-based scheme with the deformable model; and (5) capture higher-scale dependencies, using pixel- and patch-based CRFs. We use the two-scale CRF model in a tightly coupled framework with the deformable model, such that the external (image-driven) term of the deformable model eventually corresponds to the smooth probability field estimated by the CRF. We use a modified version of the discriminative CRFs presented in the study of Kumar and Hebert [35], where the MAP inference is computationally tractable using graph mincut algorithms.

10.4.1 Deformable Model Shape and Energy

In a similar manner as in Metamorphs (see Section 10.3.1, Equation 10.4), the model's shape is embedded in a higher-dimensional space of distance transforms, such that the zero-level of the scalar (Euclidean distance) function $\Phi_{\mathcal{M}}$ corresponds to the evolving front. The model $\mathcal{M}$ (interface) defines two regions in the image domain Ω: the region $\mathcal{R}_M$ enclosed by the model M, and the background $|\Omega - \mathcal{R}_M|$.

The internal energy of the model consists of three individual terms: the smoothness constraint E_{smooth}, the distance from the target shape E_{shape}, and a partitioning energy term E_{part}

$$E_{int}(\Phi_M) = E_{smooth}(\Phi_M) + E_{part}(\Phi_M) + E_{shape}(\Phi_M) \qquad (10.8)$$

The smoothness term E_{smooth}. We define the energy term that enforces smoothness along the model boundary as

$$E_{smooth}(\Phi_M) = \varepsilon_1 \mathcal{A}(\mathcal{R}_M) + \varepsilon_2 \iint_{\partial \mathcal{R}_M} \|\nabla\Phi_M(\mathbf{x})\| d\mathbf{x} \qquad (10.9)$$

where ε_1 and ε_2 are the weighting constants, $\partial\mathcal{R}_M$ denotes a narrow band around the model boundary, and $\mathcal{A}(\mathcal{R}_M)$ denotes the area of the model interior $\mathcal{R}_M$. The minimization of this energy forces the model to the position with the minimum area enclosed and the maximum first-order smoothness along the model boundary; $\nabla\Phi_M$ is defined on $\forall \mathbf{x} \in \Omega$, and is used similarly as in the Mumford-Shah formulation [6], that is, it determines the first-order smoothness along the boundary.

The partitioning energy E_{part}. The partitioning energy $E_{part}(\Phi_M)$ [26] forces the region $\Phi_M \geq 0$. (model interior, including the pixels on the interface) toward a connected form. It can be also seen as a term that minimizes the entropy of a set of particles, where the particles are assumed to be the connected components of $\Phi_M \geq 0$. The minimization of this energy forces the model toward the minimum distances between the connected components (interior particles), that is, it forces different regions (curves) on the image plane to merge. Figure 10.4 illustrates an example of the effect of this energy term: the model is initialized in three different positions on the image plane, and during the evolution, the model is forced toward a connected form. Intuitively, merging different regions (model interior) competes the data-driven terms, and therefore, sometimes the image features do not allow for this merging.

The shape-based energy E_{shape}. The role of the shape-based energy term is to force the evolving model toward a desired shape, in cases where we have a prior knowledge about the ROI in terms of its shape. This is a common approach in medical image analysis, since in many applications the goal is to segment ROIs with specific anatomic features. Introducing this term in the model energy, we combine the bottom-up approach (use image features to find a region) with a top-down methodology (use prior knowledge about the ROI to detect it in an image). This shape-based term is defined in a similar manner as in the work of Paragios et al. [48] and Chan and Zhu [49] in terms of the distance between the model and the target shape.

10.4.2 The Model Dynamics

According to the CRF-driven geometric model, the goal is to find the optimal model position on the image plane, as well as the optimal probability field of all pixels/regions. Therefore, we formulate the deformable model evolution as a joint MAP estimation problem for the model position and the image label field,

$$\langle \Phi_{\mathcal{M}}^{*}, \mathcal{L}^{*} \rangle = \arg \max_{(\Phi_{\mathcal{M}}, \mathcal{L})} P(\Phi_{\mathcal{M}}, \mathcal{L}|F), \tag{10.10}$$

where $\Phi_{\mathcal{M}}$ is the deformable model configuration; $\mathcal{L}$ is the sites' (pixels or image patches) labels, that is, $\mathcal{L} = \{-1,1\}$, with -1 and 1 denoting the background and model interior, respectively; and F is the observation set, that is, the image features.

To solve the problem of Equation (10.10), we use the simple graphical model of Figure 10.14, which integrates the deformable model with learning-based classification, namely, the CRF. The posterior probability $P(\Phi_{\mathcal{M}}, \mathcal{L}|F)$. is then estimated (using the Bayes rule) as

$$P(\Phi_{\mathcal{M}}, \mathcal{L}|F) \propto P(F|\mathcal{L}) \cdot P(\mathcal{L}|\Phi_{\mathcal{M}}) \cdot P(\Phi_{\mathcal{M}})$$

$$\propto P(\Phi_{\mathcal{M}}) \cdot P(F) \cdot P(\mathcal{L}|\Phi_{\mathcal{M}}) \cdot P(\mathcal{L}|F), \tag{10.11}$$

where $P(\Phi_{\mathcal{M}})$ is the model prior, which corresponds to the model internal energy, and $P(F)$ is the data prior; $P(\mathcal{L}|\Phi_{\mathcal{M}})$ is defined below as a softmax function of $\Phi_{\mathcal{M}}$ and represents the uncertainty between the classification and the deformable model position; finally, $P(\mathcal{L}|F)$ represents the pixel/region classification (CRF).

The data prior P(F). In a pixelwise probability field estimation, where sites indicate pixels and the observations are the pixel intensities, we define the data prior in terms of a Gaussian distribution around the *observed* pixel intensity value. In a patchwise probability field estimation, where instead of pixels we use spatially higher-scale sites, we define the data prior by directly using the pixel intensity distribution inside each site.

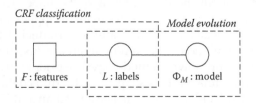

FIGURE 10.14
Graphical model for the integration of the CRF scheme in the deformable model.

The model prior $P(\Phi_{\mathcal{M}})$. We use the model energy definition of Equation (10.8) to define the model prior in terms of a Gibbs functional,

$$P(\Phi_{\mathcal{M}}) = (1 / Z_{\text{int}})\exp\{-E_{\text{int}}(\Phi_{\mathcal{M}})\}, \tag{10.12}$$

where $E_{\text{int}}(\Phi_{\mathcal{M}})$ is calculated from the energy terms described above, and Z_{int} is a normalization constant. The maximization of this prior forces the model toward a position with the minimum enclosed area and maximum smoothness along the boundary, with the smallest distance to the target shape, and the minimum *entropy*.

The likelihood $P(\mathcal{L}|\Phi_{\mathcal{M}})$. In our framework, and according to Equation (10.11), we introduce the uncertainty between the classification results (object vs. background) obtained using the deformable model configuration ($\Phi_{\mathcal{M}}$) and the learning-based site labeling (label field $\mathcal{L}$), at each instance of the model evolution. We represent this uncertainty with the likelihood term $P(\mathcal{L}|\Phi_{\mathcal{M}})$, which is formulated as the softmax (sigmoid) function,

$$P(l_i|\Phi_{\mathcal{M}}) = \frac{1}{1+\exp\{-\kappa\Phi_{\mathcal{M}}(\mathbf{x}_i)\}}, \tag{10.13}$$

where $l_i = \{-1, 1\}$ is the label of the ith pixel or region $\mathbf{x}_i$. This term indicates that the probability of a site belonging to the model interior rapidly increases as $\Phi_{\mathcal{M}}(\mathbf{x}) > 0$ increases, and converges to zero as $\Phi_{\mathcal{M}}(\mathbf{x}) < 0$ decreases; also, $P(l_i|\Phi_{\mathcal{M}}) = 0.5 \ \forall \mathbf{x}_i \in \Omega: \Phi_{\mathcal{M}}(\mathbf{x}_i) = 0$. The parameter $\kappa > 0$ regulates the slope (rate) of this change, and we usually set it as equal to 1. Also, if $\mathbf{x}_i$ is a region, we consider its center to estimate this probability, since for the estimation of patchwise probability fields we assume rectangular image patches of fixed size. In Figure 10.15, we describe this uncertainty

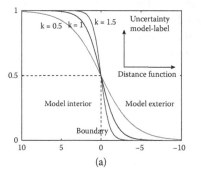
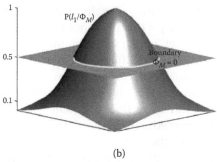

(a) (b)

FIGURE 10.15
Uncertainty between the learning-based classification and the deformable model position: (a) plot of $P(l_i|\Phi_{\mathcal{M}})$ (Equation 10.13) using a 1D distance function Φ; (b) 2D representation of $\kappa = \{0.5, 1, 1.5\}$ for the model boundary $\kappa = 1$ being circle.

term and we show how this conditional probability varies with the values of the distance function $\Phi_{\mathcal{M}}$: in panel (a) we illustrate the case where $P(l_i|\Phi_{\mathcal{M}})$ is derived from a 1D distance function $\Phi_{\mathcal{M}}$, for $\kappa = \{0.5, 1, 1.5\}$, whereas in panel (b) we show the same likelihood functional (for $\kappa = 1$) calculated using the shape representation of a circle (line) in the image domain (plane).

The remaining term $P(\mathcal{L}|F)$ in Equation (10.11) is calculated using the CRF described in the following subsection.

10.4.3 The Collaborative CRF

We use a CRF formulation [26, 50] to calculate the probability field $P(\mathcal{L}|F)$ that drives the deformable model evolution, according to Equations (10.10) and (10.11). In the collaborative formulation of this CRF, we implement *interactions* that enforce similar class labels ("ROI" or "background") between sites containing similar features. We also use *correlative* information between neighboring sites, by extracting complimentary features for classification in instances of ambiguous features. Complimentary features are considered to be features from neighboring sites, which when considered together, instead of individually, can better describe the appearance of a single ROI.

Figure 10.16(a) shows a graphical representation of our collaborative conditional random field (CoCRF). The label (ROI or background) of each site of the examined image is associated with its feature set, namely, its intensity value (site = pixel) or its intensity distribution (site = image patch); such associations (*association potentials*) are shown in red lines. Also, the unknown label node of each site interacts with the corresponding label nodes of its neighboring sites; these interactions (*interaction potentials*) are shown in blue lines. The neighboring (Markovian) property of the image sites is also applied at the observation level, that is, between the features of neighboring sites (green lines). Finally, the interactions between labels and features are governed by a third potential, what we call *correlative potential* (not shown in this figure), which enforces interactions between complimentary sites. For the mathematical formulation of this CRF, we encourage the reader to consult references [26, 50].

Figure 10.16(b) shows two different site neighborhoods for the example image in Figure 10.2(a). The neighborhood N_i of the ith site consists of the eight immediate (first-order) neighbors. In neighborhood A, some sites belong to the ROI (right ventricle) and some belong to the background, whereas neighborhood B belongs entirely to the ROI (right ventricle). The plots shown in Figure 10.16(c) and (d) illustrate the intensity distributions (features) of sites A and B, respectively; the dashed lines show the distributions of the central site and one of its neighbors, and the solid lines illustrate the joint distributions between these two sites. In panel (c), the two sites

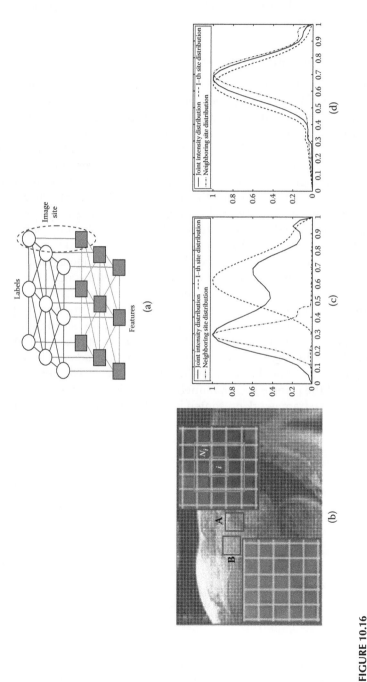

FIGURE 10.16

(a) Graphical representation of the CoCRF. (b) Two different site neighborhoods for the example shown in Figure 10.2a: some sites in A belong to the ROI and some belong to the background, whereas B belongs entirely to the ROI. The plots of (c) and (d) illustrate the intensity distributions and joint intensity distributions for two sites inside the neighborhoods of A and B, respectively (see text for explanation).

belong to different regions, whereas in (d) the two sites are part of the same region (since B is chosen from the ROI). Intuitively, and in contrast to the case in (c), the joint distribution in (d) supports the assumption that the two sites are complimentary.

10.4.4 The Classification Confidence

According to the CRF framework described above, and along with the probabilities assigned to the image sites, one can also use the classification confidence, that is, how confidently a probability is assigned to a site, for one major reason: we enforce interactions from sites classified with high confidence to neighboring sites classified with low confidence. In such a probabilistic approach, "strong" classification indicates the very high probability (low feature ambiguity) or very low probability (high feature ambiguity) of a site belonging to the ROI. On the other hand, high (low) confidence does not indicate low (high) ambiguity, but high confidence of assigning a probability. In other words, a site that is ambiguous, that is, its probability of belonging to the ROI is approximately 0.5, may be confidently assigned this probability. Therefore, in case of a probabilistic classification, confidence indicates the upper and lower values that a probability can take for a specific site.

Figure 10.17(a) illustrates the difference between the classification confidence and the class probability using a support vector machine [51]. In the feature space, two classes are shown; in each class, the strongly classified sites are marked with dots, whereas the ambiguous sites (close to the decision boundary and between the support vectors) are marked with circles. In our case, some sites from both classes are close to the decision boundary due to the noise of the feature vector, namely, the pixels intensities. According to our original CRF framework presented in references [26, 50], the classification

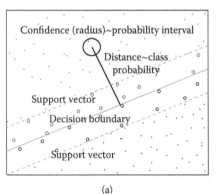
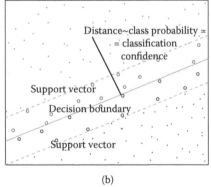

(a)   (b)

FIGURE 10.17
Classification confidence: (a) probability interval (circle radius), (b) degeneration of the meaning of confidence (confidence = class posterior probability). (See text for explanation.)

confidence indicates the high and low boundaries of the class probability: in the feature space, the probability interval can be represented with a circle around the site, and the confidence is the radius of the circle.

For simplicity, we can assume that the classification confidence indicates how strongly the classifier assigns labels, that is, for a given site with unknown label l_i and feature f_i, it is $K_i = P(l_i | f_i)$. Figure 10.17(b) illustrates this simplification.

10.5 Examples

In this section, we show a few more examples of applying Metamorphs and collaborative CRF-driven models to medical image segmentation.

To test the ability of Metamorphs to cope with objects whose interiors have a high level of speckle noise, we apply the algorithm to breast lesion segmentation in ultrasound images. Figure 10.18 shows two such examples. Because of the nature of ultrasound images, there are no clear contrast edges separating a lesion from its surrounding normal tissue. The criterion in locating a lesion is usually that a lesion contains less speckles than its surroundings. It is seen in Figure 10.18(1.c) and (2.c) that the likelihood map computed based on model-interior intensity distribution effectively captures the difference in speckle density between a lesion and its surroundings. This appearance-based region information is the key for the model to converge to the correct boundary (Figure 10.18e) despite the presence of very noisy speckle edges (Figure 10.18[1.b]) inside the lesion.

When compared to region-based segmentation methods such as region growing [52], MRFs [53], and graph cuts [9], Metamorphs is similar in the grouping property, which groups pixels whose intensities follow consistent statistics so as to be less sensitive to localized image noise than edges. The main difference is that Metamorphs is an efficient model-based approach that includes implicit smoothness constraints on the model surface and thus directly generates smooth boundary, without the need for additional postprocessing steps to extract boundary from pixel clusters and to smooth the boundary. Furthermore, Metamorphs is particularly good at segmenting an object with a gradually changing and nonuniform intensity or texture appearance. In Figure 10.19, we compare the results from MRFs with those from Metamorphs, using a synthetic example containing an object with gradually changing intensity from left to right (Figure 10.19[a–c]), and an ultrasound image with speckle noise (Figure 10.19[d–f]). The MRF implementation is based on the supervised Bayesian MRF image classification algorithm described by Berthod et al. [53]. We specified the images consisting of two classes: the *object* class and the *background* class. Given a sample patch for each class (Figure 10.19[a] and [d]), the algorithm computes

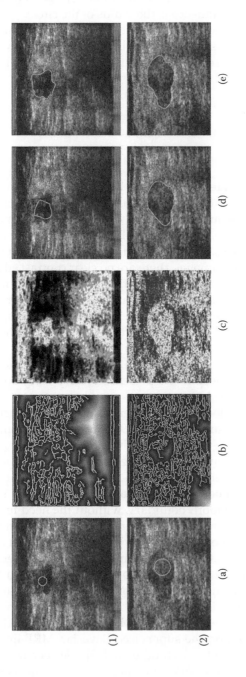

FIGURE 10.18

Segmenting lesions in ultrasound breast images. (a) The original ultrasound image, with the initial model drawn on top. (b) The shape image derived from the edge map. (c) Intensity likelihood map. (d) Intermediate model after four iterations for example (1), and 13 iterations for example (2). (e) Final converged model after 11 iterations for (1), and 20 iterations for (2).

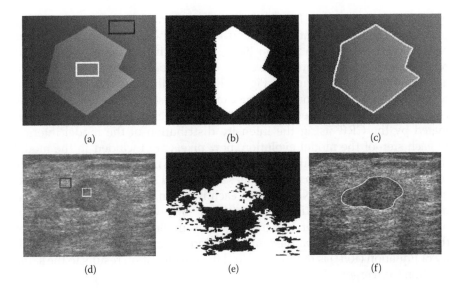

FIGURE 10.19
Comparing Markov random fields (MRFs) with Metamorphs. (a, d) Two-class initialization for MRF: object-class sample patches are enclosed by white rectangles, and background-class sample patches are enclosed by black rectangles. (b, e) MRF segmentation results using the algorithm described by Berthod et al. [53]. The main connected component of the object class is rendered in white, and the background class is rendered in black. (c, f) Metamorphs segmentation results for comparison.

the intensity mean and variance for each class, and applies MRF to perform classification. For the synthetic image, the MRF segmentation result after 268 iterations (with final temperature value $T = 0.018$) is shown in Figure 10.19b, and the result after 346 iterations (with final temperature value $T = 0.19$) for the breast ultrasound image is shown in Figure 10.19e. The temperature values and number of iterations are automatically determined by the MRF algorithm. Note that we only display the main connected component of the *object* class from the MRF result for fair comparison with Metamorphs. It can be seen that the MRF segmentation did not succeed on the synthetic image because of the heavily inhomogeneous intensity. MRF also failed on the ultrasound image because it did not separate the lesion object from part of the background that has similar statistics and it generated small holes/islands inside the object. In comparison, the Metamorphs model–based method can accurately locate the object boundaries by combining edge information, adaptive object appearance learning, and model smoothness constraints; the clean boundaries found by Metamorphs are shown in Figure 10.19(c) and (f).

Another means of overcoming the limitations of *traditional* MRF-based segmentation is to exploit the superiority of the collaborative CRF in terms of providing probability fields taking into account the spatial neighboring property of the image features. Moreover, when the CRF drives a geometric model, as we describe in Section 10.4.2, we can directly update the desired region statistics and therefore we can capture local feature variations, in an online learning manner. In Figure 10.20, we illustrate the segmentation result for the two ultrasound image examples described above. The model is initialized inside the lesion region and an initial probability field is estimated by the CRF, using the intensity distribution of the model interior. In each step of the model evolution, new pixels are included in the model interior and new probability fields are estimated using the updated model interior statistics, whereas the model's shape local smoothness is preserved by the internal energy. Note that in each iteration, we solve the MAP estimation problem in Equation (10.10) inside a narrow band around the previous model position. After 13 iterations for example (a) and 16 iterations for (b), the model converges at the image locations where the posterior probability of Equation (10.11) is maximized and the next iteration results to the same solution (convergence).

10.6 Chapter Summary

In this chapter, we have introduced medical image segmentation methods, particularly deformable model–based methods, machine learning–based classification methods, and methods that successfully integrate models and classification for robust image content interpretation. Understanding image content and extracting useful image features are critical to medical image search and mining. The introduced automated methods can be run offline on medical image archives to partition images into regions and to extract image features. Image features can then serve indexing mechanisms for efficient search. A challenge is to partition the images in a way that is close to segmenting real-world objects. The Metamorphs and collaborative CRF model–based methods are both efforts along this line since they integrate learned prior information with raw image observations.

In both Metamorphs and collaborative CRF-driven model, there are smoothness constraints that smooth out or discard pixels with incoherent appearance statistics so that the segmentation is more robust in the presence of noise and intensity inhomogeneity. The assumptions, however, sometimes complicate the segmentation of compound objects with holes. One possible solution is to keep a probabilistic mask that records which pixels inside the model have low likelihood values in the intensity probability maps. If these pixels have consistently low likelihood values for a number of iterations and they connect to cover a relatively large area inside the model, they are likely part of a hole in the model. If a hole is detected, its interior will be excluded

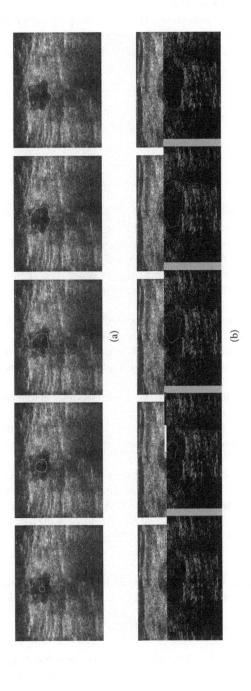

FIGURE 10.20

Segmentation of the lesions in the ultrasound images shown in Figure 10.18, using the CoCRF-driven deformable model: (a) and (b) show five instances of the model evolution for the examples of Figure 10.18(1) and (2), respectively.

from the computation of the intensity statistics of the model and the hole boundary will not affect the model evolution.

Several types of priors such as data priors and shape priors are introduced in the frameworks. However, important questions remain regarding whether to use prior or what types of prior are appropriate, given specific image segmentation and search tasks.

References

1. Shapiro, L. G., and Stockman, G. C. 2001. *Computer Vision*. Upper Saddle River, NJ: Prentice Hall.
2. Adams, R., and Bischof, L. 1994. Seeded region growing. *IEEE Transactions on Pattern Analysis and Machine Intelligence* 16(6):641–647.
3. Canny, J. 1986. A computational approach to edge detection. *IEEE Transactions on Pattern Analysis and Machine Intelligence* 8:679–714.
4. Manjunath, B., and Chellapa, R. 1991. Unsupervised texture segmentation using Markov random field models. *IEEE Transactions on Pattern Analysis and Machine Intelligence* 13:478–482.
5. Kass, M., Witkin, A., and Terzopoulos, D. 1987. Snakes: active contour models. *International Journal of Computer Vision* 1:321–331.
6. Mumford, D., and Shah, J. 1989. Optimal approximations by piecewise smooth functions and associated variational problems. *Communications on Pure and Applied Mathematics* 42(5):577–685.
7. Caselles, V., Kimmel, R., and Sapiro, G. 1995. Geodesic active contours. *IEEE International Conference on Computer Vision*.
8. Malladi, R., Sethian, J., and Vemuri, B. 1995. Shape modeling with front propagation: a level set approach. *IEEE Transactions on Pattern Analysis and Machine Intelligence* 17(2):158–175.
9. Shi, J., and Malik, J. 2000. Normalized cuts and image segmentation. *IEEE Transactions on Pattern Analysis and Machine Intelligence* 22(8):888–905.
10. Comaniciu, D., and Meer, P. 2002. Mean shift: a robust approach toward feature space analysis. *IEEE Transactions on Pattern Analysis and Machine Intelligence* 24(5):603–619.
11. Li, S. Z. 1995. *Markov Random Field Modeling in Computer Vision*. London, UK: Springer-Verlag.
12. Staib, L. H., and Duncan, J. S.. Boundary finding with parametrically deformable models. *IEEE Transactions on Pattern Analysis and Machine Intelligence* 14(11):1061–1075.
13. Metaxas, D. 1996. *Physics-Based Deformable Models*. Norwell, MA: Kluwer Academic Publishers.
14. Huang, X., and Metaxas, D. 2008. Metamorphs: Deformable shape and appearance models. *IEEE Transactions on Pattern Analysis and Machine Intelligence* 30(8): 1444–1459.

15. Yezzi, A. J., Tsai, A., and Willsky, A. 1999. A statistical approach to snakes for bimodal and trimodal imagery. *Proceedings of IEEE International Conference on Computer Vision* 2:898–903.

16. Vese, L. A., and Chan, T. F. 2002. A multiphase level set framework for image segmentation using the Mumford and Shah model. *International Journal of Computer Vision* 50(3):271–293.

17. Zhu, S., and Yuille, A. 1996. Region competition: unifying snakes, region growing, and Bayes/MDL for multi-band image segmentation. *IEEE Transactions on Pattern Analysis and Machine Intelligence* 18(9):884–900.

18. Cohen, L. D., and Cohen, I. 1993. Finite-element methods for active contour models and balloons for 2-D and 3-D Images. *IEEE Transactions on Pattern Analysis and Machine Intelligence* 15:1131–1147.

19. McInerney, T., and Terzopoulos, D. 1996. Deformable models in medical image analysis: a survey. *Medical Image Analysis* 1(2):91–108.

20. Xu, C., and Prince, J. L. 1998. Snakes, shapes and gradient vector flow. *IEEE Transactions on Image Processing* 7(3):359–369.

21. Ronfard, R. 1994. Region-based strategies for active contour models. *International Journal of Computer Vision* 13(2):229–251.

22. Huang, R., Pavlovic, V., and Metaxas, D. 2004. A graphical model framework for coupling MRFs and deformable models. *IEEE Conference on Computer Vision and Pattern Recognition* 2:739–746.

23. Florin, C., Williams, J., and Paragios, N. 2006. Globally optimal active contours, sequential Monte Carlo and on-line learning for vessel segmentation. *European Conference on Computer Vision*.

24. Huang, D., Swanson, E. A., Lin, C. P., Schuman, J. S., Stinson, W. G., Chang, W., Hee, M. R., Flotte, T., Gregory, K., Puliafito, C. A., and Fujimoto, J. G. 1991. Optical coherence tomography. *Science* 254:1178–1181.

25. Paragios, N., and Deriche, R. 2002. Geodesic Active regions and level set methods for supervised texture segmentation. *International Journal of Computer Vision* 46(3):223–247.

26. Tsechpenakis, G., Lujan, B., Martinez, O., Gregori, G., and Rosenfeld, P. J. 2008. Geometric deformable model driven by CoCRFs: application to optical coherence tomography. International Conference on Medical Image Computing and Computer Assisted Intervention, New York, NY, September.

27. Jiao, S., Knighton, R., Huang, X., Gregori, G., and Puliafito, C. 2005. Simultaneous acquisition of sectional and fundus ophthalmic images with spectral-domain optical coherence tomography. *Optics Express* 13(2):444–452.

28. Smith, W., Assink, J., Klein, R., Mitchell, P., Klaver, C. C., Klein, B. E., Hofman, A., Jensen, S., Wang, J. J., and de Jong, P. T. 2001. Risk factors for age-related macular degeneration: pooled findings from three continents. *Ophthalmology* 108(4):697–704.

29. Jones, T., and Metaxas, D. 1997. Automated 3D segmentation using deformable models and fuzzy affinity. *Proceedings of the 15th International Conference on Information Processing in Medical Imaging*, pp. 113–126.

30. Chen, T., and Metaxas, D. 2000. Image segmentation based on the integration of markov random fields and deformable models. *Proceedings of the International Conference on Medical Imaging Computing and Computer-Assisted Intervention*, pp. 256–265.

31. Samson, C., Blanc-Feraud, L., Aubert, G., and Zerubia, J. 2000. A level set model for image classification. *International Journal of Computer Vision* 40(3):187–198.

32. Chan, T., and Vese, L. 2001. Active contours without edges. *IEEE Transactions on Image Processing* 10(2):266–277.

33. Huang, R., Pavlovic, V., and Metaxas, D. 2006. A tightly coupled region-shape framework for 3D medical image segmentation. *Proceedings of the 2006 IEEE International Symposium on Biomedical Imaging*, Arlington, VA, pp. 2121–2124.

34. Lafferty, J., McCallum, A., and Pereira, F. 2001. Conditional random fields: probabilistic models for segmenting and labeling sequence data. *International Conference on Machine Learning*.

35. Kumar, S., and Hebert, M. 2004. Discriminative fields for modeling spatial dependencies in natural images, *Advances in Neural Information Processing Systems* 16:1351–1358.

36. He, X., Zemel, R., and Carreira-Perpinan, M. 2004. Multiscale conditional random fields for image labelling. *Proceedings of the IEEE Conference on Computer Vision and Pattern Recognition*, pp. 695–702.

37. Tsechpenakis, G., and Metaxas, D. 2007. CRF-driven implicit deformable model. *IEEE Conference on Computer Vision and Pattern Recognition*, pp. 1–8.

38. Tsechpenakis, G., Wang, J., Mayer, B., and Metaxas, D. 2007. Coupling CRFs and deformable models for 3D medical image segmentation. *IEEE Mathematical Methods in Biomedical Image Analysis*, IEEE International Conference on Computer Vision, Rio de Janeiro, Brazil.

39. Tsechpenakis, G., and Wang, J. 2007. CRF-based segmentation of human tear meniscus obtained with optical coherence tomography. *IEEE International Conference on Image Processing*, pp. 509–512.

40. Osher, S., and Sethian, J. 1988. Fronts propagating with curvature-dependent speed: algorithms based on the Hamilton-Jacobi formulation. *Journal of Computational Physics* 79:12–49.

41. Sederberg, T. W., and Parry, S. R. 1986. Free-form deformation of solid geometric models. In *Proceedings of the 13th Annual Conference on Computer Graphics*, pp. 151–160.

42. Faloutsos, P., van de Panne, M., and Terzopoulos, D. 1997. Dynamic free-form deformations for animation synthesis. *IEEE Transactions on Visualization and Computer Graphics* 3:201–214.

43. Huang, X., Paragios, N., and Metaxas, D. 2006. Shape registration in implicit spaces using information theory and free form deformations. *IEEE Transactions on Pattern Analysis and Machine Intelligence* 28(8):1303–1318.

44. Akgul, Y. S., and Kambhamettu, C. 2003. A coarse-to-fine deformable contour optimization framework. *IEEE Transactions on Pattern Analysis and Machine Intelligence* 25(2):174–186.

45. Duda, R. O., and Hart, P. 1973. *Pattern Classification and Scene Analysis*. New York, NY: Wiley.

46. Elgammal, A., Duraiswami, R., and Davis, L. S. 2003. Efficient kernel density estimation using the fast Gauss transform with applications to color modeling and tracking. *IEEE Transactions on Pattern Analysis and Machine Intelligence* 25(11):1499–1504.

47. Haralick, R. M., and Shapiro, L. 1992. *Computer and Robot Vision*. New York, NY: Addison-Wesley.

48. Paragios, N., Rousson, M., and Ramesh, V. 2002. Matching distance functions: a shape-to-area variational approach for global-to-local registration. *European Conference on Computer Vision*, pp. 775–790.

49. Chan, T., and Zhu, W. 2005. Level set based shape prior segmentation. *IEEE Conference on Computer Vision and Pattern Recognition.*

50. Martinez, O., and Tsechpenakis, G. 2008. Integration of active learning in a collaborative CRF. *IEEE Online Learning for Classification, Computer Vision and Pattern Recognition,* Anchorage, AK, June.

51. Cristianini, N., and Shawe-Taylor, J. 2000. *An Introduction to Support Vector Machines and Other Kernel-Based Learning Methods.* Cambridge, UK: Cambridge University Press.

52. Sonka, M., Hlavac, V., and Boyle, R. 1999. *Image Processing, Analysis and Machine Vision,* 2nd edn. Pacific Grove, CA: PWS Publishing.

53. Berthod, M., Kato, Z., Yu, S., and Zerubia, J. 1996. Bayesian image classification using Markov random fields. *Image and Vision Computing* 14:285–295.

Index